THE GOLDEN AGE
OF THE
NEWSPAPER

George H. Douglas

D0083192

Greenwood Press
Westport, Connecticut • London

Library of Congress Cataloging-in-Publication Data

Douglas, George H., 1934–
    The Golden Age of the newspaper / George H. Douglas.
      p.   cm.
    Includes bibliographical references and index.
    ISBN 0–313–31077–7 (alk. paper)
      1. American newspapers—History—19th century.   2. American
    newspapers—History—20th century. I. Title.
    PN4864.D68   1999
    071′.3′0904—dc21   98–50238

British Library Cataloguing in Publication Data is available.

Copyright © 1999 by George H. Douglas

All rights reserved. No portion of this book may be
reproduced, by any process or technique, without the
express written consent of the publisher.

Library of Congress Catalog Card Number: 98–50238
ISBN: 0–313–31077–7

First published in 1999

Greenwood Press, 88 Post Road West, Westport, CT 06881
An imprint of Greenwood Publishing Group, Inc.
www.greenwood.com

Printed in the United States of America

∞™

The paper used in this book complies with the
Permanent Paper Standard issued by the National
Information Standards Organization (Z39.48–1984).

10 9 8 7 6 5 4 3 2 1

Contents

Photo essay follows page 118

Acknowledgments

While this book is a highly personal account of a very large terrain, no such work could be undertaken without the help of many individuals and institutions. I am especially grateful for being able to use the newspaper archives of a number of libraries, most especially the University of Illinois Library, the Library of Congress, the Newberry Library, and the New York Public Library. Other insitutional help has come from the Chicago Historical Society, the Museum of the City of New York, and the Smithsonian Institution. I acknowledge with deep thanks for the help that I have received from archivists at the New York *Times*, the Chicago *Tribune*, and the Baltimore *Sun*.

At the University of Illinois I am especially grateful for services rendered by Jane Wiles, Newspaper Archivist, and her assistant, Stephanie Randall. Also I am deeply indebted to three successive Communications Librarians who shared with me their extensive erudition in the area of newspaper history: Eleanor Bloom, Diane Carothers, and Lisa Romero. A number of professors of Journalism at the University of Illinois, past and present, have looked at either part or all of my manuscript and given me encouragement and helpful suggestions. Among them are the late Theodore E. Peterson, Gene Gilmore, John C. Nerone, and Glenn Hanson. Several colleagues of mine in the English Department have read parts of the manuscript: Michael Shapiro, George Hendrick, and Chester Fontenot.

I have been able to benefit considerably by being able to talk with numerous working journalists about issues discussed in this book. I would especially like to mention my father, Halsey M. Douglas, who was on the firing line for over 40 years. Also, Andrea Lynn, Alan Branigan, Byron C. Vedder, and the late Robert Sink.

I am particularly grateful to my editor at the Greenwood Publishing Group, Heather Staines, who helped shape the final project and who made numerous suggestions, all of which have resulted in upgrading the quality of the final product.

Introduction

In the early years of the twentieth century the daily newspaper was universally accepted as one of the foundation stones of American social life. In those days real authority flowed from the printed word, and the newspaper was clearly one of our most valued cultural institutions. True, many Americans had been shocked by the excesses of sensationalism characteristic of the so-called "yellow journalism" that took root in the 1890s. Many believed that the hundreds of magazines that had popped up almost overnight were products of crass commercialism; they saw in them the greedy hand of advertising hucksters. Still, there was no denying that the periodical press—newspapers and magazines—had forged a vital link with the American people. It had given them their window on the world. Print journalism had brought our sense of national identity into being.

Today we expect much less of the printed word. Critics and historians of recent years have been quick to point out that the electronic media have diluted or supplanted the power of print. The electronic media offer the public more immediate forms of networking and cultural bonding. Marshall McLuhan, a media wizard fashionable in the 1960s, believed that television would blow the print media away by its cool immediacy and its rejection of logical thought patterns. As a benefit, he thought, television would bring us all together in a "global village." The printed page, on the other hand, was demanding, alienating, off-putting.

News by television does provide sudden confrontation and immediacy. Certainly it provokes nervous intensity. But contrary to McLuhan it does not seem to provide intimacy or any sense of community. It seldom provides real satisfaction of our needs. Television may well be capable of capturing the whole globe on a twenty-seven–inch screen, but whether this constitutes a village, or any kind of community, is an altogether different matter.

The American newspaper in its golden age ministered to a real community; in fact it had done a great deal to create that community. It had human scale; it was something you could reach out and touch. The American newspaper was nothing if not a quirky neighbor, something like the fellow next door whom you had to learn to love or endure. You always had the feeling that the newspaper, which arrived at your door as an invited guest, was written and prepared for you. Down at the newspaper office they knew who you were and where you lived. The television signal, beamed to some remote satellite, seems to inhabit its own world, to live for itself alone. It is standardized; all individuality is pumped out of it. Every news anchorman—or woman—seems like every other. We are perhaps drawn to television news because it demands no intellectual input, only passive receptivity. In the newspaper, at least in its ideal form, you were in the presence of some personality—someone like a father, a demanding school teacher, an eccentric uncle, a close friend.

This book is an attempt to tell the story of the American newspaper during its most influential years. It covers roughly a century, from the coming of the "penny papers" in the 1830s to the growth of radio news services in the 1930s. It does not assume that the newspaper died in the 1930s—far from it—but only that the electronic media changed the way we encounter the outside world. This book tries to capture the spirit of news gathering and news making in the years when the newspaper was king. This is not, however, a formal history of journalism, with comprehensive lists of newspapers, circulation figures, publishers, editors; rather it is a social history, a people's history. It tries to explain how newspapers formed a bond with the American people and helped us to discover ourselves.

Our story begins in the 1830s when Americans first began to make their way as a Democratic people. Before the 1830s newspapers were not at all newspapers in the modern sense. They were journals, dismal logs, keepers of records; they offered announcements for a commercial elite. During the early republic, columns of static commercial announcements were occasionally enlivened by political antagonism and partisan strife. This could be exciting, even incendiary, at times. But it was not news as we understand it today. With the explosion of coastal cities in the East, with immigrants pouring in from many nations abroad, there was a need to provide regular information to those who faced a rapidly changing and often inscrutable society. There was no mass education in those times—few schools and colleges—so the American newspaper had to take on the roles of schoolmaster, entertainer, and public gossip. All of these roles were avidly accepted by the penny papers and others that grew from them and were sold, not by subscription alone, but in individual copies on the street.

European visitors to the United States were astonished by the American newspaper and by the unquenchable demand for print in newly burgeoning cities. The Americans had invented lightning rotary presses from which thousands of daily copies could be produced. American newspaper circulation rapidly outstripped the long-standing leaders of London or Paris. Europeans were astonished, too, by those crazy Americans, who lugged printing presses across the Alleghenies and beyond the Mississippi, setting up newspaper offices where there were no people at all. But people would soon come, and the local newspaper was often the only cement capable of holding them together.

This is the story, then, of how the American newspaper became a great civilizing influence in spite of its many impurities. Yes, Europeans were dismayed that these Americans wanted blood, murder, and lust in their newspapers. More importantly, though, American readers simply wanted to know what was going on: how the government worked, when the new road was coming through, when a new department store was coming. These things were important because America, unlike Europe, with its rigid class structure and its older settlements, was created afresh every day. "News" thus became a passion—and a necessity.

During the last half of the nineteenth century the American newspaper rapidly became a cultural institution of undeniable force. Large metropolitan papers had increased from 4 pages to 8, then to 16, then to 32. Soon they were stuffed with supplements bursting with puzzles, comics, poems, household hints. The American people love to talk back—we all recognize the force of talk radio and television today. The newspaper could be talked to. Many readers turned first to "Letters to the Editor" or to those columns where some bright young female staffer, backed with no more authority than that of the paper itself, would attempt to provide intimate advice to the "lovelorn."

In cities like New York, Chicago, and Philadelphia, daily press runs would reach hundreds of thousands. On the other hand there continued to be rural weeklies with strong ties to the local Rotary or Grange, edited by down-home sages or "colymnists" or cracker-barrel philosophers. In any case, newspapers became purveyors of more than daily happenings. The bigger papers reviewed books, plays, and works of art. Poems and literary miscellany were a major part of most papers throughout the nineteenth century. There was hardly a poet of any importance in those days who did not publish his work in newspapers. Newspapers were also the main sources of native humor, and legions of funny men could be found working on newspapers around the country. Some have been long forgotten, but most of us remember that onetime printer's devil, Mark Twain, whose sketches, published first in newspapers, gave America an authentic voice that was heard throughout the world.

For a long time newspapers served a need every bit as important as food itself. And there were many kinds of food. This book treats the foreign language press—literally thousands of papers, some mass circulation dailies, others puny irregulars serving minuscule communities—all struggling to throw out a lifeline between the old world and the new, thus serving a function every bit as essential as the school or the church. The very word "newspaper" suggests something with deep roots in the intimate conditions of living. Yes, there were general metropolitan dailies, but there were also trade union papers, religious papers, farm papers, many special interest publications in newspaper format. In the black or African American community, in pre–Civil War days, newspapers were seen to be at the very heart of the struggle for freedom. In later years newspapers were the principal organs of the fight for equality and opportunity.

Doubtless there are many today who believe that the newspapers are doomed by the coming of the latest offspring of electronic communication: online, Internet, the World Wide Web, and so on. Of course the same thing was said when radio first edged into news broadcasting, then television. The newspaper had to die. Yet the newspaper is still here, and there seems to be nothing in sight that can replace the great skill and art of the newspaper reporter in getting hold of the news, or of the newspaper editor in deciding what the news really is. A major function of a newspaper always has been that it carves out of the chaotic fury of events the precise things that people want to know and need to know. A reader opening a newspaper does not seek a torrent of information on some one topic; he seeks a balanced meal, a reliable, structured picture of what is going on around him or her.

This book does not extend to the journalistic history of our immediate past. There is nothing in it about numerous phenomena of the post–World War II years: underground newspapers, gonzo journalism, investigative reporting in the new sense, corporate chains, or "national newspapers," like *USA Today*, with its attempt to mimic the television ethos in newspaper form. Nonetheless, as an aid to the reader, some chapters have occasionally filled in recent developments that are needed to bring the narrative full circle. Too, it provides the reader several early chapters to explain the contentious and violent beginnings of the American press in the early republic and before. For the most part, though, this book hopes to offer a portrait of the American newspaper in its most mature form. It does not attempt to glorify the subject. It keeps the warts and wrinkles in—and there are many. On the other hand, even when all of the excuses are made for sensationalism, or greedy motives, or political indiscretions, there can be little doubt that the newspaper has been among our nation's greatest cultural institutions. We Americans have made newspapers to fit our own style and personality, and, for the most part, they have been the envy of the world.

1

Penny Papers: The Printed Word for Democratic Man

When Andrew Jackson was inaugurated as president of the United States on March 4, 1829, a popular revolution was shaking the United States to its very foundations. One might call this the "real" American revolution. Before Jackson, our youthful nation more nearly resembled the princely states of Europe than the popular democracy we know today. Yes, the United States had been conceived in liberty: it had no monarch, no hereditary peerage. But the reins of power were strictly in the hands of patrician leaders—aristocratic planters of the South, sons of mercantile or banking elites in New England and the mid-Atlantic states.

President Jackson, however, brought a wholly new flavor to the front of the stage—a boisterous and often uncouth vitality, a surging sense of power that gripped the multitudes, especially the restless citizens of the new frontier states. On the day of his inaugural, thousands of rough-hewn frontiersmen swarmed over the Capitol, ran pell-mell through the streets of Washington, cheering this "Western" president who seemed to promise something new, something they could understand. When the doors of the White House were thrown open to the public—something that had never happened before—hordes of individuals streamed in, upsetting waiters and the barrels of orange punch that had been laid in for the entertainment and for the consumption of the visitors—at least those among them who had not arrived with their own jugs of hard cider.

In the near melee that followed, Jackson himself was pressed against a wall; his intimates had to link arms to protect him from the overeager voters who wanted to shake his hand. The White House, then called the Executive Mansion, or even sometimes the Presidential Palace, was looted much like the palaces and temples of ancient Rome had been by swarms of vandals and Huns. Farmers and mechanics stood on the satin-covered furniture—*their* furniture they thought—and gouged out pieces of the wainscoting to take home as souvenirs. Justice Joseph Story of the Supreme Court, born and bred of the older gentry, proclaimed, "The reign of King Mob seemed triumphant."

Whether one believed that Jackson represented the mob triumphant, or a healthy move forward for the democratic spirit, there is no question that the United States underwent an enormous social upheaval during the two terms of his presidency. A man of the people himself, and a hero of the War of 1812, Jackson was suspicious of bankers and eastern commercial interests, and his terms of office exhibited a continuing effort to put power in the hands of what was called "the plain people." The 1830s, accordingly, was a decade of revolution both in the national mood and in the style of government.

Of course it was not only in the White House that this new social impetus was felt—it was felt throughout the land: in commercial transactions, in manners, morals, language and dress. Americans were rapidly becoming a different kind of people. A pronounced revolution in men's clothing took place at this time—the old small clothes and "tie-wig" were replaced by democratic "trousers," and those who stuck to the old garb in defiance, like writer Washington Irving, soon became objects of peculiarity if not disdain. Everyone now was expected to be "of the people." The government, all social institutions, bent themselves to the will of the many, not the select few.

The Jacksonian era did not bring about a revolution in education—that revolution was yet some years off. But in one important way Americans were rapidly becoming a much better informed and more literate people, a more unified people. The decade of the 1830s—the Jacksonian era—brought about an explosion in the public prints. The printed word, which had always been a minor influence among the general population, rose suddenly to prominence and became as powerful a force as the new president himself. Newspapers and magazines sprang up throughout the land, and they were of markedly different character than those that had gone before. During colonial times the vast majority of newspapers were weeklies; magazines were few. Most books were imported from Europe. Publishing developed slowly and timidly during the presidency of George Washington and the first three decades of the nineteenth century. Now, all of a sudden, there would be a great deal of reading matter, not all of it intended for the better bred and better fed. The newspapers, especially those in large metropolitan areas, became enormously influential in American life, so much so in fact that the explosion of news readership might be considered to have played just as important a role in the "democratizing" of America as the coonskin democracy of Andrew Jackson.

The newspaper revolution, which seems to parallel the democratic revolution so precisely, was defined by the existence of a new kind of newspaper, popularly labeled by a term that would enter the language as a catch phrase: the penny paper. The very term took hold of the public's imagination and stimulated an interest in newspapers that had not been there before. As a matter of historical record, the idea of the penny paper was conceived even before papers actually sold for a penny. The term signified any inexpensive and widely available newspaper; perhaps more importantly it signified newspapers that could be bought in single copies on the street. Throughout colonial times, and actually down to the 1830s, most newspapers were sold through annual subscriptions, usually $8 to $10 a year.

Today $8 or $10 seems like a pittance, but in the 1830s these sums were forbidding to most citizens. Accordingly, newspapers were read almost exclusively by the prosperous and well-to-do—those involved in politics or the trades. Furthermore, most newspapers had little in them that would appeal to a mass audience. They were dull, stodgy, and visually forbidding. But the revolution that was taking place in the 1830s would change all that.

The drift, then, was toward "popular" papers. The term penny paper is best taken as referring to papers made widely available to the public. This development did not take place overnight. It had been possible (but not easy) to buy single copies of newspapers before 1830, but this usually involved the reader going down to the printer's office and purchasing a copy (a few were usually kept on hand beyond those mailed to subscribers). Street sales were almost unknown. However, within a few years, street sales of newspapers would be commonplace in eastern cities. At first the price of single copies was seldom a penny—usually two or three cents was charged—and some of the older well-established papers charged five or six cents. But the phrase "penny paper" caught the public's fancy, and soon there would be papers that did indeed sell for only a penny.

This new trend of newspapers for "the man on the street" did not begin auspiciously. Some of the early ventures were immediate failures. Publishers already in business, people who were owners of successful papers, had little desire or impetus to tamper with tradition and propriety. It took a few youthful daredevils to get the ball rolling.

In Boston, on July 24, 1830, Lynde M. Walter, a young Harvard graduate of some means, established a newspaper called the *Daily Evening Transcript*, which he proposed to sell for $4 a year, a silly idea it seemed at the time.[1] Walter's paper, which became a modest success, consisted of four pages in a 10 × 15-inch format. (This was the usual size; nearly all early American papers were the size of our present-day tabloids.) Other than the price there was nothing unusual about the *Transcript*. It was a conservative paper that looked pretty much like its older competitors. The first page was devoted to advertising notices, and the editorial content inside was in good taste, probably even a little dull. This was hardly a paper for "everyman." Indeed, by a curious irony of history the paper later became the leading organ of the Boston Brahmins, who continued to support and venerate it until it fell into bankruptcy more than a century later. Nevertheless, the first youthful flourish of this puny sheet that would one day be the pet of bluebloods gave rise to a phenomenon that would revolutionize American journalism.

Walter's $4 paper attracted the attention of other local publishers in the next few years, and several emulators came in with inexpensive papers of their own. Some of these would naturally be attractive to penny-pinching New Englanders. Charles G. Greene established the Boston *Morning Post* in 1831, and Capt. John T. Sleeper, the *Mercantile Journal* in 1833. Both papers prospered and enjoyed long lives in Boston, although, like the *Transcript* they were not strictly penny papers. They did, however, uncover a smoldering demand for inexpensive newspapers that would soon be more fully realized in other cities.

The first true penny paper was not the product of Boston, but of Philadelphia. Around the time that Lynde Walter was establishing the *Transcript* in Boston, Christopher Columbus Conwell inaugurated the first paper that cost only a penny. It was called, appropriately, *The Cent*. Unfortunately the venture was not a success and the paper died in 1832.

New York's first experiment along these lines was also a failure. The paper was called the *Morning Post*, launched on January 1, 1883, by Horatio David Shepard, Horace Greeley, and Francis W. Story. Greeley would later go on to become one of the giants of American journalism, but his foray into the world of the penny paper was not an auspicious beginning. A piece of bad luck might have had something to do with it. The paper made its debut in the midst of a blizzard, and the sellers who tried to peddle the first issue found the city streets nearly deserted. The paper continued for two weeks priced at a penny, after which the editors feared that the one-cent price might be offputting, so it was raised to two cents. The paper did not sell at this price either and the one-cent price was restored. But an edition of about three hundred copies could not be sold. The *Morning Post* passed into history at the age of three weeks. The experiment seemed worth continuing, but Shepard, Greeley, and Story could find no one willing to advance them credit to continue the venture.[2]

The flat failure of the *Morning Post* ought to have frightened others away, but less than a year after the *Post*'s debacle another penny paper appeared that would become an immediate success. This came about by a rather peculiar set of circumstances. Two years before, a young man with printing experience arrived in New York from Springfield, Massachusetts. His name was Benjamin H. Day. He had worked briefly as a typesetter for the New York *Evening Post*, after which he set up a print shop of his own at 222 William Street. Here he was only a job printer, working in a room 12 × 16 feet and using a primitive hand-crank press. At first he entertained no thought of starting a newspaper, although before coming to New York he had served an apprenticeship on an already distinguished paper, the Springfield *Republican*. Out on his own, Day was looking for whatever work he could get, and in the beginning there was not much. Job printing in New York became especially depressed in 1832 when a large portion of the city's population was wiped out in a cholera epidemic. Looking for something to take up the slack, Day's mind drifted to the idea of producing a small-format penny paper. He could not think of a bigger paper because this was all that his tiny shop could produce.

Day discussed the idea of a paper to be sold on a per-issue basis with two of his friends, William M. Swain and Arunah S. Abell. But both of them discouraged him from this enterprise since they knew it had not worked anywhere before. (Later both Swain and Abell suppressed their doubts and established successful penny papers in Philadelphia and Baltimore.)

Another friend of Day's had a slightly different view. A compositor for the *Journal of Commerce* named David Ramsey knew that there was a paper in London called the *Sun*, and he felt sure that a paper with that name could make a go of it in New York. What was so special about the name is not entirely clear, but Day took to the idea and laid plans to produce a New York *Sun*.

The paper made its appearance on September 3, 1833. It was a scraggly four-page sheet, 8 × 11 inches—smaller than today's tabloids. There were three columns of type. The first issue was put out by Day and a single helper named Parmlee. Most of the news was borrowed from the previous day's New York newspaper and the two printers had to stay up all night getting the first issue off the press.

The *Sun* was to be sold on the street for a penny, but following traditional practice there was a subscription offering at $3 per year. In the first issue Day explained his guiding editorial policy: "The object of this paper is to lay before the public, at a price within the means of everyone, all the news of the day, and at the same time afford an advantageous medium for advertising. The sheet will be enlarged as soon as the increase of advertisements requires it—the price remaining the same."[3]

The *Sun* was an instant success; the first day's issue was immediately sold-out on the streets, and by the end of one year the paper was selling 4,000 copies daily. What attracted the public to the paper? It was not any startling new typography, or screaming headlines, or some layout that had never been seen in newspapers before. No, rather it was an attempt to broaden the appeal of the content to reach a diverse audience. In his first issue Day remarked that New York "is nearly full of strangers from nearly all parts of the country and Europe." Most newspapers then in print had little that would pull in such a diverse audience; they appealed only to the gentry, to the commercial classes, or to those knowledgeable about long-standing and often esoteric political issues. Day, on the other hand, delivered to his readers strong "human interest" material, stories that could be easily grasped and enjoyed.

The first column on page one of the inaugural issue contained short ads, clearly de rigueur at that time. But the second column began with a feature story headed "An Irish Captain," a tale told in dialogue, not formal English. Then there was a story entitled "Wonders of Littleness," which described some miniature mechanical marvels, including a small mill that a monk could carry in his sleeve but which in one day could grind "grain enough for the consumption of eight men." Nothing of this sort would have been considered worthy material for a newspaper before the 1830s.

On page two of the paper there was a story entitled "Melancholy Suicide," which told of a young man named Fred Hall, who recently arrived from Boston and was staying at Webb's Congress Hall. He had taken his life, apparently with an overdose of laudanum. Investigation of the case revealed that the lad was aggrieved by an affair of the heart, although this motive was not discussed at length. But the story was lively enough to attract readers who were starved for information about other people like themselves, distressed souls from other lands or from upstate farms—people marooned in a rapidly growing city that was often inscrutable, uncaring, or unintelligible.

In the days and weeks ahead, the *Sun* would turn to material of a similar nature to capture its readership. The formula worked like a charm. Some other editors in New York, and elsewhere, claimed that the *Sun's* stories were lurid or sensationalistic, although they were certainly tame by the standards of today. On the other hand, these stories were invariably turned out in a clear, trenchant, and sparkling style, and when Day hired writers, as he almost immediately had to do, he gravitated toward individuals who possessed a good turn of phrase and a pungent ability for exposition and storytelling.

Not all of Day's features or his innovations were entirely original. For example, a major feature of the paper, almost from the outset, was humorous treatment of police court news. This idea was apparently borrowed from the London *Morning Herald*, a scruffy sheet that had boosted its circulation within a hair's breadth of the stately *Times* by crude renderings of the day's happenings at the Bow Street court: tales of street fights, drunken brawls, domestic disputes; the doings of petty pilferers, streetwalkers, vagrants, pickpockets, con men and other denizens of the demimonde. Some of this kind of material was already known in America through the work of George Cruikshank, the illustrator and caricaturist who had published books filled with some of these unseemly types. Cruikshank's illustrations were famous in America even before he became the illustrator of many English novels, including those of Charles Dickens.

Very early in the history of the *Sun* Day hired reporters with a knack for lively courtroom material. One of these was George W. Wisner, who was paid $4 a week to attend every afternoon's session of police court in New York. Wisner was so good at his business, and so successful were the police court items, that Day promised Wisner a share of the profits and even partial ownership, although later the two men had political differences and parted company.[4]

The police court segment consisted mostly of brief items that could be read in a few moments. But most of the other "human interest" stories of the *Sun* were also short and pithy. They were intended for readers who wanted to pick up a paper every day and enjoy these little tidbits, not so much for their informational value but as part of the day's amusements. Here was a minor narcotic, not sustenance or food for thought.

The *Sun* not only addressed the interests of the man on the street, it was sold directly to him by street vendors. The paper was not in print very long before a regular advertisement appeared in its pages asking for street sellers. The ad read: "*To the Unemployed*: A number of steady men can find employment by vending this paper. A liberal discount is allowed to those who buy to sell again."

As a matter of fact, the pay for this work was so low that most of the newspaper vendors were young boys, later called newsies, many of them orphans or children of immigrants. They nonetheless earned enough to eke out a small existence and soon became a familiar part of the urban landscape. Developing their own slang and peculiarities of speech, they were tough, independent entrepreneurs who plied their trade at prominent hotels, ferry houses, and street corners. Within a few decades these rootless children were troubling enough to civic leaders that Newsboy Lodging Houses were established offering cheap bed and board. But the newsboys (and in rare instances newsgirls) remained a vital part of the urban scene throughout the nineteenth century. Nobody could think of any other way to get mass circulation newspapers into the hands of the multitudes.

With the help of these urchins, the circulation of the *Sun* grew, month by month, much to the astonishment of New Yorkers, and much to the annoyance of the older and more orthodox publishers. Everywhere around town the paper could be found in the hands of barbers, draymen, hall porters, coach drivers, milkmen: the kinds of individuals who a few years before would have thought of newspapers as dull and remote. Clearly, the appeal of the *Sun*, many would call it sensationalism, was something that would not go away. And penny papers—newspapers for the man on the street, whatever the actual price—would be the wave of the future.

Within a year of the birth of the *Sun*, successful penny papers cropped up in other large eastern cities. Boston and Philadelphia, which a short time before had played with the idea without success, now copied Ben Day's formula and had good results. Boston saw the appearance of the *Daily Times* in 1836 and the *Herald* in 1844. The highly successful and long-lived Philadelphia *Public Ledger* appeared in 1836 and the legendary Baltimore *Sun* in 1837.

What was perhaps more important, however, was that the idea of newspapers for mass audiences did not limit itself to the original formula of the New York *Sun*. In 1835 James Gordon Bennett founded his New York *Herald* in the mold of the penny paper but quickly transcended the original formula of news squibs, police court chatter, and scanty human interest material. Bennett did not abandon the appeal of the first penny papers, but added to it much fuller news coverage, first-rate reporting, much more careful editorial treatment, as well as a good deal of the political and commercial news expected of traditional press. But he handled this traditional material with greater color and bravura than any of the old "respectable" papers. In doing so he created a newspaper of a kind that more nearly resembles the mainstream newspaper Americans are familiar with today—an informative paper of broad human appeal.

Many publishers of traditional papers complained bitterly that the *Sun* was playing with dangerous and morally corrupting materials. Stories, human interest materials, were in grave danger of stifling the search for real news—truth if you will. Were newspapers, they asked, to become nothing but vehicles for entertainment, a kind of opiate of the people? Under the guise of capturing people's attention, of entertaining them, newspapers might be deluding or corrupting them as well, and such concerns were genuine. They were as troubling in the 1830s as they are today.

On the other hand there can also be no doubt that the penny papers had helped pump life into a fusty and hidebound journalistic world. The newspapers of American cities before 1830 simply went about their stolid routines without enthusiasm or zest, except perhaps when they served as organs for incendiary political debate. Their readers were few and they were poorly informed by the news that they did receive. These older papers usually did little to engage their readers. The penny papers, and the new larger papers that followed in their wake, changed all that. Newspapers now began to draw people of a polyglot urban milieu into some kind of commonality of interest and learning. They gave people things that they could understand. As much as any other force in the Jacksonian era, the papers that began to flourish in our big eastern cities forged a new and vibrant sense of community, a sense of our own peculiar nationhood.

2

The Quest for a Real Newspaper

The penny papers, which appeared in the 1830s, were surely not great newspapers. In fact they were scarcely newspapers at all by the standards of today. Yet they were incendiary devices that helped to ignite the fires of American journalism. They helped pave the way for a new generation of newspapers that were much more inviting and much more informative than any that had been seen before.

By some standards of judgment the American newspaper had made great strides by 1830. Newspapers had existed in the United States since the appearance in Boston of the first American paper, *Publick Occurrences*, in 1690. But throughout colonial times there was no such thing as a daily newspaper; the first daily to succeed was the *Pennsylvania Packet and Advertiser*, and this did not appear until after the Revolution—in 1784.

Also, until well into the following century, nearly all papers were the product of solitary printer-publishers who got out their papers as a sideline to other more important printing business. Occasionally, in some of the larger shops, there was the help of an apprentice or other assistant. Sometimes a wife or daughter was pressed into service. But these were never news gatherers or reporters; rather they mostly aided the proprietor in setting or redistributing type or running the small hand-crank presses that prevailed everywhere in the eighteenth century.

Newspapering continued to be a small-scale enterprise right up to the Jacksonian era. In 1830 the United States had only 650 weekly newspapers and 65 dailies. During the same decade the population of the country was also growing, but not so quickly: the total population increased from 12.9 million to 17.1 million.[1] Nearly all newspapers in 1830 were four-page folios with a page size comparable to that of one of today's tabloid newspapers. Characteristically, half of the paper consisted of advertisements; in the rest there was little that could be called news. Clearly a newspaper revolution of some kind was desperately needed.

By the 1830s the demand for news and the desire to buy and read newspapers had far outpaced production. Tradition—dependence on the small one-man office and the four-page sheet—had a lot to do with keeping journalism in its long-delayed adolescence. But there were other factors as well. There were technological impediments to the growth of the newspaper: lack of paper and ink and inadequate printing presses and other mechanical equipment necessary to turn out the thousands of daily copies that we are accustomed to today. Advances in these areas came with painful slowness and in halting steps; there was a multitude of difficulties to overcome before the modern "mass circulation" newspaper could emerge.

Consider the case of paper. Paper was in very short supply in 1830; indeed it had been in short supply throughout American history. Nearly all paper in early colonial times was imported from abroad, but even in England or Holland the supplies could not be considered abundant. The first paper mill in America was not built until 1690. At that time William Rittenhouse built a small mill on the Wissahickon Creek in Germantown, Pennsylvania (now part of Philadelphia). In the century that followed, a number of other paper mills were built, most of them in New England or the northeastern states. All these mills were small, most of them having only one or two employees, and their output was hardly sufficient to meet the needs of the colonies.

But there were other serious problems in obtaining paper. The papermaking art was still in its infancy. Throughout the eighteenth century nearly all paper was made exclusively from rags, and rags themselves were hard to come by. The search for rags became almost a national obsession: mill owners were obliged to print advertisements, handbills, posters, putting out desperate calls for rags. The situation was not much better in England, where at one time laws were enacted forbidding burial of people with clothes made from cloth that could be turned into paper. In Pennsylvania, one newspaper editor expressed the opinion that every man should say to his wife, "Make a rag bag and hang it under the shelf where the big Bible is." The salvage and collection of rags took on the dimensions of a crusade or spiritual quest.

By the time of the Revolution things had gotten no better—often a good deal worse. In 1779, when George Washington was quartered at Morristown, New Jersey, he urged a man named Sheppard Kollock to begin a newspaper at nearby Chatham—the New Jersey *Journal*. Since the nearest paper mill had no rags, Washington had the army commissary collect and deliver whatever he could find to Kollock's Paper, even though by this time the regulation uniforms of many of Washington's soldiers were not much better than rags. Too, the owner of the paper mill at Springfield that supplied the *Journal* advertised that he would pay "ready money and the highest price for rags."[2]

Even if there had been an adequate supply of rags, and there never was, papermaking itself was a laborious and difficult process. All paper in the eighteenth century was handmade. There was no such thing as a papermaking machine anywhere in the world. The process had remained the same for centuries: the papermaker pulped the paper using water (nearly all paper mills were on rivers or streams), and then dried and flattened the pulp in hand presses. This was such a slow and dismal process that many mill owners dropped out of the business and sought more lucrative occupations.

There had been numerous attempts to invent some kind of papermaking machine in the eighteenth century, but all came to naught. The machine that would eventually work was invented in France in 1799 by Nicholas Louis Robert. Robert's machine was so good that its concept is essentially the same as the giant papermaking machines of our own day. But Robert got no support for his idea and he is now virtually unknown to history. He died an impoverished schoolteacher in 1828. On the other hand, Henry and Sealy Fourdrinier took Robert's invention to London in 1803 and had a few models made up. The machine, essentially a continuous "wire" with a wet end and a dry end, solved the problem of mechanical papermaking, and, of course, the machine is still called the Fourdrinier machine or the Fourdrinier process. (Alternatively, some paper today is made in a cylindrical type of press.)

The new American nation was not, however, quick to adopt the Fourdrinier machine: only a few were imported, and by 1830 only three individuals had undertaken to make them in the United States. Accordingly, during the first three decades of the nineteenth century, most paper continued to be turned out by hand.

Even if the Fourdrinier machines had been readily adopted, there would still have been a monumental paper shortage. The matter of finding a substitute for rags had not been solved, although the search had been going on vigorously for years. By the early nineteenth century desperate experimenters, perhaps hoping to make a fortune, had tried working with almost every kind of fibrous material they could get their hands on—cornstalks, bamboo, flax, jute, hemp, wood, sugarcane, even arcane and esoteric substances like ivory shavings, leather cuttings, cabbage stumps, and frog spittle.[3]

This quest for a rag substitute did not, in fact, end until after the Civil War. As late as the 1850s one enterprising manufacturer bought and imported a number of Egyptian mummies with the intention of salvaging their voluminous wrappings, while rudely disposing of the human remains within. The paper shortage was finally resolved, according to legend, when a German named Friedrich Gottlob Keller observed how in a deserted wasp's nest small fibers of wood were matted into a coarse paper substance. At Keller's suggestion, Henry Volter, a papermaker and machinist, constructed a machine for grinding wood into pulp. The design for this machine was shortly brought to America by the Pagenstecher brothers—Albrecht, Alberto, and Rudolph—and the first mill to grind wood into pulp was built near Stockbridge, Massachusetts, in March 1867.[4] Rags would continue to be used in papermaking, but now the need for them was dramatically reduced as was the cost of the paper. After the 1880s rags were no longer used in making news-paper, or newsprint as it is usually called, but they continued to be used in many high-quality papers. All this was none too soon to supply the voracious demand of newspaper publishers after the Civil War. Without wood pulping the large metropolitan dailies we know today would never have been possible.

Another technological advance that came about in the early years of the nineteenth century was the manufacture and widespread availability of printing inks. Prior to this time most printers and publishers had to make their own inks, clearly a distracting and time-consuming sideline activity. Jacob Johnson of Philadelphia was probably the first large-scale manufacturer of printing inks in the United States. In 1804 he set up a firm with his son and an associate to supply inks on a commercial scale. By 1830 this firm, Wrigley and Johnson, was the largest supplier of printing inks in the United States.

But the most important technological development during the early part of the nineteenth century was the marked improvement in the printing press. Throughout colonial times there had been no advancements over the ancient screw presses, which differed little from the designs of Gutenberg. Changes came around 1813. The first big advance was the invention in Philadelphia of the "Columbian press" of George Clymer. This substituted a series of levers for the old single-screw device.

However much an improvement this had been, the Columbian press was still essentially a human-powered operation, not suitable for the kind of rapid production that would soon be needed. What was absolutely essential was power-driven equipment. At first the power would be steam; electric motors would come on the scene only toward the end of the century. But steam-powered presses made a big difference when they arrived. The first press of this kind had been the product of a German-English inventor named Frederick Koenig. The Koenig machine, improved by David Napier, was installed at the London *Times* and then brought to America where it was used by the New York *Daily Advertiser* as early as 1825. It was capable of delivering 2,000 papers an hour. Needless to say, a press that could produce 2,000 papers an hour using steam power was not cheap. Its purchase price was between $4,000 and $5,000.[5] The day was now past when any individual could become a newspaper publisher on a shoestring.

Shortly after this time the technological initiative passed to the United States where the great Richard M. Hoe, improving upon the Napier concept, developed a double-cylinder press capable of printing 4,000 double impressions an hour. When the New York *Sun* and other papers began their rapid circulation rise in the mid-1830s, steam powered presses of this capacity were absolutely essential. But the Hoe Company, which also began supplying equipment to the *Times* of London, was only at the beginning of its long and illustrious career as a manufacturer of newspaper printing presses. By 1847 the company, which had a large plant at 29–31 Gold Street in Manhattan, developed a four-cylinder rotary-type revolving press, sometimes called the "lightning press." It consisted of a revolving printing surface in which the type form was actually locked onto the cylinder. The cylinder thus replaced the old "flat bed" known since Gutenburg's day. First employed on the Philadelphia *Public Ledger*, the lightning press was capable of printing 20,000 sheets an hour. These presses cost over $20,000—not an inconsiderable sum in the 1840s.[6]

By the 1830s and 1840s the Industrial Revolution had obtained a secure foothold in the United States as it had much earlier in Britain. The large, well-engineered Hoe Company of New York rapidly became the world's leader in the manufacture of newspaper printing presses. In 1861, at the beginning of the Civil War, the Hoe Company had on the market a rotary press that printed from stereotyped plates rather than type. This admitted the possibility of the very high-speed presses that would be necessary to produce the huge metropolitan newspapers that thrived at the end of the century.

But it was not only the advanced technological developments in eastern cities that would spur the growth of newspapers; it was a contagious feeling that newspapers were important and that any town of modest pretensions must have a paper of its own. Even in the early decades of the nineteenth century a good number of old-fashioned presses were being manufactured and shipped around the country, and more and more young people were hoping to put out newspapers.

The printing press was going everywhere, even into the western territories. Newspapers had been established beyond the Alleghenies even before George Washington took his oath of office. John Scull and Joseph Hall began the Pittsburgh *Gazette* in 1786 (the paper survives to this day as the *Post-Gazette*), and John Bradford began the Kentucky *Gazette* the following year. To be sure, publishing was a parlous business in these parts. Scull and Hall had to haul their primitive press over the mountains in a wagon, and their paper stock arrived in a train of pack horses.

But once this trend had started there was no stopping it. Soon there were newspapers in the newly admitted states of Kentucky and Tennessee. The territories of what is now called "the old northwest" had printing presses shortly after the Indian wars were over. In 1801 Wyllis Silliman began to print the Ohio *Gazette* in Marietta, which was the provisional capital of the Ohio Territory. Indiana and Illinois were hardly settled at all, and years away from statehood, but they had presses set up in 1804—in Vincennes and Kaskaskia respectively.[7]

So when the penny papers were beginning to have their impact along the eastern seaboard, newspaper fever was spreading everywhere else. The newspaper became a staple of American life wherever people went, even on the frontier. On the other hand, neither the improvement nor the dispersion of the printing press alone were responsible for the renaissance that was about to occur. It was not enough that there be more newspapers, the public also demanded that they have more in them, that they be much better.

A number of other factors had been holding newspapers in delayed adolescence for decades. One inhibiting element was the acrimonious quality of most early papers. From the time of George Washington's administration the country's major papers had been unabashed political organs, devoted to scathing and vitriolic attacks on political opponents. Papers were either rabidly Federalist or rabidly Republican (later Democrat or Whig), and the concept of unbiased news or objective reporting was unknown. Some historians have accordingly called these the dark ages of American journalism.

In the more optimistic days after the Revolution many of our founding fathers had entertained an exaggerated faith in the recently won freedom of the press. Thomas Jefferson, for example, believed that good newspapers and good schoolmasters would be the foundation of a great civilization on the American shore. But Jefferson and others did not anticipate the development of political factions or parties, which they thought they could banish in America. When parties did push in they arrived with a vengeance. The heart of newspaper "copy" for many years was nothing but political calumny or slander. Candidates for high office were lampooned and caricatured, often mercilessly. Attacks on public personages became every bit as rancorous as anything known in the twentieth century. Thomas Jefferson himself was viciously attacked by his Federalist opponents during his presidency. It was an evil-intentioned editor who researched and printed the existence of Jefferson's slave concubine Sally Hemmings. All this was too much for Jefferson's tender sensibilities; the acrimonious party press caused Jefferson to lose his faith in newspapers during his term in the White House. "The newspapers of this country," he wrote, "by their abandoned spirit of falsehood have more effectively destroyed the utility of the press than all the shackles devised by Bonaparte."

When the early newspapers were not venting malice and vituperation, they were mostly just dull. At least half of the typical newspaper in the early republic was taken up by advertisements; indeed the first page was invariably filled with advertisements in tiny agate type. In these times a great many papers had words like "Advertiser" or "Commercial" in their titles, indicating their devotion to local trade and commerce. Outside the political area such news stories as there were tended to be variants of paid advertisements—information of new business enterprise, ship arrivals, offerings, details of trade. Nearly all such "news" was brought into the printing office by those wanting to see it in print.

After the 1830s, however, all this started to change. The idea of news gathering or reporting began to take hold. The idea of the news reporter or gatherer developed slowly for at least one very obvious reason: nearly all early newspaper publishers and editors were rooted in the printing business. Nearly everyone in newspaper work had come up the ladder as apprentice printers and were tied to the craft and trade of printing. Now, however, with city newspapers expanding rapidly, many editor-publishers took employees on as newspaper writers or reporters. In the beginning most of these still had printing experience, but in a few years this would no longer be the case. The vocation of the newspaper reporter became a separate entity.

At first reporters had very specific and usually mundane duties. They brought in the news of ship arrivals, or they called on local business offices. They hoped to get a jump on their competitors. On the penny papers, and later on most other metropolitan papers, a reporter might be used to cover the jail and the courthouse. And when news of this kind got a foothold in one paper, reporters had to be hired to do the same work on competing papers. Since political news continued to be important, newspapers in Boston, New York, Philadelphia, and Baltimore discovered that they needed to maintain "correspondents" in Washington to keep on top of the news coming out of the nation's capital. So within a matter of only a few years newspapers consisted of "staffs," not merely the lone editor-publisher of yore.

The newspaper *editor* now became a more prestigious figure. Editorial writing was becoming more informational and dignified. To be sure, many editors continued to see their mission as lending support to this or that political faction, and to providing useful material for the commercial elite. But even these partisan sheets changed markedly. During the presidency of Andrew Jackson the leading paper in the nation's capital was the Washington *Globe*, established by Francis P. Blair. Blair was a devoted follower of Jackson, and got first crack at everything that came from the White House; but he was no blasphemous political hack. A Kentuckian who had edited the *Argus of the Western World* in Frankfort, Blair was a skilled writer and was well positioned to articulate the current positions of the Democratic party. He brought with him from Kentucky an even more trenchant and incisive writer, Amos Kendall. A man of scholarly habit, Kendall became the chief editorial writer on the *Globe*. As one of Jackson's rivals put it, Kendall was "the President's *thinking* machine, and his *writing* machine—ay, and his *lying* machine. . . . He was chief overseer, chief reporter, amanuensis, scribe, accountant general, man of all work—nothing was well done without the aid of his diabolical genius."[8] Whatever the partisan impulses of this new generation of journalists, many of them were good writers and reflective thinkers; they did a good deal to enhance the flow of reliable information between the government and the people.

One beneficial aspect of the politicization of newspapers in the early republic was that it tended to foster strong competition, and this in turn necessitated discipline and self-improvement. Accordingly the standard papers that came to the fore in the 1830s tended to be much better papers than those of the "dark ages" of the early republic. The political papers began taking their mission seriously. During the Jacksonian era the Washington *Globe* was the leading organ of Democratic opinion, but it was not by any means the only good Democratic paper. There were the Baltimore *Republican*, the New York *Evening Post*, the Albany *Argus*, and several others. The Ohio *Statesman* in Columbus was the leading Democrat paper in the rapidly expanding Northwest.

The Whigs were scarcely left out of the competition even with the spirit of Jackson dominating the land. Considered one by one the well-healed Whig papers were perhaps the best and most innovative of the time. The leading paper in New York was the *Courier and Inquirer*, surely as good a paper as could be found anywhere in the country at the time. In Washington the *National Intelligencer*—founded back in Jefferson's day—served up strong competition for Blair's *Globe*. Philadelphia had the *North American*, and Boston had several strong Whig papers, most of them allied to Daniel Webster. Even in Jackson's West the Whig papers were the local giants, invariably rolling over the competition. They were intensely loyal to Jackson's archenemy Henry Clay. There was the Knoxville *Whig* in Tennessee edited by "Parson" William G. Brownlow. Brownlow was a scrappy infighter who was always prepared to invoke the fires of Satan on behalf of Clay's ideas. In Kentucky there were the Lexington *True American* of Cassius M. Clay, and the Louisville *Journal* of George D. Prentice.

Probably no Whig editor in the land was better known than Thurlow Weed of Albany, New York. Weed had been involved in newspaper work in Albany for years, and he used his papers, especially the *Evening Journal*, as springboards to leadership of the Whig party. He was one of the first "kingmakers" in American politics. In 1838 Weed helped William H. Seward become governor of New York, and in 1840 he orchestrated the "Tippecanoe and Tyler Too" campaign, which brought the first Whig, William Henry Harrison, into the White House. Weed remained a major force in American politics until after the Civil War: in 1867—by then a Republican of course—he became editor of the *Commercial Advertiser* in New York City.

Probably the most influential Whig paper in the country for many years was the Springfield (Massachusetts) *Republican*, founded by Samuel Bowles in 1824, and later edited by his son, Samuel Bowles III. Beginning as a weekly, the Springfield *Republican* garnered a reputation as a solid, respectable, and even-handed sheet. It became a magnet for good writers and brisk thinkers. In time the paper had a daily and weekly edition, and the weekly edition circulated widely around the country. On the frontier, which continued to look to New England for cultural leadership, the *Republican* became, in the eyes of many, the leading national organ of opinion. In 1856, Horace Greeley expressed the opinion that the Springfield *Republican* was "the best and ablest country journal ever published on the continent."[9] Certainly the paper did much to inject into the American mind the belief that newspapers can be looked to as a source of wisdom and intelligence.

It must not be thought, however, that the quality and appeal of these papers derived solely from their editorial opinions or their pronounced political character. Nor did they necessarily reflect the ideas of their publisher owners. The chief Whig paper in New York City was the *Courier and Enquirer* of Col. James Watson Webb. Webb was one of the most hot-tempered and pugnacious editors in the American record. An army veteran of the War of 1812 and a former Indian fighter, Webb relished his combative and warlike temperament even in old age. He challenged his opponents to duels; he horsewhipped people on the street and caned elected representatives on the steps of Congress in Washington. At one time he spent two years in Sing Sing for violating the antiduelling laws. In spite of all this, the *Courier and Enquirer* was one of the best papers of its day because Webb also put much of his animus and volatile energies into beating his competitors and putting out a better paper. He spent money freely. He paid for good reporters and left them alone to do their work. (A man who spends much of his time horse-whipping people may not have the energy to micromanage a newspaper.) Using news boats and "horse expresses" he kept ahead of his competitors in New York. He always bought the latest printing presses that were available, and in the 1850s he enlarged his paper to the "blanket" size that we are familiar with today. He did this so that he could claim to have the *biggest* paper in New York.

It is probably undeniable that James Watson Webb was mostly an anachronism, a throwback to earlier times. For between 1830 and the Civil War, newspaper offices would witness the arrival of an entirely different sort of individual—the professional newspaperman. Individuals looking to get into the profession would now be drawn from all walks of life. In addition to a demand for wider circulation and more human interest news, there would be a call for some respectability. Journalism would come to be seen as a department of literature, and more and more literate individuals would make it a calling.

There was no better example of this new kind of writer and editor than William Cullen Bryant, the young poet who became editor of the New York *Evening Post* in 1829.[10] The *Post* under Bryant never became one of the circulation leaders in New York, but it became one of the most literate and highly respected papers in the country. In the 1830s Bryant was a strong supporter of Jackson, so the *Evening Post* clearly fell into the Democratic column. Bryant could turn out pungent and scalding editorials with the best of them and was decidedly prolabor and antitariff, but he was an idealist of a fundamentally liberal type, always standing up for human liberties rather than political exigencies. He abandoned the Democratic party for the free soilers in the 1850s when he saw the Democratic party falling under the control of slave state interests.

Bryant always took the high ground. A firm believer in democracy and in human betterment, he fought corruption in New York City. His paper was one of the strongest supporters of the move to set aside a large number of acres for Central Park on Manhattan Island. He might well be called the nation's first "environmentalist." He fought for every form of civic improvement from city reform politics to clean water supplies and better sanitation. Bryant was an editor of a major paper longer than anyone else in the nineteenth century. He remained at the helm of the *Post* until his death in 1878—a tenure of nearly fifty years. When he passed away he was widely regarded as the "first citizen" of New York City: the person looked to for everything from wise counsel to a polite after-dinner address. He clearly lifted journalism into polite society, not because he had created the most popular paper of the city but because of his own exemplary character. His paper was polished and erudite—always looked to for its literary notices and comments on the arts. (Bryant published poetry, not only his own but that of others.) The *Post* developed a national correspondence, it invited contributions from European papers, and it established an overall literate and refined tone, something scarcely apparent when Bryant came on the scene. If the *Post* was never one of the circulation leaders—it might have been too highbrow for that—it was something that journalism sorely needed, a moral beacon. It gave the American newspaper something to aspire to. It had integrity and class.

The New York *Evening Post* appealed to an elite. But it was not precisely the same commercial elite that had patronized the newspapers before the 1830s. We may not want to say it appealed to an intellectual elite either, for it is doubtful that such a group existed in the United States in those times. Visitors from abroad, writers like Frances Trollope and Charles Dickens, looked hard for any kind of intellectual aristocracy in their travels through America and professed to find none. On the other hand there was now a much better informed public. Literacy was rapidly expanding and the American people were looking for much more to read. People thirsted for dependable information in their books and newspapers, and by the 1840s they were getting it. Much more informative and reliable newspapers were about to roll off the presses. A profession of journalism was about to be born out of primitive and rough-hewn beginnings. This new profession would remain rough at the edges for a little while longer. But in broadening their appeal newspapers would begin to respond vigorously to a mobile, rapidly growing, and intensely curious people.

3

Giants of a New Age: James Gordon Bennett and Horace Greeley

By the 1840s New York was the leading commercial city of the United States. It had long since outpaced Philadelphia as the largest city in the country, and even though Boston continued to be venerated as the cultural capital of the nation, its image had become somewhat languid and effete; it had not kept up with the implications of the newly industrialized economy, of a diversified ethnic population, or of the rapidly rising middle class. New York was the place where the "new" America was coming into being, so it is hardly surprising that the modern newspaper had its birth there.

The penny paper had found its first success in New York. By the mid-1830s Ben Day's *Sun* was drawing readers from all walks of life. On the other hand the *Sun* was a skimpy sheet providing little more than minor diversions; few today would call it a newspaper at all. Day himself was an editor of limited vision, and he did not possess the ability or the imagination to climb the slopes to loftier heights. If real newspapers were to emerge from the public's demand for more and better coverage, it would have to come from a youthful generation of editors for whom journalism was a totally absorbing profession, an exacting vocational ideal rather than a mere offshoot of job printing.

By the 1840s two giants burst into the field, editors who would revolutionize journalism, would bring the newspaper into the modern age, and show how it could be influential in the national life. These two giants, neither of whom has been treated kindly by history, were James Gordon Bennett and Horace Greeley. Bennett founded his New York *Herald* in 1835, less than two years after the appearance of the *Sun*. Horace Greeley founded his *Tribune* in 1841. Bennett and Greeley were the most innovative editors in New York until after the Civil War. Their newspapers were the leading American papers of the day, although for completely different reasons. The two men despised each other, although not in the ways that newspaper editors had despised one another a few years before. Neither was a political hack shackled to a political party. Greeley fancied himself a public intellectual. He had strong political views, and he wanted to run for office himself, but party factotum he could never be; he bristled with ideals and causes of his own devising. Officially he was a Whig (and later a Republican), but he seldom gave comfort to his chosen party. Bennett, on the other hand, had long since cut his political ties, and although his paper covered local and national politics fully and he went after politicians with hammer and tong, Bennett was a cynic, a distruster of all settled values. He did not regard himself as an intellectual, although in fact he was better educated than Greeley. He thought himself only a hard-boiled newspaperman. Greeley was interested in ideas and in what was happening to the country. Bennett was only interested in his newspaper. He wanted to find out what the news was, what people wanted to read. And when he found out he gave it to them.

As different as Bennett and Greeley were from each other they were also curiously alike. Both stood outside the circle of polite society, even when they became prosperous, and in Bennett's case, wealthy. Both were incurable eccentrics. Neither was a gentleman. Neither conjured up the picture of a successful editor. Greeley was unkempt, always looking like an unmade bed. Even when he was nationally famous in the 1850s he resembled a clerk in a third-rate brokerage house, with slips of paper—marked-up proofs perhaps—hanging out of his pockets or stuck in his hat. He became fat, was always nearsighted, always peering over spectacles. He spoke in a piping, high-pitched whine. Not a few people suggested that he looked exactly like the illustrations of Charles Dickens's Mr. Pickwick. Greeley provided a humorous description of himself, written under the pretense that it had been the work of his long-time adversary James Fenimore Cooper. The editor was, according to this little pastiche, a half-bald, long-legged, slouching individual "so rocking in gait that he walks down both sides of the street at once."[1]

The appearance of Bennett was somewhat different but hardly more reassuring. A shrewd, wiry Scotsman, who seemed to repel intimacy, Bennett looked around at the world with a squinty glare of suspicion. His eyes did not focus right. They seemed to fix themselves on nothing and everything at the same time. He was as solitary as an oyster, the classic loner. He seldom made close friendships and few people trusted him, although nobody who had dealings with him, however brief, doubted his abilities. He, too, could have come out of a book of Dickensian eccentrics, although perhaps Ebenezer Scrooge or Thomas Gradgrind comes to mind rather than the kindly old Mr. Pickwick. Greeley was laughed at but admired; Bennett was seldom laughed at but never admired; on the other hand, he had a hard professional competence and an encyclopedic knowledge of his adopted country, an in-depth learning uncorrupted by vague idealisms. All of this perfectly suited him for the journalism of this confusing age.

Both Greeley and Bennett had served long, humiliating and disappointing apprenticeships in the newspaper business. They took a long time getting to the top, the only reward for the long years of waiting being that when they had their own newspapers, both knew what they wanted and tenaciously set about getting it. Bennett, older by sixteen years, found solid commercial success first, but with no one to offer a word of encouragement, whereas when Greeley founded the *Tribune* in 1841 he had the strong support of the Whig party and had already had a short period of modest success as an editor. When Bennett started up the *Herald* in 1835 in a dingy cellar room at 20 Wall Street he had no one behind him except himself. Fortunately this turned out to be quite enough.

James Gordon Bennett was born in 1795 in Old Town (later called New Mill), Keith, Banffshire, Scotland to a somewhat well-off Catholic family. Catholicism was alien in Calvinist Scotland so Bennett had few friends as a youth. This may account in part for his lifelong sense of isolation and his determined self-reliance. At the age of fifteen he was sent to attend Blair College, a Catholic institution in Aberdeen (later part of Aberdeen University). There he received a first-rate education, studying the classics, Greek and Latin, church history, French, logic, and general history, among other subjects. He obtained a broad knowledge of modern literature and philosophy, and he was an omnivorous reader of current European intellectual periodicals. His father apparently harbored some hope that Bennett would enter the priesthood, but in time the son's hatred of all forms of authority weakened his Catholicism. He came away with a strong liberal education but slim prospects for a vocation in the class-ridden "old world."

In his youth Bennett had read books about life in America and listened attentively to accounts of travelers who had been there. He knew that conditions in America would be crude and primitive, but the idea of starting life from scratch suited him. Accordingly, at the age of twenty-five he left the old world behind and set sail for America. Landing in Halifax, Nova Scotia, he took up a position as a schoolmaster, but was not overly pleased with

Canada. He was put off by the presence of British troops and other forms of European authority; he determined, as soon as possible, to push on to the United States. For a while he taught school in Maine, then removed to Boston where he obtained a position with Wells and Lilly, a firm of printers and booksellers.

Now Mr. Wells and Mr. Lilly were apparently kindly and intelligent men, and they instantly recognized that Bennett was a gifted and highly educated individual. But they also realized that he was difficult and demanding. He had an irritating voice, asked too many questions, and did not hide his displeasure when he failed to get a satisfactory answer. He did not get along too well with the other clerks in the store so he was given a job proofreading, which he actually preferred. Because he did not fit in socially and expressed too many offbeat opinions, Bennett formed few intimate friendships. The ugly Scotsman also had no attractions for pretty girls, although he was quite susceptible to their charms.

What was more important, he took sharp note of everything around him. He was a superlative observer. He was what his fellow Scotsman David Hume would have called an empiricist. He trusted what he saw with his own eyes. He walked the streets of Boston, peered into everything, filed everything away in his memory bank, and soon knew more about the city than anybody he talked to. For the most part he liked what he saw: Americans discovering life for themselves. He was tickled by Unitarianism, which gave the boot to traditional religion. He chortled over the idea that Unitarianism had tricked Federalist Boston by smuggling in the much despised social changes of the French Revolution under the guise of theology.

Although his Boston employers liked him and promised advancement, Bennett had a powerful desire to see more of this new country, and he soon moved on to New York, although without any firm idea of what he would do there. New York, if anything, gave him even more of an emotional lift than Boston. This city, he felt, must be the "real" America—a place with no past, living in an abundant present, waiting for a wide-open future. There were no settled institutions here, no hidebound traditions. Here, cheek by jowl, were immigrants just off the boat, displaced Yankees, stock traders, commercial enterprisers, innocents just in from the country to seek their fortune, prostitutes, swaggering frontiersmen. Here were mingled in antic confusion the accents of old Dutchmen, the Southern cotton trader, the Irish, the German, the Sephardic Jew, some of these descendants of the first settlers of New Amsterdam. All were caught up in a maelstrom, a rapidly growing society, a society that was clearly going somewhere although nobody knew precisely where.

Bennett looked for work in New York without success. A chance encounter in a coffeehouse steered him toward his life's work. Aaron Smith Willington, owner of the Charleston, South Carolina *Courier*, happened to be in New York looking to buy printing presses and other equipment. He was also looking for a new editorial assistant. Born and reared in Massachusetts, Willington was familiar with Bennett's previous employers, Wells and Lilly and, finding the young Scot to be an intelligent and ambitious fellow, offered him a job on his paper. Whether Bennett had ever thought of a career in journalism is unknown. Nor is it known why he left the metropolis that had such a strong grip on him. But something must have appealed to him in the idea of working on a newspaper, for he agreed to follow Willington to South Carolina.

Bennett could probably not have found a better place to start out. The *Courier* was one of the best papers in the South, perhaps second only to the Richmond *Enquirer*. He discovered that he had a knack for writing, particularly newspaper writing. No models from the old world held him in thrall, and he had not been party to whatever traditions of letters there had been in Boston or New York. He was an ingenious man, with a literary gift that blossomed as he went along. Starting with a clean slate in a new profession he suffered from few inhibitions. He developed a pungent sometimes combative style that seemed to fit the traditional political journalism, but added to this a prescience all his own, a sharp logic and an addiction to digging out the facts. He knew that good reporting meant leg work, and leg work had always given him joy and a sense of freedom.

Bennett liked the South. He grew overly fond of Charleston, but in less than two years he was on the move again. A kind of restlessness made him one of the first of a breed of peripatetic newspaper writers—a type that was to become commonplace later in the nineteenth century and well into the twentieth. Back in New York he worked on several papers, most importantly Mordecai Noah's *Enquirer*, for which he eventually became the Washington correspondent—in the estimation of most historians he was the first to hold that distinction. When the *Enquirer* was merged with the *Courier*, Col. James Watson Webb made Bennett his associate editor. How Bennett managed to tolerate the hot-tempered Webb is not entirely clear, but for a while the two managed to get along.

For a few years Bennett became deeply immersed in national politics. As a Washington correspondent this was inevitable, but Bennett was swept up in the Jacksonian tidal wave, and for a time he was a favorite not only of Old Hickory himself but his soon-to-be-chosen successor Martin Van Buren. Bennett shared Jackson's distrust of the Bank of the United States and wrote a series of highly trenchant articles on the subject, which gained him favor with the President. In the early 1830s, however, Colonel Webb abruptly changed his allegiance from Jackson to Clay, and the last of Bennett's articles on the bank issue were canceled. So Bennett jumped ship once again, this time with the expectation that the credit he had built up with the administration would allow him to start a New York paper of his own.

His first venture was a two-cent daily, the *Globe*. It failed almost immediately. He then purchased a paper in Philadelphia, the *Pennsylvanian*, for which he also sought aid from his political allies, but this too failed. With two major disappointments behind him Bennett became disillusioned with all attempts to build a newspaper on a political base. He was a very intuitive man, with a keen sensitivity as to how people felt about him, and he surely realized that he was mistrusted and would never be accepted as an easily managed political hack. Although his writing abilities were admitted by the Jacksonians, they rapidly reached the conclusion that he could not be relied on and thus they were unwilling to back any of his newspaper ventures. On the other hand, Bennett was distrusted just as much at the other end of the political spectrum. Webb became his steadfast enemy, a rivalry that knew no bounds after Bennett founded his own competing paper. And Thurlow Weed, leader of the New York State Whigs, developed a profound distaste for Bennett's reporting and stubborn truth-telling and would not speak to him for years.

With two failures as a publisher behind him, Bennett decided that he should abandon political journalism altogether and try something different. He was not entirely sure how he could find a journalistic formula that would succeed, but of one thing he became certain: the journalist must not be the toady of any party or faction. The journalist's ties should be to his readers; the newspaper should not be the organ of any special interest group. Bennett seems to have arrived at this notion while still working for Webb on the *Courier and Enquirer*. Writing a review of the newly established Boston *Morning Post* he remarked:

An editor must always be with the people, think with them, feel with them, and he need fear nothing. He will always be right, always strong, always popular, always free. The world has been humbugged long enough by spouters and talkers and conventioneers and legislators, *et id genus omne*. This is the editorial age, and the most intellectual age.[2]

After failures as a publisher in New York and Philadelphia, Bennett was forced to agonize long and hard over his next step. What kind of paper could speak to the people but also be substantial and intellectually independent?

By this time Ben Day had already made a clear-cut success of the *Sun* and the penny paper idea was sweeping the cities. The concept was working extraordinarily well in Philadelphia and Baltimore. The penny papers had a broad human appeal; people were really reading these papers. So Bennett concluded that he, too, should establish a penny paper. On the other hand, he was sure that readers wanted a great deal more in their newspapers than they got in the pungent but banal penny press. Perhaps there was a way to combine serious news coverage with lively human appeal. The need to find a way to bring about this mixture began to simmer in his mind.

In the spring of 1835 James Gordon Bennett was only a few months away from his fortieth birthday and had reached the time of life when a man should have gotten somewhere or nowhere. For the moment he seemed to be nowhere. At one time he had even appealed to Ben Day for a job but had been turned down. Now, however, with a life's savings of $500 he rented a cellar room in a building at 20 Wall Street. Here, with the help of some nearby printers, friends from his *Courier and Enquirer* days, he laid plans to put out his own newspaper. He proposed to call it the New York *Morning Herald*. The single basement room contained no room for presses or type cases so the printing would have to be farmed out to his generous but skeptical friends. When the *Herald* first saw the light of day, on May 11, 1835, the basement room was furnished only with a desk consisting of a plank held up by two boxes, a worn chair, and a box for files. There was but one employee: James Gordon Bennett. Yet in these humble surroundings would be born one of the great American newspapers.

The secret of the *Herald's* success was naturally due in part to the intelligence and superabundant energy of Bennett himself. But it was also due to the concept Bennett had of the paper. He knew exactly what he wanted: he wanted a paper that had the hard news of the dominant commercial papers and the liveliness of the penny press. Within weeks of the inaugural issue of his paper Bennett shared his thoughts on the local journalistic scene with his readers. He started the *Herald*, he said, because there was an obvious vacuum waiting to be filled:

The small daily papers around us were solely directed to mere police reports, melancholy accidents, or curious extracts. They indicated no mind, no intelligence, no knowledge of society at large. The larger [papers] were many of them without talent and without interest. There was plenty of room, therefore, for a cheap paper managed on our plan, calculated to circulate among all ranks and conditions; to interest the merchant and man of learning, as well as the mechanic and the man of labor.[3]

The New York *Morning Herald* made its debut looking to all the world like just another penny paper. It consisted of only four pages in the beginning. This would soon change, as would the price. Within a year the price went to two cents and the word "morning" was dropped from the title. For a number of weeks there seemed to be not a great deal to recommend the *Herald* over any of its competitors. But working day and night (Bennett seldom put in less than a nineteen-hour day), as publisher, editor, reporter, advertising manager, clerk and general factotum, Bennett pushed his struggling sheet toward the newspaper of his dreams.

But how could it have been done? In the beginning, Bennett built up his paper simply by doing a better job of the same things his competitors were doing. The successful penny papers had human interest material, so he would have it also. But he also felt that the people running the penny papers really did not know what a newspaper "story" was. The murders and courtroom dramas being presented were mostly one-shot items: here is something exciting that happened today. Bennett perceived that if you had a complex event, and it became lodged in people's minds, they would want to read about it on a continuing basis. A good news story could be milked, developed, pulled along, so that the people following the development would not only want to buy today's paper but the issue of tomorrow and the day after. It was the job of the clever newspaperman to understand what people wanted to read about on a continuing basis and what should be dropped after one day. Bennett, and those who worked for him in the years ahead, had this sense—this news sense, the sense of a story—and they exploited it to the full.

But it was not just crime news or sensationalism that Bennett wanted—he would get plenty of that and was even more heavily criticized for it than the *Sun* had been. He wanted solid news in all categories. Consider business news. New York was the center of business in America, but the commercial papers did a wretched job of covering the world of business. They were mere conduits for the information (much of it unreliable) that was passed to them. This was just a kind of advertising, not journalism. Bennett knew something about business and economics (he had studied economics in Scotland and taught it after his arrival in North America), so now he personally began to prowl Wall Street in search of "real" news. As soon as he cleaned up the first work of the day in the office he would set out for the banks and brokerage houses. He spent a good part of the day in this pursuit so that within a very brief period people began to notice that the *Herald* had all kinds of business news that could not be found elsewhere.

On the second day of the *Herald*'s publication, Bennett began writing a column called "Money Market." Scrutiny of even the earliest specimens of this column shows the information to be detailed, well researched, and analytical. One day later Bennett also began running stock prices, the first time that this had ever been done. There was a certain amount of complaint in the beginning, and some denizens of Wall Street thought that such a thing was an invasion of privacy. Within a matter of weeks, however, the complaints began to subside and New Yorkers started buying the paper for this reliable information that simply was not available elsewhere—even in the so-called "commercial" papers.

Bennett's approach to business news was succinctly explained a few years later—after the paper had become a huge commercial success—in a notice that he inserted in the paper for a few weeks running:

The spirit, pith and philosophy of commercial affairs is what men of business want. Dull records of facts, without condensation, analysis or deduction, are utterly useless. The philosophy of commerce is what we aim at, combined with accuracy, brevity and spirit.[4]

But it was not this new way of covering business alone that caught the attention of readers. Bennett expanded many other kinds of news as well. He offered much more local news, he improved the paper's foreign coverage, he introduced a column of "Theatrical Chit-Chat," and made more than a feeble attempt to cover literature and the other arts. He began to run what would come to be called "society news," and this, too, drew a large number of readers. He expanded the editorial offerings of the paper and dealt with topics other than the narrowly political. To give an outlet to his readers he inaugurated a "letters to the editor" column.

Too, Bennett became something of a crusader. He was what was much later called a muckraker, or, more politely, an investigative journalist. When he found political corruption in the city's wards, or streets not cleaned, he flayed away at the abuses he found. He carried on a campaign for a more healthy and beautiful New York. (After the Civil War, Joseph Pulitzer and the New York *World* would ride to prominence with very similar crusades, carried out on a much grander scale.) To be sure there were other editors in New York who were hoping to encourage a safer and more beautiful city. William Cullen Bryant of the *Post* had similar aspirations, but he invariably expressed them in more scholarly, polite, and genteel ways. Not so Bennett. He waded into the dirt. He hit hard. He got people upset. The role of the gentle reformer was never for him.

The *Herald* grew steadily and rapidly in circulation. What is more important, anyone who takes the trouble to look through old files of the *Herald* for its first year will see the gradual emergence of the newspaper as we know it today. It is like looking at a series of diagrams of a developing human fetus from conception to birth. This dogged and determined Scotsman was inventing what we now call news. No longer was the newspaper office a dropping-off place for moribund commercial items; now the newspaper reporter was becoming an active individual and a creator in his or her own right. Bennett's energy for discovering the news was boundless. So apparently was his ego. Two years after he established his paper he wrote, and he must have thought that he was only being matter of fact: "Shakespeare is the great genius of the drama, Scott of the novel, Milton and Byron of the poem—and I mean to be the genius of the newspaper press."[5]

Bennett's path to glory was not without bumps and pitfalls. When the paper was only three months old the printing house that was running his paper burned down in an enormous conflagration that consumed much else in the financial district. The paper had to be suspended for a while, but so confident was Bennett in his new formula that he bulled his way back in a few weeks. When the paper appeared again, the editor proudly and confidently boasted that, "We are again in the field, larger, livelier, better, prettier, saucier, and more independent than ever."[6]

But there were other forces at work against Bennett that were not so easily brushed aside. The *Herald* had put on the mantle of the penny papers and hoped to outdo them in their own field. He did not renounce news that was scandalous or titillating; rather he hoped to capitalize upon it and drain more human juices from it. If you have a spicy criminal trial you should not just notify the public that there was such a thing, you had to really cover it, get the facts behind it that are not sitting there on the court record. In such things Bennett rapidly surpassed his penny competitors. With his usual aptness of phrase he admitted that the *Sun* had a good circulation (although he was quickly closing on it) but that not many of the papers were actually read. The *Sun* was picked up by street loafers and horse tenders, but maybe it was just to dispose of their refuse. The *Sun*'s proprietors, he insisted, would not know a newspaper "story" if they saw one. They "find it as profitable to sell their paper for wrapping up tea and enveloping hog's lard, as for any other purpose."[7]

Nearly a year after the appearance of the *Herald* Bennett proved to one and all that he had it all over the *Sun* and other similar papers when it came to scandal and human interest news. A young girl from New England named Ellen Jewett was viciously murdered in a New York "boarding house"—a house that in those days was euphemistically referred to as a house of assignation. Bennett covered the investigation of the murder and a subsequent trial in full detail. He interviewed the girl's "landlady," an event that has been called the first formal interview ever run in an American newspaper. Bennett carried out his own private investigations of the case, parallel to that of the police—perhaps another first. Bennett and his reporters got the girl's whole life story. Apparently she had been an orphan from New England, adopted by a nice family, well bred, well educated for a female of the time, but she had been cast out of her genteel life after becoming pregnant. It was the kind of story that held an endless fascination for everyone in Victorian times. A girl gone wrong. An enforced slide into the city's demimonde.

Bennett looked into everything. He read the girl's letters, he traced her life story. It all appeared in the paper in full, lurid detail. This was probably the first scandalous trial in newspaper history—Bennett had made it such—and other papers were obliged to pick up the story or risk looking incompetent. The circulation of the *Herald* skyrocketed. The *Sun* was outpaced by the *Herald*, whose circulation now grew to 20,000. Bennett later insisted that he could easily have sold another 10,000 copies—or more—if his printer had had the capacity.

By 1840 the *Herald* was clearly the circulation leader in New York, an achievement that did not sit well with other publishers. Editorials in other papers attacked Bennett openly, usually for being a scandalmonger, although it was clear that Bennett's better coverage of all the news was also threatening them. For a few years there was a "moral war" on the *Herald*, and this cut into circulation for a time. Some of it emanated from the pulpit of the city's churches, but most of it came from editors of other papers jealous of Bennett's success.

Bennett never took criticism lying down, and those who attacked him were regularly assailed in the editorial pages of the *Herald*. Bennett, who had a gift for raillery and satire that was modest only in comparison with that of Jonathan Swift, took his challengers apart limb by limb. Bennett gleefully went after the weaknesses of Ben Day, Horace Greeley, and his old employer Col. James Watson Webb. Webb was so maddened by Bennett's achievements and bold contempt of his paper that he twice administered a caning to the *Herald*'s editor on the street. Bennett positively gloried in such happenings and wrote them up humorously and sarcastically in such a way that made his assailant look like the loser, and certainly the bigger fool. Bennett dealt with such situations in purely personal terms using the editorial "we" and occasionally the first person. He did not bother to disguise his shame and humiliation at being caned and his skull lacerated. He reported on it personally in an ebullient but bullying manner. His attacker, he reported, had come up from behind in a cowardly manner "and cut a slash in my head about one and a half inches in length." But he assured his readers that the event would have no effect on the editor or his paper. Webb "no doubt wanted to let out the never-failing supply of good humor and wit, which has created such a reputation for the *Herald*, and appropriate the contents to supply the emptiness of his own thick skull."[8]

Bennett never let the taunts of his competitors bother him. During his lifetime he was called, among other things, "an ink smeared Satan," a "venomous reptile," a "turkey buzzard," and other epithets too numerous to mention, but none of this abuse seemed to phase him. He answered intelligently and in good spirits. More importantly he redoubled his efforts to make a paper that would be more difficult to attack. As circulation rose he plowed back nearly all of his profits into building a top-rate news-gathering organization. He hired the best reporters, he inaugurated a European correspondence, he established a Washington bureau, he pioneered a pony express to hasten news from Washington to New York (this before the telegraph or the railroad). Anything having to do with improving news gathering, Bennett was in favor of. In the late 1840s David Hale of the *Journal of Commerce*, a man who despised Bennett but who realized that the ascerbic Scot had created the best news-gathering organization in the world, stopped in at the *Herald's* office with the idea of establishing a press association for collecting and sharing news: this would be the genesis of the Associated Press. Bennett sat down with Hale and others—even Colonel Webb!—to get the job done.

Within one year of its founding, the *Herald* had a circulation of 20,000. By this time it was already ahead of its local rivals, but this was only the beginning of its astonishing career. By 1860 it had the largest circulation of any newspaper in the world, 77,000. Of course it was not a "respected" paper, it was spat upon frequently, but its achievements could hardly be denied even by those who despised it. Bennett had built the greatest news-gathering organization in the United States. He had invented "the newspaper" as we know it today.

Bennett himself lived to a considerable age, surviving the Civil War and dying in 1872 at the age of seventy-six. When he was forty-four years old he finally gave up bachelorhood and married a comely and refined Irish girl young enough to be his daughter. Their son, James Gordon Bennett, Jr., would take over the *Herald* in the 1870s, but Bennett the elder continued his highly personal rule of the paper until the time of his death.

Throughout most of his career, Bennett's multifarious contributions to American journalism were invariably slighted because he had never lived down his reputation as a scandalmonger and "populizer" of news. Although he became wealthy through his ownership of the *Herald*, he never penetrated the upper crust of New York society, a failure that doubtless bothered him not in the slightest. On the other hand, those inside the journalistic fraternity, even those who despised him most, could hardly deny his monumental achievements. When Bennett died, Samuel Bowles, the dignified and highly respected editor of the Springfield *Republican*, did not shy away from cataloging Bennett's faults: his "lack of faith in the nobler springs of human action," his complete disinterest in idealisms or "principles," his frequently "fickle" editorial judgment. On the other hand Bowles also admitted that Bennett had no equal in organization and enterprise. He had discovered how to build and run a great city newspaper. What was more important, "under him, the *Herald* was the first of the American papers, indeed the first journal of the world, to apprehend the truth that the collection of news at any price is the first duty of journalism. . . . We must not deny to Mr. Bennett his place . . . as the great teacher and enforcer of the principle that in devotion to news-gathering lies at once the first duty and chief profit of a newspaper."[9]

One of those who commented on Bennett's death in 1872 was Horace Greeley who then would have had only a few months to live himself. Greeley was not as inclined toward generosity as Samuel Bowles. He admitted that Bennett had made the newspaper "great," but feared that he had also made it odious. Editorially, said Greeley, Bennett was "cynical, inconsistent and reckless." He was educated, but cared nothing for ideas. On the other hand, Bennett, more than any of his contemporaries, knew what the news was, and he had the ability to impress this knowledge on those in his employ. "He knew how to pick out of the events of the day the subject which engrossed the greatest number of people."[10] He knew what a news story was, and he knew how to follow it and develop it to the satisfaction of the multitudes. In this area he had no equal in his own time.

The deep suspicion in which Bennett was held by Horace Greeley was not entirely the product of professional jealousy, but rather of a wholly different concept of the goals and purposes of journalism. Unlike Bennett, Greeley was a reformer and an idealist. He believed himself to be an intellectual, a man of ideas. He believed that it was the job of the newspaper to improve the world, to make some kind of moral order out of the flux of events. Not only must the newspaper present the news, it must select, analyze, and interpret the news. The newspaper must not be a mere collector of

information, it must be a progressive force. To this endeavor Horace Greeley devoted his career, although during the years of his prime he often received little more thanks for his noble efforts than Bennett received for
more popular ones.

Greeley, who became the most widely known newspaper editor in America during his lifetime, was born near the village of Amherst, New Hampshire, on February 3, 1811. From an early age he helped his father eke out a
meager living on a rocky, sterile, barely productive farm. Apparently a
bright boy and an inveterate reader, young Horace was considered something of a "prodigy" or boy wonder by the neighbors, some of whom offered
to take up a collection to send him to nearby Phillips Exeter Academy and
perhaps later to college. The family was too proud to accept this charity,
however, and the offer was never taken up. On the other hand, Horace read
everything he could get his hands on. With the encouragement of his
mother, by the age of five he was reading Shakespeare, the Bible, and various works of the classics.

When Greeley was eleven his father lost the farm in Amherst and the
family had to flee New Hampshire ahead of a bankruptcy judgment. His father's alcoholic excesses apparently played a large part in this misfortune,
something that Greeley would remember all his life—the temperance
movement became one of his many near-fanatical causes. His father, Zac-
cheus (or Zack) Greeley, settled the family in the northwestern corner of
Vermont, only a few miles from the New York State border. It had already
been decided that Horace was not destined for a life as a farmer, so he was
apprenticed to Amos Bliss, editor of the *Northern Spectator*, in the nearby
town of East Poultney. The *Spectator* was a scraggly, ill-endowed sheet, and
Greeley barely scraped by on $40 a year. But since he was already inured to
a scant, hardscrabble existence, this seemed tolerable enough. He learned
typesetting and began to write. In his spare time he read everything he could
find in the local library.

Doubtless Greeley had his first exposure to politics at this time. Far away
from the refinements of Boston and Cambridge, East Poultney was nonetheless completely in the grip of the Federalist-Whig mentality. To Greeley,
this meant an unbounded faith in Henry Clay's ideas of internal improvements and a strong national economy. (In the election of 1828 the village of
East Poultney gave 334 votes to John Quincy Adams and 4 to Andrew Jackson.) Always a warm-hearted man, deeply concerned with the fate of individuals such as the subsistence farmers around him, Greeley nurtured the
idea that only the national government could ensure the prosperity of those
who were not already well endowed. Like most of his neighbors he became

a firm believer in the tariff. He was suspicious of individualism and laissez-faire policies, which he was sure would lead to anarchy and poverty.

The *Spectator* where Greeley spent his apprenticeship failed in 1830 when Greeley was nineteen. By this time the rest of his family had moved on to western New York where Zack tried, with no success, to make a fresh start. After the failure of the *Spectator* Greeley wrapped up his worldly possessions, tied them to a stick, and trudged the many miles to western New York. He helped with the farm for a while, but soon sought out another newspaper job a few miles away in Erie, Pennsylvania. This employment—on the Erie *Gazette*—lasted only five months, at which time Greeley decided to set off for New York City. In the hot summer of 1831 he traveled by foot, canal boat, and paddle-wheel steamer to New York with a total of $15 in his pocket. He arrived in the city at dawn on August 17, 1831, an ungainly, ragtag scarecrow of a figure with a round, innocent face—a face that would surely fail to inspire confidence in any potential employer. Only the most fertile imagination could have predicted that stepping off the boat that summer morning was a man destined to become one of the best-known Americans of his day.

Although Greeley would spend the rest of his life in New York City, there was nobody ready to hire him in 1831. He applied to the *Journal of Commerce* but the editor there thought he was a runaway apprentice and suggested it would be best if he returned to his master. For a year or so Greeley survived on whatever odd jobs he could find, but in the process he became well acquainted with the problems of metropolitan life and made up his mind that in this city he would one day be able to do some good, and that eventually he would have his own newspaper. Shortly Greeley made the acquaintance of another young printer named Francis Story, and the two of them started a small printing business at 54 Liberty Street on a shared capital of $200. The firm's chief source of income in the beginning was some printing business for the New York State lottery.

At the beginning of 1833 Greeley and Story began their ill-fated *Morning Post*. The following summer Story accidentally drowned, another severe setback for the new printing firm. But Story's place was taken by his brother-in-law Jonas Winchester and the business plodded along. Horace Greeley, although quite capable of running a printing business, was determined to put out his own newspaper, to get his ideas into print, and his new partner was willing to go along. The following year, 1834, they ventured upon a second publishing venture, this time a weekly rather than a penny daily. The paper was called the *New-Yorker* and it made its debut on March 22, 1834. Greeley's stated objective was to publish a family paper (it more nearly resembled what we would today call a magazine) devoted to current literature and politics, and designed to reach the masses and elevate their taste.[11]

The *New-Yorker* did fairly well in almost every way except financially. It was quite a hit in New York and eventually had mail subscribers around the country. Within six months there were 2,500 subscribers, and by 1837, 9,000; this was, in fact, a larger circulation than that enjoyed by any other literary magazine of the day.[12] The *New-Yorker* published essays, poems, stories, songs, as well as criticism of the popular arts. A scissors-and-paste operation in the beginning, contributions from established writers eventually came dribbling in. Greeley tried his own hand at nearly all the literary genres himself, turning out the occasional poem or story, but he soon discovered that his talents did not lay along these lines.

Being himself a strong-minded reformer, Greeley devoted most of his time to editorials of a political character. The paper claimed no firm political alliance (and it shunned religious controversy), but it was Greeley's intention to get people to think about the serious issues of the day; he did what he could to serve up his personal prejudices with "sweetmeats and pepper sauce."[13] A pungent writer, quite as lively as Bennett but usually less acerbic, Greeley's editorials attracted widespread notice.

In general Greeley's new literary miscellany appeared to most people to have a prominently Whig coloring, and in the end it was his political attachments that allowed the paper to survive. During the "panic" of 1837 Greeley was facing bankruptcy procedures that would have been every bit as humiliating as that suffered by his father in New Hampshire; subscriptions had been canceled; in distant areas of the country people tried to pay for their subscriptions using wildcat currency—if they paid at all. But Greeley the writer had attracted the attention of some of the Whig leaders of New York State, especially Thurlow Weed, editor of the Albany *Evening Journal*, who was the undisputed Whig boss of New York State. Weed was hoping to run his good friend William H. Seward for governor of New York the following year, and he wanted to start up a campaign newspaper to that end.

Out of the blue one day, Weed, who had not met Greeley before but had read his zesty and forceful editorials, showed up at Greeley's print shop, then located in a dismal attic in downtown Manhattan. Weed, a cheery, outgoing man, sometimes called "the Jolly Drummer," was surprised to see the pale, gangling, moon-faced Greeley setting type. He had a hard time believing that this was the author of the numerous neatly phrased editorials he had read. But the two men hit it off and went down the street to enjoy a meal at a nearby oyster house.

As a result of this meeting Greeley agreed to put out a campaign newspaper on behalf of Seward. The paper, called the *Jeffersonian*, published under Greeley's editorship, did the job: Seward was elected governor of New York in 1838. Two years later Greeley performed the same function for presidential candidate William Henry Harrison. With the help of another Greeley-edited campaign paper called the *Log Cabin*, Harrison became the first Whig candidate elected president. These political papers had the effect of tying Greeley to the political arena, most especially the Whig party, for which he became a prominent (although admittedly eccentric) publicist. Greeley kept his political attachments all his life (much to the scorn of the independent Bennett), and these would prove as injurious to his later career as they were advantageous in the beginning.

With the success of his political ventures and a modest income from these, Greeley was able to turn his mind once more to the idea of publishing a daily paper. He continued to be attracted to the idea of a penny paper—a paper within the reach of honest workingmen—although he believed that what people wanted (and needed) in such a paper was uplift, and moral direction. After the *Log Cabin* had accomplished its useful purposes in the election year of 1840, Greeley began laying plans for starting up an independent daily paper—with Whig leanings of course. The time for such a paper seemed ripe. The recent "moral war" against the *Herald* was fresh in everybody's mind, and Greeley hoped to cash in on the repeated demands for a "good" cheap paper, a demand not met—at least in his mind—either by the *Sun* or the *Herald*.

The paper he had in mind was the New York *Tribune*, which made its appearance on April 10, 1841. The product was a four-page paper of five columns, and it was well edited and printed. The name itself suggested the paper's goal, which was to engage the minds and talents of the people. The *Tribune* would stand first and foremost for progress and reform. Its job would be to elevate the character of its readers. It was to be a political paper, but not harnessed to any particular political party or interest. It would take on the particular and specific topics that troubled the city or the nation at the moment. It would bubble over with its reform notions and causes. It would be "Anti-Slavery, Anti-War, Anti-Rum, Anti-Tobacco, Anti-Seduction, Anti-Grogshops, Brothels, Gambling Houses."[14]

Hoping to compete head to head with the *Sun*, Greeley doubtless realized that he could not adopt a purely lofty tone like William Cullen Bryant at the *Post*; he would have to cover crime, seduction, drunkenness, and the other excesses of urban life. But he was determined to do this in a way that would point up some lesson; there should always be some moral precept to be taken from all reports of crime, adultery, or violence.

Conceived this way the paper was an immediate success. It sold 5,500 copies after four weeks and 11,000 after seven weeks.[15] At no time, however, did the *Tribune* ever exceed the *Sun* or the *Herald* in circulation. Furthermore, like Greeley's earlier journalistic ventures, the *Tribune* showed no signs of making money, probably because Greeley had little competence as a business manager. This situation improved after four months when Greeley took on a partner, a Whig lawyer named Thomas McElrath, who bought a half-interest in the paper for $2,000. McElrath, who stayed with the paper for sixteen years, put the *Tribune* on a sound financial footing and freed Greeley to do what he did best: write and edit.

Curiously, though, it was not the daily morning *Tribune* that brought national fame to Horace Greeley. Rather it was a weekly edition of the same paper that was started five months after the daily. Called the *Weekly Tribune* and sold mainly by subscription at $2 a year, the *Weekly Tribune* was a successor to the *New-Yorker*, which was folded into it, bringing along some of its popular features. Also folded into the new weekly was the campaign paper, *Log Cabin*, which was still alive in the fall of 1841, although William Henry Harrison, whom it had elected president the year before, died after only one month in office. Keeping the features of the *New-Yorker* meant retaining many of the magazine's literary qualities and an air of belle lettres, even though the new weekly would mainly be an organ of current ideas and political opinion.

It is probably fair to say that the *Weekly Tribune* was the nation's first national newspaper. It circulated around the country and was read and discussed in country general stores, in offices, and in legislative chambers. It was dropped off trains and stagecoaches in the West and eagerly awaited at innumerable post office windows around the country. Within a few years this national paper would make Horace Greeley the best-known newspaperman in the country. He was the only newspaperman in the land who was known wherever he went, and his popularity was quite understandable. He was not a political hack; he was nobody's toady in spite of his Whig alliances. He regarded himself as an educator. He talked up to people, not down to them. He encouraged them to think. Furthermore, as a countryboy himself, he knew what people were worrying about, he knew what they were saying around the cracker barrel in front of the old general store. If Bennett had a genius for knowing what news would excite and enflame people, Greeley had a genius for knowing what things were troubling people. What should we do about slavery? Was the United States destined to become an industrialized nation, or should it struggle to maintain its pastoral and agrarian beginnings? Should we have labor unions? Strikes? What should we do about unsanitary cities? Horace Greeley was not content to report these problems, he wanted to deal with them, he wanted to solve them. And he wanted to solve them in high-minded and visionary ways.

To be sure he was often called a crackpot. His editorial policies occasionally caused him to get into deep water as a public thinker. Too, Horace's crusades were a frequent burden for those who worked for him. For example, Greeley was insistent that whenever some scandalous situation had to be covered it must be used to reinforce a specific moral ideal. Greeley was particularly adamant on the subject of alcohol. In one especially characteristic Greeley story he stated: "A man by the name of Tibbetts, a short time since, jumped into a river and eternity at one and the same time. Cause: intemperance!"[16]

Greeley's broad taste in ideas and issues for reform ran to the peculiar to say the least. He was attracted for a while to Fourierist socialism and other kindred experiments like Brook Farm—these as solutions to the problem of urban decay. He was drawn inter alia to labor unions (although he could not accept strikes), vegetarianism, pacifism, and spiritualism. He was an advocate of providing free homesteads for settlers in the West and continually touted western migration. He was one of the nation's most vociferous abolitionists in the 1850s, although as the Civil War approached he could not make up his mind how the South should be dealt with.

Nonetheless, Greeley's reforming zeal had the effect of attracting to his staff some of the best newspaper talent of the nineteenth century. Among those who got their start on Greeley's *Tribune* were Henry Jarvis Raymond, who would go on to found the New York *Times* in 1851; Charles Anderson Dana, who would make the *Sun* one of the great American papers after the Civil War, and Whitelaw Reid, who would be publisher of the *Tribune* following Greeley's death. The number of writers who used the *Tribune* as an early training school could be infinitely extended. There were Henry James, William Dean Howells, Bayard Taylor, Margaret Fuller, Walt Whitman, George Ripley, Richard Hildreth, William H. Fry, James S. Pike, Solon Robinson, Edmund Clarence Steadman, Carl Schurz, and many others.

Greeley's eccentricity bothered some people; his championship of poor farmers and working-class people in the cities sometimes bothered the middle class. But in seeking solutions to the problems of the day, he was always open to ideas wherever they might be rooted. This was probably part of the reason so many younger writers and thinkers were drawn to his staff. Here was Greeley, nominally a Whig, later a Republican, hiring none other than

Karl Marx as a European correspondent for his paper in the 1850s. It is perhaps important to see that Greeley was basically a down-to-earth pragmatist and dabbler in ideas rather than a philosopher. This was put very forcefully by V. L. Parrington, the famous historian of American social thought, when he remarked that Greeley, "far from being the visionary he was so often accounted . . . was the most practical of men, accepting fact and seeking to square theory with reality; as ready to adopt new social machinery as the mill owner to adopt a new invention."[17]

Greeley's paper—certainly the *Weekly Tribune*—became a national clearinghouse of ideas in the 1840s and 1850s, always anxious to accept ideas from here and there, however peculiar. Before he even started the *Tribune* Greeley had married a young schoolteacher from Connecticut named Mary Youngs Cheney. The two had set up housekeeping at 124 Green Street, New York, where Mary made an effort to entertain distinguished visitors and intellectuals. Mary was herself very much interested in *The Dial* and faithfully read the works of Emerson, Margaret Fuller, Bronson Alcott, and Theodore Parker. She encouraged Greeley in 1844 to offer Margaret Fuller a job as literary critic on the *Tribune*. Fuller accepted and actually lived in the Greeley home for a time. She was the first woman to be a full-time writer on an American newspaper.

Fuller and Greeley did not always get along, but in the two years she served on the *Tribune* before moving to Europe, Greeley gave her complete freedom to express her ideas and cheerfully acknowledged that she was a superlative literary critic. Too, he shared her views on the equality of the sexes. On the other hand, Fuller expected chivalry from men, which Greeley found logically inconsistent. On one occasion Fuller asked Greeley to arrange an escort to walk her home after dark. Greeley threw up a quote from her book, *Woman in the Nineteenth Century*, "Let them be sea captains if they will!" That sarcasm, Greeley acknowledged, "did not tend to ripen our intimacy."[18] There was always a "friendly antagonism" between the two, in Greeley's words, but Fuller was always completely free to express her views in the *Tribune*.

There were plenty of criticisms of Greeley during his lifetime, although he became a popular figure around the country where he was familiarly known as "Uncle Horace." He was a person who could be trusted in spite of his eccentricities. The biggest complaint against his ideas and his editorials was that they did not add up to anything, that there was no coherent philosophy behind them, or even that they were irrational. As the Civil War approached, and during the war, Greeley seemed to become even more mercurial and unpredictable. The vagaries of his opinions began to trouble people.

Greeley made a wonderful cartoon figure with his shabby clothes, sticking-out hair, moon face, and falling spectacles, and when political cartoons became common in presidential campaigns, malicious artists could seldom resist poking fun at the *Tribune* editor. Greeley's fellow editors never ceased teasing him as well. James Gordon Bennett regularly referred to him as "poor Greeley," and "Greeley the Horace," or "the philosopher Greeley," always dripping with scorn. Bennett admitted that Greeley was "well intentioned," but felt that he had no consistent view of society or human nature.

Truthfully Greeley never was a philosopher, and his views of the world were undoubtedly mercurial and erratic. But in the 1840s and 1850s America was an erratic and rudderless nation. The country was struggling to orient itself in turbulent and chaotic times. The most that Greeley could do was cast about for whatever usable ideas were presently in circulation, and this he always did to the best of his ability. People eagerly waited to hear what he had to say, because everyone instinctively knew that "Uncle Horace" was nobody's hired man.

Greeley's last years were filled with sorrow and disappointment. He was constantly held up to ridicule during the Civil War. Later, in 1872, his defection from the Republican party and his attempt to launch a "Liberal" party as an antidote to the corruption of the Grant administration were noble failures as was his presidential candidacy in the last year of his life.

On the other hand, by this time Greeley had already made his mark, and his merit was universally acknowledged. He had shown the people that journalism was serious business and that newspapers could provide a genuine forum for important ideas. If he had not always been successful in solving the problems of the world, no one, even his most dedicated enemies, ever doubted that he had been in there trying.

Horace Greeley and James Gordon Bennett were the true founders of American journalism, each in his own peculiar way. Both were stubborn individualists who refused to be tied to the traditional ways of doing things. Both were eccentric and strong-willed enough that they made fools of themselves on more than one occasion, and the growing pains of their respective papers could be unseemly and embarrassing. On the other hand, their combined force pulled American journalism out of the mud in which it had long been stuck: alliance to commercial interests on the one hand or political forces on the other. In both men there was a stubborn insistence on the independence of the newspaper to speak to the people directly. The newspaper had to be an entity in its own right. Both editors repeatedly declared that their first dedication was to the reading public. In no small measure these two inspired but flawed geniuses revived Thomas Jefferson's early faith that the newspaper could be a way of educating and uplifting the populace, a way of allowing the people's voices to be heard.

4

Newspapers Move West—Ferment in the South

In the 1840s nearly all of the major newspapers of the United States were in the large cities of the East—New York, Philadelphia, Boston, Washington, Baltimore, Charleston. Some of these papers, however, were national in scope. Greeley's *Weekly Tribune* had subscribers all around the country: in the South, in New England, and in the rapidly growing western states. But the appetite for news was so great that almost all of the important eastern papers had mail subscribers far from their editorial offices and printing plants.

But this domination by the eastern press could not last. Newspaper fever had swept the land and no self-respecting town could afford to be without its own newspaper. Printing presses had been hauled across the Allegheny Mountains into Kentucky, Ohio, Indiana, and Illinois, when all of these were still merely territories. Just as the new towns and territories of the West had to have their own railroads, their own colleges—even one-building "universities"—they also had to have their own newspapers, "booster" newspapers they have sometimes been called.

It was all part of an infectious spirit that Europeans could never understand. Why build a railroad to places where there were no people? Why have colleges in tiny hamlets? Why have newspapers where there were no people to read them? The exuberant and untraditional Americans looked at things quite differently. If you build a railroad, if you have a newspaper, the people will come. This was the pattern of development almost everywhere in the West. Printing offices, newspapers, were there almost before the settlers. For example, before Minnesota was admitted as a state in 1858 there were printing offices (many with newspapers) in over forty towns and villages. Farther west this oddity was even more apparent. By the end of 1867 there had been at least four newspapers in Cheyenne, Wyoming, a town that had a population of only 800, and the whole Wyoming Territory had fewer than 9,000 people. In 1870, nearly two decades away from statehood, the very sparsely settled Dakota Territory already had seven newspapers.

Such things made foreign visitors shake their heads in disbelief. There was first of all the mysterious question of how printing presses could have been shipped out West in such great numbers. In pioneer times there were more presses in Minnesota and Wisconsin than there had been in all of England at the middle of the eighteenth century. Of course in England, and in most European countries, the number of presses had always been severely restricted by the government, which insisted on licensing printing establishments. In America, with its constitutional guarantees of freedom of press, the old licensing restrictions blew out the window after the Revolution. Anybody could own a printing press, and they could move it wherever they pleased.

The existence of the "portable press" was the clue to the profusion of newspapers in pioneer times. To be sure, most of the presses that found their way into the territories were manufactured in the East. And these models were far from being the Hoe "lightning presses" already being used in New York. They were hand-operated "army presses" which one man could carry by himself and which could easily be moved to the hinterlands on flatboat or stage. Because of the proliferation of these little devices the United States had become the leading "printing" nation of the world by the 1840s.

Still, what person in his right mind would think to set up a press and start publishing a newspaper in a tiny village where there were only a few dozen individuals, or sometimes no individuals at all? The answer is that the pioneers of the West regarded the newspaper as the essential instrument that would make civilization possible. Capt. Henry King, who worked on pioneer papers in Illinois, Missouri, and Kansas, and was for a long time the editor of the St. Louis *Globe-Democrat*, explained how it was that Kansas had a flock of newspapers even before it was admitted as a state. (Curiously the first newspaper in Kansas was a missionary sheet written in the Shawnee language!) King admitted that it seemed "illogical, fantastic and preposterous" to start newspapers before there was any news to print, but folks did it eagerly in Kansas. The newspaper was regarded as the herald of progress, not the product of it.

For the first time the press manifested the pioneering instinct and proposed to lead and not follow the course of progress—to become itself a part of the history of settlement and development. . . . The novelty of it was infectious. A second paper was soon established at Kickapoo. Early in 1855 two more appeared here in Lawrence. Others followed as new towns were founded. The printing press preceded all of the usual agencies of society. It did not wait for the rudimentary clutter of things to be composed and organized. The spirit of adventure thrust it forward ahead of the calaboose, the post office, the school, the church, and made it a symbol of conquest.[1]

The western newspaper was not merely the result of spirit and drive, it was quite simply a practical necessity. It was not that these small communities needed daily local news. As far as that was concerned, most citizens knew what was going on in town as soon as the editor of the local paper, if not sooner. The newspaper was needed in these sparsely settled areas to let people know what services were available or being introduced. The newly arrived settler just swinging down from the stage or railroad coach and hoping to make a living in a growing community had to have a way to make his talents known. Is he a tooth puller, a dry goods salesman, a druggist, a teacher, an evangelist? The best way to make these vocations or services known was through the local news sheet. Most of the contents of the early western papers were advertisements. They were the life blood of the printer, even more than in the East.

Too, advertising was important to these rapidly growing communities as a way of reaching the outside world and stimulating further migration and settlement. Very often the pioneer newspaper was supported by local land companies and business promoters. Such papers were sent to places at distant remove—the East Coast certainly, even Europe. They frequently offered land at reduced prices or boosted get-rich-quick schemes. They often wrote glowing descriptions of the localities and climate of the area, not shying away from flights of fancy that were wildly at variance with reality.[2] Many outsiders were taken in by such descriptions, as was Charles Dickens who savagely lambasted them in his travel book *American Notes* and in his novel *Martin Chuzzlewit*.

From an economic point of view, these early printing and newspaper enterprises were shaky ventures. Many of them failed either because of particular local problems or the operator's lack of ability. But presses that failed were usually followed by others that did succeed. There was nearly always quite enough business on the frontier to keep printing establishments going. This was because the majority of them were taking on the old responsibilities of the "publik printer," and there was a great deal that had to be printed in the rapidly growing territories. There were legal documents, posters, legislative enactments, court papers, and so on. The volume of such material could be staggering.

Newspapers themselves were involved in much "legal" work. In the boom-lot towns newspapers had the task of printing legal notices for homesteaders. People hoping to take possession of land were obliged to "prove up," which meant running notices in the local newspaper as many as six times declaring that they had lived up to all the government requirements. Newspapers charged exorbitant fees for such notices—from $6 to $10—and this naturally resulted in lucrative income for the printer. In areas where there were disputes over land, newspapers also ran "contest notices," notices that were even more profitable. When the Big Sioux reservation was first opened up in the Dakotas, one enterprising printer set up thirty presses in different locations so as to get all of the "proving up" and "contest" business in the area.[3]

As shoot-'em-up settlements gave way to towns, and as some degree of permanence and civility set in, there was a lot more for local printers to do. There were almanacs, manuals of navigation, even books of elementary instruction. Printed sermons were always in demand in the nineteenth century, especially in communities where rival churches were being erected and producing heated doctrinal disputes. There were endless minutes of the meetings or proceedings of religious organizations. The life and career of many a pioneer printer can be traced through his imprint on a pamphlet or the minutes of some local association of Baptists.

Of course the story of the West is not simply the story of frontier outposts. By the 1840s and 1850s there were sizable cities in the West, and many of them had established dailies that became influential in their own right. The first dailies were highly dependent on the powerful eastern press for national and international news. For this they sometimes had to wait several days or even weeks for important news to arrive by stagecoach, riverboat, or pony express. As soon as telegraph lines were strung in the 1840s, western newspapers made eager use of them. Telegraph lines reached St. Louis in 1847, and Chicago and Milwaukee in 1848.[4] In Chicago's case the telegraph arrrived the same year as the railroad.

The major cities of what was once called the "old northwest" naturally established important newspapers in quite early times—long before the appearance of the telegraph. By the beginning of the nineteenth century, for example, Cincinnati, the Queen City of the Ohio, already had a long newspaper history. In 1793, William Maxwell, a Revolutionary War soldier of Scottish parentage, established the *Sentinel of the North-Western Territory*. By the 1840s Cincinnati was anything but a small town. In fact it was the fifth-largest city in the United States, with two major daily papers, the *Ga-zette* and the *Commercial*. In the next decade the city had eight to ten dailies. By 1860, Cincinnati was a major cultural center publishing twenty-six monthlies, semimonthlies, and quarterlies.[5]

St. Louis, too, had influential newspapers early in the nineteenth century. There were ten daily newspapers by 1860, the most important being the *Missouri Republican* and the *Missouri Democrat*. The former was particularly influential in the Midwest through a widely distributed weekly edition.

Many midwestern communities grew with lightning quickness, and papers developed from one-man operations to influential daily operation in only a few years. Once again this was due to the booster spirit, which caused Minnesotans to change the name of Pig's Eye to St. Paul after vague plans were made to build a cathedral there. St. Paul, located on the Mississippi River, was the jumping-off place and center for migration to the Minnesota territory. In 1849 James M. Goodhue, a recently arrived Yankee, established the first newspaper in St. Paul (and Minnesota). In honor of the hoped-for cathedral, he planned to call his paper "The Epistle of St. Paul," but friends objected that this might sound sacrilegious. He chose instead the very appropriate name, the *Pioneer*. It was a paper that grew rapidly and survives to this day as the St. Paul *Pioneer Press*, one of the country's best-known newspapers.

Chicago newspapers, too, grew with breathtaking speed. At the time of the War of 1812, Chicago was nothing but a little stockade on Lake Michigan called Fort Dearborn. As late as 1830 the population was only thirty people.[6] But the newspaper expansion in Chicago was fairly typical for the time and locale. By 1833 the little community had grown to 350 people, at which time John Calhoun, a journeyman printer, established a tiny four-page weekly using an "army press." It contained descriptions of Indian life, news clipped from eastern papers, articles about the editor's hero, Old Hickory, and a dollop of local news. After the opening of the Erie Canal in New York State many people began taking the "overland route" to the West, and Chicago began to grow in population. One of those who came to town with the new migration was "Long John" Wentworth, a young Dartmouth graduate who had intended to take up the law but instead, with the encouragement of some local friends, bought the *Weekly Democrat*, improved its quality, and boosted circulation. Wentworth went on to become a leading citizen of the town. He served as representative in Congress for twelve years and mayor of Chicago for two terms. His paper grew explosively like the city itself. It became a daily by 1840 and was running news from the telegraph by 1848.

A competing Chicago paper was founded in 1847. This was the Chicago *Daily Tribune*, which was started by John L. Scripps, a great-uncle of E. W. Scripps, the founder of the famous twentieth-century newspaper chain. A few years later the paper was taken over by a vigorous Ohio Whig, Joseph L. Medill, who had owned papers in Coshocton, Ohio as well as in Cleveland—the *Leader*. Eventually he gained control of the *Tribune* and folded the older *Democrat* into it. Medill became one of the major figures in nineteenth-century journalism. Like "Long John" Wentworth he became a mayor of Chicago, but, more importantly, he would continue to dominate the *Tribune* until his death in 1899, making this one of the most prominent newspapers of the Midwest. For a long time, too, he was a major force in the Republican party. He has sometimes been credited with having "discovered" Abraham Lincoln—certainly he was one of Lincoln's staunchest supporters both in his campaign for the Senate in 1858 and the presidency in 1860.

It only stands to reason that the larger cities of the Midwest would have major papers as early as the 1840s and 1850s. But even before most of these papers became dailies, others had found their way across the breadth of the North American continent. For example, before large areas of the Southwest were joined to the United States by the Mexican War, an effort had been made to publish a Spanish-language newspaper for the residents of Arizona, New Mexico, and California. This was *El Crepusculo de la Libertad*, which appeared in Santa Fe in 1834. But English-language papers were not slow to arrive in the Southwest. (In the early years most were printed with Spanish and English sections.)

The first paper in California was the *Californian* published in Monterey in 1846. In the beginning it was a small sheet, about the size of a letterhead, and printed only on one side. After a brief time the paper was moved to Yerba Buena (later called San Francisco), where it had competition from a newly established Mormon paper, the California *Star*. These two papers were later combined into a new paper known as *Alta California*. It became California's first daily paper in 1850. Both papers had been started long before Sutter's gold brought hordes of fortune seekers to the West Coast.

There were also newspapers in the Pacific Northwest during the 1840s. The *Oregon Spectator* appeared in 1846 and the *Weekly Oregonian* of Portland in 1850. The first paper printed in Nevada was the *Territorial Enterprise*, which was born in Genoa, moved to Carson City, then Virginia City. The *Territorial Enterprise* became a new kind of booster paper in that it served the mining interests of the Comstock Lode. The *Enterprise* would go down in American history for an entirely different reason, however. Mark

Twain was the paper's "city editor" in the early 1860s, and he here began some of his famous spoofs and literary hoaxes. Many of these were picked up by eastern newspapers, which made Twain a famous figure in the popular imagination while he was still a young man.[7]

During the 1850s, when the Pacific Coast was far removed from the rest of the United States and it was often quicker to send news around Cape Horn than overland,[8] another kind of restlessness was becoming manifest back East and was beginning to occupy the attentions of the country's major newspapers. This was the growing sectionalism and the tension between the North and South over the issue of slavery. There had, of course, been tensions before the 1850s, but after the Kansas-Nebraska Act of 1854, and especially after the Dred Scott Decision of 1857, these tensions flared into outright conflict that no longer seemed capable of resolution.

Many newspaper editors in the North were fiercely opposed to slavery, and some, like Greeley and Bryant, were trumpeting the cause of abolitionism long before the 1850s. For the most part, however, they had handled this matter very gingerly until the eve of the Civil War. In the thinking of most of the northern reformers, the abolition of slavery was a distant goal, and they urged it circumspectly with the hope of gently nudging the South into reform.

On the other hand, there also had grown a small but very vociferous "abolitionist" press that sought to bring the whole issue to a head. The efforts of the abolitionist papers were often bullheaded, sometimes even violent. The abolitionist movement began peacefully enough around 1814 when a Quaker named Benjamin Lundy in Greenville, Tennessee, began publishing a quarterly *Manumission Journal*, the purpose of which was to encourage slave owners to free their slaves. Thus, the first serial publication of this kind came from the South itself, and, as historians often do not make clear, there were quite a few antislavery advocates in the South until sectionalism became overpowering and acrimonious in the 1850s.

Perhaps the most influential antislavery editor of the pre–Civil War era was a New Englander named William Lloyd Garrison. Garrison joined with Lundy to publish an abolitionist paper in Baltimore in 1829, but by this time there were also nearly a dozen other abolitionist papers around the country, some in the North and some in the south. Garrison's most famous paper was the *Liberator*, which he began publishing in Boston in 1829. Garrison was a forceful writer and tremendously effective organizer. During the early 1830s he managed to organize antislavery societies in nearly every city in the North. His *Liberator*, too, went everywhere, and he became passionately hated in the South. At one time the state of Georgia offered a $5,000 reward for his capture, and almost every day he received letters threatening his life.

The *Liberator* remained the leading abolitionist paper for the next thirty-five years, and many people saw Garrison as a fiery individual. Interestingly, before the Civil War, his crusade was wholly a moral one. He did not believe in political means to abolish slavery. He never advocated war. At one time he suggested that the North should secede from the Union since the Union permitted slavery to continue. Garrison was persistent rather than fiery. Still, he drew a lot of criticism even in the North. In 1835 a mob dragged him through the streets of Boston, and he was barely saved from lynching. This mob was not necessarily composed of proslavery advocates, but rather of individuals fearful of antagonizing the South and beginning some kind of sectional conflict.

At least one abolitionist editor did lose his life in the cause. The Rev. Elijah P. Lovejoy, a Presbyterian minister in St. Louis established a religious paper called the St. Louis *Observer* in 1835. The paper had strong abolitionist tendencies. Feeling threatened in Missouri he moved across the Mississippi River to Alton, Illinois, where three times in one year a mob broke into his shop and threw his press into the river. A great many people, even in the free state of Illinois, were troubled by what they regarded as Lovejoy's incendiary activities. As he was setting up his fourth press in 1837 a pitched battle arose and Lovejoy, caught in crossfire, was shot and killed.

Meanwhile, blacks in America, slave and free, were also active in the abolitionist cause and some of them founded newspapers of their own. Undoubtedly the most famous of these was Frederick Douglass, the son of a black slave and a white father. At the age of seven, Douglass was sent to Baltimore where he learned to read and write while working as a house servant. Still later he ran away to New York and later to New Bedford, Massachusetts. In 1847, when he was thirty years old, he began publishing the *North Star* in Rochester, New York, which, along with William Lloyd Garrison's *Liberator*, was one of the most prominent abolitionist papers of the pre–Civil War period. A well-educated man, with a keen sense of irony and a powerful oratorical style, Douglass eventually parted company with the "moral crusade" of Garrison and recommended political activism in support of abolition.[9] As the Whig party began to disintegrate in the early 1850s (the Whigs had always vacillated on the issue of slavery), and as free-soilers began to gravitate toward the newly formed Republican party, Douglass threw his support behind the Republicans.

It is important to remember that in the 1850s there were a great many free blacks in the United States, the largest percentage of them in the North, but a number in the South as well. Many of the freedmen were involved in anti-abolitionist groups and other political organizations. Accordingly, Douglass's *North Star*, although the most prominent black paper before the Civil War, was not the only one, nor was it the first. The first was *Freedom's Journal*, published in New York in 1827, a four-page weekly edited by John B. Russwurm and Rev. Samuel Cornish, a Presbyterian minister. Cornish eventually went on to publish three other such papers.

Almost every important northern city had black liberation papers. David Walker published the *Appeal* in Boston in 1829. Between 1830 and the Civil War there were a number of black-edited papers in New York. Philadelphia had the *Christian Recorder*. In Pittsburgh, Martin R. Delaney, the first of his race to graduate from Harvard, found that the local newspapers would not run his articles on abolition, so he started his own paper there, *The Mystery*, in 1843. There was the *Alienated American* published in Cleveland by W. H. Day, a graduate of Oberlin College. And, as incredible as it may seem, there were such papers in the South as well. The first black daily in the South was the New Orleans *Daily Creole* founded in 1856.[10]

During the early years of the nineteenth century the South itself maintained a discreet silence on the issue of slavery, the prevailing belief being that their "peculiar institution" was not a suitable topic for genteel discussion. On the other hand, with men like Garrison and Douglass brewing trouble everywhere, the South had its own bellicose advocates. Among the best known of these—they came to be called "fire-eaters"—were William Lowndes Yancey, Edmund Ruffin, and Robert Barnwell Rhett, Jr. The most volatile of the lot was Rhett, who owned the Charleston *Mercury*. Sometimes called "the father of secession," Rhett had recommended as early as 1832 that the South remove itself from the Union, for which view at the time he was as much castigated in the South as was Garrison in the North. As the Civil War drew near, Rhett moved to center stage as a leader of the secessionist cause, making South Carolina the tinder box of the war between the states.

It is important to realize, however, that the South also had moderate papers as well, and some of its editors urged restraint right up to (and even after) Fort Sumter. Lincoln himself, elected as the first Republican president, began his term of office in a conciliatory tone. He did not belong to the abolitionist wing of his party and was willing to settle for slavery continuing in the states where it already existed.

Nonetheless, the war did come, with tragic consequences for both North and South, but it would also bring about yet another transformation in American journalism—a revolution perhaps—one that would be even more monumental than the arrival of the penny press two decades before. The handling and processing of news would now definitely become a large-scale industry, calling for better and more efficient presses and other new equipment. The war would raise troubling questions about censorship, about freedom of the press, and about the relationship between the state and the press in a democracy—questions never before encountered.

Above all, there would suddenly be a great deal to report—news of battles, of soldiers killed at the front, of loved ones lost—and all such information would have to be reported quickly and efficiently if it were to be of any value to the public. The Civil War would promote the once lowly field reporter to the forefront of the newspaper world, and the reporter would have to invent a new craft. He would have to learn to write with brevity and precision, qualities that had not previously been held in high esteem. These new skills would completely transform American journalism. More importantly, the modern newspaper would now begin to emerge and transform the American mind. In the course of only a few years the newspaper would alter forever the ways of American speech and thought.

5

The Civil War—The Indispensability of News

The Civil War provided us with one of the most traumatic and earthshaking periods of transition in American history. Our survival as a nation, the very notion of the "United States," was put to a brutal test. In the years just before the war most people feared that if the issues that divided the North and South were not resolved, the republic itself would fall apart. Here was a nation, said Abraham Lincoln in his Gettysburg Address, "conceived in liberty and dedicated to the proposition that all men are created equal . . . engaged in a great civil war, testing whether that nation or any nation so conceived and so dedicated can long endure."

The nation's newspapers, some of them long-established and flourishing, would play a major role in that war—a more vital role than in any of our wars before or since. The newspaper, which in times past had been an important source of public information, suddenly became crucial and indispensable to all citizens. Most major dailies in the country were now making use of a revolutionary development in communication: the telegraph. Nearly all the big papers would employ reporters or war correspondents to cover events on the battlefields—some employed as many as forty such correspondents, or "specials" as they were then called. Reporting became much more important to newspaper publishing than it had ever been before, and the quality of reporting became crucial to the war effort itself and to the governments of both the Union and the Confederacy. Since the art of military intelligence was only in its infancy, generals and cabinet officers often learned from newspapers what was going on in the battlefields before they found out through the chain of command.

Above all, the people lived by and through the newspaper during the four dreadful years of war. The newspapers described the battles in full detail, explained and analyzed the implications of the drift of events, published maps, and ran lists of dead and injured. For those not actually involved in the battles themselves, the newspaper evoked the full reality and horror of the war. As Oliver Wendell Holmes put it at the time, "Only bread and newspapers we must have. Everything else we can do without."

This is not to suggest that newspapers had an entirely beneficial influence on the war effort. Editorially the newspapers of both North and South were difficult, stubborn, and petulant. It would not be an exaggeration to say that Abraham Lincoln found the nation's newspaper editors as big a thorn in his side as he did his most wayward or incompetent generals. In the South, Jefferson Davis was repeatedly pummeled and smeared by editors, even though they were dedicated to the Confederate cause.

In the decade or so before the Civil War, the major metropolitan newspapers had become large business organizations and powerful influences on public opinion. Most of the leading papers had sizable staffs and large press runs. There was a rising tide of news, and by the 1850s advertising, once an important presence on page one, was banished to back pages, even though it provided an increasing source of revenue. During the war itself advertising was banished almost completely from the first page, and in some papers it would not return to that place thereafter. Nearly all daily papers had a greater number of pages. The four-page penny sheet was a thing of the past in big city journalism. By the time of the Civil War, and indeed throughout the war, the New York *Herald*, which was the circulation leader among the major dailies, printed a triple-sheet, twelve-page paper, 22×32 inches in size. The price of a single copy was going up. The *Herald* went from two to three cents in December of 1862, then to four cents in August of 1864.[1]

There were important technological advances in the war years that would sharply offset rising costs of labor and materials. A few days before the war began, Greeley's *Tribune* began printing from "stereotyped plates" cast from a mold of the original type bed. This development would make for much faster press runs on rotary presses. Within a short time nearly all of the other major papers were printing from stereotyped plates. Circulation rose accordingly. During December 1860 James Gordon Bennett's *Herald* had the largest circulation of any daily in the world. It printed an average of 77,107 weekday papers, 25,000 more than the *Times* of London. The *Trib-*

une had a circulation of about 55,000; the *Sun* about 60,000; Bryant's staid *Evening Post* around 20,000.[2]

New York was clearly the newspaper capital of the nation in 1860, just as Washington was the political capital. In lesser newspapers around the country, the words "From the *Herald*" or "From the *Tribune*" were understood by everybody to refer to the New York newspapers of that name. By this time both were national newspapers. They were sent by mail all over the country and emulated and copied everywhere. Both newspapers offered home delivery daily in Washington D.C., as well as the New York area.[3] Greeley's weekly edition was still the most widely circulated paper around the country with an astonishing circulation of nearly 300,000.

Before 1860, however, the two leading national dailies were getting strong competition from another New York paper. This was the New York *Times*, founded by Henry Raymond in 1851. Raymond was a former *Tribune* editor, once a right-hand man to Horace Greeley, and, like Greeley, a native Vermonter. He had a concept for a newspaper different from that of either the *Herald* or the *Tribune*. He wanted to establish a penny paper for mass circulation, but he expected to operate it along conservative lines, avoiding the scandal and cynicism of Bennett on the one hand or the loose and volatile crusading of Greeley on the other. It would be pragmatic rather than partisan, dispassionate rather than pugnacious. Raymond believed that for all of their achievements both Greeley and Bennett were held in suspicion by many Americans, and that what was needed was a newspaper that was above suspicion, that could be relied upon to present the news impartially.

Raymond was right. His paper did not overtake the two leaders during the Civil War period (it had a circulation about half that of the *Herald*), but many people began to appreciate the even-handed editorial policies of the *Times*. Raymond made two things clear from the beginning; he wanted nothing to do with sensationalism, and he wanted nothing to do with crusading. He could appreciate the satiric bite and literary flamboyance of Bennett, but he wanted to avoid Bennett's cynical indifference to ideas. On the other hand, the mercurial and incoherent qualities of Greeley's idealisms must have been one of the reasons Raymond quit the *Tribune*. In introducing the *Times* he stated his editorial philosophy with brisk determination:

We do not mean to write as if we were in a passion, unless that shall really be the case, and we shall make it a point to get into a passion as rarely as possible. There are very few things in this world which it is worth while to get angry about, and they are just the things that anger will not improve.[4]

This was Raymond's journalistic credo in 1851, and it would pay rich dividends almost immediately. His paper's circulation rose to 10,000 after only ten weeks, which was astonishing for any newly established newspaper of the time. Conventional, conservative New Yorkers who were not pleased with the rantings of either Bennett or Greeley and wanted a paper that would not "tear a passion to tatters," got it from Raymond. The *Times* would begin a slow but steady climb to national prominence.

As to the two great New York editors during the Civil War, both of them came out looking badly, most especially Greeley, who had long been held in high esteem as a sage and public philosopher. Greeley's problem was rooted in politics and in his old Whig ties. He had long been a supporter of the abolitionist cause so that he naturally switched to the Republican party as soon as it was founded. During Lincoln's run for the presidency in 1860, Greeley had avidly supported Lincoln above William H. Seward, now one of Greeley's enemies. Greeley, of course, had once been a Seward booster and edited the campaign paper that got him elected governor of New York in 1838. But Greeley had broken with both Seward and his ally Thurlow Weed when they did not reward his own political ambitions. (One can hardly fault them since Greeley would have made a terrible politician.) When Lincoln triumphed in the 1860 presidential convention it looked as if Greeley would now sail into smooth waters with his favorite candidate entering the White House. However, when Lincoln made up his cabinet he included Seward as secretary of state—all in the interest of party unity. Greeley was crushed by this development, and the relations between the president and the *Tribune* editor were never quite the same again.

Greeley had long been an abolitionist, although never of the fire-breathing variety. After Lincoln's election he urged the avoidance of war with the South at all costs. He suggested that the government not respond to the taking of Fort Sumter, thinking that the South could still be reconciled. After the war was underway Greeley generally supported it, although he continually carped about this or that field commander or tactic and complained about the results of the North's battles. He was a regular scourge and thorn in the president's flesh. Too, Greeley began pressing for an immediate Emancipation Proclamation, which was not forthcoming. In the later years of the war Lincoln must have been exasperated by Greeley, who, on several occasions, made furtive peace overtures to the South and recommended restoration of "the Union as it was," this at a time when victory was finally in sight. Greeley lost a good deal of his credibility with the general public when he went to Canada to meet with southern representatives on a fruitless peace initiative. After the war, Greeley's reputation slipped still further when it became known that he signed the bail bond of the former Confederate president, Jefferson Davis.

Greeley was at his worst in these years as his various idealisms clashed with one another, and his personal feuds short-circuited his good intentions. His heart was in the right place—he sought a much kinder reconstruction in the South—but his mind was too cluttered with unresolved issues and political conundrums. Nonetheless, the *Tribune* did a generally good job of covering the war. The paper continued to be thought by many to be the leading American newspaper.

Greeley aside, most of the Republican papers in New York strongly supported the administration's policies during the war. Certainly the *Times* did. Raymond was such a strong supporter that he was elected chairman of the Republican National Committee in 1863, and later elected to Congress, a goal once coveted by Greeley but repeatedly denied. Bryant's *Post* was a reliable "Republican" paper, although after the war it would return to its "Democratic" roots. Lincoln also invariably had the support of the *Commercial Advertiser*.

The situation with James Gordon Bennett's New York *Herald* was somewhat more complicated. Strictly speaking the *Herald* was nonpartisan, and the acerbic old Scotsman at the helm carried none of the political baggage that regularly dragged Greeley down. On the other hand, the *Herald* was every bit as much a nuisance to Lincoln as the *Tribune*. The *Herald* was the biggest newspaper in New York—in the world for that matter—and it had a widespread national and international circulation. Before the war no northern newspaper had more subscribers in the South, and many people felt that Bennett had strong sympathies with the southern cause. He had never been an abolitionist and had urged resolution of the differences between North and South. After the secessionist movement picked up speed he at first recommended letting the South go its own way. When the war began he branded both sides as "revolutionaries." Subsequently he grudgingly supported the Union cause.

On the other hand, Bennett caused no end of pain to Lincoln during the war years and regularly assailed the president and his policies in his usually adroit and satiric language. Lincoln often spoke to his cabinet and other advisers about finding ways to "sweeten up" Bennett. He wrote politely to the New York editor and received polite replies in return. Lincoln made strong efforts to see that the army cooperated with the *Herald* and its war correspondents. Lincoln knew the *Herald* was the most widely read daily paper. It was also the most popular American paper in England and all over Europe. Since the British government made regular overtures to the South, which supplied its mills with cotton, Lincoln wanted to make sure that the northern position on issues was well represented in Whitehall. Furthermore, even after the war began, the *Herald* was widely read and quoted—and to some extent trusted—in the South. So the contents of the *Herald* were of utmost concern in Washington.

In one other way the *Herald* was indispensable to Washington during the war. It had the best news-gathering organization in the nation with the largest staff, the greatest number of and probably the best war correspondents. Bennett was always scrupulous about getting straight news and never allowed his own petty hatreds or flights of fancy to creep into the business of gathering and presenting the news. The editorial page and the news columns were kept entirely separate. There may not have been any man, any idea, any prevailing attitude to which Bennett could give his wholehearted support, but he offered unqualified allegiance to straight news.

Bennett was a generous and grateful employer. If there was anything to the myth of the tight-fisted, penny-pinching Scotsman, the myth did not apply to Bennett. He paid the highest wages in the business; he rewarded his reporters with bonuses and lavish praise for scoops and for any work well-done. Nothing was too good for the men in the field. There was never any grudging scrutiny of expense accounts, no grumbling about dead or injured horses, or the extravagance of steamboat charters or special locomotives. In instances where *Herald* reporters were taken prisoner their salaries were continued and their families taken care of by the paper. James Parton, one of the early biographers of Horace Greeley, knew Bennett well and answered the frequently uttered charges that Bennett was mean-spirited. No publisher of the day, he said, got more out of his reporters because none was more solicitous of their welfare and appreciative of their efforts: "There is no newspaper in the world where real journalistic efficiency is more certain to meet prompt recognition and just reward than in this."[5]

There was far more news in the *Herald* than in any other paper. The casualty lists were the most complete and dependable; detailed coverage of battles was nowhere more exhaustive. On one occasion the *Herald* ran the muster-roll of the entire Confederate Army, a coup of unbelievable proportions. Horace Greeley in his anger suggested that this was because Bennett was a traitor, or had friends in the War Department in Richmond, or hired spies. The truth was that Bennett paid a lot of money to get this information from advertisements and lists published in southern papers, all of which were then brought through the lines by his reporters.[6]

It is not hard to understand why the *Herald* was the one paper that was indispensable in Washington. It invariably contained more information than the War Department could get from its own intelligence sources. Nor is it hard to understand why the *Herald* was the one paper that Abraham Lincoln read every day.

Bennett was sometimes called "a traitor" in Washington, probably not a few times by Lincoln himself. On several occasions Secretary of War Edwin M. Stanton recommended censoring the *Herald*, especially because complete news coverage of battles and troop movements would give more information to the rebels than they could get from their own paid spies and observers. On the other hand the *Herald* was a loyal paper, and when asked to withhold certain secrets the staff did so willingly.

But there were plenty of newspapers around the country that proved a much greater threat to the war effort, and these provoked some limitations on freedom of speech and the press unknown in earlier days of the republic. There was in the North what came to be called the "copperhead press." The name was derived from the very poisonous snake of that name that makes no rattling noise and is thus able to sneak up silently on its victims. (The term has also been attributed to the wearing of lapel pins made of the heads of copper pennies.) These copperhead newspapers, while not precisely treasonous, attacked the war and the administration in Washington on a more or less regular basis.

Most of the copperhead papers were Democratic papers which before the war had strongly advocated the preservation of the Union by leaving the South to its own way of life. To be sure, a number of Democratic papers supported both the war and the federal government and were no more troublesome to the president than many of his own "Republican" papers.

New York City was a center of copperhead activity, as hard as that might be to understand. Active at the time were near-seditious groups like the Knights of the Golden Circle. Even the city's mayor, a Tammany Democrat named Fernando Wood, was himself a copperhead. He regularly attacked the war, the government, the draft, and the abolitionists. Probably the most important copperhead paper in New York was the *World*, originally established as a religious paper in 1860. It later merged with the old *Courier and Enquirer* but never became a moneymaker in these years. Although originally Republican in outlook it was taken over by individuals closely allied to Tammany Hall and was bankrolled by millionaire August Belmont and Mayor Wood himself. But there had already been another Tammany paper in New York, the *Daily News*, founded in 1855. During the war years this was run by Benjamin Wood, the brother of the mayor, and it became an even more overt copperhead paper than the *World*. Other New York papers thought to have copperhead leanings were the *Journal of Commerce* and the

Day-Book. And there were other papers nearby that fell into the same column: the Brooklyn *Eagle* (Brooklyn was a separate city from New York until 1898), and across the river in New Jersey there was the Newark *Journal*. The foreign-language papers in New York had copperhead leanings, most especially the German *Staats-Zeitung* and the French *Courrier des Etats-Unis*. On the other hand, the New York *Express* and the *Sun*, while Democratic, remained loyal.

There were copperhead papers throughout the North. In Boston, the *Courier* was seen to be copperhead. And the Midwest was a virtual hotbed of copperheadism. An Ohio politician and editor named Charles Laird Vallandingham might well be called the original copperhead editor. He had published an antiabolitionist paper in Dayton, Ohio, since 1847 and won a seat in Congress in 1858. During the war he proved so troublesome that he was arrested by Gen. Ambrose E. Burnside and sentenced to prison for sedition. On Lincoln's order, however, he was banished behind the Confederate lines.[7]

The copperhead papers were fairly easy to identify and their editorial content predictable. The complaints most often heard from them was that the war was a mistake and that there was no way that it could be won. In addition, they regularly disparaged the northern army, most especially its generals, and tended to play up battle losses. On the other side they glorified the southern forces and generals. They mercilessly attacked Lincoln and his cabinet as well as the military and financial management of the war, often making use of slanders (most of them untrue) that had been reported in southern papers. Most destructively they railed against every call for a fresh draft of troops, warning that more young men were being led to the slaughter by the butchers in Washington.

These attacks did not go over too well in Washington, and there were repeated requests from various generals and from the War Department to close down or censor the copperhead papers. Lincoln had been granted strong, almost dictatorial, powers during the war; he was even permitted to suspend the writ of *habeas corpus*. But he used these powers only sparingly. He always tried to treat the press with kid gloves, unlike some of his generals who, when provoked, had an occasional war correspondent taken into custody or even sent to prison. Gen. William T. Sherman distrusted nearly all members of the press and believed that most of them were effectively serving as spies. Lincoln did not go that far; however, on one occasion he did confess that "The enemy behind us is more dangerous to the country than the enemy before us."[8]

Sometimes the patience of the authorities was sorely enough tried that publishing was suspended by military order. In New York the *World* and the *Journal of Commerce* were closed down for several days in 1864 when they printed a fake presidential proclamation calling for another 400,000 men. Apparently they had gotten this piece of fiction from Joseph Howard, city editor of the Brooklyn *Eagle*, who dreamed up the hoax hoping to make a profit in the stock market. The papers resumed publication, but the editors were given very severe warnings about the dire consequences of a repetition.

Another suspension during the war was of the rabid copperhead paper *Crisis* in Ohio. The paper's editor, Samuel Madery, was a stooge for C. L. Vallandingham. He was indicted and thrown in jail. He died before coming to trial, but his office had already been destroyed by a mob. One of the most virulent leaders of the copperheads in the Midwest was Wilbur F. Storey of the Chicago *Times*. The *Times* was a more or less loyal Democratic paper until the Emancipation Proclamation, after which Storey went on a wild binge of attacking Lincoln and his generals. The *Times* was closed down by Gen. Ambrose Burnside, then commanding the military department of Ohio (which included Illinois), but a few days later Lincoln rescinded the order. Partisans of the *Times* were quick to point out that the paper had been bankrupt and that the circulation improved considerably in the wake of its suppression. The *Times* and Storey both survived the war as weak sisters on the Chicago journalistic scene.

Whatever the political indiscretions of editors great and small during the war years, there was one bright spot in the history of the American newspapers during this period. The news-gathering process was greatly enhanced and improved; papers learned how to sift the wheat from the chaff. There would be a much greater volume of news, and novel methods were devised to handle it expeditiously. Nearly all of the major metropolitan papers now had large professional staffs, so that the processing of straight news was carried out according to accepted and uniform protocols. Whatever the vagaries of editorial opinion, the leading papers managed to do a good and honest job of presenting the dispatches available to them. Above all, the business of news reporting became a respectable profession, and it began to attract good men, many of whom would later become famous journalists in the post-war years.

The Civil War was not the first war to have war correspondents, or "specials." There were a number of these in the Mexican War, and some of them gained notoriety. George Wilkins Kendall was one of the stars in the Mexican War. Editor and publisher of the New Orleans *Picayune*, Kendall reported the war news himself, and his dispatches were picked up by papers around the country. Most newspapers did not have reporters on the scene during the Mexican War, but some of them made good use of the pony express, steamers, and the newly introduced telegraph, so that rapid transmission of the news became a highly prized goal of most editors. Newspapers had become so good at collecting war news that an astonished and frustrated President James K. Polk received news of the victory at Vera Cruz not through military channels but through a telegram from Arunah Abell of the Baltimore *Sun*.

Papers in Great Britain learned a great deal about "war correspondence" during the Crimean War (1853–1856), but the scale could hardly compare with that which the Civil War developed in America. There were hundreds of reporters in the field, covering the battles themselves and also, as necessary, the War Departments, munitions, prisons, hospitals, and many other behind-the-lines venues. Some major papers had dozens of "specials" by war's end as well as stringers, miscellaneous informers, and other helpers. The two great competing papers, the *Herald* and the *Tribune*, would often have as many as a dozen correspondents covering a particular battle. Reporters at the front developed numerous and complex arts of getting the news through the lines by hook or crook, making use of the telegraph and the railroad when possible, or whatever other means were available when telegraph lines were down or rails ripped up.

Being a war correspondent seemed an attractive occupation to some in spite of its hazards. So good was war news for the health and prosperity of the newspapers back home that some publishers spent time at the front themselves. Henry Raymond of the New York *Times* was present at the Battle of Bull Run. Joseph Medill of the Chicago *Tribune* spent considerable time at the front, and, more importantly, he swiftly learned the art of organizing war news. He thereby made his paper one of the strongest in the Midwest. Included among the war correspondents were several who would go on to be newspaper publishers after the war. One was Whitelaw Reid of the Cincinnati *Gazette* who proved such a brilliant reporter at the Battle of Shiloh that he was hired by Horace Greeley and eventually became Greeley's successor as publisher of the *Tribune*. Another was German-born Henry Villard who worked for both Bennett and Greeley, reporting on several major battles including Bull Run, Fredricksburg, and the Wilderness. Villard made a fortune in railroading after the war and then purchased the New York *Evening Post*, which he and his son Oswald Garrison Villard ran for many years.

But there were numerous other correspondents who earned big reputations for themselves during the war. Some of them earned their reputation through specialization. Such was the case with B. S. Osbon of the New York *Herald*, who became in essence the first naval correspondent, covering the campaigns of Adm. David Farragut. He also served as Farragut's signal officer, and therefore was closely involved in the war effort—probably part of the reason for his spectacular success. Other correspondents won praise for their usefulness to military commanders. George W. Smalley, later to become famous as one of the first "foreign correspondents," covered the war for the *Tribune*, but he also acted as a dispatch rider for General Hooker at the Battle of Antietam. During the battle Smalley had two horses shot out from under him, but he managed to be the first to get the news of the battle to Washington where Lincoln was anxiously awaiting some hopeful outcome that would justify his Emancipation Proclamation.[9]

Some "specials" became noted for their bravery, or at least for their indefatigable energy. Some were imprisoned on being caught behind enemy lines; a few were actually hanged. It was reasonable to suppose, after all, that anyone reporting on troop movements, battlefield formations, or methods of supply was a spy for the other side, and sometimes this supposition was correct. In any case, the "special" war correspondent became a legendary figure—the stuff that dime novels would be made of. A good example of the "star reporter" in the Civil War was Charles Carleton Coffin of the Boston *Journal*. Coffin was one of the few correspondents who covered the war from beginning to end, and he seemed to have a talent for turning up everywhere at precisely the right moment. He was highly esteemed by all of his colleagues for his integrity; once he rode forty miles to verify a single report. He was completely trusted by military commanders not only because of his accuracy but because he was skilled in engineering and surveying. A biographer offered a description of Coffin that might be be highly suggestive to some movie casting director: "His tall figure and his equipment—cape, overcoat, binoculars, watch, pocket compass and notebooks—were soon familiar to the men of both West and East."[10]

It has sometimes been said that the Civil War brought about a new era of reporting, that it lifted the role of the reporter to great heights by raising professional standards. This may be something of an exaggeration. There were more reporters now, and they would be much more important cogs in the wheels of large and complex news-gathering organizations. As one media historian put it, "journalism in the Civil War was not so much different as bigger, more prominent, and as people anxiously followed campaigns that involved their husbands and brothers and sons, more important to ordinary people."[11] Newspapers were read more eagerly than at any other time in American history.

In one way that is often overlooked, Civil War journalism *did* provide a revolution in American life. The reporter, the war correspondent, may well be considered responsible, at least in part, for a wholly new way of writing and even thinking. The war required efficiency in writing as in all things, so that the newspaper reporter began to invent a clipped, telegraphic style. In part this style might have been enforced by the telegraph itself, which demanded short transmissions and brevity of expression. The reporter, anxious to reach his home office as quickly as possible with summaries of dramatic events, learned the art of writing in a concise, dramatic style. He abandoned the rich effusions and leisurely editorial digressions that usually characterized earlier newspaper prose.

Newspaper stories changed greatly during these years. Editors now called for "summary leads" for stories. These were insisted upon because telegraphic communication frequently got cut off and the lead would leave the editor with the main part of the story if that was all that came through. But shorter, more dramatic writing was also demanded by paper shortages as well as the sheer flood of news coming in from the front.

Newspaper writing was probably having a powerful effect on all of American writing during this perod. Edmund Wilson in his book *Patriotic Gore*, a superlative history of the literature of the Civil War, speaks of a "chastening" of the American prose style, which affected all domains of literature from sermons, to political speech-making, to fiction writing.[12] In the novel, for example, America moved, within only a generation, from the prolixity of James Fenimore Cooper to the simple colloquial style of Ambrose Bierce and Mark Twain.

All these changes can be easily seen in the appearance of American newspapers during the Civil War period. Anyone who takes the trouble to look at files of most American newspapers before 1860 will notice the monotonous columns, page after page of dreary ribbons of type, unbroken by ornament or other visual relief. During the Civil War small headlines became frequent, and text was occasionally broken up by maps and other visual presentations. There were photographers active during the Civil War, including the famous Mathew Brady, but it would be several more decades before a means would be found to reproduce their work in newspapers. Still, it was possible at this time to run line drawings, and more and more newspapers began to rely on the work of artists to liven up the news stories with depictions of battle scenes or other prominent events. (Quite frequently, too, pen and ink artists copied the work of on-the-spot photographers like Brady.)

These newspaper artists, now greatly increasing in number, would bring about the visual liberation of newspapers in the years after the war. Newspapers during the war, restricted as they were by space limitations, also had competition from weekly magazines that could afford to use more of the material coming from the throng of journalistic artists. The most prominent pictorial weeklies—forerunners of today's picture news magazines—were *Frank Leslie's Illustrated Newspaper*, and *Harper's Weekly*, both founded in the 1850s. These lavishly illustrated periodicals gained enormous circulations at this time.

There were numerous technological advances during the war years that also resulted in marked improvement in the quality of newspapers. Printing from stereotyped plates made possible much faster printing as well as longer press runs. In 1863 William Bullock introduced the web perfecting press, which allowed the printing of both sides of a continuous roll of paper on a rotary press. Too, syndication or sharing of news now became a widespread practice. The Associated Press, founded as a local organization in New York in 1848, became a vital clearinghouse for news—a boon to small or regional papers with limited reporting staffs.

It is probably fair to say that the Civil War brought a dramatic transformation to the very idea of news. Yes, of course, newspapers became big very rapidly, with press runs of newspapers like the *Herald* running to over 100,000 following a particularly important battle. More importantly, reading the news became a necessity, a habit that could not be broken by the average literate American. The wartime newspaper achieved something that had never been accomplished before in American life. Here was a war splitting the country apart; the newspaper alone could provide awareness of what was going on everywhere in the country. The early American republic had been regional, segmented, with citizens attending to their own affairs. Now people in Boston knew where Vicksburg and Charleston were; people in the South knew about the daily affairs of Abraham Lincoln. In the days of John Quincy Adams the affairs of the president of the republic were remote and mysterious.

The Civil War created a kind of nationwide consciousness, a sense of unity and coherency even in the face of political disintegration and the horrors of war. The newspaper, more than any other institution, was responsible for this birth of a national consciousness that remains with us today.

6

Dana and the New York
Sun—The News Story as Art

The years immediately following the Civil War opened a new chapter in the history of American journalism. It was as if a page had been decisively turned and a wholly new era revealed. In some ways, of course, this new era was only quantitatively different from the one before it. Newspapers would soon have many more pages, larger circulations, more advertising, more vested capital, larger physical plants. The nation was growing rapidly, and newspapers, especially in the larger cities, would become big businesses. Gone forever were the days when a man could start a newspaper in New York or Chicago in a basement room with one desk, a few benches, a hand press and a printer's job case. The United States was entering the Gilded Age, and even newspapers would have their gilt-edged stock certificates.

What was still more important historically was that the great editors of the 1840s, 1850s, and 1860s were nearly all about to pass from the scene. Horace Greeley and James Gordon Bennett both died in 1872. Henry J. Raymond, founder of the *Times*, died even earlier—in 1869. William Cullen Bryant continued to serve as editor of the New York *Post* until his death in 1878. His tenure had been longer than that of any major American editor before or since—forty-nine years.

It would be impossible to make any account of these years without mentioning the old New York *Sun*, the city's first penny paper. In 1837, after running the paper for less than five years, Ben Day, the founder, sold it to his brother-in-law Moses Y. Beach, whose family ran the paper for the better part of the next three decades. The *Sun* continued to be a very meager sheet, although it had strong street sales and a nice share of the city's working-class readers. It made good money for a while, and Ben Day sorrowfully declared in later years that "selling the *Sun* was the silliest thing I ever did in my life."[1] After the Civil War the sin and scandal formula became tiresome and the Beach family, probably not having too much to be proud of in the scraggly paper, looked around for a buyer.

By a curious twist of fate, in a new garb, the New York *Sun* would become a great newspaper after all. Not only did it last long into the twentieth century, in the 1870s it would begin to thrive. It never became a journal of national opinion like Greeley's old weekly *Tribune* or a "newspaper of record," like the Ochs *Times* of a future day; nonetheless it became an institution of pivotal importance in the history of American journalism. Perhaps more than any paper of its time it influenced the style and mood of American journalism; it was to have an impact on American writing that went far beyond that of its modest ambitions and its local audience. By 1880 the *Sun* was frequently referred to as "the newspaperman's newspaper," which was neither a modest nor an exaggerated tribute.

This later *Sun* was the work of a new publisher and editor, Charles Anderson Dana, who bought the paper from the Beach family in 1868. By this time Dana was already a well-known individual with an eminent journalistic background—sufficiently eminent one would suppose that his purchase of the *Sun* struck many people as peculiar in the extreme. For many years Dana had been a right-hand man of Greeley's at the *Tribune*. Before the war he had risen to be managing editor of that paper, the first individual to hold such a title in the United States. But he had serious disagreements with Greeley, and as the war developed the two could not get along. Dana was pushed out. At the risk of oversimplification, their parting did have a straightforward explanation. Dana was an unequivocal supporter of the war, whereas Greeley, with his conflicting and capricious idealisms, blew hot and cold on the war and repeatedly squabbled with the administration in Washington over policy issues.

Partly as a reward for his strong editorial support, Lincoln appointed Dana assistant secretary of war, a position he held with some distinction. At war's end Dana returned to journalism as the editor of a new Chicago paper, the *Daily Republican*. This paper thrived and became the forerunner of the *Inter-Ocean*, which would be a major paper in the next decade. But Dana apparently got tired of Chicago and returned to New York. Undoubtedly he had his heart set on running a great New York paper.

Dana was a well-educated man, but, like Greeley, his youth had been difficult and spartan. Born on August 8, 1819, in Hinsdale, New Hampshire,

Dana came from a poor but well-established pre-Revolutionary family. By dint of having studied Latin and Greek he was able to attend Harvard for two years, using up his meager savings. Worried about poor eyesight he moved to Brook Farm where he spent part of his time reading, part in manual labor, milking cows, and waiting on tables. In his spare time he taught Greek and German. Later he contributed articles to the *Dial* and the *Harbinger* and came to the notice of the most illustrious New Englanders of the time: Emerson, Hawthorne, Theodore Parker, Margaret Fuller, and George Ripley.

Before he left Brook Farm, Dana had married Eunice McDaniel, and perhaps of equal importance had caught the eye of Horace Greeley, who would shortly bring him to New York as city editor of the *Tribune*, earning fourteen dollars a week—just a dollar less than Greeley himself.[2] Before long Dana, with a sure hand at detail, and the intricacies of daily journalism, was running the paper as managing editor.

Working for Greeley probably had an important effect on Dana's character. Undoubtedly before the Civil War, surely by the time the two men parted company, Dana had had his fill of moral crusades and intellectual disputes and was ready for a new kind of journalism, probably more like that found in the *Herald* than the *Tribune*, although Dana undoubtedly shared the common contempt of Bennett's vulgarities. When Bennett died in 1872 Dana praised him for emancipating the American press of "sects, parties, cliques, and what is called society,"[3] and he obviously believed that Bennett was right in attempting to create a fresh and lively paper that responds intuitively to the wants of its readers.

But it must have come as a surprise to many people that when Dana decided to buy his own paper he picked the *Sun*, which was, in 1868, as it had always been, a frivolous little four-page sheet of no intellectual pretensions. Here was a man who had climbed the heights of journalism by buying a "saloon paper." It was the equivalent of the editorial page editor of today's New York *Times* buying into a supermarket tabloid. The *Sun* was almost never seen in fashionable parlors or on the steps of brownstone mansions. Furthermore, Dana was of a somewhat conservative and patrician mind-set. So what was he doing buying a paper whose readership (slogging along with a circulation of about forty-three thousand) was composed of workmen, mechanics, barbers, clerks, and keepers of livery stables?

Dana obviously had something in mind. For a time he had toyed with the idea of starting a newspaper from scratch. In buying the *Sun* he had strong backing from a group of prominent local Republicans including Roscoe Conkling, William M. Evarts, Salem H. Wells, A. B. Cornell, and Cyrus W. Field. With the aid of these benefactors the *Sun* moved into a new building at the corner of Nassau and Frankfort Streets facing City Hall Park—the city's rapidly developing "Newspaper Row." (The *Tribune* would build an elaborate Florentine palace right next door; the *Times* was two doors away.) By a curious irony the building purchased by the *Sun*'s Republican benefactors had long been the home of Tammany Hall, the city's Democratic headquarters, an odd coincidence that did not prevent Dana from tarring the outrageous Tammany criminals of the next decade.

Dana made some changes in the *Sun* almost immediately. The paper's masthead was changed from Roman to Old English lettering, and the accompanying emblem was redesigned. This new masthead lasted during the entire run of the paper—well into the twentieth century. There were some changes in typography and a consistent headline practice. Several important things were not changed: the paper continued to be a folio (four pages) and it continued to sell for two cents at a time when the leading competitors were getting four cents. Dana was going to hold on to the original *Sun*'s idea of a cheap newspaper for the multitudes. To be sure, most of the papers that were charging more were bigger papers with twice as much in them. If the *Sun* was to gain the edge it would need to do something better in its four pages.

And this was precisely Dana's idea. In the beginning he did not want to sacrifice the four-page format, although in later years competition forced the paper to grow. This size was just right for his purposes. What he wanted was a small, condensed, but well-thought-out paper that would have a feel of intimacy about it. Every single thing in the paper was to pulsate with life; Dana's idea was that the reader would want to read every item in the paper because all of it was lively, colorful, and condensed in a masterly manner. Naturally some news items would be more interesting than others, but Dana was determined not to have a single story that was not compelling to the reader. And if there was an important item that seemed as dull as dishwater, you transformed it or condensed it or found some other way of getting it to sparkle. In part the *Sun* would continue to be devoted to what was referred to as "human interest" news, and yes, to use those ugly words, sex, and scandal; accordingly there would be people who complained that the new *Sun* was not much different from the old. But "human interest" was a great deal more than naughtiness, and it was, Dana believed, the business of the newspaper editor to find what this much larger field of human interest was. With the passage of time Charles Anderson Dana became the ultimate connoisseur of human interest news, and he trained several generations of newspapermen to identify it and launch it into glory.

A newspaper person, certainly one who was going to work for the *Sun*, had to begin by knowing what the news was. A reporter, Dana believed, ought to have a good general education, to have read widely, and experienced life. On the face of it, a lot of what is published in newspapers is neither new nor fascinating, so it is up to the writer and editor to make sharp discriminations about what is new and riveting to the attention. Colorful news is not a series of static or closed-end events. An historian of the *Sun* put it quite well:

To Dana life was not a mere procession of elections, legislatures, theatrical performances, murders and lectures. Life was everything—a new kind of apple, a crying child on the curb, a policeman's epigram, the exact weight of a candidate for president, the latest style in whiskers, the origin of a new slang expression, the idiosyncracies of the City Hall clock, a strange four-master in the harbor, the headdresses of Syrian girls, a new president or a new football coach at Yale, a vendetta in Mulberry Bend—everything was fish to the great net of Dana's mind.[4]

Dana always emphasized the "new" part of the word news. He wanted to fill his paper with items that people hadn't heard before: "freshness," became the byword at the *Sun*, and nothing could make up for news that was borrowed, hackneyed, or stale. It was always one of Dana's favorite axioms that "all the goodness of a good egg cannot make up for the badness of a bad one."

Furthermore, it was not just scandal that people were interested in but all things of compelling human interest, and it was better that these things would be small, intimate, and close at hand rather than pompous, remote, and abstract. John B. Bogart, a longtime city editor of the *Sun* in the Dana era gave one of the most memorable and oft-quoted definitions of the news: "When a dog bites a man that is not news. But when a man bites a dog, that's news."[5]

Not only must the newspaper reporter be able to identify fresh angles on the news and ferret out stories of human interest, he or she must be able to write them with verve and dash after finding them. The art of the newspaper story was paramount to Dana. A lot of people today, even some journalists, have forgotten that in the profession it has long been customary to call the newspaper article (undoubtedly the preferred layman's term) a "story." The news writer who has just written an item about the latest peccadillo of the governor will approach his editor's desk and say, "Here's my story about the governor." More than anyone else in journalistic history Charles Anderson Dana can take credit for the persistence of this term among the journalistic fraternity, for what he hoped to encourage in his staff was the ability to write the newspaper story as an art form, as a form of literature.

A reporter attending a criminal trial or a society banquet had to be the eye, the ear, and the emotions of the reader. There was no courtroom television in those days to allow the reader to see whether the defendant sweated in the witness box, or whether the prosecutor looked stunned when he received an unexpected answer. Of course any newspaper can produce a bland, straightforward catalog of facts about a trial, or a street encounter, or a society ball, but this was precisely what Dana did not want. He wanted the newspaper writer to *write*, to use imagination, wit, instinct, education, and then to create an ambience, a world perhaps, for every story.

It is probably true that today's newspaper reporters have neither the leisure nor the propensity to write news stories as strong amalgams of fact and imagination, although the best of the breed may still be influenced by the old craft of the New York *Sun*. A *Sun* story had to have the facts, to get things correct, but if that was all it had, it would not receive praise from the editor's desk. Here are two examples of stories that illustrate the *Sun's* art form at its best. The first, written by Will Irwin, one of the best newsmen of a later day, is the lead to a story about the great San Francisco earthquake and fire, headed "The City That Was." All of Irwin's stories from the San Francisco quake were subsequently printed in book form, but the opening lines alone have often been quoted in textbooks of journalism:

The old San Francisco is dead. The gayest, lightest-hearted, most pleasure-loving city of this continent, and in many ways the most interesting and romantic, is a horde of huddled refugees living among ruins. It may rebuild; it probably will; but those who have known that peculiar city by the Golden Gate, and have caught its flavor of the *Arabian Nights* feel that it can never be the same.

It is as though a pretty, frivolous woman had passed through a great tragedy. She survives but she is sobered and different. If it rises out of the ashes it must be a modern city, much like other cities and without its old flavor.[6]

That is the *Sun* at its best in a mellow, contemplative mood. But the *Sun* was also beyond compare in handling the light or frivolous "action" story. At a critical juncture during the Populist Political Convention of 1896 the suspenders of the sergeant-at-arms broke—as reported by the *Sun's* W. J. Chamberlin:

He clutched, but he clutched too late. He dived, and grabbed once, twice, thrice, but down those trousers slipped. Mary E. Lease was only three feet away. Miss Mitchell of Kansas was only two feet away. Helen Gougar was almost on the spot. Mrs. Julia

Ward Pennington was just two seats off, and all around and about him were gathered the most beautiful and eloquent women of the convention, and every eye was upon the unfortunate Deacon McDowell.

Then he grabbed, and then again, again, and again they eluded him. Down, down, he dived. At last victory perched on him. He got the trousers, and with a yank that threatened to rip them from stem to stern, he pulled them up. At no time had the applause ceased, nor had there been any sign in a let-up in the demonstration. Now it was increased twofold. The women joined in.

McDowell, clutching the truant trousers closely about him, attempted to resume his part in the demonstration, but it was useless, and after frantic efforts to show enthusiasm, he retired to hunt up tenpenny nails. When it was over an indignant Populist introduced this resolution:

"Resolved that future sergeants-at-arms be required to wear tights."

The chairman did not put the resolution.[7]

This was reporting from an older, simpler, more relaxed America than we are familiar with today. It was a time before war, drugs, deficits, concentration camps, the atomic bomb. There were, to be sure, things to worry about, and the *Sun* did cover politics, economics, and social affairs, but mainly it was Dana's belief that the average American, hard at work, wanted the newspaper to provide him or her with a little pleasure: lighthearted stories, sentiment, tenderness, wit. The paper was not, in fact, devoted to smut and scandal, although some people who demanded high seriousness naturally tended to think so. Many people quoted Mrs. Frederick P. Bellamy, who despaired of the New York newspaper scene back in the days of Dana and E. L. Godkin: "What can you expect of a city in which every morning the *Sun* makes vice attractive, and every night the *Post* makes virtue odious?"[8] In fact, the *Sun* only made vice attractive to the extent that the entire range of human affairs was attractive. It devoted itself to the warm and simple side of daily life, to a kaleidoscopic presentation of the passing show.

The *Sun* very rapidly became a leading paper under Dana. Occasionally during the 1870s it nearly overtook the *Herald*. In the early years it would be somewhat hindered by its abbreviated format, but that was eventually remedied. So successful was the morning *Sun* that an afternoon edition of the paper appeared in the 1880s and this was highly successful for many years. There also was a weekly edition of the paper that had a large mail circulation all over the country, although it never pretended to serve as an organ of opinion like Greeley's old weekly *Tribune*.

What is more important historically, many of its best characteristics—and some of the *Sun*'s most talented writers—would be taken over by Joseph Pulitzer's New York *World* in the 1880s and by other major metropolitan papers. During its best years under Dana the *Sun* became a veritable breeding ground of journalism, a magnet for young writers who wanted to learn the art and craft of the newspaper story. The rich vein of colorful and humorous news writing displayed so well in the *Sun* has largely dried up in the twentieth century, probably to our detriment. To be sure, the *Sun* could not take all of the credit for this renaissance of news writing in the last quarter of the nineteenth century. Who can forget the stories of Mark Twain and many other contemporary top-flight newspaper writers who made contributions in the same vein? But the daily papers emanating from the *Sun* building on Nassau Street set the standard for a kind of journalism that perfectly fit the mood of an untroubled and self-confident American people. To some extent the gay light of the *Sun* shone on many American newspapers from the 1870s until the 1930s.

It goes without saying that the *Sun* attracted some of the best-working newspapermen of the day. Among the more important were W. J. Chamberlin, John R. Spears, Julian Ralph (who covered the famous Lizzie Borden trial), Amos J. Cummings, John B. Bogart (he of the "man bites dog" fame), Franklin Fyles (who covered the trial of the world-famous Brooklyn preacher Henry Ward Beecher), Edward Payson Weston, Henry Mann, Chester S. Lord, Tom Cook, and Louis Siebold. One of the giants of American journalism, Arthur Brisbane, showed up at the *Sun* when he was eighteen, knowing nothing at all according to city room legend; in two years it was believed he knew everything.

In a somewhat later period, and well into the twentieth century, the *Sun* continued to be a roost for legendary reporters. One was Will Irwin; another Montgomery Schuyler. Among the best was James Ward O'Malley ("O'Malley of the *Sun*") who joined the paper in 1906 after having been an illustrator and writer of light verse. A grand master of what was called the "feature story," O'Malley is said to be the originator of the supreme newspaperman's philosophy: "Life is just one damn thing after another." He is also credited with coining the word "brunch" for the newspaperman's breakfast-lunch combination. With the usual fey humor that characterized the *Sun*'s best years, O'Malley once wrote a sketch of his own newspaper career: "Reporter, New York morning *Sun*, for fourteen years, thirteen of which were spent in Jack's Restaurant."[9]

While the *Sun* was decidedly not an intellectual's paper, it is easy to overlook the exemplary literary quality of the *Sun*'s editorials and also the fact that the paper had some of the best editorial writers in the business. There was, for example, Edward P. Mitchell, who later succeeded Dana as editor. Mitchell was a first-rate craftsman and a polished writer. He wrote exceedingly erudite editorials, but he was also one of America's first science fiction writers. He published his stories anonymously in the *Sun*; some of them only came to light in the 1970s. (One story, "The Clock That Ran Backward," has been said to be the inspiration for H. G. Wells's *The Time Machine*.) At the *Sun* Mitchell was a very deft, graceful, and even-handed editorial writer.

And there was an army of editorial writers who later went on to glory with other papers: Henry M. Armstrong, at the *Times*; Henry J. Wright, editor of the *Globe*; Willis J. Abbott, editor of the *Christian Science Monitor*; and William L. Chenery, who went to *Collier*'s magazine. There was "night editor" Carr V. Van Anda who subsequently went on to fame as the builder of the "modern" New York *Times*. There was Henry B. Stanton, husband of the famous early leader of the feminist movement Elizabeth Cady Stanton. There were Frank Herbert Simmons, Louis Springer, Grant Overton, Mayo W. Hazeltine, W. O. Bartlett, Edward M. Kingsbury, all of whom earned distinguished professional reputations.

One of the *Sun*'s great editorial writers was Francis P. Church, who wrote probably the best-known newspaper editorial of all time, "Yes Virginia, There Is a Santa Claus." An eight-year-old Manhattan girl named Virginia O'Hanlon wrote to the *Sun* in 1897 and asked the question: "Some of my little friends say there is no Santa Claus. Papa says, 'If you see it in the *Sun* it's so.' Please tell me the truth, Is there a Santa Claus?" Edward P. Mitchell, then managing editor, admired Church's Addisonian literary style and wondered if he might like to answer the letter. Church was not too keen on the idea. But when he finally made up his mind to do it the piece turned out to be a masterpiece, a tribute to the overriding dominance of faith, love, fancy, romance, and imagination over mere fact. The piece has been reprinted more times than any other single newspaper editorial.[10]

If anyone wished to establish the point that the *Sun* was only a "light paper"—certainly it was always lighthearted—one would have to forget that it employed James Gibbons Huneker, one of the most scholarly writers of criticism ever to work on any American newspaper. (His books on music are still reprinted and read today.) One would also have to forget the many well-known literary figures who at one time or another contributed to the *Sun*, many of them regular visitors to the offices on Nassau Street: Henry James, Robert Louis Stevenson, Walt Whitman, Rudyard Kipling, Bret Harte, Ella Wheeler Wilcox, and William Dean Howells. David Graham Phillips and Samuel Hopkins Adams had themselves been on the *Sun*'s staff at one time.

Dana died in 1897, but his paper continued with much of its glory intact for the next two decades. Edward P. Mitchell was editor-in-chief of the paper from 1903 to 1920. In 1916 the paper was bought by Frank Munsey, the rising newspaper magnate and merger king. While Mitchell was active there was little diminution in the quality of the *Sun*; thereafter the paper went into a slow decline. In the 1940s the paper was merged into Scrips-Howard's afternoon *World-Telegram*, which shortly went to its own grave.

Throughout Dana's life, however, and surely for many years thereafter, the *Sun* was called the "best school of journalism in the United States," and this not only by those who had been trained by Dana personally, but by many who read the paper around the country and modeled their writing on the *Sun*'s style. One devoted follower of the *Sun* was Joel Chandler Harris of the Atlanta *Constitution*, whose Uncle Remus stories in that paper became world famous in book form. Another *Sun* devotee was St. Louis–born Eugene Field who became renowned for his "Sharps and Flats" column in the Chicago *Daily News* in the 1880s and 1890s. Field seldom passed through New York without stopping in at the *Sun* offices.

What is even more important, the *Sun*'s style influenced generations of working newspapermen. Much of the glitter of Pulitzer's *World* when it was founded in the 1880s could be traced to the influence of Dana and his staff of writers. So, too, much of the writing that was found in the *Herald*, the Hearst papers, and, yes, even the more stolid *Times*. The *Sun*'s style seeped into the famous humor magazines of the late nineteenth and early twentieth centuries—*Judge*, *Puck*, the old *Life*. When Harold Ross founded his famous *New Yorker* magazine in 1925 he got off the ground by hiring young men who had been a part of the New York newspaper scene in the early years of the twentieth century and had the talent for writing "casuals" that sparkled. That was the very talent that Ross wanted. Within a few generations the *New Yorker* staffers believed that they themselves had invented the "casual" or the journalistic familiar essay. But the word "casual" was recognized in the *Sun*'s city room in the 1880s, and the art form surely had its birth there.

Dana's death on October 18, 1897, was observed by only two lines placed at the top of the editorial page. It was all that the great editor wanted in the way of an obituary, all that he thought a newspaperman needed: "Charles Anderson Dana, Editor of the *Sun*, died yesterday afternoon." Journalists all over the country knew that a giant had passed, and the praise was heartfelt. But the best tribute to Dana and his paper had already been written by Eugene Field whose column "Sharps and Flats" gave a Dan-aesque sparkle to the Chicago *Daily News*. It was a little jingle in dialect that probably summed up the feelings of everyone who knew Dana or who had ever worked for his paper:

> But bless ye, Mr. Dana! May you live a thousan' years
> To keep things lively in this veil of human tears;
> An' when it comes your time to go, you'll need no Latin chaff
> Nor biographic data put on your epitaph;
> But one straight line of English truth will let folks know
> The homage 'nd the gratitud 'nd reverence they owe;
> You'll need no epitaph but this: "Here sleeps the man who run
> That best 'nd brightest paper, the Noo York *Sun*."[11]

7

Newspapers in the Gilded Age

In the 1870s and 1880s American newspapers, at least in the country's major metropolitan areas, were rapidly becoming big businesses. In part this was because business itself was becoming big. The nation was drifting away from the old agrarian ways to the new and often bewildering values of an urban society. It was an age of business triumphant, of capitalism rampant—an age of large corporations, of trunk line railroads, of trusts, of investment banking, of robber barons, and rags-to-riches millionaires.

Since there was a dramatic shift in the character of society, and because cities were filling up with new waves of European immigrants, there would be a need for more newspapers everywhere (many in foreign languages), and a need for existing papers to increase their number of pages and their circulations.

In a city like New York, now the principal port of embarkation for those arriving from abroad, an unhealthy bursting at the seams had already been apparent for a long time. Even before the Civil War the city was being tested to its limits. Between 1840 and 1860 the population of New York increased from 312,000 to 813,000—and this did not include nearby independent communities like Brooklyn and Queens, which were themselves large cities and did not become part of the Greater City of New York until 1898. If you added the populations of these places and nearby suburban areas in New Jersey, Long Island, and Connecticut, you had a metropolitan population of 1,600,000 by 1860.[1]

Of course the same painful growth was going on in all of the nation's major cities. Chicago's growth before the great fire of 1871 was even more rapid than that of New York. Elsewhere, small and medium-sized cities were expanding dramatically, nearly always at the expense of smaller rural communities. Census figures show that the number of American towns and cities having more than 8,000 people doubled between 1880 and 1900. By 1900 cities having more than 8,000 people accounted for 32.9 percent of the total population of 76 million.[2] Thomas Jefferson's old dream of a nation of well-spaced agrarianists was now a fading memory.

These population shifts had a great deal to do with changes in the national character and the American way of life. The rapidly increasing wealth of the city had a tendency to mask a great diversity of social problems. There were enormous disparities in wealth. There was an emerging high society or "Four Hundred," as it was called. Mansions were being built, as were posh shops, department stores, clubs, opera companies, theaters, and many new services and provisions of comfort for those who could afford them. Naturally all these delights for the multitudes required that they be promoted through advertisements, a burgeoning form of communication that would now begin to assume a prominent role in the nation's newspapers and magazines. Since advertisements paid the way for both newspapers and magazines, they began to appear in ever-increasing numbers. Advertisements had always been a major source of revenue for newspapers, but the rapid increase in volume helped boost the newspaper's economy into the larger sphere of big business.

For some time after the Civil War, newspaper advertisements continued to be uninviting ribbons of agate type without illustrations or other display devices. On the other hand the fact that many papers continued to run them on the first page gives a clue as to their indispensable nature. The increasing volume of ads and their importance to local business enterprise did not escape notice. The first advertising "agent" came upon the scene in 1841. He was John L. Hooper of New York. Shortly thereafter Volney B. Palmer was selling advertising space in Boston, Philadelphia, and New York. These early agents did not write the ads themselves but acted as middlemen or space brokers. They bought up large chunks of ad space and then sold parts of them at a slightly higher price to customers.[3]

Within a few decades, however, all this would change. One of the most important developments was that advertisers in metropolitan newspapers were no longer only local merchants drumming up trade or announcing services. Companies that manufactured consumer products began to see the advantages of display ads. Suddenly there were advertisements for products such as Castoria, Scott's Emulsion, Lydia Pinkham's Female Compound, or Hood's Sasparilla, "for that tired feeling." There were display advertisements for baby powder as well as for hernia trusses and magic curing belts. In the early 1880s Harley T. Procter of Cincinnati began to find success with the so-called "advertising slogan." Procter & Gamble's Ivory Soap was huckstered with the slogan "it's 99.44/100 percent pure." In a phrase that stuck, Procter added: "It floats."

In addition to these consumer product ads, and perhaps even more important as a source of revenue to newspapers, there were local department store owners who wanted to purchase gigantic display ads. Three great merchant princes led the way: John Wanamaker in Philadelphia, Marshall Field in Chicago, and A. T. Stewart in New York. It was John Wanamaker who placed the first full-page newspaper ad—this in 1879.[4] Full-page advertisements did not become commonplace immediately, but by the 1890s they were found in nearly all big city newspapers. There were vigorous developments in other advertising areas as well. The Philadelphia *Public Ledger* was supposed to have introduced "classified" advertising shortly after the Civil War. That is to say the *Ledger* was the first to have a department specifically for the purpose of soliciting such business.[5]

Because of the easy availability of paper, and because of the increasing demand for both advertising and news, most metropolitan newspapers increased their numbers of pages dramatically in the 1880s and 1890s. The old folio sheets were passing from the scene, even though some editors such as Charles A. Dana had a sentimental attachment to the four-page format. Soon there would be papers of twelve pages, then sixteen, then, in the twentieth century, twice and three times that number.

What was even more important, with population growing rapidly and literacy on the increase through the spread of public education, the demand for reading matter pushed up the circulation of newspapers in the last quarter of the nineteenth century. In the early 1870s only a few papers in the country had circulations above 100,000—probably only the New York *Sun*, *Daily News*, and the *Herald*. A decade or so later Pulitzer's *World* had entered the scene, and by 1892 it was the leader of the pack, with a daily circulation of 375,000. In all of the leading cities—New York, Philadelphia, Chicago, St. Louis, Baltimore, and a few others—there were major dailies with huge circulation figures. Of course there were other cities of considerable size with newspapers having circulations no greater than 20,000. But there was an increase in the aggregate circulation of American dailies of 222 percent between 1870 and 1890, this at a time when the country's population only increased by 63 percent.[6] The figures offer some testimonial to the rapidly increasing demand for reading matter.

Papers with more pages and higher circulations meant one thing without a doubt. The modern daily newspaper had to become much more fully industrialized. It would now require more typesetters, more printers, more pressmen, more deliverymen, more personnel at every stage of production. Already before the 1870s high-speed presses had been in operation on most big city papers. There was a certain amount of competition among manufacturers of presses, but the R. Hoe Company of New York continued to be the leading manufacturer of high-speed presses.[7] By the 1880s the Hoe Company had developed a "double supplement perfecting press," which consisted of two presses operating simultaneously, printing supplements of one segment fed into the other by means of a turning bar. By 1889 the Hoe Company had developed a "sextuple press," which was fed by three giant paper rolls. Such presses could turn out 48,000 twelve-page papers or 24,000 twenty-four-page papers per hour. In these same years there were also better presses being developed for smaller newspapers. Starting in 1884 the Duplex Printing Press Company put on the market a flat-bed, web-fed press that eliminated much of the old hand labor.

Naturally with the development of high-speed presses, all kinds of new cutting, pasting, and folding equipment had to be developed. During the 1880s highly advanced ink pumps were put on the market. Also, new machines were developed to cut, fold, paste (when needed), and convey twenty-four-page papers at high speed. Also, it was not good enough to print newspapers at high speed if you could not get them out of the plant, so high-speed conveyor systems were needed. In most big city newspaper plants papers could be bundled and perhaps delivered to waiting horse-drawn carriages at street level, usually by gravity chutes.

The size and speed of presses would continue to increase: in the 1890s there were Triple Web, Octuple, and Double Sextuple Presses, and by the early years of the twentieth century such presses would be capable of delivering 60,000 papers per hour.[8]

But it was not only the pressroom that saw mechanical advances in the post–Civil War years. Advanced machines were soon found in the editorial offices as well. Several years after the invention of the telephone by Alexander Bell in 1875, newspaper offices began to perceive the importance of this device. At first even the largest papers might only have one telephone for the whole office; several decades later numerous telephones were found in large city rooms, and they became an indispensable part of the journalistic world. Of equal importance was the invention of the typewriter. E. L.

Sholes, a one-time editor of the Milwaukee *Sentinel*, built the first practical typewriter in the mid-1860s. It had severe limitations, however, and was not widely adopted in newspaper offices. The arms manufacturer, E. Remington & Sons, put a superior model on the market in 1876, but it was only after the Remingtons developed their Model 2 in 1881, which could print both capital and lower-case letters, that large numbers of newsrooms adopted the machine. Many older individuals, both reporters and editors, continued to write their copy by hand until the turn of the century, and in some places beyond.

By the 1880s there was one area of newspaper production that remained dramatically untouched by machine technology and that was typesetting. As papers grew larger, the setting of type by hand became an intolerable burden. Every letter, every comma, every hyphen, every period, every space between letters had to be set out of a printer's box or job case, one by one. Huge numbers of typesetters were needed to put out a metropolitan daily, and a visit to a newspaper office must have been an awesome and even terrifying experience with hundreds of arms flailing about, diving into type cases much like sandpipers diving for fleas. If labor had not been cheap at the time such work could not have been accomplished at all. This was skilled journeyman work so that the speediest individuals commanded premium wages. But the process had nearly reached the limit of human endurance.

By the 1880s a number of inventors had patented machines for setting type and some of them were installed in newspaper offices. But there were defects in nearly all of them—they were too slow, they broke up the type, whatever. Prizes were offered for the invention of a good machine, but the difficulties in finding one were enormous. The machine that finally worked had been sweated over for several years by a young German machinist named Ottmar Mergenthaler. A former watchmaker's apprentice, Mergenthaler was working in Baltimore as a builder of patent models when he made the acquaintance of James Clephane, a Washington court stenographer who had been interested in perfecting the typewriter as a means of making multiple copies of court documents. Mergenthaler, like many others, toiled to develop a usable typesetting machine, although the project nearly drove him to madness. Success finally came with the invention of a gravity system by which small brass matrices, one for every character to be set, dropped down a channel into place at the touch of a key on a typewriter-like device. His machine assembled these matrices into a single line of type, cast the whole line, and then redistributed the matrices. A line of type could now be set and justified in a matter of seconds.

This machine was first demonstrated at the New York *Tribune* on July 3, 1886, and Whitelaw Reid, the paper's publisher, christened the new machine the "linotype." Some people made fun of the device, calling it "Reid's rattle box."[9] For a time other newspapers continued to experiment with other things. Eventually, however, the linotype machine took complete command of the market and became the body and soul of all commercial typesetting. It remained such for the better part of a century.

The heavy industrialization of newspapers in the years following the Civil War meant the same thing in the world of journalism that it meant in any of the rapidly growing industries of the period, namely a sharp separation of management from labor and a certain amount of unrest over wages and working conditions. The labor unions of printers, typographers, and pressmen became more powerful and more aggressive. The National Typographical Union (later to become the International Typographical Union) was founded in 1850, and by the time of the Civil War it had 34 locals and 3,500 members. In the 1840s and 1850s many newspapers encouraged the development of unions and looked with favor on their fraternal functions. After the war, however, the relationship between the papers' owners and shop workers became more heated and adversarial. By the mid-1870s a number of the larger papers had already experienced strikes—usually with only small benefits to the workers. Most were of short duration.

By the 1880s labor unrest had become extremely rancorous in places like New York and Chicago. Publishers made concerted efforts to break the strength of the various craft unions. In 1887 the United Typothetae was formed for the purpose of giving companies that hired print workers a bulwark against the typographical union and its demands for higher wages. There was much unrest in newspaper plants in the mid-1880s. For the most part workers did not find their demands being met; nonetheless their wages were generally good when compared to unskilled workers of the period. By 1890 most typographers were earning $4 for a nine-hour day.[10] This is a wage that would have been pleasing to some, even to young reporters, who typically earned $12 to $15 a week for their white-collar, but nonunionized, jobs.

The separation of functions and the industrialization of the post-war era made the newspaper office a much different place than it had been back in the 1830s and 1840s. The "personal" newspaper, like Greeley's *Tribune* or Bennett's *Herald* had now nearly passed from the scene. To be sure, one-man control had not disappeared, but the publisher of this later time was usually a man of some wealth, and he could become far removed from the day-to-day operation of the paper. Of course it was still usual for these publishers—or "press lords" as they were occasionally called, to have climbed up the ladder in the newspaper business, but it was no longer a requisite. The publisher could be an individual who made his money in some other field and used his capital to start a paper or buy one already that existed. So the older pattern of the owner-printer-writer-editor was becoming a thing of the past. Moreover, by the early twentieth century there would be extremely wealthy owners of newspaper chains—men like E. W. Scripps, William Randolph Hearst and Frank Munsey, who might never even visit the offices of some of their less important papers. They may or may not have exercised control of editorial content, but certainly they were not running a highly personal institution the way Greeley once ran the *Tribune* or as Dana ran the *Sun* in the 1870s and 1880s.

It was easy now to see most of the publishers of major metropolitan newspapers as corporate executives rather than newspapermen. To be sure, it continued to be the case that most of the publishers of this tumultuous age had newspaper backgrounds and were qualified by experience to hold their positions of power; nonetheless their position at the top frequently made them remote from the daily workings of the papers they headed.

No better illustrations of this tendency can be found than in the careers of Whitelaw Reid who took control of the New York *Tribune* after the death of Greeley, and of James Gordon Bennett Jr. who became the owner of the *Herald* after the death of his father. Both men were quite sufficiently prepared for their executive roles, both knew a lot about the newspaper business, both exercised their authority with vigor and determination, but in both cases there was an eventual falling off of hands-on leadership.

As to Whitelaw Reid, nobody ever suggested that he was unsuited for leadership; there was not the slightest doubt about his credentials as a newspaperman. A midwesterner by birth, Reid had a sound classical education: his uncle ran a private academy near Xenia, Ohio, and Reid studied there and later at Miami University of Ohio, where he had a brilliant academic record. Deciding on a newspaper career, he joined the Cincinnati *Gazette*, one of the best papers in the West, and quickly rose to city editor. He was an uncommonly good writer as well, and his editorials received a certain amount of national notice. He proved to be an able correspondent during the Civil War—one of the stars—and at war's end he rose rapidly in the hierarchy of his paper. Horace Greeley had followed Reid's career closely and brought him to New York in 1868 at the age of thirty-one. Reid quickly became chief editorial writer and then managing editor of the New York *Tribune*.[11] He was a far more efficient and capable executive than Greeley, and by the time Greeley made his futile run for the presidency Reid was essentially running the paper.

The *Tribune*'s stock was widely held and upon Greeley's death the paper was up for grabs. Eventually, however, Reid wheedled full title to the paper. Six years later, now a dignified conservative and prim bachelor, Reid married Elizabeth Mills, twenty years his junior, and the daughter of Darius Ogden Mills, a prominent Californian who had made millions in the gold rush. The Mills's fortune was quite sufficient to buy the *Tribune* outright and sustain it for many years.

Under Reid's management the *Tribune* was a very well-run paper, probably far better run than it had ever been under Greeley. It was the leading Republican paper in New York, the paper most likely read by the city's commercial elite. With the passage of time Reid became somewhat hidebound in his outlook and his paper took a consistently conservative stance on most political issues. He was strongly antiunion, and his fierce desire to develop a typesetting machine had been partly due to acrimonious relations with his typesetters. A standoffish, patrician type of individual, Reid became more remote from the workaday world of journalism as the years went by. Too, like Greeley, he was drawn to politics. What is more important, he enjoyed some of the political success that had always eluded his predecessor. In 1889 President Benjamin Harrison appointed him minister to France, and three years later he accepted the vice presidential nomination under Harrison.

Reid lived on until 1912, probably one of the best-known public figures in America. In the last years of his life he was ambassador to Great Britain in the reign of King Edward VII. But he continued to be editor of the *Tribune* until the time of that appointment in 1905. He ran a very solid, genteel, and dull newspaper: a bulwark against the sensationalism and the vulgarities of yellow journalism in the 1890s. He always insisted on having the best journalistic talent in the land. He hired college graduates for his paper almost exclusively, an approach that would have annoyed Greeley. He always knew what was going on at the paper even when he was abroad. On the other hand, much of the personal element of an earlier day had receded from newspaper management. For all his culture and journalistic savvy Reid was more like the corporation executive we know today than the ink-bespattered publisher of a few generations earlier.

The tragi-comic life of James Gordon Bennett Jr. took another pattern that was probably also characteristic of the Gilded Age. It might be a temptation to report that the younger Bennett illustrates the difficulties that arise when a stupid and spoiled son takes over the father's business and finds it beyond his competence. Bennett the younger may well have been spoiled and undisciplined but he was far from stupid, nor was he indolent. He was, in fact, endowed with executive talent and showed flashes of brilliance and bravura. Yes, he was the son of a very wealthy man; he had been educated in Paris and thoroughly trained by his father to take over the reins of the New York *Herald*. Unfortunately by temperament and disposition he was also what is today universally called a "playboy"—addicted to fast horses, fast women, ardent spirits, and all of the dubious pleasures of the high life. Some of his escapades would provide scintillating copy for newspapers not unlike his own.

James Gordon Bennett Jr. was born in 1841 and taken abroad early by his mother to escape the suffocating social circles which the atrabilious elder Bennett had never been invited to join and never aspired to join. Young Bennett attended the Ecole Polytechnique in Paris. During the Civil War he accepted a commission in the navy, after which he joined his father on the *Herald*. He was almost immediately given high responsibilities, becoming managing editor at the age of twenty-five. The following year the Bennetts established an evening paper in New York, the *Evening Telegram*; Bennett the younger was put in charge of it. When his father died in 1872 he took over as publisher of both daily papers.

Unlike his father, James Gordon Bennett Jr. was a handsome man of smooth manners; accordingly he was eagerly welcomed into New York society. Although he made a determined effort to manage his father's properties, he was a capricious individual and his riotous living occasionally dampened his effectiveness.[12] He was a very eligible bachelor in New York, and in the mid-1870s he became engaged to a society girl, all of which seemed to portend a charmed life as a conventional American millionaire. Unfortunately, on New Year's eve in 1876 he attended a party at the Manhattan home of his fiancée's parents. Arriving in an advanced state of merriment, he apparently mistook the living room fireplace for a bathroom fixture—all in full view of the ladies' present. This outrage naturally caused his engagement to be broken off, and Bennett was effectively drummed out of New York society. While still welcomed at his men's clubs he was never again invited to gatherings where women were present, an isolation that was undoubtedly excruciating to this outgoing and fun-loving individual. (His father would probably not have been bothered by such a banishment.)

Shortly thereafter Bennett moved to Paris, surely a more forgiving place, and lived there for forty years—the rest of his life. He thus became an absentee owner, although he was far from being an uninvolved owner. Indeed he made every effort to run the paper as intimately as if he had been in New

York. He bombarded his editors with daily telegraph messages. Nobody could be hired or fired without his permission. He received every single issue of his papers and criticized them laboriously. At editorial conferences in New York there was always an empty chair for him at the head of the table, and documents were placed there even though he was never in attendance.

Bennett ruled his papers in a dictatorial and arbitrary manner, and he could be cruel, but as a publisher he was not without his flashes of insight and high intelligence. The *Herald* remained a good paper, particularly strong on military, nautical, and society news and European news. Bennett was responsible for the laying of a trans-Atlantic cable (the Mackay-Bennett cable), and his upbringing and later residence abroad made him much more interested than any of his contemporary publishers or editors in international developments. Bennett was very alert to all of the possibilities of world news and even promoted various global exploits. In 1870 he sent one of his correspondents, Henry M. Stanley, to find the explorer David Livingstone, who had apparently become lost in "darkest Africa" while seeking the headwaters of the Nile and Congo Rivers. Naturally the "find" was an exclusive to the *Herald*.

Stirring exploits of international character became a much prized staple of the *Herald* under Bennett's incessant prodding. He bankrolled the *Pandora*'s search for the Northwest Passage, and the DeLong Expedition to the North Pole, which ended in disaster. Military coverage was always unexcelled in the *Herald*. The paper had Joseph L. Stickney with Dewey in the Spanish-American War. Richard Harding Davis covered the Boer War and Oscar King Davis and W. H. Lewis the Russo-Japanese War.

Bennett was always ready to dip into his bank account to subsidize stunts and heroic exploits of any kind. In 1875 he paid Commodore Vanderbilt $1,000 to run a fast train between New York and Chicago so that Chicagoans could have the Sunday *Herald* first thing on Sunday morning.[13] This sort of thing (always producing news) became habitual with Bennett. He donated cups for a balloon race in 1906 and for auto and airplane races in 1908. An avid sportsman, Bennett is credited with bringing the sport of polo to the United States. He personally competed in the first trans-Atlantic yacht race in 1866.

Although Bennett was a tyrannical, capricious employer, who hired and fired people on whims, the *Herald* thrived under his leadership—at least for a while. It remained the circulation leader in New York during the 1870s although often challenged by the *Sun*. When Pulitzer and the *World* appeared on the scene in the 1880s the *Herald* slipped slightly. Bennett did not get into labor entanglements with his own workers as did Whitelaw Reid. He got into trouble with the street news sellers instead: he tried to cheat them out of their profits on an occasion when he lowered the price of his paper to compete with the *World*. In spite of this, the *Herald* remained competitive, and it was profitable until the last few years of Bennett's life.

Bennett continued to live the high life in Paris until his death in 1918. One of his most notable achievements was the establishment of a Paris edition of his paper, which survives to the present day; it was for a long time a familiar icon of American civilization abroad—the Paris *Herald*. Altogether, Bennett can hardly be considered a failure as a publisher in spite of his absentee status. He was abroad many more years than Whitelaw Reid and ruled more effectively than Reid did as an expatriate owner.

The life of James Gordon Bennett Jr., nonetheless, illustrates one more instance of the dangers that beset newspapers as they moved from the old highly personal management of the pre–Civil War years to the age of big business. The separation of the entrepreneur and the editorial functions is not impossible, or necessarily bad, but always parlous. Bennett, through his malicious energy and keen-sighted enterprise, was able to keep his paper fit and trim for over forty years. Troubles only arose toward the end of his life. But perhaps the falling off that finally came was inevitable.

One should not conclude from the examples of Reid and Bennett that the newspaper business was falling into the hands of rich, remote, and pontifical capitalist bosses. The New York *Herald* and the New York *Tribune* were among the circulation leaders of the nation, and it was unlikely hereafter that large papers like this could grow without capital. And it was inevitable that some papers would be owned by those who had inherited wealth or married wealth, or achieved it by the kinds of chicanery that was common in the Gilded Age. On the other hand, the patterns of Reid and Bennett the younger, although representing a tendency, are not wholly characteristic of the era. Newspapers could and would grow from tiny seedlings as they had in earlier times and as they have in our own day. With very little capital Dana had taken over a weakling and made a great paper of it, and Joseph Pulitzer and E. W. Scripps began newspapers on shoestrings in these years and later became giants in the field.

Nor would it be correct to say that newspapers were moving completely away from the older personal style of journalism. Papers continued to express the ideas and eccentricities of their dominant leaders. Even the papers of Reid and Bennett were highly personal enterprises, albeit with attendant weaknesses, which grew with time. For the most part, the younger editors and publishers who came to the fore in these years were anything but remote from their papers. They may not have started with ink-besmeared fingers, but the vast majority were working newspapermen who put the stamp of their own personality on their enterprise. Part of the reason for this is that few American cities had large newspapers at the time of the Civil War and for some years thereafter. In the 1870s cities like Chicago, San Francisco, Cleveland, and Kansas City were still in their infancy as centers of newspaper activity and were thus ripe for youthful genius and enterprise. To a large extent the editors and publishers in these cities were closely tied to the civic life of their community. For example, Joseph Medill, publisher of the Chicago *Tribune*, had been mayor of Chicago and one of that city's prime boosters. His civic leadership was as important to him as his newspaper ownership.

The decades after the Civil War saw the appearance of some of the greatest editors and publishers of the American record, but their stature was due not to their national prominence but to their devotion to their cities and states, and often to their involvement in local and state politics. Even more importantly, however, nearly all the news giants of this age had served rugged journalistic apprenticeships of one kind or another.

Another example from Chicago might be sufficient to establish this point. Melville E. Stone, who founded the Chicago *Daily News* in 1876, had served a long apprenticeship as a newspaper reporter and editor in numerous cities around the country. The *Daily News* was launched with the aid of Chicago financier Victor F. Lawson, but the inspiration was nearly all Stone's. Stone brought to Chicago during the 1870s and 1880s some of the best journalistic talent in the United States: Eugene Field, Slason Thompson, Finley Peter Dunne (Mr. Dooley), George Harvey, George Ade, and many others. In a mere nine years the *Daily News* achieved a circulation of 100,000.

Naturally around the country major newspapers were growing from seed but led by long-standing newspaper veterans. In Atlanta, Georgia, Henry W. Grady made one of the great American newspapers of the Atlanta *Constitution*, a paper on which he had once worked as a reporter. In the true booster spirit of the time Grady became not only the leading editor of Atlanta, but a spokesman for the "New South," a term he himself coined in 1886.[14] Grady was nationally recognized as an indigenous sage of his region and was called upon to offer his views whenever any questions about the South arose in national politics.

Of the journalistic giants of this age, not all had strictly come up from the reporting ranks, but most had some kind of identification with the rudiments of newspaper work. No better example of this could be found than the career of William Rockhill Nelson of the Kansas City *Star*. Nelson had never been a reporter like Grady or Melville Stone but he clearly deserved the monumental newspaper success he enjoyed: no prizes just fell into his lap. He had been a lawyer and building contractor in Indiana before buying a small paper in Fort Wayne in 1879. The following year he moved to Kansas City, then a dusty cattle town that was jerry-built, politically corrupt, and naive—an overgrown frontier gathering place for drovers, saloon keepers and three-card monte players. Nelson saw great promise in the town and established a two-cent daily that was fresh and lively but avoided sensationalism.

While Nelson had never been a writer, he recognized the centrality of reporting to the newspaper and gathered around him the best reporters he could find. Nelson lived until 1915, the very picture of a newspaper patriarch. On the other hand, the reason for the prominence of his paper and its circulation leadership was that he determined early on, and saw to it with indefatigable energy, that the *Star*—his paper—*was* Kansas City. The city and its paper grew up together. The heart of the *Star* was its regular crusades—crusades for everything: sanitation, paved roads, parks, municipal services, and modern housing. Nelson swooped down on gamblers and crooked politicians. Nothing escaped his scrutiny, and no irregularities in city management could evade his withering attack.

Nelson was surely a "press lord" if ever there was one. On the other hand, in the Midwest the newspapers and their leaders were not alien from the social life; they dug in tenaciously; they breathed life into the world around them. Nelson had continued on a grand scale, the old formula of the western press: newspaper first, civilization afterward. The *Star* was an example of the power of the press, and if anyone was tempted to complain about the unbridled reign of capitalism in the Gilded Age, or the dominance of robber barons and money changers, they can only do so by forgetting the many glories that this age so conspicuously produced: the native newspaper genius of men like Melville Stone, Henry Grady, and William Rockhill Nelson.

8

Dangerous Crossroads: Pulitzer and Hearst

In 1883 Joseph Pulitzer, at one time a penniless immigrant from Hungary, bought up a moribund New York newspaper, the New York *World*, and made of it, within a scant few years, the most envied and widely copied paper in America. As circulation leader in New York it rapidly crushed all of its competitors, and what is more important, it did more to create the American newspaper as we know it today than any other paper in our history. The formula of the *World* was not entirely new; it drew much of its inspiration from James Gordon Bennett's *Herald* and from the penny papers of an earlier day. It was clearly intended to grab the masses with large doses of sensationalism, but there was more, much more, than scandal, gossip, and titillation. The *World* also established itself as a substantial paper. It was intelligent, wide-ranging, curious, vibrant. It hummed with the energy of the myriad manufacturing plants that were transforming the country into an industrial giant; it crackled like the electrically charged telegraph wires strung along the railroad lines which now penetrated every nook and cranny of the land.

Above all the *World* was big. Everything about it was big. Starting with a circulation of only 15,000, within a few years it would tax to the limit the latest and fastest Hoe rotary presses. At the end of the first year of Pulitzer's management the paper had risen to a circulation of 60,000. Pulitzer quickly established a Sunday edition, which in four months had a circulation of 100,000. To celebrate this achievement Pulitzer staged a grand promotional event, presenting each of his employees with a tall silk hat. He had one hundred cannon shots fired in City Hall Park. The number of pages leaped upward: the daily edition rose from 8 to 12, then to 14 pages; the Sunday edition from 36 to 44 pages. As early as 1884 the *World* bested the *Herald* of James Gordon Bennett Jr. in columns of advertising. (Pulitzer allowed local department stores to place ads with illustrations, while Bennett continued his "type only" policy.) By 1886 the paper was running sixty columns of advertising a day in a fourteen-page paper; nearly half of the Sunday paper of thirty-six to forty-four pages consisted of advertisements.[1]

After only three years of Pulitzer management, the *World* was the most profitable newspaper in the nation, and Pulitzer was a wealthy man. By 1890, a mere seven years after taking over the *World*, Pulitzer was erecting on Park Row a 310-foot, 16-story, bronze-domed office building to house his paper's offices and presses. Not only was this the tallest office building in New York at the time, it dramatically underscored the solid success of the paper by towering above all the buildings on newspaper row, including those of the *Herald*, the *Tribune*, the *Times*, and the *Sun*.

The New York *World* seemed to represent a giant leap forward for American journalism from the very first day under Pulitzer's ownership on May 11, 1883. Historians of journalism have spoken of Pulitzer's innovations in the *World* as giving birth to a "new journalism," a term that may seem a bit exaggerated to some, but neither is it completely unjustified. There was no single thing entirely new about the *World* in 1883, but Pulitzer, a man of keen intellect and fierce determination, took hold of every aspect of his paper and whipped it into a form previously unknown anywhere in the world.

The *World* was a paper that reached out to the masses. It was a blatantly popular paper. Front-page headings in the weeks after the arrival of Pulitzer give some notion of the lurid appeal of the news stories. There were, inter alia, "All for a Woman's Love," "A Bride but Not a Wife," "A Mother's Awful Crime," "Love and Cold Poison." On the other hand, Pulitzer was not interested in these stories solely for their prurient appeal but as a part of a wider picture of metropolitan life. More often than not Pulitzer used his news pages to uncover social problems: child abuse, political corruption, poverty, crime, filthy and underfunded city asylums, and so on. There was a large dosage of sympathy and human compassion beneath the *World*'s headlines, and the paper's readers—hordes of day laborers, newly arrived immigrants, and tenement dwellers—quickly perceived that Pulitzer was on their side, was pulling for them.

Still more important, much of the success of the *World* can be attributed to its crusades. Always a Democratic and "reform" paper, Pulitzer projected his ideas into the forefront of the now dawning progressive era. Daily he attacked monopolies, tax luxuries, the lifestyles of the rich, child labor, repressed wages, conspicuous consumption, the misuse of corporations and trusts. He called for civil service reform and the punishment of corrupt officials. He exposed vote buying, bribery, and graft. The *World*, in essence, gave birth to what would later be popularly known as "muckraking," and it started some authors on their way as well-known muckrakers, such as David Graham Phillips.

In addition to muckraking and crusading, the *World* attracted its readership by means of campaigns, escapades, and stunts. When it was announced in 1885 that France was about to ship the disassembled Statue of Liberty to the United States and it was revealed that there was no suitable pedestal for the heroic sculpture to stand upon, Pulitzer championed the cause; his paper took up a collection for the pedestal, announcing that he wanted the money to come from ordinary people, just as had the gifts from the French people had for Liberty herself. Within months the *World* managed to raise the $100,000 needed, and the pedestal was erected on Bedloe's Island in New York harbor.[2]

Another reason for the *World*'s rapid and spectacular success was that Pulitzer broadened the scope of the newspaper's functions. He wanted his paper to be both informative and entertaining in large measures. The increased size of the paper allowed Pulitzer to include more items that might be called recreational and had not previously been part of daily newspapers. He introduced into his papers (which included an evening edition established in 1887) features such as women's pages, puzzles, sections for young readers, sections for sports enthusiasts and other special interest groups. Even before photography made its way into daily journalism the *World* was offering its readers generous use of line drawings, starting with single column cuts of well-known people, later two-column cuts, including maps, scenes of crimes with an "X" marking the place where a body lay. During the presidential campaign of 1884 the *World* began running large-sized political cartoons.

Pulitzer was himself a man of some culture and refinement, so he was personally dubious of the increasing use of illustrations, cartoons, and the like. But he found that when they were removed the readers howled, so they were immediately restored and multiplied. With a big splurge, on Sunday November 19, 1893, the *World* introduced the first colored Sunday supplement, printed on a new press especially designed for the purpose. Among the features appearing in this new supplement was a cartoon called "The Yellow Kid," drawn by R. F. Outcault. It gave birth to what we now call the comics, or the "funnies." Other cartoon features followed and were subsequently introduced into the daily *World* as well.

There was probably not one, or two, or even a half dozen novelties that made the New York *World* the most innovative newspaper of its day. It was, rather, the incessant push, day after day, to revolutionize the way newspapers looked and responded to the world. Joseph Pulitzer, a man of intense and superabundant nervous energy, personally managed his paper step by step, retaining what worked and discarding what did not. For a number of years he was essentially both the editor and publisher of his paper—thus giving the lie to the notion that the "personal" journalism of Greeley and Bennett had vanished. Newspapers were much larger now, much more difficult to manage down to their last detail; nonetheless, for nearly a decade Pulitzer managed to do it. In the end his health was broken under the strain, but while he was in full possession of his faculties he was able to direct the force of his considerable intellect to creating a newspaper of commanding presence.

Who was this Joseph Pulitzer who took the newspaper world by storm in 1883? Curiously, only thirty-six years old, he had already made a mark in the newspaper field as publisher of the St. Louis *Post-Dispatch*, which he had bought at a bankruptcy sale five years earlier and transformed in a scant few years into a highly successful institution. Pulitzer himself was clearly something of a dynamo and wonder-worker. He had been born in Mako, Hungary, on April 10, 1847, son of a Magyar-Jewish father and an Austro-German (Catholic) mother. His family was rather well-to-do and cultured, so he received a solid private school education. After this, with the prodding of two officer uncles, he decided upon a military career. This turned out to be a terrible choice. As a seventeen-year-old youth Pulitzer was scrawny and had poor eyesight, so there was no room for him in the Austro-Hungarian Army. He was equally unsuccessful in finding a place in the French Foreign Legion and the British Indian Service. Finding that recruits were needed in the Union Army during the last year of the Civil War, Pulitzer migrated to America, where he served eight months in the cavalry under Gen. Philip Sheridan. Apparently a prickly oddball, Pulitzer did not get along well with his officers and fellow recruits. Accordingly, after spending the final months of the war as an orderly, he gave up his dream of a military career and found himself in New York, nearly penniless and without prospects.

Because of his guttural accent and shaky English, Pulitzer decided that he ought to trek out to the American heartland where there was no German spoken, only plain American English. Somebody, probably a practical joker, recommended St. Louis, a predominantly German city at the time. He arrived there without a clue as to his occupational prospects. It has been said that he worked as a waiter in a German restaurant for half a day. After this he held a job as caretaker for sixteen Missouri mules. Years later Pulitzer recalled those mules. "Never in my life did I have a more trying task. The man who has not cared for sixteen mules does not know what work and troubles are."[3]

A number of equally menial jobs followed, but meanwhile the insatiably curious Pulitzer was frequenting the great St. Louis Mercantile Library, reading everything he could get his hands on in his spare time, living in run-down boardinghouses. He soon formed a connection with the Deutsche Geselschaft, founded by Carl Schurz and Emile Preetorious to assist young Germans in the city. This connection led to more dignified positions. Pulitzer now began reading law and was subsequently admitted to the Missouri bar. His energy and intelligence so impressed Schurz and Preetorious that they offered him a job as a reporter on their *Westliche Post*, probably the most prominent German-language paper in the Midwest. This was in 1868, and Pulitzer was twenty-one years of age.

As a reporter Pulitzer must have seemed a comic, Dickensian figure as he raced around town, a long, lanky individual with a pencil behind his ear, coattails flying. When he arrived at a political meeting or some other place of breaking news he rushed in and began asking questions of everyone in sight, which caused him to be the butt of jokes of reporters on the English-language papers. But the editors of those other papers were soon finding things in the *Westliche Post* that were not in their papers that should have been. Pulitzer's competitors found that it was better to copy the volatile scarecrow "Joey" than make fun of him. Alas, Pulitzer's frenetic energy was more easily admired than duplicated. The young whiz was never at rest: he worked every day from 10 A.M. to 2 A.M. without cessation and involved himself in every aspect of his paper's news coverage.

Rising rapidly on his paper with the support of Carl Schurz, Pulitzer eventually became a part owner of the paper. But he was also drawn to politics and was elected to a term in the Missouri state legislature as a Republican. Here he proved to be as stubborn as those Missouri mules he had once taken care of. He was shot in the leg by one of his fellow legislators after a nasty tiff. In 1872 Pulitzer passionately devoted himself to Horace Greeley's "liberal Republican" challenge to the corruption of the Grant administration. Later, however, breaking with his mentor Schurz, he turned Democrat and supported Samuel J. Tilden for president in 1876.

By this time Pulitzer had probably made up his mind that his future was not in politics but in journalism. He sold his share of the *Westliche Post* and moved east where he worked for a time as Washington correspondent of the New York *Sun*. (Being somewhat of an admirer of Dana and the *Sun*, Pulitzer was prompted to propose that he put out a German-language edition of the *Sun* in New York, but the idea was never taken up.) While he was in Washington Pulitzer fell in love with and married Kate Davis, a beautiful and accomplished young lady of an old southern family. They sailed to Europe on their honeymoon, but Pulitzer was now determined to provide for his wife as a newspaper proprietor.

After the honeymoon he returned to St. Louis, a place he knew well. His guttural accent had faded, and he now effected a more patrician air, although his nervous energy and seething ambition had only been plowed under. At the end of 1878, Pulitzer bought at a sheriff's sale a miserable little paper, the St. Louis *Dispatch*, which had started in 1864 and was then fading away to nothing. Pulitzer paid $2,500 for the paper, although it did have one redeeming feature, a membership in the Associated Press. Several days later Pulitzer formed an alliance with the St. Louis *Post*, owned by one John Dillon. For a year or so Dillon remained a partner of Pulitzer's but then sold out to him. The St. Louis *Post-Dispatch* was then a Pulitzer property.

St. Louis was already a strong newspaper town when Pulitzer entered the field. The area was dominated by two powerful and influential morning papers, the *Missouri Republican*, and the *Globe-Democrat*. The latter had a nationwide reputation: its editor-publisher Joseph B. McCullagh was the first newspaperman ever to be granted a formal interview with a president of the United States, the president being Andrew Johnson.[4] But the *Post-Dispatch* had little room to maneuver, since it was an evening paper, and not much to work with in the beginning. The old *Post* did not even have a press of its own; its pages had been turned out in off-hours at the *Globe-Democrat*. The *Dispatch* had hand-me-down equipment at 111 North Fifth Street, but it was in these shabby quarters that Joseph Pulitzer began his path to glory as a newspaper publisher.

As was his way, Pulitzer plunged in at a furious pace, sometimes working sixteen- or twenty-hour days. He would be driven to work in a brougham, usually accompanied by his lovely young wife who had few other occasions to be with him. He would have a quick sandwich and a glass of beer at a nearby restaurant for lunch, then go home to dinner. But an old friend recalled that on passing Pulitzer's office at 11 P.M. the light was always on. The editor was a gushing fountain of ideas for his staff to act upon. He sat in a little alcove off the main editorial room of the paper, separated from the reporters only by a curtain, from behind which many times a day he would unexpectedly leap, like an elongated Rumpelstiltskin, always with some new idea to be followed up on.[5]

What made the St. Louis *Post-Dispatch* such an immediate success was Pulitzer's determined effort to put his paper at the disposal of the people. Although now nominally a Democrat, he lashed out at political corruption as a spokesman for the public, never allying himself with any interest groups. A newspaper, he believed, should be its own center of focus. What made his paper popular, some have said, were Pulitzer's regular crusades: his usual targets were crooked politicians, wealthy tax dodgers, police-protected gambling rings, and self-serving public utilities. Not content with merely pointing out such malefactors, and not content with superficial treatment of things, Pulitzer always demanded in-depth coverage. His philosophy as expressed to his staff was: "Never drop a thing until you have gotten to the bottom of it. Continuity! Continuity! Continuity! until the subject is really finished."[6]

Pulitzer put together a top-flight staff. Probably his most important acquisition was Col. John A. Cockerill, a widely experienced and hard-boiled newspaperman whom Pulitzer brought to St. Louis in 1880. Cockerill was particularly strong on sniffing out stories having to do with murder, sin, sex, lynchings, and other sensational events that would sell papers—and it was an essential part of the Pulitzer philosophy that newspapers ought to sell. Cockerill was also a man endowed with determination and organizational skills. This would later become useful to Pulitzer when he was trying to whip the *World* into shape in New York. Even before Cockerill came on the scene, however, the *Post-Dispatch* was a success, and Pulitzer was on his way to becoming a wealthy man.

Making a success of the *Post-Dispatch* was nerve-wracking, and by 1883 the high-strung Pulitzer was on the verge of a physical breakdown; his eyesight, never good, was failing him. His reputation in the close-knit St. Louis society had long ago been tarnished, and it was not improved in the slightest when Cockerill shot and killed a lawyer who had been attacked by the paper. (Cockerill got off on the grounds of self-defense.) In the spring of 1883 Pulitzer decided to take a long rest in Europe, leaving his newspaper in the hands of his lieutenants. But in passing through New York he learned that the New York *World* was for sale, and all of his competitive urges as an entrepreneur were stirred up. He recalled that he had always wanted to run a leading paper like Dana's *Sun*, and he must have been especially piqued by the fact that his younger brother Albert had recently started a newspaper in

New York, a frivolous sheet called the *Morning Journal*, and had made a minor success of it.

The *World* that Pulitzer bought had once been a leading paper in New York, although it had come through a rather tortured history. Originally established in 1860 as a moral and religious organ by a Philadelphian named Alexander Cummings, the paper went on to absorb the old *Courier and Enquirer*, a longtime leader in New York. But the paper was not successful and eventually fell into the hands of a group of wealthy New Yorkers active in Democratic politics: Fernando Wood and August Belmont. They brought in as editor (and later owner) Manton Marble, who in time became one of the most highly respected editors in New York. The *World* certainly paid its way for a while. In 1876, however, Marble got tired of the paper, or politics, or both, and sold out to a group headed by Thomas A. Scott of the Pennsylvania Railroad. Later, as part of a railroad swap, Scott's group turned the paper over to the notorious railroad tycoon Jay Gould. Gould probably wanted the paper to cover and explain some of his nefarious financial exploits, but he knew nothing about the newspaper business, so the *World* started losing money—as much as $40,000 a year.[7]

This was how things stood in the spring of 1883. Pulitzer paid a call on Jay Gould at his Western Union Building at 195 Broadway, and Gould offered to sell the *World* to Pulitzer for $346,000. This seemed rather steep considering the paper's recent losses, yet Pulitzer agreed, and he promised to come the next morning to clinch the deal. He was booked to sail for Europe the following day, and in the evening he got cold feet, even contemplated backing out. His brother Albert might have had something to do with his doubts. Albert stormed into Pulitzer's hotel room and insisted that New York could not harbor two Pulitzer newspapers. Furthermore, Joseph knew that this was no small pond like St. Louis. He would be up against powerful and probably vindictive competitors. Kate Pulitzer, however, laughed at her husband's fears, and, unhappy as she was in having to give up her vacation, convinced him to stay and do what he really wanted to do.

Accordingly the next day Pulitzer plopped down an initial payment on the $346,000 that he had pledged to Gould—an amount Gould insisted should cover his own purchase price plus his losses. The down payment came out of recent *Post-Dispatch* profits, and the remainder was subsequently paid off from the windfall profits of the next few years. There was no written contract, only a handshake on the deal. Whether Gould had any doubts about Pulitzer's ability to pay off his debt has never been recorded.

After leaving Gould, Pulitzer paid a short visit to the shabby *World* offices on Park Row. Undoubtedly he froze the blood of some of his new employees when he proclaimed, icily, "Gentlemen, you realize that a change has taken place in the *World*. Heretofore you have all been living in the parlour and taking baths every day. Now I wish you to understand that, in future, you are all walking down the Bowery."[8] Several of the staffers, including Editor William Henry Hurlbert, who had been putting out a dignified but totally unadventuresome paper—its circulation only 11,000—quit on the spot. The first issue under the new management was that of May 11, 1883, and it contained a letter personally signed by Pulitzer that set forth his goals as publisher:

There is room in this great and growing city for a journal that is not only cheap but bright, not only bright but large, not only large but truly democratic—dedicated to the cause of the people rather than that of the purse-potentates—devoted more to the news of the New than the Old World—that will expose all fraud and sham, fight all public evils and abuses—that will serve and battle for the people with earnest sincerity.[9]

With a huge debt hanging over him, Pulitzer had no choice but to appeal to the masses. But he was not cynical in making this appeal. He genuinely believed that a cheap, bright paper, colorfully written, would "hook" the public, after which he could educate them and appeal to their reasoning minds. The editorial page from the very beginning would be markedly more serious and intellectual than the rest of the paper, making for a rather odd contrast in style and tone. Pulitzer respected and admired the editorial page of the old New York *Post*, now edited by E. L. Godkin. But for his own part he would not be satisfied addressing only an intellectual elite: "I want to talk to a nation, not a select committee."[10] He also admired the literary traditions of Dana's *Sun*, but again he did not want a staff composed of writers who spent their time polishing their own literary style. He disdained amber prose and good-natured whimsy; he wanted snap, crackle, and pop. He wanted news stories that would get readers leaping out of their chairs in indignation. To be sure he wanted good writing, and to this end he freely lured reporters from the staff of papers like the *Sun* and the *Herald*, but he did not want his reporters relishing their own metaphors, he wanted them wandering through the lower east side, imbibing the welter and the phantasms of daily life.

The *World*'s success was probably not due to a single formula, or to its particular mix of sensational news and crusading; it was due to Pulitzer's instinctual sense of what his reading public wanted, his insight into the driving force of the polyglot masses that were daily arriving through the gates at Castle Garden down at the Battery. The *Herald*, the *Sun*, the *Tribune* all had their formulas, and they worked; the impulsive and hard-driving Pulitzer accepted no pat formula; he created his paper day by day, column inch by column inch.

Whatever the formula, it worked. Within a year and a half, the *World* was the circulation leader in New York, and it was in fact only beginning its rise. In his early months in New York Pulitzer had a difficult time recruiting staff, but as circulation figures soared he was able to hire good men away from major New York newspapers like the *Sun* and the *Herald*. For example, he stole a brilliant editor named Ballard Smith from the *Herald*, making him managing editor. S. S. Carvalho came over from the *Sun* to edit the *Evening World* when that paper made its appearance in 1887. And with his rising eminence Pulitzer was able to raid papers all around the country. As chief editorial writer he brought in William H. Merrill from the Boston *Herald*. Most importantly, Pulitzer raided his own St. Louis *Post-Dispatch*, bringing on board Col. John A. Cockerill as editor-in-chief. Cockerill added the same flair and daring to the *World* that he had imparted to the *Post-Dispatch*.

The lightning-quick success of the *World* did not sit well with the publishers of other New York papers, most of whom suffered at Pulitzer's expense. Dignified papers like the *Times* and the *Post*, read only in well-furnished parlors by "elites," suffered little. But the *Sun* and the *Herald* were seriously injured. Circulation loss caused James Gordon Bennett to lower the price of his paper by a penny. He foolishly tried to pass this loss on to newsdealers, which caused a further drop in circulation.

Needless to say, the competing publishers were not at all pleased with Pulitzer's rapid rise. There were moral crusades against the *World* as there had earlier been against the *Herald*. Neither Whitelaw Reid of the *Tribune* nor Bennett of the *Herald* nor Jones of the *Times* had to worry about the *World* being found in fashionable drawing rooms on Fifth Avenue; nonetheless, the paper was the city's circulation leader by the mid-1880s. Dana was positively virulent in his attacks on Pulitzer and took snipes at him whenever he could. Bennett believed that the Pulitzer bubble would eventually burst. "Poor, misguided, selfish vulgarian," roared Bennett. "Can't last."[11]

The *World* did, however, last. It was not a flash in the pan. It remained a major force in American journalism long after Pulitzer's death in 1911, although by the early 1890s, severely troubled by ill health and finally blindness, Pulitzer was forced to relinquish day-to-day control of his paper. In spite of his infirmities, though, Pulitzer, an autocratic man if ever there was one, did keep his paper on a short leash and was probably more in control than the absentee proprietors Bennett and Reid. The overwhelming success of the *World* may be a little difficult for a twentieth-century reader to understand because the strange elixir of a serious editorial page and sensationalistic news coverage does not exist in any newspaper today. But the precise mix of forces put together by Pulitzer formed an ideal combination in the 1880s and 1890s.

But Pulitzer and the *World* did not go unchallenged for long. By the mid-1890s the *World* had a serious challenger—a challenger that if he had been younger and in better health Pulitzer might have been able to repel with ease. In fact he did respond vigorously, although not with total success, and with certain unhappy consequences. By a cruel irony, this challenge came from a paper that Pulitzer earlier had had no difficulty pressing into the ground—his own brother Albert's *Morning Journal*. By the early 1890s Albert had vacated the newspaper field, selling out to John R. McLean, the ambitious publisher of the Cincinnati *Enquirer*. But McLean was no more successful in competing with the dynamic *World* than Albert Pulitzer, and, in 1895, admitting that he had failed in New York, McLean sold the paper at a tremendous loss to a young lad from California—William Randolph Hearst.[12]

Hearst was only thirty-two years old at the time, but he was already an old hand at the newspaper business by this time. He was beginning one of the longest tenures as a newspaper publisher in the American record, a tumultuous career that would go on until 1951—over half a century. Already in 1895, however, Hearst had been the successful editor of the San Francisco *Examiner*, a paper that had been purchased by his millionaire father, U.S. Senator George Hearst. When young Hearst took over as editor of the *Examiner* at the age of twenty-four, he had already worked as a cub reporter on Pulitzer's New York *World* and had carefully studied its methods. He tried to make over his California paper in the image of the *World*, with considerable success. By the time he got to New York Hearst was fully intending to get to the top by out-Pulitzering Pulitzer, if such a thing was possible. With the passage of time Hearst would own a great many newspapers and become a far greater newspaper tycoon than Pulitzer ever aspired to be, although his contributions to journalism are far more tawdry and open to skepticism. Tycoon he was indeed, although there are some who will say that in attaining his various triumphs Hearst considerably diluted the quality and the ethical standards of the American newspaper.

Still, Hearst was an epic, larger-than-life character, and certainly not without gifts as a newspaperman. He was born in San Francisco on April 29, 1863. His father, who had already become a wealthy man by that time, provided him with a sheltered and even pampered existence as a child. George Hearst had come up the hard way and was already in his forties when William Randolph, or Willie, was born, but he must have provided his son with some of his own wildcatting instincts as an entrepreneur. George Hearst himself was a Missouri farmboy who briefly attended mining school and unprofitably attempted for a good number of years to work the lead mines in his native state. He moved to California in 1850 in the wake of the gold rush, but for a while he did little better. Later, however, in 1859, an indefatigable energy and his own self-taught methods brought him riches in the Comstock Lode of the Sierra Nevadas. Still later he became a multimillionaire by his success with some of the West's richest mines: Ontario, Homestake, and Anaconda.

George Hearst had quite sensibly married a plain but rock-ribbed Missouri schoolteacher, Phoebe Apperson, a woman who would become a well-known California philanthropist in later years, a woman of uncommonly good sense, with only one defect of character, an inability to deny anything to her cherished only-child, Willie. George Hearst remained, until the end of his days, a bearded, tobacco-chewing Missourian, crude of diction, although warm and picturesque. When he took his seat in the U.S. Senate in 1886 he was universally liked by his colleagues because of his natural dignity and forcefulness of expression.

The Hearsts wanted their son to have only the best in the way of an eastern education, so, at the age of nineteen, he was shipped off to Harvard. His main pursuits there were not scholarly, however, and his academic record was undistinguished. Nonetheless, he developed a serious interest in publishing and a respect for the written word and became business manager of the college's humor magazine the *Lampoon*. He was an avid reader of the Boston *Globe*, a morning paper founded in 1872, at first a failure, but upon being taken over by Gen. Charles H. Taylor, a lively sheet set up against the old reliables of Boston—the *Evening Transcript*, the *Daily Advertiser*, and the *Herald*. General Taylor had cut the price of his paper to two cents, focused on sensationalism, big headlines, and features, and did everything he could to draw in ordinary folk. (One of Taylor's tricks was to print the names of as many of his subscribers as he could in each issue.) Hearst was taken by the playfulness of it all.

Playfulness and antic behavior seemed to have been the controlling impulses during Hearst's years at Harvard. Many of his fellow students believed that he had more money than was good for him, and he spent much of his allowance on pranks and other light diversions. He was particularly drawn to fireworks and pyrotechnic displays, which he purchased in great abundance. On one occasion he introduced a flock of roosters to the college yard. They provided a cacophony of noise with the coming of dawn—much to the annoyance of professors and students. He kept an alligator in his room for a while, which he kept drunk on champagne. The animal staggered to campus parties with him on the end of a leash.[13]

None of this should suggest that Hearst was a loud-mouthed, arrogant college-type boy. Tall and blond, he had a shy disposition and an ever-so-polite manner that seemed out of character with these wild antics that seemed to come in spurts. This curious admixture of traits would follow him throughout his life. Even as a great newspaper press lord in later years he was never a mogul of the type known to movie central casting. He remained somewhat languid, always polite, self-effacing, and shy, a manner that would actually hold more terror for his subordinates than the roaring and desk-pounding editors of popular legend.

Hearst's youthful high jinks, however, were enough to get him kicked out of Harvard in his junior year. The final prank that brought about his ouster was when he ordered a number of chamber pots inscribed in scrolled letters with the names of his professors and delivered the offensive souvenirs to their homes. Phoebe Hearst was grievously distressed by her son's dismissal; she tried to get the decision reversed but without success. By this time her son was well prepared to move his playfulness into the bigger and wider outside world. And his movement into the newspaper field that so fascinated him was not long in coming.

Rejecting his father's appeal for him to take part in managing some of the family mining and real estate businesses, he boldly asked to take over the San Francisco *Examiner*, which the senator had purchased in 1880, believing that the paper would aid him in his quest to become Democratic governor of California. The *Examiner* had not made money, however. It had to endure stiff competition from the highly popular *Chronicle*, which did a superlative job of boosting California, and had at times used the talents of Mark Twain and Brete Harte, among others. George Hearst had little faith in newspapermen and he was not too keen on his son going into this line of work. Most likely prodded by his wife, who still could deny her son nothing, he relented. The wily old prospector probably summed up his son as well as anyone when he observed: "There's one thing that's sure about my boy Bill. I've been watching him and notice that when he wants cake he wants cake, and he wants it now. And I notice that after a while he gets the cake."[14]

Accordingly, at the age of twenty-four, William Randolph Hearst took over management of the *Examiner*. He was, surprisingly, no layabout. He worked sixteen-hour days, just as Pulitzer had on the St. Louis *Post-Dispatch*. He was also an eager learner, and he knew what he wanted. He wanted a San Francisco version of the New York *World*, with its sensationalism, stunts, and crusades. Like his father (and Pulitzer), Hearst was a Democrat, and he lambasted the big-moneyed interests in California, especially the Southern Pacific Railroad and its leading figures, Colis P. Huntington, Charles Crocker, and Leland Stanford. (The Hearst silver fortune, doubtless, was never seen as "ill gotten gain.")

As was his practice throughout life, Hearst hired the best people he could get and paid them salaries way out of line with prevailing rates. He brought in as managing editor Sam S. Chamberlin, who had worked for both Pulitzer and Bennett. And in the ranks were Ambrose Bierce—later well known for his short stories—who wrote a sharp and acidic column called "Prattles"; Arthur McEwan, who helped devise the style of the Hearst editorial pages; Homer Davenport who became famous for his political cartoons, and Winifred Black (who wrote under the pen name Annie Laurie), the first in a long line of newspaper sob sisters; it was said that "Annie Laurie" could get in "a sob for the unfortunate in every line."[15] The *Examiner* was clearly a paper of youthful exuberance, as befitted its youthful owner, and its circulation doubled in one year. Senator George Hearst died in 1891, but by that time he must have been not a little astonished that his spoiled and impulsive son had made a paying proposition out of a paper that he himself had failed to invigorate.

By the mid-1890s, with success in San Francisco behind him, Hearst could not resist the temptation of invading the New York newspaper field. With an impetuosity that occasionally bordered on megalomania, Hearst felt sure that Pulitzer was very vulnerable, stricken as he was with blindness and other unclassifiable neurotic maladies and complaints. Accordingly, in the fall of 1895 Hearst plopped down $135,000 for the New York *Morning Journal*.

Combating Pulitzer would not be easy, and Hearst's techniques for doing so did not pay off right away. Almost immediately after taking over the *Journal* (the word *Morning* was soon dropped), Hearst lowered the price of the paper to one cent. Since advertising revenues were scanty this meant that for a time the paper would be losing a torrent of money. However, Phoebe Hearst made up the deficits while the paper was getting on its feet. It has been estimated that over a period of at least three years she sank $7 million into the paper. A good deal of it just went down the drain. During most of this period other New York publishers were certain that Mrs. Hearst would soon tire of her son's spending spree and turn off the faucet. But this never happened, and eventually little Willie did manage to make a success of the paper—a smashing success at that.

And, yes, what worked was the use of even more blatant techniques than those employed at the *World*—bigger headlines, more sensationalistic treatments, more sin and sex, more outrageous crusading, larger pictures, and something Pulitzer had not stooped to: overt manipulation and distortion of the news. To help him get the effects he wanted he brought most of his best people with him from San Francisco, including Sam Chamberlain, Homer Davenport, "Annie Laurie," Ambrose Bierce, and Arthur McEwen. McEwen, a tall Scotsman with a goatee, provided much of the pungency of the *Journal*'s editorial page, explaining that the essence of the Hearst journalism was the "gee whiz" effect. Any issue of the paper that didn't cause the average reader to jump out of his chair and proclaim "Great God" after looking at the front page just wasn't getting the job done."[16]

It was not, however, the "gee whiz" emotion alone that would be needed to steal the circulation laurels away from Pulitzer. Hearst clearly understood this to be the case. In the mid-1890s the fulcrum of the *World*'s power was the paper's Sunday edition with its simple-minded features, its pseudoscientific stories, its colored comic section, its dozens of pages of retail advertisements, and its extra plump doses of weekend sensationalism. The Sunday *World* by now was a fixed institution in New York with complete dominance of the field—certainly among the working classes, although everybody knew that many regular readers of the more genteel papers liked to take a peek at the Sunday *World* as well.

Early in 1896 Hearst laid secret plans to lure away the whole staff of the Sunday *World*. Once again he made liberal use of his mother's open checkbook and offered huge salary increases to bring them over. Nearly all of them came, most importantly the paper's innovative editor Morrill Goddard. Stunned, Pulitzer attempted to negotiate with his crew as it was abandoning ship, but Hearst raised the ante once again and nearly everyone jumped. To counter this loss Pulitzer put the Sunday *World* in the hands of a brilliant youngster named Arthur Brisbane, whom he had lured away from Dana's *Sun*. Brisbane in fact worked further wonders with the Sunday *World*, driving the circulation of the paper to over 600,000, the largest in the world at that time.[17] A year later, however, after secret negotiations with Hearst, Brisbane also jumped. He received an enormous salary to become the top Hearst editor, a position he held for nearly forty years.

The losses to the Sunday *World* were painful, and Pulitzer's attempts to counter the losses served only to dramatize and exaggerate them. One of the most popular Sunday features was the comic strip called "The Yellow Kid," drawn by Richard F. Outcault. Originally called "Hogan's Alley," it caricatured the life of New York tenement kids, and the color specialists of the

World decided to give the most prominent and raucous kid on the block a long yellow apron or bib, so eventually the strip took his name. The "Yellow Kid" was the most popular feature in the Sunday "funnies" so when Richard Outcault took off for the *Journal*, Pulitzer knew he could not abide the loss. Accordingly, he hired another artist, George B. Luks, to start drawing the feature. There were now two "yellow kids," one in the *World* and the other in the *Journal*.

The rival "yellow kids" stood as a symbol of the rivalry of the two papers. For a time the rivalry even extended to the newsboys who sold the papers on the street. Occasionally they decorated their carts with yellow banners or bunting, ramming each other as they sought out their respective corners; sometimes fisticuffs broke out among the boys, each of whom believed that *his* "yellow kid" was the real one.

This rivalry did not make much difference among the more literate members of society, but the "dignified" papers used the fracas to raise yet one more moral crusade against the forces of sensationalism. Ervin Wardman of the *Press* was apparently the first to use the term "yellow press" when referring to the *World* and the *Journal*, and the term stuck. It was picked up and used relentlessly by Dana's *Sun*, which was happy to be able to tar its arch enemy the *World* with the same brush as the *Journal*. The *Journal*, most people believed, was bereft of all journalistic principle. Now Pulitzer was going down the same road.

Strong public doubts about the yellow press came to a head in 1898 with the Spanish-American War. It has become commonplace to say that the war was as much the product of the jingoism and journalistic saber-rattling of the *Journal* and the *World* as it was of strained relations between Spain and the United States. Some historians have called the Spanish-American War "Hearst's war," which might be stretching things a bit, but certainly not a great deal. It is true that there was a good deal of tension between the United States and Spain over the issue of Spain's repressive regime in Cuba and over the insurgency movement that had begun in 1895. Most Americans had an instinctive sympathy for the insurgents in Cuba, and some pressures had been put on Spain under the administration of Grover Cleveland. Furthermore, after coming to office in 1897, the weak but well-intentioned William McKinley seemed to be getting somewhere with the situation through diplomacy. In the fall of that year a new premier took office in Spain. He recalled Governor-General Valentine Wyler, who had been hated by the Cuban insurrectionists, and called a butcher by many. The new government in Madrid also promised to release political prisoners held in what were called concentration camps. Spain even agreed to offer some kind of home rule to Cuba.

None of this was good enough for William Randolph Hearst, who had sent whole platoons of correspondents and artists to Cuba with the express purpose of keeping up the war fever, describing atrocities, sometimes imagined or fictitious. Scarcely a day went by during 1897 and early 1898 when the New York *Journal* did not have a front-page story about some fresh atrocity in Cuba—babies killed, women raped, dissidents imprisoned. A number of these stories were either greatly exaggerated or, in fact, outright lies. All of Hearst's reporters and artists were under strict orders to dig up as much dirt about Spanish rule as they could, truth being only a secondary consideration. The story has often been told that one of the men Hearst sent to Cuba was the famous illustrator of Western scenes, Frederic Remington. He arrived at a time when things seemed to be calming down. Bored and restless, after a few days he cabled to Hearst that he wanted to come home. Remington was said to have cabled "Everything is quiet. There is no trouble here. There will be no war." Perhaps it is apocryphal but Hearst is said to have replied: "Please remain. You furnish the pictures and I'll furnish the war."[18]

If Hearst did not actually use these words, they give some clue to the approach he was taking. He had in effect decided that a nice little war with Spain would be great fun—much like the effects of the firecrackers he so fondly used as a college student—and he was not going to be content until he had his war.

An entire book could be written about Hearst's efforts to sound the trumpets of war in 1897 and 1898. Endless stories about circumstances in Cuba were either grossly distorted or made up out of whole cloth, and in the days before photojournalism, newspaper artists could tell lies as well. A very shocking and sensationalistic picture appeared in the *Journal* documenting a story of several American girls, leaving Havana on a ship of U.S. registry, who were stripped naked and searched by Spanish agents. Remington did a very lurid picture of this inquisition, with one young lady standing totally naked while lusty-looking Spaniards went through her clothing. But the event had never happened that way: the young ladies had been searched by matrons, and Remington the artist had been given false information by another Hearst operative that was never checked. Distortions of this kind appeared day in and day out in the *Journal*.

In early 1898, two events played into Hearst's hands. First, he turned up a purloined letter from the Spanish ambassador in Washington that literally called President McKinley a moron. It was published on page one of the

Journal on February 9. The allegations of the letter caused great indignation when it was republished around the country. But there was worse. Six days later, the battleship *Maine*, on an ostensibly peaceful and friendly visit to Cuba, was blown up at anchor in the Havana harbor. There was never any evidence that Spaniards were responsible, and certainly there was no Spanish motivation for such an act since they were then making strenuous efforts to appease the United States. Nonetheless, the explosion, which caused the deaths of 260 American seamen, was hard to disregard, even by the more conservative press, which heretofore had been contemptuous of Hearst's warmongering.

After the sinking of the *Maine*, war seemed inevitable. A good many Europeans (Spaniards most of all perhaps) believed that all the posturing that went on was merely a pretext to annex Cuba, and, although this was not the case, many historians have treated the Spanish-American War as an excessive misuse of American expansionism and imperialism. In fact it is better seen as an example of blundering in Washington, with President McKinley unable to stop the rampaging of the Congress and the press. At war's end, McKinley remarked: "But for the inflamed state of public opinion, and the fact that Congress could no longer be held in check, a peaceful solution might have been had."[19]

After the sinking of the *Maine*, even the more tranquil and conservative papers had to join in the chorus, and after Congress passed a war resolution on April 18, there was universal support for the action. Most Americans, during and after the war, were seemingly in agreement with Secretary of State John Hay, who referred to the five-month rout of Spanish military and naval forces as "this splendid little war." Naturally both the *Journal* and the *World* were exultant that the war they had been pushing had come to pass. Hearst was positively jubilant. As early as 1897, when he was beginning to stoke the fires of jingoism, he introduced banner headlines to the American newspaper—headlines that ran the entire width of the paper. In the months to come, the *World* joined the trend toward "banner" headlines, and when the *Maine* blew up on February 15, the *World* not only had a single banner head, but many banner-length lines of display type and an enormous and probably fanciful drawing of the event.

Pulitzer's attitudes toward Spain in the year before war broke out are difficult and even painful to characterize. One suspects that if there had been no Hearst that Pulitzer, a blind and ailing man, isolated on his yacht or his home in Bar Harbor Maine and connected to his editors only by telegraph, would have avoided the extremes of jingoism. But he and Hearst were now locked in a struggle like the horns of two elks. Pulitzer, who probably knew

better, had no choice but to match Hearst trick for trick. Pulitzer, always the
far-seeing businessman, perceived that the *Journal* was his principal competition in New York and that he could not back away from it without losing
the game. The battle, however, must have been severely stressful to Pulitzer,
who was not, at heart, a setter of firecrackers and a college playboy on the
loose. Pulitzer had used sensationalism as a way of drawing a mass readership into his own higher goals of reform and progress; now he was caught up
in a whirlwind. In the vortex there was no higher purpose, no philosophical
center of focus.

The long struggle with Hearst for supremacy must have been especially
disturbing to Pulitzer since he now found himself under indictment in the
journalistic fraternity, smeared with the label of "yellow journalist." That is
what yellow journalism had become: Hearst and Pulitzer, Pulitzer and
Hearst—Tweedledum and Tweedledee. For E. L. Godkin of the *Post*, the
Journal and the *World* represented the lowest point in the history of American journalism. Godkin, one of the few editors who continued to call for restraint after the *Maine* disaster, excoriated the utter recklessness of New
York's two yellow papers. He wrote:

Gross misinterpretation of the facts, deliberate invention of tales calculated to excite the public, and wanton recklessness in the construction of headlines which
even outdid these inventions, have combined to make the issues of the most widely
circulated newspapers firebrands scattered broadcast throughout the country. . . . It
is a crying shame that men should work such mischief simply in order to sell more
papers.[20]

Denunciations of this sort would probably not have bothered Hearst at
all. His rumpus-room mentality and his sheer joy in upsetting applecarts
had no intellectual need to respond to criticisms of his methods. But to Pulitzer, who had been dragged into yellow journalism and who had set a somewhat different course in the beginning, censure by the nation's intellectuals
and serious organs of opinion must have been deeply painful. But with his
weakened physical condition and his neurotic fears for the future of his beloved newspaper, there was no easy route of escape.

Interestingly enough, the war itself had a curative effect on some of the
worst ills of yellow journalism. Reporting on both the *World* and the *Journal* was more reliable and factual than it had been, no doubt partly because
there was more genuine news to report. There certainly were a great number
of stellar correspondents in the field: men like Stephen Crane, Richard
Harding Davis, Frank Norris, Stephen Bonsal; artists like Frederic Remington and John T. McCutcheon. There was still some distortion of fact. The

Spanish-American War was an all-boys roundup, and many of the correspondents saw themselves as participants rather than objective outsiders. Richard Harding Davis, although a reporter for the New York *Herald* and *Scribner*'s magazine (he had quit Hearst in disgust), led a charge in Cuba; Hearst's own James Creelman led an attack on a fort at El Caney.

Unable to resist the itch to fight himself, Hearst sailed his yacht the *Buccaneer* into the Caribbean, leading a small flotilla of hired tugboats and steamers and bearing a motley collection of newspaper artists, photographers, and assorted roustabouts. After one naval battle, Hearst's amateur navy spied a group of Spanish sailors on a beach—refugees from a sunken battleship. Hearst stripped off his trousers and waded ashore, brandishing a revolver. The group was taken prisoner and later turned over to the "real" navy.[21]

The little pushover war of 1898 represented the high watermark of yellow journalism. With the war over and the country sailing into relatively tranquil waters, there was little for the rival papers to cannonade one another over. Of course there were still scandals, and there was still room for political crusading, but there was no longer a need for rival papers to shout each other down. In any case, coverage of the war, bringing an endless number of "extra" editions, had proven exorbitantly expensive for the *Journal* and the *World*. Both papers found themselves wallowing in red ink even though during the months of the war both had circulations above a million daily. The deficits of the *Journal* were made up by the ever-generous Phoebe Apperson Hearst; Pulitzer, with a much smaller fortune, was not so pleased to be paying for a "newspaper war" out of his own pocket.

Even before the war Pulitzer had decided to pull out of the competition with the *Journal*, and he wrote a memo to his top manager, Don Carlos Seitz, making his determination clear: "You can tell every night editor, city editor, managing editor & editorial writer, *to let the Journal alone* as long as they let us alone—and possibly even longer." In the wake of this directive, Seitz called his whole staff in and admitted that things had been too rushed, there had been too many fake or inaccurate stories, and that Pulitzer had decided that it was time for the *World* to become a "normal paper" again.[22] A few years later Pulitzer had the paper's monster typefaces broken up, and for the most part he kept his resolve to abandon the competition with Hearst and to avoid the worst excesses of "yellow journalism."

To be sure, the "yellow" fever did not subside elsewhere around the country for the better part of a decade. With Pulitzer and Hearst pushing them from New York in the late 1890s, a good number of newspapers joined the yellow brigade. Among them were Hearst's San Francisco *Examiner*, of course, and the Boston *Post*. Even the Philadelphia *Inquirer* took on the yellow hue for a while. One of the most scrofulous sheets in the nation was the Denver *Post* of Fred G. Bonfils and Harry Tammen, which sometimes showed flights of imagination that put Hearst to shame. On the other hand, most of the New York papers had sagely resisted the urge, as had the papers of Baltimore, Washington, and most of the South. William Rockhill Nelson's Kansas City *Star*, while devoted to ferment and reform, had no truck with lurid headlines and fictional journalism.

With the war over, Hearst, his enormous energies undiminished (and with Pulitzer backing away from combat), devoted himself to starting up or buying other papers around the country, beginning with the afternoon Chicago *American*, which he founded in 1900. Over the next three decades Hearst put together an enormous media empire, which by 1937 consisted of twenty-five daily papers; seventeen Sunday papers; and over a dozen magazines, including *Good Housekeeping, Cosmopolitan, Harper's Bazaar, House Beautiful, American Weekly*, and others; ten radio stations; two wire services, International News Service, and Universal Service; several press syndicates including King Features and International News Photos; and a newsreel company (Hearst Metrotone News).[23] Although this empire got into financial straits during the Depression, mostly because of Hearst's profligate spending habits, it held together for the most part until the publisher's death in 1951.

Hearst continued to rule his empire until the end, always continuing to jerk his editors like puppets on the end of a string. On the other hand this pulling of strings was intermittent and without informed direction as Hearst interested himself in other things. For several decades he was deeply involved in politics on his own behalf. He served two terms in Congress as a Democrat from New York (1903–1907) and even entered the presidential race in 1904. Here he actually received 204 votes at the Democratic convention, but lost the nomination to Judge Alton B. Parker. His political star declined from that time on, although he continued to have political aspirations until the 1920s, losing close races for mayor of New York in 1905 and 1909, and governor in 1906. Beginning around World War I Hearst began to be involved with the movie business, hobnobbing with movie folk in California, and eventually moving his base of operations to his "castle" at San Simeon, which he shared for over thirty years with his "film" mistress Marion Davies. (Hearst was *publicly* a "good" family man, having five sons by his wife Millicent Willson, a New York actress whom he married in 1903, and to whom he remained married until his death.)

Yellow journalism subsided after 1910, although it enjoyed a strong revival with the appearance of tabloids in the 1920s. Gone for a while were shrieking headlines, the full-page pictures of some gruesome crime scene. As far as Joseph Pulitzer was concerned, yellow journalism died with the Spanish-American War, although it took several years for the *World* to regain its voice. It did this in great measure in the last years of Pulitzer's life even as the old man's body decayed and his mental state sometimes approached madness. In 1903 Pulitzer chose a brilliant young editor, Frank I. Cobb, to run the editorial page of the *World*, and Cobb served the paper with distinction until his unexpected death in 1923. Under Cobb's even hand the *World* retrieved much of its former greatness, returning to crusading, now carried out in depth and with high seriousness of purpose.

Pulitzer and Hearst were surely giants of the American press. It is unlikely that we shall ever see their like again. But their personal lives took on a tragic dimension that would have taxed the dramatic powers of a Sophocles or an Aeschylus. Pulitzer, in his neurotic rages and unsuccessful search for silence, made a botch of his family life, hectored his wife and daughters, and completely misread his three sons. His youngest son Herbert, whom he seemed to favor and who received the lion's share of the *World*'s ownership, had neither drive nor ability. His eldest son, Ralph, whose life was always made miserable by his father, became Publisher of the *World*, a job to which he keenly aspired and for which he had a modest measure of talent. Pulitzer's middle son, Joseph Jr., in whom the elder had no faith, was given the St. Louis *Post-Dispatch* as a sop, and turned it into one of the great American papers. Joseph Jr. became a far better business manager than his father had ever been, and perhaps his equal as an editor as well.

Pulitzer, who died in 1911, is perhaps better known today for his wise philanthropy in creating the Pulitzer School of Journalism at Columbia University and the famous Pulitzer Prizes by which the achievements of generations of American journalists have been marked for posterity. Moreover, his best instincts were good for journalism. He had a philosophical cast of mind and a strong sense of purpose. He attempted to forge a strong bond between the press and the people, and, when not hobbled by neuroticism and physical complaints, he cemented that bond in a way that has never really been duplicated.

Hearst, of course, was an altogether different case. He left no great legacy of thought or action. He was tremendously resourceful, he was talented, but essentially he was a hollow man, guided by the opportunities of the moment. Pulitzer made the lives of those around him miserable. Hearst, on the other hand, was an indulgent father and employer. His quiet blue-eyed charm successfully masked the fact that somehow he had never quite grown to maturity. He remained until the end of his days the spoiled rich man's son who set off firecrackers and released roosters in the college yard. He wanted so much to be loved, but never quite succeeded. He spent a lifetime building castles, spending money on art treasures, suits of armor, things that he never looked at but that instead had locked up in a huge two-block warehouse in the Bronx. He believed that as a newspaperman, as a reformer, as a Democrat, he could do people good, but he never paused long enough to reflect what the good was. He was perhaps the product of a more carefree America that has passed by never to return. There was a youthful zest and grandiosity in the man that did the nation some good, and the same may be said about the "yellow journalism" of the fin de siècle. It may have served as a kind of wake-up cry to a somnolent and indolent America. It might also have served to remind Americans that the road to good newspapers is always a difficult one, fraught in each generation with fresh dangers that, once they infect the air, are not easily overcome.

James Gordon Bennett's New York *Herald* as it appeared in 1847. Circulation wars were already underway and Bennett is here touting a circulation of 40,000—an inconceivable figure a generation before. Courtesy of the University of Illinois Newspaper Archives.

James Gordon Bennett, the flinty-eyed Scot who found out what Americans wanted in a newspaper—and gave it to them. Photo courtesy of the Library of Congress.

Horace Greeley, as neatly fitted up as he ever got. In spite of the vagaries and eccentricities of his opinions, most Americans trusted "Uncle Horace" to explain the complex and painful changes in American life during the 1840s and 1850s. Photo courtesy of the Library of Congress.

The Hoe lightening press as it appeared on the eve of the Civil War. Such mighty machines, and the much greater behemoths that came after, made possible the giant metropolitan newspapers with circulations in the hundreds of thousands. Courtesy of the University of Illinois Library.

Charles A. Dana, shown here in his days with the Lincoln administration. After the Civil War his revived New York *Sun* developed the high art of newspaper writing. A paper more charming than Dana's *Sun* probably never existed in America. Photo courtesy of the Library of Congress.

Mark Twain, a former printer's devil, rode to fame as a newspaper humorist on the back of his celebrated jumping frog of Calaveras County. Twain's frog story first appeared in the New York *Saturday Press*, on November 15, 1865. Photo courtesy of the University of Illinois Library.

Joseph Pulitzer, the lion of New York publishing in the 1880s. A man of tremendous intellect and ingenuity, nervous and physical ailments clouded his career in later years, but never his resourcefulness or insight into the mind of the reading public. Photo courtesy of the Library of Congress.

The New York *World* of January 2, 1886, boasts a circulation of "over a million a week." Illustrations, although not yet photographs, are now a major part of the formula. In its best days, even after Pulitzer, the *World* forged an enduring bond with the New York reading public—a kind of intimacy that has never been matched by any large newspaper. Courtesy of the University of Illinois Newspaper Archives.

Nellie Bly, with her Scotch check ulster and ghillie cap about to embark on her 1889 voyage around the world in less than eighty days—the fictional record set by Jules Verne's hero Phileas Fogg. Nellie Bly's stunts for Pulitzer opened the floodgates for women in the field of journalism. Photo courtesy of the University of Illinois Library.

New York's "newspaper row" and "printing house square" in the late 1890s. The famous Pulitzer dome is on the left of the tall buildings. Then, far below, the diminutive *Sun* building, the *Tribune*, and the *Times*. New York's City Hall is on the far left. Photo courtesy of F. H. Douglas.

A Chicago newspaper dynasty. Seated in this 1890s picture is the legendary Joseph Medill of the *Tribune*. Around him are his grandchildren, Robert R. McCormick (seated left), and Medill McCormick (upper right) both later publishers of the *Tribune*; Joseph Medill Patterson (seated right), founder of the New York *Daily News*; and Cissy Patterson (standing left), publisher of the Washington *Times-Herald*. Photo courtesy of the Chicago Historical Society. Used with permission.

The battlements of the Tribune tower, built in the early 1920s. Scorned by architectural critics, the building, with its matchless locale looking down on Lake Michigan, seemed a suitable home for Colonel McCormick's bellicose sheet which immodestly labeled itself "The World's Greatest Newspaper." Photo courtesy of George H. Douglas.

The New York Times.

"All the News That's Fit to Print."

VOL. LXI...NO. 13,561.

NEW YORK, TUESDAY, APRIL 16, 1912.—TWENTY-FOUR PAGES.

ONE CENT

THE WEATHER.

Unsettled Tuesday; Wednesday, fair, cooler; moderate southerly winds, becoming variable.

TITANIC SINKS FOUR HOURS AFTER HITTING ICEBERG; 866 RESCUED BY CARPATHIA, PROBABLY 1250 PERISH; ISMAY SAFE, MRS. ASTOR MAYBE, NOTED NAMES MISSING

Col. Astor and Bride, Isidor Straus and Wife, and Maj. Butt Aboard.

"RULE OF SEA" FOLLOWED

Women and Children Put Over in Lifeboats and Are Supposed to be Safe on Carpathia.

PICKED UP AFTER 8 HOURS

Vincent Astor Calls at White Star Office for News of His Father and Leaves Weeping.

FRANKLIN HOPEFUL ALL DAY

Manager of the Line Insisted Titanic Was Unsinkable Even After She Had Gone Down.

HEAD OF THE LINE ABOARD

J. Bruce Ismay Making First Trip on Gigantic Ship That Was to Surpass All Others.

Biggest Liner Plunges to the Bottom at 2:20 A.M.

RESCUERS THERE TOO LATE

Except to Pick Up the Few Hundreds Who Took to the Lifeboats.

WOMEN AND CHILDREN FIRST

Cunarder Carpathia Rushing to New York with the Survivors.

SEA SEARCH FOR OTHERS

The California Stands By on Chance of Picking Up Other Boats or Rafts.

OLYMPIC SENDS THE NEWS

Only Ship to Flash Wireless Messages to Shore After the Disaster.

LATER REPORT SAVES 866.

BOSTON, April 15.—A wireless message picked up late to-night, relayed from the Olympic, says that the Carpathia is on her way

William Allen White, editor of the Emporia
Kansas *Gazette* from 1899 to 1944, was the very
picture of a genial country editor. A perceptive
critic of the national scene, he was looked to by
presidents for sage advice. But White sought
above all else "the sweet intimate story of life."
Photo courtesy of the Library of Congress.

H. L. Mencken, the Sage of Baltimore. He spent nearly his whole career with
the Baltimore *Sunpapers* but became a national literary figure as well.
Probably no better newspaper stylist has been found on the American shore.
Robert Frost called him our greatest essayist. Photo courtesy of George H.
Douglas and Culver Pictures.

9

The Rise of the New York *Times*

Even as the worst effects of yellow journalism swept the nation's metropolitan newspapers in the late 1890s, there were correcting forces at work. Even in the most raucous days of the Spanish-American War, many papers held out against screaming headlines and sensationalism, against the coloration and distortion of the news. Many large papers resisted the yellow plague entirely; certainly the vast majority of small city and rural papers did so. Most of them were not locked in cut-throat circulation wars and never took up the garish flights of fancy adopted by some of the papers of New York, Boston, Philadelphia, and San Francisco. Furthermore, shortly after the turn of the century many papers that had adopted the yellow hue began slowly backing away. Even Joseph Pulitzer gave orders to "leave Hearst alone" and had his monster type faces broken up. After 1905 the New York *World* promptly retrieved lost ground and once again became a newspaper of the first rank.

More importantly, even as Hearst and Pulitzer were locked in their deadly embrace during the Spanish-American War period, another New York newspaper would confront the demons of sensationalism head on. Even as a large number of editors were at least pretending to mimic the techniques of the *Journal* and the *World*, one newcomer to the New York newspaper scene was decisively turning his back on everything that Pulitzer and Hearst seemed to stand for. The newcomer was Adolph S. Ochs, who in 1896 bought the struggling and impoverished New York *Times*, bringing with him new and resolute ideas of what to do with this once distinguished paper.

In 1896 few in New York knew anything about Adolph S. Ochs, a young man who had recently arrived from Chattanooga, Tennessee, where he had successfully doctored another paper called the *Times* and made of it one of best papers in the new South. In 1896 Ochs was thirty-eight years old and had been in the newspaper business since he was fourteen. But he did not arrive in New York with a fat bankroll, as did Joseph Pulitzer in 1883. Ochs's Chattanooga *Times* was a successful paper to be sure, but in the early 1890s Ochs had gotten into trouble with real estate speculations and seemed on the verge of losing the paper he had worked so long to build up. Ochs saw New York as a possible solution to his financial embarrassments. He thought that if he could build up a large circulation paper there he might be able to pull himself out of the quagmire he had been in since the depression year of 1893. Strapped for cash, there was no way that Ochs could buy a really healthy paper, so he looked around for whatever he could get. In 1895 he met with the owners of the New York *Mercury*, which was then in a shambles and losing $2,000 a week. Ochs was offered half ownership in the *Mercury*, but when he looked into the conditions and prospects of the paper, his cautious nature caused him to back away. The paper folded shortly thereafter.

The next year Ochs was back in New York negotiating for the New York *Times*, a paper that he felt he could be genuinely proud of, even though for some years it had been on a downward spiral. The *Times* had been founded in 1851 by Henry J. Raymond, one of Ochs's boyhood idols. Raymond's philosophy in starting the *Times* was to produce a paper that would keep itself free of political ideology and avoid the sensationalism of the early *Sun* and the *Herald* of Bennett the elder. The *Times* was nominally a Republican paper, and Raymond himself was very active in party politics, but the founder kept strictly to the idea that a newspaper should always be impartial, always get the facts straight.

Unfortunately, after a strong start in the 1850s and 1860s, the *Times* went downhill. Raymond himself died at an early age in 1869 and ownership went over to George Jones, who had been one of the paper's cofounders in 1851. Jones was a fairly successful owner and manager, although he never served as editor of his own paper. Under Jones's management the *Times* had some notable successes, mainly its exposé of the Tweed Ring in the 1870s. By the 1880s the paper was running into trouble. It remained a Republican paper, but it was now recognized as a mugwump: it supported Cleveland against James G. Blaine in the 1884 election. Thereafter the *Times* lost much of its loyal readership—and some of its well-healed advertisers as well. Still the paper was modestly successful up until the time of George Jones's death in 1891.

During the early 1890s the *Times* was in the hands of Charles R. Miller, who had been Jones's editor since 1883. Miller, a New Hampshire-born graduate of Dartmouth and former staffer on the great old Springfield *Republican*, was a skilled editorial writer but an inept business manager. In 1893 he and a few other staff members and outside investors bought the paper from the Jones family for a million dollars, but the paper slumped badly in the next few years. By the time Adolph Ochs appeared on the scene the paper was in a sorry financial condition. It had the lowest circulation of any morning daily in the city: there was a daily press run of 23,000 but apparently only 9,000 copies were actually being sold. At this time Bennett's *Herald* was selling 140,000 papers; Pulitzer's morning *World* sold 200,000.[1]

Adolph Ochs had studied the *Times* carefully and he convinced Miller and his associates as well as their New York bankers that he had the ability to turn the paper around. The financiers hoped to talk Ochs into a very complicated deal in which Ochs would advance some of his own funds and receive a $50,000 salary as publisher. Ochs insisted, however, that current salary was of no interest to him; he had not come to New York to find employment. "Unless I am put in absolute control of the property and of all who are employed therewith, I would not undertake the management at any price," he adamantly told the New York financiers.[2] But he would also not expect control until he had turned the paper around. After many months of negotiation, and with his Chattanooga paper on the table along with $75,000 of his own money, a deal to his liking was struck on August 13, 1896. The risk for Ochs was great—everything he had—and Ochs was not a risk taker by nature. He had bought the *Times* because he believed he could make it pay.

Thus, there arrived on the New York newspaper scene one of the nation's great publishers. Ochs was also one of the last men of the press who rose to the top in the old Horatio Alger, rags-to-riches, tradition. His career was not very different from that of Greeley, Bennett, or Pulitzer. At the age of fourteen he had been taken on at the Knoxville *Chronicle* as chore boy and printer's devil, and he climbed the ladder slowly and decisively. Unlike many of the great publishers of an earlier generation Ochs seemingly had no literary ability. He completely lacked Bennett's sharp and brilliant way with words. His talents lay in another direction, he was a great manager, an even hand at the tiller, a far-seeing judge of men. Unlike Pulitzer, who was a nervous jackrabbit always on an impetuous headlong plunge to somewhere and anywhere, Ochs had the temperament of a giant tortoise. He was capable of making mistakes and occasionally fell in a hole (as he had in his real estate dealings), but with firm determination he pulled himself up and began again on whatever path he had laid out for himself.

Ochs had been born in Cincinnati in 1859, the oldest of six children in a German Jewish family. His father, Julius Ochs, had come to the United States in 1845, served in the Civil War, then moved his family to Tennessee in a covered wagon. For a while Julius prospered in Knoxville, but by the time Adolph was nine, his father's business had failed and the family was drifting aimlessly. Julius, a dreamy, visionary individual, hoped that his sons would seek careers as scholars or artists, but in this age of Horatio Alger it was work not contemplation that seemed to be the route to success. Accordingly, Adolph, or Mooley as he was called, delivered papers, clerked in a store, then was apprenticed to a druggist.

At the age of fourteen, his schooling over, Ochs presented himself at the offices of the Knoxville *Chronicle* and asked its publisher, Capt. William Rule, for a job—any job. The only job available was that of chore boy, but Captain Rule must have been sufficiently impressed with this blue-eyed stripling with tight black curls, that he gave him the job. The lad proved so industrious in cleaning up the office that at the end of the day Rule virtually had to chase him home. Ochs moved forward briskly over the next several years, learning every aspect of the printing side of the newspaper business. At seventeen he got a job on Henry Watterson's Louisville *Courier-Journal*, and here he tried his hand at reporting. While in Knoxville Ochs had caught the attention and strong admiration of Col. John E. MacGowan, publisher of a paper rivaling the *Chronicle*, who believed that there was room for a good daily paper in the rapidly growing town of Chattanooga. At the time Chattanooga was a mud-flat town with no sidewalks and a population of only 12,000.[3] Filled with many disgruntled Confederate veterans, it was a typical frontier outpost with saloons and the usual shoot-outs. Newspapers had made no headway here: of the sixteen papers started in the previous forty years, all but one had failed, and that one, the *Times*, was also on the verge of extinction.

Buying up a half-interest in the paper for $250, with an option on the other half if he made a success of it, Ochs took over a tiny printing building with splintery floors, cases of worn and broken type, and a hand-pump press. This was in July 1878. Ochs was twenty years old. Once again, however, his industry saved him. By itself the paper might have failed like all of its predecessors, but Ochs solicited job printing to tide him over—he put out a business directory, public notices, and the like—so that when the city did begin to prosper and gather at least some semblance of gentility, the *Times* became a money-making institution. Eventually Ochs brought his brothers and even his father into the business; by the early 1890s the Chattanooga *Times* was a thriving institution. At the age of twenty-five, now an important man-about-town, Ochs married Effie Miriam Wise, a young girl he had met on a business trip to Cincinnati. Miss Wise, well-read and intelligent, became the *Times*'s book reviewer and spent much time at the paper with her husband until family duties called. (Only one child of this marriage survived, a daughter named Iphigene.)

Ochs's venture in New York was naturally different in one important respect from that of Chattanooga eighteen years earlier. The newspaper field was crowded; there were strong competitors and they could be vicious. Ochs, however, was nothing if not determined, and, as with everything he undertook, he had a clear-eyed vision of what he wanted to do. He had a plan to bring the New York *Times* back from oblivion, and he immediately put it into effect, never wavering from his vision and his goals.

Being a cautious and conservative individual, Ochs made no rapid moves to shake the *Times* to its foundation. He kept most of the staff, including Editor Charles R. Miller who remained a stockholder. Eventually Ochs put Miller in charge of the editorial page where his talents showed to best advantage. From the first, Ochs's firm resolution was to avoid being drawn into the orbit of the yellow press. He was convinced that what New York wanted and needed was more and better straight news. Just as Henry Raymond's early *Times* had made its way by resisting the sensationalism of the 1840s, Ochs decided to resist the formulas of Pulitzer and Hearst while finding what new things the intelligent New York reader wanted in his or her newspaper. To emphasize his intentions, several months into his management, Ochs had printed on the editorial page of his paper "All the News That's Fit to Print," and he subsequently offered a prize to his readers to come up with a better slogan. The prize was won by a reader in New Haven, Connecticut, who sent in "All the World News, But Not a School for Scandal." Ochs liked this a lot, but in the end preferred his original slogan. Accordingly, on February 10, 1897, he moved the slogan to the front page of the paper where it has remained ever since.[4]

Ochs immediately called for more comprehensive coverage of local and national news and inquired of his staff what areas of the news might lend themselves to expansion. Ochs picked everyone's brain, but he was especially drawn to the view of City Editor Henry Lowenthal. Many evenings of the week, after the major decisions of the day had been made, Ochs and Lowenthal would take a light meal at a nearby restaurant like Hitchcock's or Child's, then walked the streets of New York, discussing the problems of the paper. Lowenthal made the suggestion that expansion of business and financial news might bring back some of the paper's old readers. Some other staffers thought this was a route to disaster. Claiming that the paper was already too boring, many reporters thought that more business news would certainly kill the paper. Nonetheless, following Lowenthal's instincts, the business and financial sections of the paper were beefed up. Almost immediately Ochs began a feature called "Buyers In Town." Although it was a long and somewhat dull list, the *Times* had offered something that was not available anywhere else. (In the 1890s the *Wall Street Journal* was nothing but a four-page afternoon newsletter.)

Lowenthal could have pointed out to Ochs, but probably did not, that James Gordon Bennett Sr. had used just such a technique to get his paper off the ground in the 1830s. Noting the very poor coverage of business news in New York papers—ships' arrivals being about all there was—Bennett initiated a much fuller treatment of activities on Wall Street, this along with his front-page sensationalism. His circulation leaped forward.

So Wall Street and the financial district now became an important beat for the *Times*. Reporters were reassigned to business news, and additional men were hired to cover the area. Many new departments were opened up: real estate transactions, market reports, relevant political and judicial news. Within a year or so the New York *Times* was coming to be recognized as the "business bible" in New York and that was no mean accolade in this the financial capital of the nation. What is more important, no other paper stepped into the breach. The *Tribune*, which might have done so, was adding a few yellow touches as Whitelaw Reid's way of dealing with the changing newspaper scene—surely the wrong way to go for the staid *Tribune*. By default, business news became the province of the New York *Times*.

Ochs, however, was working on a great many fronts. He completely redesigned the paper, ordered new type faces, widened the spaces between lines of type, bought better newsprint and inks, banished a lot of unsightly advertisements for quack remedies and magic cure belts. He insisted on "dignity" in the advertising sections as well as the news pages. In such areas Ochs, who had come up through the composing room, needed no advice: the visual changes in the paper were mostly the products of his own taste and intelligence.

Of equal importance, Ochs began to expand other features of his paper. On September 5, 1896, he introduced a halftone Sunday supplement that was an immediate success. Less than two months later he added a Saturday book review supplement, which naturally had the effect of greatly increasing the number of book advertisements—one more important source of revenue. The paper greatly augmented its coverage of education, the arts, theater, and cultural affairs. On October 18, 1896, the paper inaugurated a front-page column "The News Condensed," a helpful device that also pointed up the fact that the *Times* was packing its pages with more hard news, both local and national.

The circulation of the paper rose, although not dramatically in the beginning. A year after his takeover, the daily *Times* was selling 22,000 copies, the Sunday *Times* 28,000—far better than under the old management, which had been selling only half of its press run. What was more important, advertising revenues were up sharply.

By 1898 the *Times* was widely recognized in New York as a solid and reliable paper, and some of its competitors were getting a little uneasy. Pulitzer complained that the *Times* was the toy of the sugar trust, of Wall Street bankers, or perhaps even of Tammany bosses. It is true that Ochs's instincts were conservative—he was a "gold Democrat" and had no respect for William Jennings Bryan and his silver frenzy—but he also succeeded in keeping himself independent of financial and political power brokers. Unfortunately, during the Spanish-American War, the paper was hurting because it could in no way hope to compete with the war coverage provided by the wealthy Pulitzer, Hearst, and Bennett organizations.

But Ochs found a way to turn this disadvantage around. In October 1898 he announced that the price of the *Times* would be reduced from 3 cents to 1 cent (both the *World* and the *Journal* were selling at 2 cents). Many people predicted disaster from this. Competing publishers believed that the *Times* must be on its last legs. Some journalists, even those on the *Times* staff, thought that the paper was about to venture into yellow journalism. But Ochs immediately made clear that he had no such intention. "It is the price of the paper and not its character that will change."

This price reduction brought about a miracle. Within a year the circulation of the *Times* rose from 25,000 to 75,000.[5] Ochs's instinct had been correct. Many people, finding they could buy a solid, dignified paper for only a penny, switched their allegiances. By 1900 nearly 100,000 copies of the daily paper were on the press, and in August of that year, four years after taking over, Adolph S. Ochs took full control of the New York *Times*. Had he wished at this time, Ochs could have laid back and enjoyed some of his own wealth, but he never developed the sybaritic tastes of Pulitzer or Hearst. It was his way, and would always be his way, to keep only modest profits for himself and plow most of his gains back in the business.

Indicative of this generosity toward his own business enterprise was the grand new building he built for his paper only a few years after he gained control of the company. The old plant and offices at 41 Park Row had been dilapidated and outmoded when Ochs took over and needed to be replaced, even though much new equipment had been installed there. Once again seeing into the future with a clear eye, Ochs bought a plot of land way uptown, far from Newspaper Row, at a place called Long Acre Square. Here he began building a tall Florentine-style office tower on a peculiar triangular parcel of land at 42nd Street, where Broadway and Seventh Avenue crossed. Some people in the newspaper trade thought that Ochs had lost his senses in going so far off the beaten track; others worried that he had extended himself dangerously—all of his ready cash went into this risky project.

Yes, the choice of the locale did seem odd in 1902 when Ochs purchased the land. Long Acre Square had been a nondescript neighborhood of carriage dealers and out-of-the-way shops. But there were already signs of change in the neighborhood. It was clear that the city's rialto was moving up this way. The Metropolitan Opera House had moved to 39th Street and Broadway in 1893. In the late 1890s great impresarios like Oscar Hammerstein and David Belasco had built new and ornate theaters on 42nd Street. Across from the Times Building would be the luxurious Astor Hotel with a soon-to-be-fashionable roof garden.[6] Even more important, the planned New York subway would come through here, and when it was opened in 1904, only months before the Times Building itself, Ochs convinced the subway owners to name the station Times Square. After this the old name Long Acre Square faded into oblivion. Far from being off the beaten track, the new Times Building was in the very epicenter of the modern city of New York. When the presses began to roll in the new building on January 1, 1905, many copies of the paper were delivered to distant parts of the city by means of the newly built subway.

In 1905, however, the greatest years for the *Times* were still ahead. While the paper's reputation was secure, the mighty news-gathering organization that would make the *Times* one of the world's great newspapers was still in the making. Largely responsible for putting together this great organization was a new managing editor who had arrived on the scene in 1904, Carr V. Van Anda. Van Anda was probably the best managing editor in the history of American journalism; his selection revealed yet another example of Adolph Ochs's ability to pick the right man for a job. Seldom inclined to make public appearances or pronouncements about his work, Van Anda possessed a mind that was curious, analytical, intuitive, and energetic: a splendid combination for running a huge news-gathering army.

Van Anda came on board as managing editor after sixteen years as an editor at the New York *Sun*. Born in Georgetown, Ohio, in 1864, Van Anda had studied science and mathematics at Ohio University. Had the fates played a different hand, he might have had a great career for himself in the sciences, but early in life he had been bitten by the newspaper bug. At the age of six he was pasting news items on sheets of paper and selling them for ten cents a copy. At ten he made his own wooden press and later solicited job printing. The world of learning waylaid him for a while at Ohio University, but he left college early to work on the Cleveland *Herald* and other Cleveland papers. He worked for the Baltimore *Sun* for a time before moving to the New York *Sun* in 1888.

Van Anda is one of those editors to whom the word "legendary" has been freely applied. He was not, however, a table-thumping editor of the type so beloved of Hollywood central casting. It was true that he had a cold, piercing glance that one of his reporters referred to as the "Van Anda death ray," but essentially he was an unflappable, well-organized individual of scholarly mien and habit of mind. Much of his success was due to sheer energy and dogged pursuit of the news. At the *Sun* Van Anda had been the night editor, and when he came to the *Times* he insisted on holding this job as that of well as managing Editor. He stayed at his desk throughout the night, planning the news coverage and layout until the wee hours of the morning when the paper was actually on the presses.

Foresight and perhaps some kind of intuitive vision were at the heart of Van Anda's genius. Some of the stories that are told about his foresight may be apocryphal. It is said that on one occasion Van Anda asked a reporter to go to a particular street corner and wait. Something might happen. Shortly thereafter a man leaped from a nearby tall building and the reporter got the scoop. For the most part, though, it was not "scoops" of that kind that made Van Anda's reputation. Rather it was a dogged and persistent attention to detail and awareness of unfolding events that was the key to his success.

A more characteristic example of Van Anda's "foresight" took place shortly after his arrival on the *Times*. The Russo-Japanese War was in progress. On May 29, 1905, at 4:31 A.M., news came that Admiral Togo's battleships had practically annihilated the Russian fleet. At 4:31 A.M. Van Anda was still riding the news in anticipation of just such an event. He had already marshaled all of the background material and was ready to go with full coverage and headlines. The regular edition of the paper had already been printed and was being delivered, but in 19 minutes Van Anda had another edition of 40,000 copies on the presses, and horse-drawn wagons had been asked to stand by at the curb outside the Times Building. At dawn not every newsstand in the city had copies of this battle extra, but all the major hotels and newsstands had them. The other morning papers had nothing.[7]

In 1912 Van Anda's quick thinking resulted in the first announcement of the sinking of the *Titanic*. At 1:20 A.M. on April 15, the Associated Press reported that the *Titanic* had hit an iceberg and had put out an SOS. When no further messages came through, Van Anda assumed that the ship had sunk on its well-publicized maiden voyage. Van Anda, as usual, was on top of the rapidly moving events. By 3:30 he and his staff had completely organized the story and once again had the jump on all the morning papers around the country. By resourceful use of radio, and even the help and participation of the radio's inventor Guglielmo Marconi, Van Anda scooped all of the other papers over the next three days with the lists of survivors on the incoming ship *Carpathia*.

Curiously, even the afternoon papers later in the day had the news wrong. Misled by knowledge that the ship was "unsinkable," and deceived by the secrecy of the White Star Line (which Van Anda's staff quickly penetrated), the *Evening Sun*, had a banner headline announcing: ALL SAVED FROM TITANIC AFTER COLLISION. Smaller headlines announced, "Liner Is Being Towed to Halifax."[8] It was the kind of goof that would never occur at the *Times*.

To be sure, many of the triumphs of the *Times* after the arrival of Van Anda were due to the generosity of Ochs in building up the news organization and in supporting Van Anda in all of his needs. The celebrated *Times* feature writer Meyer Berger in his book *The Story of the New York Times* remarked that "there may have been somewhere in newspaper history a more perfect publisher-managing editor team than the Ochs-Van Anda set-up, but none comes to mind."[9] Both publisher and editor had a craving for news and they wanted it to be fast, complete, and well documented. Both went to great lengths to satisfy this craving. Ochs never stinted on staff, giving Van Anda all the reporters he needed; too he supplied all the white space necessary to get fully documented news in print.

In the first few decades of the twentieth century, both Ochs and Van Anda were well aware that there was a great deal more to the news than scandal; they knew that the public had a large appetite for it. In those years the automobile, the radio, and the airplane were rapidly making the United States into a wholly different place. To survive, a modern newspaper would have to cover the latest developments in science and technology. Few, if any American newspapers then bothered about science news, although years earlier, under Henry Raymond, the *Times* had been a pioneer in the coverage of science. With the scientifically trained Van Anda at the helm the *Times* once again moved to the forefront. It was the New York *Times* that introduced Albert Einstein and his "theory of relativity" to the American public in the period right after World War I. Van Anda personally steeped himself in these matters, although he now employed trained people on the science beat. In the early 1920s, when Einstein had come to Princeton to deliver some lectures, Van Anda questioned an equation that was sent in to the paper and asked his reporter to check it. Although naturally hesitant to question anything done by the greatest scientific mind of the age, the reporter timidly advised Einstein that his "editor" was puzzled by a particular equation. Einstein was astonished, but looked at the notes. "Yes, Mr. Van Anda is right," he said. "I made a mistake in transcribing the equation on the blackboard."[10]

Van Anda was managing editor of the *Times* for twenty years, retiring in 1925. He lived on another twenty years as a lingering memory and legend at the New York *Times*. There were always detractors. There were those who said that Van Anda did not care that much about writing, and that the *Times*, in spite of its complete coverage, was heavy or elephantine in style. Clearly the *Times* was not as well written as the *Herald*, the *World*, or the *Sun* in those years, but such charges never bothered Van Anda or Ochs, neither of whom saw a newspaper as a spawning ground for free-wheeling poets.

The *Times*'s recognition as the American newspaper of record was probably cemented for all time during World War I. It was then that the *Times*'s large news-gathering organization pulled ahead of most of its American competitors. It was not size alone that mattered, but, once again, planning. Hearst-like escapades and color reporting counted for nothing in this war. Van Anda was at his best now, poring nightly over maps of Europe, dispatching his minions by means of radiotelegraphy. In the characteristic fashion of Van Anda's legend, *Times* men often arrived at the scene of a battle before the troops. But the stage had been set for this long before America's entry into the war. The *Times*, which had worked out very elaborate exchanges with European papers and news bureaus, had the most comprehensive coverage of what was going on in Europe. At this time it also began the practice of publishing, in full, white papers, speeches of political leaders of the various countries, a policy that led to its becoming the leading American reference newspaper in the minds of librarians, scholars, government officials, and probably other newspapers as well.[11] The appearance of the *New York Times Index*, published continuously since 1913, reinforced the paper's stature. But it was clear long before World War I that Adolph Ochs had created a newspaper of the first rank, that he had fully realized the ideals that Henry Raymond first expressed back in 1851.

As early as 1904, while traveling in Germany, he met at long last his one-time detractor Joseph Pulitzer. Ochs was very impressed by Pulitzer the man, calling him a great philosopher, and concluding that if it were not for Pulitzer's blindness and other afflictions he would have been one of the most eminent men in American life. Ochs also found Pulitzer very complimentary about the *Times*, which he had once attacked as the toady of the sugar trust and as "keeper of the deficit." The two men met a short time later at Aix-les-Bains and parted in the manner of two genial ambassadors. Pulitzer spoke disparagingly of his own New York *World* and expressed strong admiration for the *Times*. "You have a very, very able editorial page," he ventured.[12] More importantly perhaps, he admitted that whenever he wanted to get the day's news himself he turned to the pages of the New York *Times*.

10

Of Evenings, and Sundays, and Funnies, and Such

The path taken by the New York *Times* under Adolph Ochs was hardly typical of the metropolitan newspaper at the turn of the century. To be sure, most papers did not go to the extremes of Pulitzer's *World* or Hearst's *Journal* in serving up lurid and sensational human interest stories; on the other hand, by the 1880s, most newspaper editors believed that the public wanted more from their daily paper than straight news. In these years, before the arrival of the electronic media, people expected newspapers to provide a wide variety of entertainment. In this sense the modern newspaper began to take shape in New York during the 1880s. It was Pulitzer, on taking over the *World*, who discovered that readers wanted a richer diet than a daily dose of facts; they wanted games, puzzles, contests, stunts, humor, household tips. They wanted useful information for coping with modern life.

These are the things that today's newspaper editors call "features," although that word has never been capable of easy definition. Since Pulitzer's time, and down to our own, few newspapers have failed to provide these other staples in their daily fare. Even the staid New York *Times* caved in, although only a little, when it introduced a crossword puzzle in its Sunday magazine. But that was not until 1942, seven years after the death of Adolph Ochs.[1] (Eight years later this enormously successful feature, which the *World* had introduced back in 1913, also appeared in the weekday *Times*.) History cannot record what Adolph Ochs would have thought of the crossword puzzle. Perhaps he would have liked it, as did many *Times* readers.

The vast majority of American newspapers went much further into this area of recreational journalism; a few became positively besotted with it. The growth of "features" in the daily press followed the greater availability of newsprint after the Civil War, the development of bigger and better presses, more readable typefaces, and finally technological developments which permitted lavish illustrations and color supplements. The increasing number and size of display advertisements probably also had a great deal to do with this expansion of format.

There were other trends in the newspaper field that had a lot to do with the burgeoning of entertainment features. One was the shift, during the 1870s and 1880s, to evening newspapers. Before the Civil War, most urban dailies were morning papers, although there had long been afternoon papers as well. In New York, the *Evening Post* and the *Commercial Advertiser* were afternoon papers. So too the *Evening Transcript* in Boston and the *Evening Bulletin* in Philadelphia. But in the post-war period many new evening newspapers were launched. The development of the telegraph probably had much to do with the trend. Most news "broke" during the day, and with late-breaking news capable of being released on lightning presses, the afternoon time slot became much more attractive to newspaper proprietors.

Moreover, competition was pushing morning publishers to issue later and later "extras"; some of these were essentially afternoon editions. Also, there was another technique that publishers of morning newspapers could use to ride the trend toward afternoon newspapers: they could put out "early editions" of their morning papers. James Gordon Bennett used this ploy as early as the 1840s. The next step became inevitable: by the 1880s morning papers began issuing their own separately administered afternoon editions. In 1887, when he felt himself jostled by the popularity of Pulitzer's *World*, Charles A. Dana introduced an Evening *Sun*. It had its own editor and staff. This was the first lively, compact, one-cent afternoon paper. Not to be outdone, Pulitzer introduced his own afternoon *World* seven months later. By 1890, about two-thirds of American daily papers were published in the afternoon.[2] This trend would eventually be reversed, but not until the latter half of the twentieth century.

One of the reasons for the success of the afternoon papers beginning in the 1880s was the appearance in many homes of oil lamps—later gas and electric lights. Reading small print in poor light posed noticeable discomforts until such time as the home parlor could be well illuminated in the evening. With adequate illumination available, a strong demand for reading matter of a more leisurely nature was bound to arise.

But it was the creation of the plump Sunday paper, stuffed with full-page ads, that truly opened the door to a multitude of new entertainment features, many of which had never been dreamed of before. There were columns for women, including advice to the lovelorn, features on etiquette, fashion, home decoration; there were articles on dogs, horses, gardening, sporting events; there were puzzles, comics, stories for children, poems, and every imaginable kind of ephemera. The Sunday paper finally gave rise to "supplements"; whole sections for women, children, sports enthusiasts, theater-goers, society watchers. In the late 1890s the Chicago *Tribune* was even publishing a "Worker's Magazine."

It is not, of course, true to say that "non-news" features had been invented by Pulitzer in the 1880s: they had been there all along in somewhat smaller quantities. Even in the early republic newspapers published literary miscellany, humor, japes and pasquinades, poems, essays, and sketches of every imaginable sort. Newspapers sometimes printed stories and even serials. Long before the 1880s there had been book reviewing, and serious articles on religion, art, and theater. But there would be major changes in the nature of these materials over time. A random walk through the newspapers of the nineteenth century is a surprising experience. Consider the case of poetry. Poems appeared in newspapers during colonial times and were commonplace in the early republic. During the stormy days of party strife poems were often political or satirical in nature, but they were nonetheless considered to be important to the editorial mix. Some writers—Philip Freneau was a good example—moved from newspaper editing to poetry. Others moved the other way. It was not considered odd in 1829 that a poet of the stature of William Cullen Bryant would take on the editorship of a newspaper. During his nearly half century as editor of the New York *Evening Post*, Bryant published a good deal of verse, sometimes his own, although he was scrupulous in avoiding the appearance of using the *Post* as a vehicle for his own poetry.

There was a good deal of poetry in American newspapers during the Civil War—on both the northern and southern sides: poems about John Brown, Harper's Ferry, Bull Run, Gettysburg, Lee's surrender. Walt Whitman, a longtime newspaper writer and former editor of the Brooklyn *Eagle*, wrote some of his greatest poetry in the wake of Lincoln's assassination. Even Bryant did not fail to publish in the *Post* his own memorial poem, "The Death of Lincoln."[3] The Civil War made a reputation for a number of poets—Edmund Clarence Stedman in the North and Henry Timrod in the South to name but two. After the Civil War newspaper poetry became somewhat less important, but nearly all of the major American poets of the nineteenth century contributed poems to newspapers—Poe, Emerson,

Whitman, Longfellow, and Lowell. John Greenleaf Whittier was even called the "newspaper poet" because of his long association with the abolitionist cause.

In the twentieth century there has been much less poetry in American newspapers, but it hardly became rare until after World War II. Perhaps poetry disappeared because of changes in public taste, or because poetry itself became more esoteric. But popular poets found their voice in newspapers for many years. James Whitcomb Riley began writing his homespun poetry about "punkin's," butter churns, hay ricks, and hobgoblins in the Anderson, Indiana, *Democrat*, and later became a regular contributor to the Indianapolis *Journal*.

Even as the nineteenth century waned, younger poets were coming along who used newspapers as their chief outlet. Wilbur D. Mason wrote poems on a daily basis for the Baltimore *American*, and later the Chicago *Tribune*. Probably the most widely circulated newspaper poet of all time was Edgar A. Guest, who began writing poems for the Detroit *Free Press* in 1899. His work subsequently appeared all over the country in syndication. Never held in high repute among the literati—having written lines such as "life is just a bowl of cherries," and "it takes a heap o' livin' to make a house a home"—Guest nonetheless wrote some 11,000 poems before his death in 1959. The vast majority of these were first published in newspapers.

The most common form of entertainment feature in newspapers before the 1880s was humor, which doubtless includes the musings of crackerbarrel philosophers, prose poets, and small-town sages. Nearly all papers, even rural weeklies, tended to have their own whimsical bards, and the effusions of such notables often became the feature of the paper the average reader turned to first. Before widespread syndication of features early in the twentieth century, most newspaper humor and whimsy was of local origin. On the other hand, humorists of the first rank did become known nationally. The most famous newspaper humorist was, of course, Mark Twain. A newspaperman born and bred, Twain had worked on his brother's paper in Hannibal, Missouri, as a boy, and then moved around the far West as a wandering printer. He became a nationally known figure soon after publishing "The Celebrated Jumping Frog of Calaveras County" in the New York *Saturday Press*, on November 18, 1865.[4]

While Twain was undoubtedly the best-known humorist of his day, he was by no means the only one in the public eye during the latter half of the nineteenth century. It was, one might say, a kind of golden age of folk humor in America. Most of the native humorists of the period wrote for newspapers, some of them as full-time employees. One such newspaper humorist was Charles F. Browne, a New Englander by birth, who later moved on to Ohio as a tramp newspaperman. While working for the Cleveland *Plain Dealer* he began writing a series of letters using the name Artemus Ward, supposedly an old showman with a "marvlus collecksion of Wild Beasts." With his antic spelling and his strange use of dialect he managed to poke sly fun at modern people and their ways. Another newspaper humorist who used a similar technique—letters to the editor—was David Ross Locke, who gained fame under the name of Petroleum V. Nasby. Locke worked himself up the newspaper ladder to become editor and owner of the Toledo *Blade* after the Civil War. During the war he invented the character of Petroleum Nasby, which was based on a town loafer and drunkard he had met while working in Findlay, Ohio. Since the drunken Nasby was a Copperhead, with all sorts of deliciously ignorant and bigoted southern stereotypes roaming in his head, his outrageous mouthings seemed very amusing to northerners during the war. Many of "Nasby's" splendid spurts of ignorance were collected in book form after the war and became best sellers.[5]

Many of the newspaper humorists of the late nineteenth century were regionalists, but a few made their small-town papers famous. There was James Montgomery Bailey of the Danville (Connecticut) *News*; there was Brick Pomeroy of the (La Crosse) *Wisconsin Democrat*; there was Bill Nye of Laramie, Wyoming, who named his newspaper after a major comic character, "Boomerang"—his pet mule. (The "Boomerang" stories appeared daily for a time, but most of Nye's humor circulated in the weekly edition.) There was George W. Peck, later governor of Wisconsin, who invented "Peck's Bad Boy," for *Peck's Sun* in La Crosse. There was Robert J. Burdette of the Burlington (Iowa) *Hawkeye*. There was E. W. Howe, owner of the Atchison (Kansas) *Daily Globe*, who became a celebrated aphorist, memorist, and paragrapher. He was known nationally as "The Sage of Potato Hill." There was Opie Read who began his *Arkansas Traveller* in 1882. Read's paper attained an amazing circulation of 85,000 with its backwoods or "up the creek" humor.

This is not to say that the big cities did not have their share of newspaper humorists. There was Charles B. Lewis who wrote for the Detroit *Free Press* under the name M. Quad; there was Charles Heber Clark who wrote for the Philadelphia *Inquirer*; there was Joel Chandler Harris who for twenty-four years wrote humorous sketches, southern in ambiance, for the Atlanta *Constitution*. Naturally, too, some of the country funny men found their way to the city. George W. Peck moved to Milwaukee; Opie Read became a contributor to Pulitzer's *Sunday World*, and so did Bill Nye. The

Hawkeye humorist Bob Burdette moved east to the Brooklyn Sunday *Eagle*.

Chicago was a veritable magnet for humorists at the end of the nineteenth century. Perhaps the best of the lot was Missouri-born Eugene Field, who conducted the "Sharps and Flats" column in the Chicago *Daily News* from 1883 until his untimely death in 1895. A man of genuine literary talent, he had an exquisite light touch and an exuberant youthful playfulness. Like Mark Twain, he could handle the poignant and the satirical with equal deftness. It was probably top literary talents like Fields that made Chicago a "port of humorists" in those years, drawing in lighthearted columnists who continued to be popular well into the twentieth century. From Indiana came John T. McCutcheon and the sharply ironical George Ade. From Michigan came Ring Lardner. From Chicago itself came Franklin P. Adams (F.P.A.), who later moved on to New York; and Finley Peter Dunne, who began his literary career with the Chicago *Post*. Dunne created for the *Post* his most famous character "Mr. Dooley"—saloon keeper, economist, philosopher—who still delights people after the passing of nearly a century.

The rural humorists and street-corner philosophers have for the most part disappeared from the newspaper scene in the twentieth century, as have regional dialects, errant spellers, and talking mules. But newspaper-based humorists have not completely disappeared; one recalls men like Christopher Morley and Don Marquis in the 1920s and 1930s and numerous others in the years since. Today newspaper humor is mostly an occasional flavoring for op-ed pages and is more firmly rooted in current events, but there have been very masterly writers like Art Buchwald and Russell Baker who have nourished long careers as humorous or at least "light-side" columnists.

By the time Pulitzer began building up the Sunday *World* in the mid-1880s it was clear that there was no way that a paper of this heft and girth could be filled up with humor or literary miscellany. Finding new things for the Sunday pages would be a prime necessity. Pulitzer turned in his quest to a young Dartmouth graduate named Morrill Goddard who had already established himself as a live-wire reporter. Goddard once interviewed James G. Blaine in his home in Maine and then burst into the kitchen to interview the servants.[6] He was nothing if not resourceful, and with Pulitzer's approval he began foraging about for new material to fill up the Sunday *World*. He had an undoubted skill at discovering a "features angle" in all kinds of news stories and in the most slender of trivia. Goddard was so successful that he has often been called the "father of the Sunday paper." Sunday papers were not new, to be sure: James Gordon Bennett had instituted a regular Sunday *Herald* as early as 1841. But the giant Sunday paper we are all familiar with today was a product of Goddard's fertile imagination in the 1890s.

Goddard relied heavily on the sorts of things *World* readers were already familiar with: narratives of sex, crime, scandal, and dabblings in pseudo-science. Crusades, perforce beginning on the news pages, were puffed up and covered from fresh angles. Goddard's ace in the hole, so to speak, was illustration. By the 1890s no one doubted that pictures sold newspapers, so Goddard made sure that the Sunday *World* had plenty of them. Generally the rich abundance of illustrations were gathered in separately printed Sunday "supplements." Goddard had no monopoly on supplements—the *Sun* and the *Herald* had them, so did papers like the Boston *Globe* and the Philadelphia *Inquirer*. One of the advantages of supplements was that they could be printed a few days early if necessary—and inserted later among the news pages. Techniques for reproducing photographs in newspaper printing had not yet been developed and had to wait for the arrival of rotogravure, a German import, around 1913. But newspaper artists flourished in the 1890s and there was never a dearth of illustrated material to fill up the Sunday pages. There were maps of crime scenes, line drawings of abandoned children or betrayed wives, and so on. Goddard was also fond of pictures of dancing girls or female acrobats in tights, or women in skimpy attire or windblown dresses.

The most dramatic development of the Sunday paper was the debut of the colored comics. The first of these appeared in the New York Sunday *World* on November 19, 1893. Richard Outcault's snaggle-toothed street urchin of "Hogan's Alley," already enormously popular, was now seen prominently sporting a broad yellow apron. Pulitzer, as usual, was out at sea in his yacht when Goddard and editor-in-chief Arthur Brisbane first thought of running a colored Sunday supplement. They cabled Pulitzer and received a one-word response: "Experiment."[7] But there were not many doubts that the experiment would succeed; the circulation of the Sunday paper, already the biggest in the country, leaped forward once again.

As to the birth of the comics or the "funnies" in American journalism, the form developed not in one grand leap, but in a series of stages. "Hogan's Alley" (later changed to "The Yellow Kid") has usually been acknowledged as the first newspaper comic drawing. But one must be cautious of using the words "comic strip" for in the beginning comics were only single panels—and remained so for a while even in the Sunday color supplement. The comic strip, with several panels—and with bubbles that allowed characters to speak their words—did not develop until the end of the 1890s. Naturally the comics as we know them had their ancestral types. The art of caricature existed in ancient Rome and flourished in England early in the nineteenth century. English masters of the form were artists like Thomas Rowlandson and George Cruikshank.

Too, American newspaper readers were already accustomed to cartoon drawings because single-panel political cartoons had appeared in newspapers since colonial times. (Benjamin Franklin was in fact the first American cartoonist. He printed a political cartoon as early as 1747.)[8] Political cartooning, using the techniques of caricature, was thereafter always a part of the American newspaper and nearly all of our presidents and other political figures suffered the indignity of being caricatured. On the other hand, the political cartoon as a daily feature of the editorial page had to wait until the 1890s.

Political cartooning on a regular basis had been a feature of weekly illustrated papers during and immediately after the Civil War. The most famous American cartoonist of the day was Thomas Nast, who drew for *Harper's Weekly* the famous caricatures of "Boss" Tweed that demolished the Tammany leader and made his name synonymous with political malfeasance throughout the world. Nast, who could be cruel and sulphurous, also had a mellow side: he created the visual attributes of the jolly Santa Claus that we know today. He also created the most enduring political symbols in American history: the Republican elephant and the Democratic donkey.

Political cartooning got a big boost in the public prints by the appearance of three major humor magazines during the 1880s: *Puck*, *Judge*, and *Life*. These magazines owed a great deal to European models such as the English *Punch* and the German *Simplicissimus*, and much of the popularity of these magazines was due to bold full-page political cartoons using the new technique of color printing known as chromolithography.

Political cartoons did not become a *regular* feature of daily newspapers until the presidential election year of 1884, when a cartoonist named Walt McDougall began supplying cartoons to a short-lived New York paper called the *Extra*. That same year McDougall did a vivid anti-Blaine cartoon that was rejected by *Judge*. Later he dropped the drawing off with the elevator boy at the World Building saying that Joseph Pulitzer could have it for free if he wanted it. Pulitzer plastered it on page one of the *World*, full size, not realizing that it was supposed to be reduced. Without reduction "it looked like the crab's eyebrow," said McDougall. But Pulitzer was tickled with the results (and an increase in sales of his paper), so he hired McDougall to do political cartoons on a daily basis at a handsome salary of $50 a week.[9] Within a few years nearly all self-respecting urban newspapers had to have their own political or editorial page cartoonists. A long newspaper tradition was thus begun.

The "comic strips" of the late 1890s did not wholly grow out of the political cartoon. They were more closely allied to the literary folk humor that was so prominent at that time. Eventually they would need a narrative element or story line and a recurrent group of characters. There had been a regular group of characters in "Hogan's Ally" ("The Yellow Kid") but no story development for a long time, just that single panel. In Europe, however, there had been a rich tradition of "picture stories." In France artists like Rudolphe Topffer and Georges Colomb cultivated this art form. (To this day picture storybooks—romances and such—are much more popular in France than in the United States.) In Germany an artist named Wilhelm Busch had created two humorous characters, "Max and Moritz," who were regulars in a pictorial series. Inspired by these characters, a beginner in New York, Rudolph Dirks, began a strip called the "Katzenjammer Kids," which made its debut in the New York Sunday *Journal* on December 12, 1897. It was the first strip containing a series of panels and a recurrent cast of characters with well-established individual personalities. The Katzenjammer kids, Hans and Fritz, were two "bad boys" of the kind well known in American folklore at the time, but adding to the humor they lived in a fanciful German colony of Africa and spoke in comical German-English accents. They hated all forms of authority, including schoolteachers and state officials. Their guiding philosophy was "Society ist nix." "Katzenjammer Kids" was not only the first comic "strip" in the modern sense, it has been the longest running strip of all time.

Naturally there were numerous other artists who immediately devoted themselves to this very profitable art form. Among the pioneers were James Swinnerton who drew "Little Jimmy," Charles E. Schultze, the creator of "Foxy Grandpa," and George Herriman, creator of "Krazy Kat." An extremely fertile artist of the early days was Frederick Burr Opper who drew a number of strips: "Happy Hooligan," "Her Name Was Maud," and "Alphonse and Gaston." Happy Hooligan was a clown; Maud a stubborn mule who always got the best of her owners (certainly the last kick); Alphonse and Gaston were two Frenchman whose exaggerated politeness drew them into ludicrous mishaps.

In the 1890s many Americans referred to the Sunday supplements as the "funny papers," although a lot of other things appeared there beside comics. But early in the twentieth century strips also began appearing in the daily papers. The first such was Bud Fisher's "Mr. A. Mutt"—later "Mutt and Jeff"—which began in the San Francisco *Chronicle* on November 15,

1907.[10] Responding to public demand, artists came up with a variety of new ideas. Richard Outcault, having left both Pulitzer and Hearst, created a new little boy, "Buster Brown," inhabiting a much more genteel environment than that of "Hogan's Alley." Buster Brown was a neatly dressed youngster with blond hair, usually accompanied by his brindle bull pup, Tige. Buster Brown would, in time, become a much greater draw than "The Yellow Kid," and ran until 1926. Buster's clean-cut little face was picked up by advertising people and used to sell everything in sight—children's clothes, hats, shoes, even cigars and whiskey! In time there were enough of these products to bring about the establishment of a Buster Brown Museum in New York, at 119 East 36th Street.[11]

It quickly became apparent that the "funnies" could be concocted to amuse adults as well as children. One of the early comic strip artists was George McManus, creator of "Bringing Up Father," popularly called "Maggie and Jiggs." McManus was a superlative draftsman and an incisive social critic who offered sparkling commentary on a social-climbing wife and daughter always trying to interest "father" in higher things with snob appeal such as opera and ballet. Father, of course, preferred the company of his old cronies and simple restaurants of his Irish neighborhood where corned beef and cabbage were served. "Bringing Up Father" was one of the most enduring strips. After McManus's death in 1959 it was continued by other artists. It appeared in 500 American newspapers as well as forty-three foreign countries, and was said to have had some eighty million readers. The rolling-pin wielding Maggie probably did more than anyone else to convince Europeans that *at home* American men were completely dominated by their wives.

By 1910 the demand for comic strips was enormous and many new avenues were being explored. The funnies no longer needed to be funny. Strips were devoted to fairy tales, melodrama, mythological fables, science fiction, even to domestic situations that were not unlike today's soap operas. Adventure and melodrama were especially important, and by the 1930s the "funnies" were filled with a multitude of slouch-hatted sleuths, phantoms, crime reporters, supermen, super boys, super girls, adventurers in far away jungles, even in outer space.

The comics were successful in part because a younger generation of newspaper artists responded to the vigorous public demand for their strips. But they also increased in number because of the latent potential for reaching mass audiences through syndication. If an artist like George McManus or Bud Fisher could appear not in one paper but in dozens, even hundreds, their incomes could go through the roof. Some of them became wealthy men.

It was syndication in fact that made possible the great triumphs of the Sunday papers and the spread of feature material in the daily papers. In the first few decades of the twentieth century most of the comics were distributed through Hearst's giant King Features Syndicate and the Chicago Tribune Syndicate. But the idea of syndication had historical precedent. For several decades before the turn of the century the native humorists and "colymnists" were read around the country because of the spread of "ready-print" services that supplied pre-prepared material or "boilerplate" to smaller papers.[12] The idea of syndication began during the Civil War when many papers, particularly in the Midwest, found their printers and typesetters drafted into the army. They purchased prepared materials (usually half-sheet supplements) from larger papers. Good coverage of war news was made possible to these hard-pressed papers. By the 1890s, however, a great deal of boilerplate was feature material—comics, humor, household advice, travel articles, whatever.

Among the most assiduous readers of feature material in both Sunday and daily papers were, of course, women, just as they were of the magazines that began to flourish in the 1890s. Even before Hearst established his own syndicate, magazine publishers, and like S. S. McClure and Edward W. Bok of the *Ladies' Home Journal*, hired women with newspaper experience to help them, such as Ella Wheeler Wilcox, who began conducting a weekly column in this period.

By the time that the big Sunday supplements were appearing in the New York papers, the newspapers themselves were making use of their own women reporters and feature writers to churn out materials for feminine readers. William Randolph Hearst was alert to the importance of "women's viewpoint" material and brought from San Francisco to New York "Annie Laurie," one of the first newspaper "sob sisters." Also, within a few years he had established (and distributed through his syndicate) the column "Advice to the Lovelorn," written by Beatrice Fairfax (the pen name of one Marie Manning), which began on July 20, 1898. The popularity of features of this kind can hardly be doubted: "Miss Fairfax" sometimes received as many as 1,500 letters a day during the height of her career.[13] Of course at this time, too, the bulging Sunday paper also offered practical household information for women as well as articles on fashion, child rearing, and other subjects, much of it boilerplate.

In the days before radio and television, newspapers also published, especially in evening or Sunday editions, stories or games for children. Indeed among the first items sent out by S. S. McClure's newspaper syndicate were stories that had been published previously in the *St. Nicholas* magazine for children. The Cincinnati *Commercial Tribune* offered an entire tabloid supplement for children entitled "Our Boys and Girls." Not a few newspaper writers had a soft spot for the juvenile audience and made attempts to write for it, some with enormous success. About 1910, Howard R. Garis, a reporter on the Newark *Evening News*, began to write a series of "Bedtime Stories" for children. These stories featured Uncle Wiggily, a "rabbit gentleman" in whom the traces of ebullient boyhood had never been eradicated. Garis wrote 15,000 "Bedtime Stories," until his retirement over forty years later; they were syndicated in hundreds of newspapers. Garis also wrote some 700 other children's books, some under his own name and some under pen names—he contributed many titles to series like Tom Swift, the Motor Boys, the Bobbsey Twins, and numerous others.[14] He was capable of writing a children's book in one week.

A visitor to America or a newly arriving immigrant at the beginning of the twentieth century would surely find the American newspaper to be unlike anything found in the nations of Europe, most of which stuck tenaciously to long-established newspaper formats. "American journalism," commented an English observer, "has reached its highest development in the Sunday newspaper. There is no parallel to it in England or in any other country. It is at once a newspaper and a literary miscellany, a society journal and household magazine."[15]

The Sunday paper also offered clear proof, once more, of the American genius for casting aside worn-out conventions and inventing new ones, often in defiance of all the staid old proprieties.

11

Newspaper Chains and Press Associations

The first decade of the twentieth century was witness to a gigantic concentration of power in the world of American business; it was an era of conglomeration and amalgamation, of monopoly and cartel; it was a time when the word "trust" was on everyone's lips. There was a sugar trust, a beef trust, a tobacco trust, even a shoe trust. Huge corporations, more powerful than any known in history, were being forged into still larger corporations. Gobbling up most of their former competitors were monopolistic behemoths like Standard Oil, the American Tobacco Company, the American Sugar Refining Company, all set up as a means of elbowing their way to dominance in their respective industries. In 1901, in the library of J. P. Morgan, the nation's premier merchant banker, the United States Steel Corporation was patched together as a way of setting prices and waging a ruthless war on any independent company that threatened to undersell the market. As late as 1890 the American steel industry had been highly competitive; now 66 percent of steel production was under the umbrella of this single giant corporation.

Newspapers did not, of course, join in this march toward conglomeration, at least not in any significant number. Partly this was due to the fact that newspapers were intimately tied to their local communities and aspired to no national market. Too, they were usually run by highly idiosyncratic owners who valued their fierce independence. More importantly, no tidal wave of conglomeration swamped the newspaper world because newspapers were seldom truly large businesses to begin with. To be sure, men like

Whitelaw Reid and Joseph Pulitzer in New York, or Victor Lawson and Joseph Medill in Chicago had become wealthy men in pursuit of newspaper enterprise, but for the most part they were quite content with the power and prestige—even national authority—they enjoyed as rulers of influential organs of opinion.

In time, however, there did appear concentrations of power in the newspaper business and a trend toward the creation of newspaper chains, where one company or one individual owned a group of newspapers. The trend was very weak in 1900, at which time there were only eight groupings of daily newspapers. Even these held only twenty-seven papers (1.3 percent of the total number of papers) and perhaps 10 percent of circulation.[1] Of this small number of chains, some of the most prominent held only two papers. This was, in fact, the extent of ownership by Joseph Pulitzer, William Randolph Hearst, and Adolph S. Ochs. To be sure, in a few years Hearst would begin his madcap acquisition of newspapers, but this reached a fever pitch only in the 1920s. Between 1900 and 1910 Hearst was distracted by his political ambitions—he ran for Congress, the presidency, the governorship of New York—so his newspaper empire grew only by slow degrees.

Curiously, newspaper chains are a more important part of the American scene at the end of the twentieth century than they were at the beginning. We live today with such giant chains as Gannett, Knight-Ridder, Newhouse, and Times-Mirror, Rupert Murdoch—all of them products of the past half century. In 1900, ownership of newspapers by some far distant individual or by a holding company seemed unnatural and unhealthy. Even some of the wealthiest newspaper owners—men like Whitelaw Reid, James Gordon Bennett, Jr., and Joseph Pulitzer—had not the slightest desire to reach beyond their own flagship papers.

Accordingly, when chains did arise in the newspaper business they made their appearance in a most peculiar way. They did not come from the top down, with a few powerful players dealing all of the cards; rather they grew from the ground up. Nor did they come from the East as one might well have expected. The first effort toward chain control of papers came from the Midwest, and it was the work of an individual who had no desire to invade the great cities with flashy papers, but preferred instead to create modest "people's papers" in midsized cities. The individual who took this route nevertheless became one of the great American publishers. He was Edward Wyllis Scripps, who was born on a farm near Rushville, Illinois, in 1854.

Scripps was the thirteenth child of a thrice-married Englishman named James Mogg Scripps who had failed as a bookbinder in London and emigrated to the Rushville farm with little to his credit except a large and vigorous family. The elder Scripps had a number of children by two English wives, and some of these had already reached adulthood when Edward Wyllis Scripps was born to his father's third wife—an American. Three of the children of James Mogg Scripps's second wife played a significant role in American journalism: one son, James, founded the Detroit *News*; another son, George, was involved in several newspaper ventures over the years, and Ellen, eighteen years older than E. W., was something of a surrogate mother and a trusted mentor to Edward, who eventually became the most illustrious member of the Scripps family.

So it was James Scripps who brought the family into the newspaper business. James left home early and served a newspaper apprenticeship in Chicago, then moved to Detroit where he became a part owner of the Detroit *Advertiser* (later *Tribune*). When this paper's plant burned in 1873, James used $20,000 of insurance money to found his own paper, the Detroit *News*. Before this, however, he had brought Edward and Ellen into the business, and in setting up the *News* convinced his brother George to sell his farm in Illinois and put $15,000 into the venture. The *News*, a two-cent evening paper, was not an immediate success—its strongest competitor was the morning *Free Press*, which had held a strong grip on Detroit since 1831. Surely there were times when George, Edward, and Ellen must have thought that farm drudgery could have not been much worse than the newspaper business. On the other hand, James was not lacking in newspaper sense. He made of the *News* a sprightly little paper just at the time the evening newspaper trend was beginning to develop. By 1877 the paper was making a nice profit; a decade later it had a comfortable circulation of 40,000.

E. W. Scripps received his newspaper education at the hands of his brother, for whom he began working at the age of seventeen. He developed circulation routes for the *News* and served for a time as city editor. But Edward and James had temperamental differences and probably ideological differences as well. James was conservative and plodding, E. W. was bold, impulsive, and imaginative; furthermore, E. W. considered himself a friend of the growing labor movement and unalterably opposed to city political machines and the concentration of wealth. By the time he was twenty, Edward decided to go off on his own and looked for a nearby city that might need a paper. He settled on Cleveland, Ohio, where, on November 2, 1878, he issued the first copy of the Cleveland *Penny Press* (later called the Cleveland *Press*). The paper was owned, however, by James and George who had contributed $10,000 to the start-up costs.

The *Penny Press* was an afternoon paper as were most of Scripps's later papers, and it had tough competition from the city's leader, the *Plain*

Dealer. Nonetheless, the paper, a one-cent four-page sheet, was on a paying basis at the end of a year. Much of the success of the paper can be attributed to Edward's sensitivity to the needs of this industrial city. The *Penny Press* was unabashedly pro-labor, but it also presented the news in a condensed, easy-to-read form.

The young Edward, a hard-driving, hard-drinking, restless individual, lost interest in the Cleveland *Penny Press* as soon as he felt that it was traveling on the right track. He urged his brothers to start a paper in St. Louis, a venture that was only a modest success in a market overwhelmingly dominated by the *Post-Dispatch* and the *Globe-Democrat*. But the Scripps brothers also bought a partial interest in papers in Buffalo and Cincinnati, thus beginning what was the first American chain of daily newspapers. This was not, however, the origin of the great chain of Scripps newspapers known to the twentieth century. That organization had to await the 1890s, by which time Edward had become free from all financial ties to his half-brothers.

It was not only restlessness that caused E. W. to leave Cleveland; he did not see eye to eye with his brothers and wanted to be on his own. Accordingly, for a number of years the Cleveland *Press* was not in his orbit at all, and management of that paper reverted to George and James.

Doubtless urged on by his free-spirited sister Ellen, Scripps bought a controlling interest in the failing Cincinnati *Penny Paper*, whose name he changed to the *Post*. The year was 1883 and Scripps was twenty-nine years old. Here he began to develop his distinctive approach to newspaper publishing, which was, in effect, an extension and refinement of methods that he had brought to success in Cleveland. It was also an expression of the "new journalism," which this very year Joseph Pulitzer was unleashing in New York. Like Pulitzer, Scripps wanted his papers to reach the ordinary workingman, and he was keenly devoted to political and economic reform. He differed from Pulitzer in that he had no attachments to any political party. Holding to the philosophy that the newspaper was the only "schoolroom" available to working-class people, Scripps demanded that his "people's papers" should stand as an advocate for city laborers and artisans. "The first of my principles," he once proclaimed, "is that I have constituted myself the advocate of the large majority of people who are not so rich in worldly goods and native intelligence as to make them equal, man for man, in the struggle with individuals of the wealthier and more intellectual class."[2]

In spite of much local opposition, Scripps's formula of a one-cent afternoon paper devoted to the workingman caught on in this blue-collar community. The *Post*'s circulation rose rapidly; by 1891 it had a circulation of

70,000. Two years later its circulation was 105,000, making it one of the biggest papers in the Midwest.[3]

While he was in Cincinnati, Scripps began a working partnership with Milton A. McRae, a capable business manager who had come down from the Detroit *News* to help put things in order at the *Post*. Scripps and McRae worked very well together, although they were of distinctly opposite personalities. McRae was an affable outgoing individual, a joiner, always a member of service and civic organizations who could easily mend fences with the business community. Scripps, who referred to himself as "a damned old crank," was an eccentric individualist, a nonjoiner, who would only have ruffled the feathers of potential advertisers. There was an ideal division of authority, with E. W. setting news policy and picking the editorial staff, and McRae running the business side.

Within a short period of time E. W. began buying newspapers on his own, completely independent of his brothers. In fact he had not owned the Cincinnati *Post* very long before he bought the Kentucky *Post*. Then he began looking around for other papers to buy, applying to them his own philosophy of newspaper expansion. It was his policy to get a newspaper standing on its legs, after which he turned the editorship over to some trusted individual and looked around for another city in which to start up. He and McRae, his collaborator in these ventures, used a simple and consistent approach. They scouted around for a rapidly growing industrial city that had only weak newspaper competition and started a new daily there, putting up a modest amount of capital and taking into the business some young and ambitious editor who would be paid a small salary and promised stock if the business succeeded. Scripps always insisted on retaining effective control—51 percent of the stock. If the young editor made good he could conceivably become a wealthy man; if not, Scripps would take the loss. He might then scrap the business or find someone else capable of making a success of it. Since the cities for these ventures were well chosen and Scripps a good judge of newspaper talent, and since nearly all of the papers were inexpensively produced evening papers, few actually failed.

By 1889 there were enough of these healthy little "people's papers" that Scripps and McRae formed the Scripps-McRae Newspaper League. Its purpose was to share talent and information; it did not entail a financial combination. A year later Scripps felt satisfied enough with the way things were going that he decided to retire to California. He planned and built a grand ranch near San Diego, which he called Miramar, and settled down to enjoy life. He did not, however, aspire to live like a grandee or potentate in the manner of William Randolph Hearst. The high life meant little to him, although he had become a wealthy man. Scripps's idea of the good life was lollygagging around the house in old clothes. His idea of luxury was being able to smoke big black cigars and scatter the ashes on his carpet.[4] But Scripps could not bring himself to keep away from the newspaper business altogether. With McRae managing the growing number of papers in the Midwest, Scripps began buying up papers on the Pacific Coast on his own, making of these a separate chain. While he was doing this the Scripps-McRae chain was continuing to grow; there would be thirty-four of these papers by the time of Scripps's death in 1926, although not all survived.[5]

In the later years of his life Scripps often proclaimed that the achievement he was most proud of was the establishment of the United Press Association. Perhaps if it had not been for this contribution to national journalism he would be a much less well-known figure historically. After all, until the last years of Scripps's life nearly all of his papers were minor dailies in the Midwest and West. His establishment of the United Press, however, shows something of his feisty and indomitable spirit. The United Press had as its purpose the sharing of news among a group of papers—in the beginning mainly Scripps's own papers. Scripps's reason for entering this arena was once again characteristic of the man's distrust of the big boys and of monopolies. When he founded the United Press Association he was responding to the overweening power and influence of the nation's leading press association, the Associated Press. And at this moment in history when trusts, monopolies, and cartels were bearing public scrutiny, Scripps was taking his own stand against an association that had the power (even if never fully exercised) to control and harass the owner of any newspaper that was not held in favor.

Long before the twentieth century it had become apparent that the enormous volume of news—news that was not only nationwide but worldwide—required the pooling of news-gathering resources among the nation's papers. If there was, say, a major train wreck in Sandusky, Ohio, with dozens of people killed, the matter was of nationwide concern. But a newspaper editor in Portland, Oregon, had no reporters on the job in Sandusky, Ohio. The information about the wreck had to come to him over the telegraph wire—so too did many other items of news from around the country. The only way that the editor in Portland could get information about what was happening in Sandusky was through the existence of some kind of pooling agreement among newspapers. Local editors would continue to develop their own spot news (and share it if it was important), but would need to depend on an association of their peers to collect the news from around the nation and the world.

This idea of cooperative news gathering was hardly new in 1900; the need for it was obvious even before the Civil War. As early as 1848, Moses Y. Beach, then owner of the New York *Sun*, made a proposal to fellow New York City publishers that they pool their harbor news. Before this time, every paper in the city had to maintain a news boat to sail out into the harbor to meet incoming vessels from abroad. The practice was costly and inefficient since all of the reporters would return with essentially the same information. Accordingly, Beach and his fellow publishers formed the Harbor News Association to share the day's harbor news takings—one news boat could be sent out instead of six or seven.[6]

Even before the formalization of this arrangement, there had been other attempts made at the pooling of news. During the Mexican War, the Baltimore *Sun*, the New York *Herald*, and the Philadelphia *Ledger* established a pony express service to bring war news from New Orleans. It was clearly a cooperative venture, albeit only a temporary one. However, shortly after the establishment of the Harbor News Association in 1848, the major publishers in New York City sat down and worked out an even more elaborate pooling organization. This organization became the nucleus of the Associated Press, although that name was not formally adopted until the 1860s. The invention of the telegraph had a good deal to do with the practicality of this kind of arrangement. On May 13, 1848, Henry J. Raymond, then of Greeley's *Tribune*, wrote to a telegraph agent in Boston expressing the desire of six New York papers "to procure foreign news by telegraph from Boston in common," agreeing to pay a stipulated amount for news brought on incoming steamships or other news forwarded from Halifax. Part of this agreement was that the "Associated Press" would also make this news available to papers in Philadelphia and Baltimore.[7]

For a number of years the Associated Press was a small organization; even during the Civil War it consisted of nothing more than a manager, a few telegraph operators, and messenger boys to get the news out to member's offices. The association was not incorporated until the 1890s; it served simply as a "mutual association" for the benefit of its members whose principal obligation it was to pay the bills as they came in. By 1880, however, the association, housed in the Western Union Building at Broadway and Dey Streets in New York, was a fairly sizable organization, taking up six rooms, sending reports to 355 member papers, and paying $392,000 to Western Union for its services.[8]

But the paths taken by the Associated Press were anything but smooth in the early days. There was a certain amount of unrest among the managers of papers, particularly those in the West who felt they were being slighted by a monopolistic association run mainly for the benefit of a half-dozen New York papers. Accordingly a Western Press Association was founded based in Chicago. Its moving spirits were Victor F. Lawson and Melville E. Stone of the Chicago *Daily News*. The schism between these two competing associations was eventually healed, however, and, in fact, Melville Stone became general manager of the Associated Press, a position he held with distinction for many years.

There were a few other news services providing competition at the end of the nineteenth century, but these made little headway against the Associated Press behemoth. For a while there had been an agency called the United Press, but it was hardly united and pretty much a weakling. It would actually become defunct before the name itself was revived by Scripps. There was also the Laffan News Bureau closely allied to the New York *Sun*, and there was another struggling association in the East called the Publisher's Press. But nearly all of these were regularly blown out of the water by the vast Associated Press, which now had a worldwide scope through agreements with European agencies like Reuters in England, Wolff in Germany, and Havas in France.

It was at this time, with all of the minor players struggling or dying, that the curmudgeonly Edward Scripps mounted the national stage. What annoyed Scripps the most about the Associated Press was that it catered flagrantly to morning newspapers. To be sure the Associated Press had what was called a "day report," but the most important breaking news of the day was held back so that the morning papers could get the choice items. Since the papers of the Scripps-McRae league were afternoon papers, this kind of favoritism irked the egalitarian-minded Scripps in the extreme. Here was one more chance to take a swipe at the "big boys." Accordingly, in 1897, Scripps jumped into the press association picture with his own "report," called the Scripps McRae Press Association. He also founded a second organization, the Scripps News Service to serve his western papers. In 1907 Scripps bought up the Publisher's Press and merged it with his own associations, reviving the old name United Press for this new organization.[9]

The revived United Press brought a infusion of competition in the press association business. It seemed to revive E. W. Scripps personally and give him something to live for. By 1900, he was stagnating in Miramar, a seemingly doomed alcoholic. He was aged, stooped, nearly blind from drinking a huge jug of whiskey daily. He gave up alcohol (although never his fat black cigars, which he enjoyed to the end of his days) and threw himself into the new work. Despising the "mutual" or "membership" type of approach, Scripps immediately decided that his United Press would be a stock company and would offer its services to anyone who wanted it; no one was to be excluded. There were a fair number of takers almost immediately.

The United Press probably went out of its way to minister to the afternoon papers which were looking for more feature material. Its correspondents were given bylines (which the AP did not then do), and there was a wealth of leisurely feature material and emphasis on distinct fields such as sports, politics, and gossip from the nation's capital, much of it called "undated cable" or "time copy." Later the UP would take the lead in graphic news-feature stories and in news photography.

A year after its founding the United Press got a forceful leader in the person of twenty-five-year-old Roy W. Howard, who would subsequently go on to prominence as partner in Scripps's newspaper chain and one of the most prominent newspapermen of the twentieth century. Howard's meteoric rise to power was no doubt due in large measure to his own intrinsic abilities. But his early discovery also illustrates Scripps's rich gift for identifying newspaper talent. Scripps was fond of saying that one of his pleasures in life was to visit the offices of his papers and look around for bright eager youths who might one day rise to the top and take a management role. Newspapers, he believed, could only be kept going if they maintained a fresh infusion of talent. It was a philosophy quite at odds with that of William Randolph Hearst, who never wanted anyone else jostling around at the top. Roy Howard was discovered by Scripps during a visit to the offices of his Cincinnati *Post*. There were other bright faces in the city room no doubt, but Scripps immediately picked out Howard as one who would go to the top:

He was a striking individual, very small in stature, a large head and speaking countenance, and eyes that appeared to be windows for a rather unusual intellect. His manner was forceful and the reverse of modest. Gall was written all over his face. It was in every tone and every word he voiced. There was ambition, self-respect, and forcefulness oozing out of every pore in his body.[10]

Roy W. Howard would go on to be the true heir of E. W. Scripps. The Scripps chain eventually became the Scripps-Howard chain (this after the death of Milton McRae). It would be Howard rather than Scripps who would invade the field of large eastern newspapers. But Howard won his spurs on the United Press while still in his twenties. As general manager of the association he hurried around the country establishing UP bureaus; he also set up bureaus in every major European capital and forged alliances with foreign newspapers and news agencies not having connections with the Associated Press. By 1914 over 200 papers were subscribers to the UP's full daily service; another 300 subscribed to an abbreviated service.[11] It was brisk competition for the AP indeed.

The first decade of the twentieth century saw the appearance of yet another major press association, the Hearst-controlled International News Service. Under the leadership of Richard A. Farrelly in its early years, the INS was never as comprehensive in its coverage as the AP and the UP, but it had a very feisty spirit and a gift for assigning top-flight writers to cover major news events. Together with the King Features Syndicate which distributed boilerplate features—puzzles, comics, columns—the Hearst associations gave a far greater prominence to the simple-minded Hearst newspapers than they would have enjoyed in their own right.

Clearly, by the time of World War II, there was strong competition among American news associations. At the same time, among newspapers themselves, there seemed to be a growing faith that no single large chain would ever dominate newspaper publishing. The kind of conglomeration that worked so well for steel or tobacco would not work in the newspaper field. E. W. Scripps would come to own a large number of papers, but during his own lifetime nearly all of them were located in the Midwest and far West. These papers had only a small influence on the national scene. William Randolph Hearst did aspire to own a chain of papers in many of the major metropolitan areas, but his chain had been slow to get off the ground between 1900 and 1920 when Hearst was devoting most of his energies to his political career. In the 1920s he gobbled up newspapers at a furious pace, but most Hearst papers were of the second rank, devoted to sensationalism, and if Hearst's own political failures are any indication, never highly influential nationwide.

One thing always worked against the development of really powerful newspaper chains in America. No matter who tried to tame newspapers, no matter who desired to fit them into a stereotyped mold, a newspaper by its very nature had to keep a strong local and individual identity; whatever its faults, E. W. Scripps had always been adamant about this. You could not just string together newspapers like grocery stores or five and dime stores, all of them carbon copies of one another. During the years that Scripps was expanding his loose and informal chain, much more highly structured and centralized chains were being established in the retail field—Sears, A&P, Woolworth, Kresge, and numerous others. Unified and stereotyped management of such chains made good sense. But it made little sense at all in the newspaper business, and Scripps knew it.

To be sure the years that witnessed the triumph of the huge corporation did not pass without some attempts at buying up and organizing newspapers as if they were merely "properties," businesses to be run for a profit—for the benefit of the "bottom line," as they say today. Aside from Hearst and Scripps, the most prominent buyer of newspapers in the first two decades of the twentieth century was a man named Frank A. Munsey, who had made a small fortune as a magazine publisher and then greatly increased his wealth through real estate and stock speculation. Munsey acquired a good number of eastern newspapers, some of them prominent and with long histories. He tried to tame them, to operate them with modern efficiency, but with not one of them did he work any great magic. With none did he repeat his considerable success in the magazine field. He merged papers, or killed them outright. For this he probably made himself the most hated man ever to enter the newspaper field—at least from the perspective of the workingmen of the press. Most importantly, he was living proof that such roguish aggrandizement in the newspaper business just was not worth the effort.

Even if he had not thrown reporters and editors out into the street, Munsey would never have made of himself a beloved figure in newspaper offices. Still, the economic message he delivered was perhaps greater than his cultural legacy, which was probably nil. This was because Munsey was not wholly mistaken about what was wrong with the newspaper field in the early years of the twentieth century. There were far too many newspapers. Most big cities had a dozen or more English-language dailies—too many to be efficient and profitable. Most of them were struggling gamely along with their own individual charm and distinction, but they were chasing a readership that just was not there. Munsey put his finger on this problem, and acted on it, although no one ever loved him for his perspicacity.

Munsey was the perfect embodiment of the Horatio Alger, rags-to-riches myth which laced the American dream in the years of his youth. He was born in 1854 near Mercer, Maine, the son of a penniless farmer-carpenter. With little in the way of education he got a job as a telegrapher with Western Union, and, at the age of twenty-three, became the manager of the office in Augusta. In 1882 he arrived in New York with $40 and the dream of becoming a magazine publisher. The dream would be a long time in realizing itself. Munsey's first venture in the field was called *Golden Argosy*, a children's magazine. It struggled desperately without making any money for five years, building up an enormous pile of debt. Often with no money to pay his authors, Munsey wrote a lot of the articles himself, and he was not a good writer.

Striking out in a different direction, Munsey next began an adult magazine which he gave his own name, *Munsey's*, but this, too, was an instant failure. By the panic of 1893 he was saddled with $100,000 in debt and facing ruin. Munsey did not really care very much what was in his magazines, but through trial and error he had learned a great deal about the magazine business. He reasoned, and correctly as things turned out, that if you lowered the price of a general magazine to reach the multitudes you could run up your circulation and pull in advertisers. He dropped the price of his magazine to a dime in October 1893 and sold 40,000 copies; by 1895 *Munsey's* was selling 500,000 copies a month.[12]

By 1900 Munsey was sure enough of his own abilities as a publisher that he turned his attentions to the newspaper field. In 1901 he bought two newspapers, the New York *Daily News* and the Washington *Times*. Neither were important papers. The following year, however, for $600,000 he bought the Boston *Journal*, one of the leading papers of New England. He had admired its gold-domed building when he first visited Boston as a ragged lad. The *Journal*, a solid, respectable paper going back to Whig days, was clearly in need of an overhaul: it was stodgy in character and continued to run advertisements on the first page, a practice that most metropolitan newspapers had given up decades earlier. Accordingly Munsey began a makeover of the paper, and at first this met the approval of his staff and the leading citizens of Boston. He cut down the unmanageable size of the paper and provided more pictures and colorful headlines. He spent freely on new presses and other equipment.

These efforts at modernization were probably sorely needed. But the circulation figures did not improve to Munsey's satisfaction. The *Journal*, as sacred as the Bible at many New England hearthsides, was not the same paper that it had been, and many habitual readers drifted away. Munsey continued to tamper with the formula of the paper in the hopes of finding the route to success. (Probably to a certain degree he was influenced by the recent sensationalistic triumphs of the Boston *Post*, run by an old Pulitzer protégé, Edwin A. Grozier.) But Munsey was seldom on the scene: he ordered his changes from New York over the telephone from a grand suite of offices in the Flatiron Building. He usually made these changes without consulting his key editors and mainly on the basis of his own fly-blown notions of what would work. Over a period of several years he killed the evening edition of the paper, then revived it, later killed it again. He tried various formulas with the Sunday paper and then killed that also. In 1913 he sold the whole business at a loss and left Boston for good. Munsey never saw his ill-considered tamperings as the reason for his failure in Boston. He insisted to Hearst's chief lieutenant Arthur Brisbane that "there isn't enough advertising in Boston to grease a fly's ear."[13]

Even before giving up on the *Journal*, Munsey was harboring hopes of establishing a chain of newspapers in large eastern cities. He bought the Baltimore *Evening News* and the Philadelphia *Evening Times*. The former he sold in 1914, the latter he killed. In New York Munsey went on a virtual binge of newspaper buying. Among the papers he bought were the *Press*, the *Globe* (successor to the *Commercial Advertiser*, the oldest American daily), the *Evening Mail*, and the *Evening Telegram*. His most important acquisition in the years before 1920 was the *Sun*, which continued to be edited by the peerless Edward P. Mitchell, although it had suffered a slump in later years. To strengthen the *Sun*, Munsey merged the *Press* into it.

Before he died in 1925 *all* of Munsey's New York papers were merged or liquidated. The greatest newspaper in his stable was the New York *Herald*, of which Munsey was inordinately proud. He bought this paper (and its Paris edition) from the estate of James Gordon Bennett Jr., who was one of Munsey's idols. Even this paper was later merged, but not by Munsey, and its future success, a great chapter in the history of American journalism, was one that Munsey himself would not write, and could not have written.

From a business standpoint Munsey's newspaper career was not completely unsuccessful. Munsey often proclaimed that New York had 60 percent more newspapers than it needed, and he was probably right. On the other hand, his successes in cutting down the field cannot disguise the fact that seldom did Munsey's Yankee thrift result in the rise of better newspapers. His merged papers were, for the most part, weaker than the ones they replaced. Too, one has to remember that killing a newspaper is in some sense killing a spirit. A newspaper is a cultural icon—and many of the papers Munsey killed or merged had been good papers—dead they could only be mourned by a readership for which they held some special appeal. Nor could one forget the hundreds of reporters, pressmen, and others thrown out on the street all in the name of efficiency.

Munsey's greatest defect as a publisher is that he was not a newspaperman himself and could comprehend neither the independence nor creativity of the men who worked for him. He did recognize talent, but usually only after it had been pointed out by others. William Randolph Hearst could be despotic in his dealings with his underlings, but he had a sociable side and more frequently tended to be indulgent with the rank and file. Munsey tended to be authoritarian in his relations with his employees, although his despotism was kept in check by the diversity and far-flung nature of his enterprises.

Frank Munsey's name was mud among the newspaper fraternity throughout his life. There was no escaping the fact that he was only a man who had money to buy and dispose of newspapers. When Munsey died there were some weak tributes paid to him in a few papers around the country, although in city rooms everywhere you could doubtless have heard cries of jubilation. Out in Emporia, Kansas, William Allen White probably best expressed the views of newspaperdom in his bitter tribute:

Frank Munsey the great publisher is dead. Frank Munsey contributed to the journalism of his day the talent of a meat packer, the morals of a moneychanger, and the manner of an undertaker. He and his kind have about succeeded in transforming a once noble profession into an 8 percent security. . . . May he rest in trust![14]

Maybe a bit heavy-handed, maybe a bit unfair, nonetheless, White was expressing the aversion that newsmen have to the capitalistic freebooter who comes in from the outside and thinks he knows how to run a paper, and who essays to do so through arbitrary fiats, thunderings, and remote telephone calls. The American newspaperman could always accept autocratic rule from the top, even the eccentric domination of a Greeley, a Bennett, or a Scripps; but they had to know that those in charge had once held a paste pot in their hands, or set a line of type somewhere, or interviewed a fire captain. They would not accept the man with the balance sheet, and history has shown that no one has ever been a successful newspaper publisher only by tinkering with the accounts.

This is the reason, no doubt, why combinations, amalgamations, and chains of newspapers have only been successful when the organization has been loose and somewhat anarchic. In spite of Hearst's spasmodic desire to enforce editorial policies on his papers, his attempts were never uniformly successful and usually had the air of *opera buffa* about them. And it is still impossible to escape the conclusion that the best and healthiest newspapers in America have been single, independent papers with their own stubborn and individual charm, ever on guard against tampering from those on the outside.

12

Fantasy and Reality: The Newspaper Reporter

At the dawn of the twentieth century it was doubtful if press lords or newspaper moguls held any fascination for the popular imagination. Publishers or owners could no longer hope for the kind of personal identification with a paper that was once enjoyed by Horace Greeley or James Gordon Bennett. One-man control or ownership had not died, of course, but even in the case of a magisterial figure like Pulitzer, it was no longer possible to think of a newspaper as being an emanation of a single man's soul. In the 1840s the *Tribune was* Greeley and the *Herald was* Bennett. People would pick up the *Tribune* and proclaim, "let's see what Uncle Horace has to say today." But that era was gone forever.

The newspaper was now the product of its diversified and often far-flung minions—its reporters and correspondents, its telegraph editors, its copydesk men and rewrite men, its sob sisters and sports columnists, its editorialists and pundits, its feature writers and fashion reporters, its artists and photographers, its advertising space sellers, its pressmen and linotype operators. It was the working newspaperman or woman, not the publisher, who brought the newspaper to life day in and day out. However much of an autocratic spirit might have filtered down from the top, the newspaper was now the product of a large cadre of hard-toiling professionals without whose effort no large daily paper could have come into existence.

The indispensable figure in the modern newspaper was the newspaper reporter or writer, the man or woman who chased the ambulance, who sat through a whole murder trial, crystallizing it into story form, who took down the mayor's actual words at city hall, who rushed to the scene of a flood or a fire, who rode out on a revenue cutter to interview a diva or famous author arriving from Europe. The bigger newspapers became—8 pages, 16 pages, 32 pages, 64 pages—the more of these stalwarts there would need to be. They would drift in from the small towns, the farms, the suburbs; they might have recently passed through the gates at Castle Garden or Ellis Island. They were inventing a vocation that had something peculiarly American about it, something exhilarating and liberating—satisfying enough in any case to make many beginners overlook the fact that the pay was usually low, the hours long, and the work frenetic and backbreaking.

At the end of the nineteenth century the newspaper reporter was emerging as a professional, or perhaps a quasi-professional. It had become obvious to newspaper editors and publishers that it was impossible to get out a newspaper without trained individuals, without people who knew their business. More often than not reporters were trained on the job had served an apprenticeship on a country paper or did time as a "copy boy," or "cub," before being allowed to spread their wings. But training was now essential. Still, the apprenticeship for newspaper work was loose, amorphous, and anarchic, the reporter himself tending to be an airy and wayward individual. Too, in the gaslight era, in the days of O. Henry, the footloose quality of the reporter's work gave the profession a colorful or even heroic patina. Every newspaper reporter was suspected of being (at the least) a hard drinking man with a flask of gin on his hip. At his worst he might be a felon on the loose; at his best a flashy rake or a failed novelist. A great many Americans probably accepted the judgment of President Charles W. Eliot of Harvard who believed reporters to be "drunkards, deadbeats, and bummers."[1]

A few decades later, in the era of the flivver and the speakeasy, the image of the newspaper reporter had not changed much; if anything it had become crystallized, probably with the aid of Hollywood screenwriters, not a few of whom had acquired familiarity with the trade on the hoof. Stanley Walker, a well-known city editor of the 1920s who was more than a little knowledgeable about the animal, offered a splendid summary of this movie stereotype:

Thanks to the motion pictures, a few plays, and the antics of a handful of the gentlemen of the press in real life, the popular conception of the news-gatherer seems, if anything, a shade more scrofulous than before. Today the reporter is supposed to smash all furniture in sight when invited to a home. He prefers to climb the chandelier before beginning an interview with the Chairman of United States Steel. He gets his greatest scoops while sleeping off a drunk in some boozy haven in the red light district. He writes best on twelve Scotch highballs. He insults everybody in earshot and is rewarded handsomely for his bad manners. He is happiest and most heroic when he has been thrown down a flight of stairs. He has one wife whom he rarely sees and always mistreats an ex-wife in Peoria who has never been able to collect alimony, and a honey in Brooklyn Heights who regards him as a misunderstood Zola. Quite a lad.[2]

However overdrawn and melodramatic this account, there can be no doubt that the newspaper reporter was an exciting and colorful figure in American folklore. There was always a touch of wild romanticism about the life of the working newspaperman—or woman. This was a calling, a vocation, never just a job or even a profession. The reporter was drawn to the newspaper the way a fly is drawn to honey, even though, more often than not, there was not really much honey. If you wanted to feed a family of four you probably needed to "move up" to something better—publicity, public relations perhaps, maybe the proverbial great American novel that it was thought all reporters were writing.

Much of the attractiveness of reporting—particularly general-duty reporting—was that it allowed the adventurous youth to drink deep of all the adventure, the comedy, the tragedy, the foolishness of the human race. One did not need to be a knight in shining armor to partake of this growing public world of surprise, mischance, and valor. At five dollars a pair one could be a knight in shiny pants. Where else could a boy from the country, often with only a passable education, rub shoulders with the faker, the morgue manager, the crooked politician, the abandoned damsel, the stuffed shirt, the society matron, and the unfrocked priest hauled up on charges of carnal abuse? You could not enjoy this world if you took up a job slaving away in a cubicle in some office building, stamping documents in and out. No, the newspaper reporter had a gleeful finger in every pie and loved every minute of it.

The short duration of the apprenticeship for becoming a newspaper reporter in the early years was one of the nicest things about being in the trade. Almost everyone in the newspaper business simply wormed their way in by hook or by crook. All that seemed to be required of the novice was a keen desire and basic literacy; almost everything else could be learned on the job from the ground up. It is good to keep in mind that what was wanted in those days—and perhaps in our day too—was the generalist, the avid observer of human folly in all of its diversity. Few reporters were hired because they had specialized knowledge of finance or science or cloakroom politics. If you got assigned to cover such matters you would learn something about them after you got on the job, and you would learn quickly.

In 1900, and for many years thereafter, few newspaper reporters had college educations. Even on the big metropolitan daily the city editor was not at all opposed to interviewing a bright-eyed youth just out of high school, especially if he looked fresh, curious, energetic, and willing to work. There was no need to think about "advancement," or climbing the corporate ladder; the newcomer was thrown in and either succeeded or failed.

Henry L. Mencken, who went on to become one of the most famous journalists of the twentieth century, got his indoctrination in the typical manner when he walked into the city room of the old Baltimore *Morning Herald* on a Monday evening in 1899. His father had died the previous Friday and Mencken abruptly decided to take up newspaper work. This greenhorn eighteen-year old was a recent graduate of the Baltimore Polytechnic Institute and had been at the top of his class. His father, a well-to-do cigar manufacturer, could easily have sent him to a first-rate college or university, or he could have been accepted without hesitation into the family business. But Mencken had no interest in business, and all his life he had no desire to surround himself with pedagogues; he hoped to find a kind of higher education that was infinitely more agreeable and romantic. Thus his visit to the offices of the *Morning Herald*.

There was probably a little more behind Mencken's boyish choice of a career. He was a bookish lad who loved to read and write and did both prodigiously. Too, at the age of seven, his father gave him as a gift a self-inking printer and font of type. He did his best to put out his own newspaper, but, more importantly he recalled in later years: "I got the smell of printer's ink up my nose at the tender age of seven, and it has been swirling through my sinuses ever since"[3]

When Mencken walked into the city room of the *Herald* he was able to get the attention of the city editor, Max Ways, who seemed to be in a particularly good mood after a pleasant and undisturbed dinner. Ways could not promise anything, and uttered the editor's usual defense that "nothing is available right now," but perhaps he saw some glimmer of hope in this callow applicant. He questioned the lad about his education, his interests, his writing, all with a kind of wry smile. He urged Mencken to keep his day job at the family cigar factory, but he also suggested that it would be all right to stop by every evening around 7 o'clock, on the remote possibility that something might turn up.

Mencken showed up the next night without fail, and the next, and the next. Usually Ways would wave him aside, sometimes abruptly, sometimes wistfully. But nothing seemed to have developed. After more than a month of sitting in a corner of the city room with diminishing expectations, one snowy evening Max Ways beckoned to him. "Go out to Govanstown, and see if anything is happening there." Govanstown is now part of Baltimore, but was then a remote suburb at the end of a trolley line. "We are supposed to have a Govanstown correspondent, but he hasn't been heard from for six days."

Not much was in fact happening out in Govanstown. The volunteer fire-men were playing pinochle in the firehouse and had nothing to report. When Mencken returned to the *Herald* office around 11 o'clock, he told Ways that there were only two stories. Because of the snow the Improved Order of Red Men had postponed their oyster supper until March 6. Max thought it was better to forget that one. But there had apparently been a horse theft, and Mencken was told to write it up. He was shown a vacant desk in the far cor-ner of the room, and he sat down to write the story. It was a trivial little item, but for the moment it seemed to be the most important thing in the world. Mencken ran it through the typewriter several times to get it just right. The next morning shivers ran up and down his spine as he picked up a copy of the *Herald*. There was his story, exactly as he had written it.

A horse, a buggy and several sets of harness, valued in all at about $250, were stolen last night from the stable of Howard Quinlan, near Kingsville. The county police are at work on the case, but so far no trace of either thieves or booty has been found.[4]

It is hard to imagine anything more vacuous—except perhaps the item about the Improved Order of Red Men and their oyster supper. But seeing this story in print the next day provided Mencken with the rush of all rushes. "There ran such thrills through my system as a barrel of brandy and 100,000 volts of electricity could not have matched."[5]

This rush did not entirely wear off in the weeks ahead. Mencken, as a newcomer, indeed as a "temporary," was assigned stories that would try the patience and endurance of all but the most determined neophyte: meetings of the Women's Christian Temperance Union, installations of ministers, in-terviews with YMCA secretaries or "bores" just back from Europe, organ recitals, chalk talks, funerals, minor political rallies. These assignments were tedious enough to shake loose all but the most tenacious cub reporter. But Mencken, whose brilliant literary style spoke as loudly as his youthful energy, became a "regular" on the *Herald* after serving as an unpaid volun-teer for only about a month. On a day when some boozy old timer dropped off the roster, Max Ways pointed to a shabby desk that Mencken could share with another reporter, promised to round up a typewriter from somewhere, and said those all important words or a reasonable facsimile, "You're hired." The salary was to be $7 a week to start with the promise of an early raise for good performance. Mencken also received a book of passes for trolley cars and some expense vouchers. The moment of truth had arrived. Henry L. Mencken was a newspaper reporter.

But $7 a week? That was probably just barely a living wage in 1900. A lad still living with his parents could probably swing it. To be sure, the *Herald* was itself a struggling sheet, not a leading paper like the *Sun*. Perhaps the *Sun* would be able to pay a beginning reporter $10 a week in 1900. In New York a young police reporter might expect to receive $15 a week. A seasoned general assignment reporter might fetch $25 a week on the *World* or the *Tribune*.[6] But three or four decades later, in the golden age of press journalism during the 1920s, many reporters on a New York paper could still not expect to receive more than $15 or $20 a week; seasoned veterans might pull down $35 a week,[7] although there was always vague talk about "star" reporters lured away by Hearst at the incredible sum of $100 a week. Usually this was nothing but that—talk.

Continuing low wages probably account for some of the fluidity, the discontents, the vagaries of the reporting life. Things may be somewhat better today, but certainly not markedly. The profession continues to appeal to the young, but with only a few jobs at the top there has always been a tendency for good men to drop out and look for something better elsewhere—in public relations or advertising, or lobbying, or political speechwriting. The general assignment reporter always just got by and started a family only at his own peril. Low wages and irregular hours probably accounted for the wayward quality of the reporter, perhaps the tendency to wind up in a neighborhood tavern at the end of the day, and the tendency to shift hobolike from paper to paper, hoping that something better might turn up. Those who truly loved the work might still be covering the courthouse at the age of sixty; the vast majority, however, would have burned out, gone over the edge, or found something better in another field.

Preparation for employment as a newspaper reporter was vague, informal, and mysterious. Literacy was required as was a good pair of legs, probably at least a modicum of ability to rub shoulders with the multitudes. For the most part, at least in the early days, a reporter was not required to be prepared with specialized expertise. He was a generalist and his skills were acquired on the job. Many believed that there was no other way of learning the business than by apprenticeship, a system known since time immemorial. In the twentieth century this would change, albeit slowly; schools and colleges of journalism would make their appearance, although they were not immediately welcomed; old timers continued to believe that the only possible training for a youngster could be obtained in the office—sink or swim. Show him where his desk was, the men's room, the morgue (i.e., library), give him fleeting instructions about how to organize a story, get the facts, verify them, keep within the space limitations, be concise—and hope for the best.

In time, though, there would be pressures from editors and publishers to find a way to produce a better-educated more professionally trained newspaperman. It came to be admitted, slowly and almost always grudgingly, that the apprenticeship system was costly and inefficient, and that some formal method of training journalists might add stature to the profession, and perhaps do something to counter the notion that the reporter was a wastrel or deadbeat waiting his turn to fall in the gutter. By the 1880s there was considerable talk about making journalism a "profession," and publishers like Whitelaw Reid, himself a college graduate, expressed a preference for hiring men with college degrees, although even for a wealthy paper this was a practical impossibility at the time.

Talk about schools and colleges of journalism had been heard for a long time, although the concept seemed comical or grotesque to the vast majority of working newspapermen. Apparently the first suggestion along these lines came from Gen. Robert E. Lee in 1869. The former Confederate general was then president of Washington College (later Washington and Lee), and he suggested a plan whereby boys intending to enter journalism could earn their way through college—the typical classical curriculum—by working at the printing trade.[8] (Perhaps Lee had enjoyed a better press during the war than some of his contemporaries, since his attitude was completely at variance with that of William Tecumseh Sherman, who viewed journalists as little better than spies—or lice.) Unfortunately Lee's idea was never fully implemented, and no courses in journalism appeared at the time.

Most people in the newspaper business, hearing of General Lee's ideas, were skeptical if not downright scornful. The usual response was that of Frederic Hudson of the New York *Herald*, who expressed the dominant view of the time that "the only place where one can learn to be a journalist is in a great newspaper office."[9] Even E. L. Godkin of the New York *Evening Post*, well disposed toward education, found the idea of courses in journalism to be an absurdity. Still, the idea gradually took root. The first actual courses in journalism to be offered in an American university were two offered in the period 1878–1885 at the University of Missouri.[10] The first organized curriculum in journalism seems to have been offered at the University of Pennsylvania around 1893. It was headed by Joseph French Johnson, a former financial writer for the Chicago *Tribune*. The University of Illinois began offering a four-year program in journalism in 1904, and the first separate school of journalism appeared at the University of Missouri in 1908, with a newspaperman named Walter Williams as its dean.[11]

There was, quite naturally, a good deal of ambivalence and irresolution on this matter. In the early 1890s, flush with the success of his *World*, Joseph Pulitzer contacted President Seth Low of Columbia University with an offer of funds to start some kind of school of journalism. But the trustees of Columbia were reluctant to accept money for such a purpose, so the offer was politely refused. At this time the classical curriculum still held sway in higher education, although it was giving ground slightly in land-grant universities. The prevailing view was that such workaday matters—mere job training—must not be allowed to defile the liberal arts.

As a matter of fact, even though he was willing to put up money for a school of journalism, Pulitzer himself was skeptical about the value of a college education for working journalists. His charitable offer was partially motivated by a suspicion of the colleges which he believed to be populated by playboys and sons of the idle rich, and also, no doubt, by the uselessness of the classical curriculum. He was deeply suspicious that lazy college students would get the idea that a college degree carried a promise of professional achievement. On the other hand, Pulitzer was solidly behind education and wanted to upgrade the quality of working journalists. He once pithily explained his personal philosophy in the matter, and it was probably not too different from that of other editors and publishers at the time. "The best college is the college of the world . . . the university of actual experience." As to a college education his belief was that "a college education is valuable, but it is not indispensable."[12]

In 1904 Pulitzer made another overture to Columbia University, which by this time had moved its campus to Morningside Heights and was rapidly expanding under its new go-getter president Nicholas Murray Butler. After some further foot-dragging, Columbia was induced to accept a Pulitzer gift of $2 million to establish a school of journalism, the money being provided in Pulitzer's will and made available on his death in 1911 (along with another $250,000 for the world-famous Pulitzer prizes). The Pulitzer School of Journalism began its activities in the fall of 1912. Pulitzer's gift opened the floodgates to other beneficences of a similar character. William J. Murphy, publisher of the Minneapolis *Tribune*, established an endowment for a school of journalism at the University of Minnesota in 1918; the family of Joseph Medill established the Medill School of Journalism at Northwestern University in 1921.

It is probably true that until well into the twentieth century the majority of newspaper reporters were not college graduates, even in the face of a rapidly developing trend to establish journalism schools, especially in public and land-grant universities. It is probably also true that there was a stubborn and continued resistance on the part of hard-boiled city editors who had come up from the city streets or from some ink-spattered rural apprenticeship to make fun of journalism schools. E. W. Scripps, who never attended college, probably held the most typical attitude among rustic publishers when he remarked that if you wanted to become a blacksmith you should spend time in the smith's shop. If you wanted to be a newspaperman you should enter a newspaper office. A college, Scripps thought, was fine if you wanted to be a professor.

This was a persistent and tenacious attitude. It brings to mind a well-known cartoon showing a smirking city editor asking a young job hopeful, "And what, may I ask, is a school of journalism?" The same question was still being asked in a 1958 Paramount movie, *Teacher's Pet*, with Clark Gable and Doris Day. Gable, the hard-bitten city editor without college training, propounds his knock-about-the-world theory of education in opposition to the book-learning theories espoused by journalism professor Doris Day. Both views are given full vent before the story dissolves into the expectedly romantic blending and harmony of the two views.

It could also be added that even if there had been no impetus to establishing schools and colleges of journalism in the twentieth century, education for journalism would have been expanded in any case. By the turn of the twentieth century many high schools were offering courses in journalism and providing outlets for students to learn the business by establishing school newspapers. However gentle and undemanding the apprenticeship of the school paper might have been, it doubtless had the effect of exposing many a youngster to the newspaper virus. A classic example might well be Ernest Hemingway, who wrote for his school paper, the *Trapeze*, at Oak Park (Illinois) High School and then, instead of going on to college, took a job as a cub reporter for the Kansas City *Star*. In those same years of the early twentieth century there were many other educational avenues that funneled the young into newspaper work. A great many high schools offered courses in printing (mostly only for boys) as part of their programs in manual training, and perhaps thousands of individuals were propelled into newspaper work after getting ink on their hands in school print shops or setting type from a California job case.

Even if the newspaper reporter's education was spotty in the early days of the twentieth century and college courses in journalism were few in number, the profession was developing other supports and underpinnings. The appearance in many large cities of "press clubs" tended to give a lift to the professional aspirations of lowly reporters. They were certainly more uplifting than bars or other watering holes. The first such club was the New York Press Club, founded in 1873. Among the most famous was the Gridiron Club organized by the Washington press corps in 1885. Professional journals also began to appear. The best of the early ones was the New York *Journalist*, founded in 1884 and edited for many years by Allan Forman. (It was later merged into *Editor and Publisher*.)

One type of journalist's organization that did not take root for many years was the craft union. The newspaper reporter continued to be vastly underpaid until well after World War II, and probably still is in relation to printers and typesetters. The reporter or editor had as his only solace the knowledge that he was a "white-collar" worker, a creative writer, a freestanding individualist, perhaps even a poet, while the better-paid pressman was only a factotum. But the dark depression years of the 1930s saw a strong impetus to provide some kind of union support for newsmen and-women, as well as improvement in such matters as sick pay, minimum wages, overtime pay, severance pay, annual holidays, and improved working conditions. The Newspaper Guild, established in 1933, rapidly signed up some 8,000 members, and a scant few improvements were noted as a result of the guild's activities; on the other hand after a year's existence the guild had signed only a single contract. By 1938 some seventy-five contracts with newspapers had been signed, but this was still regarded as an insignificant number.[13]

It is probably tempting to think of the slow start of unionization among working reporters as being due to stiff resistance from publishers and their organizations, especially during hard economic times when jobs were being eliminated right and left. But there was also a certain amount of resistance from the reporters themselves. Many continued to think that their white-collar profession was above and beyond the workaday world. In spite of low wages it was sometimes possible to accept a life of shabby gentility as the price one had to pay for being a "professional" and a freestanding individual.

In short, one of the reasons why the union movement took so long in reaching the reporter is that reporters refused to think of themselves as laborers. They may not have been management either, but it was hard to forget that in a very important sense they *were* the newspaper. Too, socially speaking, the newspaper writer or reporter cut across class lines: in America this was a profession that attracted farm boys, blue bloods, intellectuals, the hangers-on of cafe society or the demimonde. Newspapermen, or women, may have been hirelings, but they never *felt* like hirelings even when oppressed.

One of the distinct advantages of the journalistic profession, certainly at the end of the nineteenth century, was that it knew few class boundaries and was magically adapted to the fluidity of American life. Almost anyone with common sense, a modicum of literary talent, and the requisite physical and psychic energies could use newspaper work as a means of self-discovery and accomplishment, goals foreclosed in so many workplaces. Consider the case of Theodore Dreiser, a lanky, ungainly, half-educated Indiana boy with gauche manners who went on to become one of the great American novelists. At sixteen he left Warsaw, Indiana for Chicago where he failed at almost everything he tried from dishwasher, to freight-car checker, to installment collector. A sympathetic former high school teacher staked him to a year at Indiana University, but Dreiser, a hopelessly uncontrolled romantic spent the year falling in love and got little out of college. He had, of course, been a reader all of his life, and back in Chicago, failing again, he became attracted to the "Sharps and Flats" column of Eugene Field, which gave him the feeling that maybe, just maybe, he could write. He began putting down the impressions he had had as a penniless wanderer of Chicago streets.[14]

Having not the slightest idea of how to break into newspaper work, he answered an ad for part-time work with the Chicago *Herald*, a job that turned out to be nothing more than handing out toys to needy children at Christmastime. Still later he was able to finagle a job with one of the city's weakest papers, the *Globe*, where a kindly city editor broke him in by slow degrees. In the next few years Dreiser wandered the country as a kind of tramp newspaperman, working in St. Louis, Toledo, Cleveland, Pittsburgh, and finally in New York. At one time he thought of buying into a small-town Ohio weekly, the *Wood County Herald*, but when he saw the shabby office, the primitive printing press, and the broken-up type, he left after one day. In Pittsburgh, with a fair amount of free time on his hands, Dreiser began reading Balzac, which probably gave him some intimation of his real life work. Sitting in the darkening gloom of the Allegheny Carnegie Library in this city of smoke and greed he also began reading Spencer and other social philosophers whose ideas he could only turn into intellectual sludge. On the other hand, his year abroad had given him the materials out of which he would eventually craft his very realistic portraits of American life.

Dreiser was not a success as a newspaper reporter. In fact he failed miserably in New York where he did space work on Pulitzer's *World*, then got fired. He determined that he would never again have anything to do with the newspaper business. He tried his hand at freelance magazine writing with more success during the magazine boom of the 1890s. But in another sense, the years as a tramp newspaperman had been the making of Dreiser. It gave him his entry into the world of letters, the only entry he could have afforded, but, more importantly perhaps, the only entry that could have delivered to him the raw and inchoate world of capitalism and industry that was to be his subject matter as a novelist.

Dreiser was not alone among those budding writers who found in the daily newspaper a key, an opening, into the welter of American life. The only way to understand the cruelly changing America of these days was simply to report on it, to tell the story of those who lived through it. Accordingly, a great many writers of this time got their start in newspaper work, among them Frank Norris, Jack London, Stephen Crane, Ambrose Bierce, George Ade, Richard Harding Davis, Frank Stockton, Edgar Lee Masters, Carl Sandburg, Willa Cather, Lafacadio Hearn, Bret Harte, O. Henry, Eugene O'Neill—yes, even O'Neill, who spent time as a reporter on the New London *Telegraph*. These names can be added to those of others who had already climbed Parnassus—William Dean Howells and Mark Twain, for example—and had served their time on newspapers in more tranquil years.

In a very real sense newspaper work was both a school and a proving ground for many of these writers. It was both a place where they could sharpen their skills and begin the process of communication with a larger public. It is also important to remember that throughout most of the nineteenth century schooling was offered only in a rudimentary form, which caused many people to see journalism as one of the few legitimate forms of providing knowledge and shaping public opinion. Both Joseph Pulitzer and E. W. Scripps were of the opinion that the newspaper was the only form of education within the reach of all; newspapers were the people's school. It is no wonder then that newspapers also served to open the careers of many writers who would be at the center of the reform movement in America after 1890. Both Pulitzer and Scripps put reform activities at the center of their thinking, and so did Hearst in his own opportunistic and self-serving way. For the New York *World* of the 1880s and Hearst's *Journal* of the next decade, reform was served up as a form of popular entertainment and as a way of selling papers, but, in addition, most of those who went on to be the leading muckrakers—expanding their reputations as writers of magazine articles or full-length books—had gotten their start on newspapers. Among these were Lincoln Steffens, Jacob Riis, Ida Tarbell, Ray Stannard Baker, David Graham Phillips, George Kibbe Turner, Charles Edward Russell, and Will Irwin.

In the early twentieth century, with metropolitan newspapers augmenting their feature and opinion sections, with the establishment of book reviews and other departments dealing with the arts and ideas, the newspaper also proved to be a major staging point for serious intellectual writers. Alan Nevins, James Truslow Adams, Samuel Hopkins Adams, and Mark Sullivan moved into history through newspaper work. Writers and critics of the arts like James Gibbon Huneker, Christopher Morley, Henry Seidel Canby, Carl Van Doren, and Edmund Wilson got their starts on newspapers and always preferred to think of themselves as journalists as well as men of letters. Major political thinkers and critics of American life—Walter Lippmann and H. L. Mencken for example—were associated with newspapers for their entire careers.

Whatever truth there may have been behind the running stereotype of the newspaper reporter as the hard-drinking, foul-talking, free-living, cocked-hat vulgarian, there is also a great deal to suggest that the profession was keenly attractive to first-rate individuals for the better part of a century. In a nation where traditional folkways, where class, where older forms of propriety meant little and where millions of newcomers to the country's shores were changing and remaking the country year by year, sometimes it seemed week by week, the newspaper was the only reliable guide to the kaleidoscopic experience that constituted this new democratic experience.

For years the typical newspaper reporter was better positioned than anyone else to watch the passing parade and make sense of it. If he (and shortly, she) did not always have the luxury of reflection enjoyed by the scholar or intellectual, he could be less easily fooled about what was really going on. Living life on the edge of daily events, the newspaper writer was, and probably still is, accepted as one of the few people in society capable of ripping the cover off all manufactured essences, all political and professional scams, all fake proprieties. He may only rarely have partaken of the bounty of the American dream, and gentility may often have eluded him, but it is possible to accept him as what Emerson might have called a representative American man. He was a hero of no mean proportions since he was one of the few who could speak to all of us in a society that is infinitely segmented and only loosely coherent. Since his appearance on the American scene, the newspaper reporter has been one of the few individuals we have trusted to give us some insight into the frantic and mysterious life we Americans live day by day.

13

When the Women Marched In

Reporters. Writers. Newspaper*men*. In any superficial account of the history of American journalism one might get the idea that women journalists did not exist until the later and more enlightened years of the twentieth century, but nothing could be further from the truth. Although women were not represented in great numbers in the journalism of the nineteenth century, they were far better represented than they were almost everywhere else in the workforce. To be sure, women were slow to appear in offices of any kind. Women were shunned in the learned professions. Even secretaries were male until long after the invention of the typewriter. On the other hand, women were irresistibly drawn to newspaper work from early times. Those who entered the field believed that they belonged there, and, for the most part, their male colleagues came to believe it too. What is more important, they made a more powerful impact on all print media than any mere numbers might suggest.

There are probably several reasons why women found the door slightly ajar in the newspaper field. One of the most important is that women had been found in printing and newspaper offices since colonial times. The acute shortage of labor in the sparsely settled American colonies often required that printers train their wives or daughters in typesetting and printing; not a few women also acted as editors or proofreaders. In England, although women could own businesses, the print shop was never considered a place for genteel ladies, so no tradition of women printers developed, even though a few could be found here and there.

In America, women as owners of printing establishments or newspapers were not rarities, although their ownership typically came about when their husbands died or became incapacitated. When John Peter Zenger was arrested for seditious libel, in colonial New York, his wife, Anna Catherine Zenger, put out the New York *Weekly Journal* during his confinement. She also ran the paper for a few years after his death in 1746. Mrs. Zenger was preceded as a female newspaper publisher by Elizabeth Timothy, who published the South Carolina *Gazette* for seven years following the death of her husband in 1738. Anne Franklin, the widow of James Franklin, took over Rhode Island's first newspaper—the Newport *Mercury*—in the 1760s and ran it expertly along with her two daughters. Mrs. Franklin was skilled enough at her work that she was appointed printer for the colony; she and her daughters, with family servants, pressed into service, printed an edition of colonial laws filling 340 pages. And there was a scattering of other women printers of distinction in colonial times. While most were widows of established printers, they often proved to be businesswomen of considerable skill.[1]

In addition to this tradition of women as printers and publishers—a tradition that continued even after the Revolutionary War—there were certain characteristics of the American woman herself that explained her journalistic aspirations. As most early European observers noted, there was a spirit of adventure and tenacious independence in the American woman; as maiden, wife, or mother she seldom allowed herself to be closed out of anything, always insisting on being at the center of social activities. Whatever there was of the "men only" way of life quickly eroded on the American soil. Alexis de Tocqueville, author of *Democracy in America*, still probably the best book ever written about the United States by a foreigner, observed in the 1830s that nowhere in America do women of any age display childish timidity or ignorance. Nowhere in the world, said de Tocqueville, "are young women surrendered so early or so completely to their own guidance." In America, with customs fleeting, public opinion unsettled, paternal authority invariably weak, and maternal authority always contested, repression of women was a hopeless task. As to the American woman:

She has scarcely ceased to be a child when she already thinks for herself, speaks with freedom, and acts on her own impulse. The great scene of the world is constantly open to her view; far from seeking to conceal it from her, it is everyday disclosed more completely and she is taught to survey it with a firm and calm gaze. Thus the vices and dangers are early revealed to her; as she sees them clearly, she views them without illusion and braves them without fear, for she is full of reliance on her own strength, and her confidence seems to be shared by all around her.[2]

This was hardly a minority view; a great number of European observers at the time were saying much the same thing. American women were curious, robust of imagination, lacking in the hesitation and girlish diffidence of their European contemporaries. Above all they were fearless about going out in the world. When the Camden and Amboy Railroad put its first train on the tracks in 1831, several women hopped on board the cars, whereas many men, fearing that "John Bull" the locomotive, giving off smoke and sparks, would blow up, hid discretely in the bushes nearby. And later, when hot air balloons made ascents at public fairgrounds, many women were moved by an overpowering urge to go up. When automobiles appeared women were immediately drawn to these flimsy and dangerous machines and insisted on being taken out in them. So too with the airplane; women not only begged rides, they demanded the right to fly the early kitelike planes themselves. Many of them had pilot's licenses—some as teenagers—even before women got the right to vote. And by all accounts the early women pilots were every bit as fearless, and competent, as the men.

So the American woman, always game, always hardy, always anxious to push to the center of some activity, would never be kept away from newspaper work that provided access to the political and social scene and carried with it the promise (if not always the reality) of personal independence. As a practical matter, of course, there was no large influx of women into journalism in the first half of the nineteenth century. Yes, they continued to function occasionally as they had in colonial times, as printers in small newspaper offices, helping a husband or son perhaps, even taking over when necessary. But when big city dailies began to attain large circulations in the 1830s, very few women were involved as reporters and editors. Some justification was given for this at the time. The major metropolitan dailies were nearly all morning papers before the Civil War, and evening work was considered unseemly for women. Too, the frenetic bursts of activity needed to put out daily papers and the knockabout life of the reporter seemed to preclude female employment, although undoubtedly there were more than a few women who might have been willing to give it a try anyway.

Accordingly, when women did break in during these years it was invariably under exceptional circumstances. One such exceptional circumstance was merely an extension of the tendency for women to take over publishing businesses owned by their families. Thus, for example, the first woman to be an editor of an important daily paper in America was Miss Cornelia Walter who edited the Boston *Transcript* from 1842 to 1847. Once again, though, she had taken over from her brother, the paper's founder, Lynde M. Walter.

There were a few other exceptional circumstances where the door was left slightly ajar for women in these years. In a few instances women were allowed to serve on major city papers as editorial writers, a position that would naturally remove them from knockabout reporting, and, in some circumstances, might even allow them to work at home. For example, Ann S. Stephens was both an editorial writer and a literary critic for the New York *Evening Express*, positions she filled with considerable dignity for forty years starting in 1837. Jane Grey Swisshelm edited the Pittsburgh *Saturday Visitor* for five years, and before that she won the distinction as the first woman accepted as a member of the Washington press corps.

No doubt the most important woman journalist in the first half of the nineteenth century was Margaret Fuller, hired by Horace Greeley in 1844 to write for the New York *Tribune*. Fuller wrote three articles a week on literary and social topics. These articles appeared not only in the daily *Tribune*, but also in the nationally distributed weekly edition of the paper, which gave Fuller a great deal of national exposure. Greeley did not hire Fuller to discourse on "women's" topics or to oversee a woman's page. He hired her because he respected her as a thinker, because of her associations with the New England poets and intellectuals he admired, and because she had already been an editor of the transcendentalist magazine *The Dial*.

After a few years working in New York and even living in the Greeley household—certainly a trying experience in the extreme—Fuller decided to travel to Europe where she became, in essence, the first woman foreign correspondent. She eventually became involved in the revolutionary movement in Italy, married an impoverished Italian nobleman by whom she had a son, but was forced to flee the country when the revolution failed. She was returning to the United States in 1850 when her boat was shipwrecked off Fire Island, New York. She, her husband, and her infant son were all lost. But her few years on the *Tribune* nonetheless represent a kind of pinnacle for women journalists in that era.

Women like Margaret Fuller and Ann Stephens were safely ensconced in the mainstream, but they were surely atypical. On the other hand they were not by any means the only women who made an impact on American journalism during those years. Beyond the genteel boundaries set for them in nineteenth-century life there was a hardy band of women, usually eccentrics, who kept the flame alive even if it meant bringing scorn on their own heads. If one pauses to wonder what happened to the free-wheeling, irrepressible, self-determined women that de Tocqueville found so prominent in American life, they were there, and they made themselves heard, though history has not always paid them their due.

A perfect example of the type was Anne Royall who published her own paper in Washington D.C. for twenty-three years beginning in 1831. Royall was a widow in her fifties when she began life as a journalist. She got into the business because her husband died and left all his money to his children. Royall went to Washington to see if she could request a pension for her husband's Revolutionary War service. She stayed on to be the capital's first visible woman journalist. In a time when reporters never dreamt of approaching the president of the United States for an interview, Royall went down to the banks of the Potomac River where President John Quincy Adams was wont to fling off his clothes and bathe in the nude. Royall sat on his clothes and refused to allow Adams to emerge with presidential dignity until he had answered her questions.

Needless to say, Royall did not make a big hit in Washington. Windows and doors were invariably closed to her. One of the victims of her barbed pen whacked her on the head; another threw her down a flight of stairs. At one point she was arrested as "a common scold and termagant," for which she could have been sentenced to the ducking stool. Because of her age and penury, she was let off with a $10 fine.[3] While Royall was never welcomed in the halls of power, she earned a certain amount of grudging respect. Even poor President Adams, who found her a pest, could not help liking her. He called her "a virago errant in enchanted armor."

Unable to find steady employment with any paper, Royall began her own weekly, *Paul Pry* (its name was later changed to *The Huntress*). This paper was never a great financial success, and the publisher had to keep it going by writing travel books that *were* highly successful and very well written. Still, as a newspaper publisher, she was bold and aggressive. Within a year she had agents all over the country handling her paper. She attacked political corruption, backed sound money, liberal immigration and tariff laws, and better conditions for wage earners. She called for the abolition of flogging in the navy. She also continued to campaign for her widow's pension but never got it. She died in 1854 and was buried in the Congressional Cemetery, although there was no money to mark her grave.

Anne Royall hardly belonged to the mainstream. But it was virtually impossible for women to storm the bastions of the big city press during the first half of the nineteenth century. Accordingly, the role of mischief maker or virago seemed to offer one of the few outlets for women of forceful or eccentric personality. Another individual somewhat in the mold of Anne Royall was Victoria Woodhull, who in the 1870s put out a five-cent paper in New York called *Woodhull and Claflin's Weekly*, a raucous sheet which gleefully exploited the kind of news for which the penny papers had long been chastised.

Unlike Royall, Victoria Woodhull was not a writer. Apparently she was only half literate and was said never to have read a book in her life. Her paper, which started in 1868, was mostly written by two men fascinated and probably awestruck by this irrepressible vixen. Born in Ohio as Victoria Claflin she was married briefly to Canning Woodhull, but she then started off on her own as a fortune-teller and stump spellbinder. Later she stormed New York with her sister Tennessee Claflin and received the backing of Wall Street financiers to put out their paper. *Woodhull and Claflin's Weekly*, devoted to topics such as free love, prostitution, social disease, medical malpractice, all subjects that were deemed "improper," "indecent," and "unwomanly" at the time. Woodhull was a woman of inescapable charisma and charm—eerie, raffish, a glowing figure in flounces. Her sister Tennessee was apparently a woman of considerable beauty. Such was the notoriety of the *Weekly* that Victoria Woodhull attempted to run for the presidency in 1872 against Grant and Horace Greeley. She won no electoral votes, but nonetheless considered her campaign for women's suffrage a notable success. How much Victoria's campaign for the ballot and free love was real and how much of it was mere playful mischief is a matter of conjecture. A woman typesetter from another paper sought a job on the *Weekly* but found all of the typesetters and clerks to be male. Victoria Woodhull brushed the applicant aside with the remark: "We won't have our paper spoiled by women."[4]

Woodhull and Claflin's Weekly lasted only eight years—until 1876. By this time the two sisters were doubtless tired of their paper, which, it is said, they seldom if ever read. They moved on to England where they took London society by storm. Men of the English gentry flocked around these two raffish American females. Victoria married a wealthy banker and the beautiful Tennie eventually married a baronet and became Lady Cook. Victoria Woodhull died in 1927 at the age of eighty-nine, "full of years and honors."[5]

It might be easier to see Victoria and Tennessee as stars of the theater—the theater of life perhaps—than as stars of the journalistic firmament. Their actual contribution to the history of American journalism was slight. But even as they were publishing their scrofulous sheet in the 1860s and 1870s, the door was being opened to women in mainstream journalism. It did not fling violently open to be sure, but opened enough for a few capable professional women to squeeze in. The most characteristic route of entry was through part-time space work, or freelance writing of a kind that could

often be carried out at home: travel pieces, literary criticism, essays on society and manners. With the rapid growth of newspapers and expansion in all
departments after the Civil War, a great many newspapers were willing to
accept occasional pieces from women writers. All around the country
women with writing aspirations were sending furtive messages to newspaper editors asking for assignments or even showing up at the office during
off hours.

With that trend established, it was only a matter of time before bolder
women came looking for jobs as reporters. They got them, too, although not
in large numbers at first. By the late 1860s a few women had managed to
talk their way onto newspapers in New York, Boston, Chicago, Philadelphia, and Baltimore. One such was eighteen-year-old Sally Joy of Vermont,
who wrestled a job on the Boston *Post* in the late 1860s, insisting that she
wanted "to be treated like a man." For the most part she was. If there was any
strong resistance on the part of the males in the city room it took the form of
overly solicitous behavior. After a matter of weeks the men in the office
were lining the floor with papers to keep her white satin gown from picking
up dust. Too, on days when Miss Joy had to attend functions after seven
o'clock in the evening, the youngest male reporter in the office was assigned
to go along as an escort, a humiliating experience that probably brought the
lad some good-natured ribbing from his pals.

Matrimony eventually claimed Sally Joy as it did so many other women
of her time and class. But like many women of the press bitten by the bug
she did not give up her career after marriage. She later became "Penelope
Penfeather" of the Boston *Herald*, writing on fashions, the home, and other
"women's" topics. She became the first president of the New England
Woman's Press Association and helped to found the General Federation of
Women's Clubs.[6]

Not all women were as gently introduced to the profession as Sally Joy.
The vast majority of editors believed that the city room was no place for
women, and that the gentle sex ought to be kept out of general duty reporting. It was common to attempt to shake women loose by giving them assignments that were either disagreeable or completely trivial. As late as 1920
the editor of a midwestern newspaper sent a young woman reporter, fresh
from work on a college paper, to a hanging, hoping that this revolting experience would bring her career to a swift end. It did not, and within a year the
young lady was made Sunday editor. This was a sidetrack, but one which
gave at least grudging admission to her talent as well as her grit.[7]

By 1920, however, women workers had become commonplace in
America's newspaper offices. Already by the 1880s and 1890s they were no

longer kept on the fringes of the profession or seen as obstreperous outsiders in the manner of Anne Royall and Victoria Woodhull. Although initially few in number, the "girl reporter" was beginning to make her presence known in city rooms, often breaking in much the way Sally Joy had done at the Boston *Post*. For a long time women's presence was unsettling and they seldom achieved bylines. But in 1890 a spectacular round-the-world trip brought one female reporter to the attention of the general public and people all over the world. After this the "girl reporter" was a permanent fixture in the public mind—an image that could no longer be denied.

This young lady was twenty-two-year-old Elizabeth Cochrane, who attempted to encircle the globe in less time than the fictitious character Phileas Fogg in Jules Verne's novel *Around the World in Eighty Days*. Cochrane, who had adopted the pen name "Nellie Bly," from the Stephen Foster song of that name—one of the most popular songs of the nineteenth century—had appeared two years before out of thin air but now suddenly became the best-known reporter in America, if not the world.

Elizabeth Cochrane was as far as you could get from a termagant, a *femme fatale*, or a mischief-maker. She was a mild-mannered, seemingly timid girl, barely 5'3", neither beautiful nor dramatically appealing. If her hair had not recently been put up she would have resembled nothing other than a polite schoolgirl. Yet behind her gray eyes, and hidden by her self-effacing manner, there was a bold, even fearless personality. She was the kind of person willing to try anything. And she did.

Elizabeth Cochrane, or Nellie Bly, arrived in New York in the summer of 1887 when she was only twenty; she stormed the offices of Joseph Pulitzer's *World*. At first clerks and subeditors headed her off so she never got in to see Pulitzer or his major domo, John A. Cockerill. Before this she had already had several years of solid newspaper work under her belt and might have been hired if she had been a man. Cochrane was born in Cochrane Mills, Pennsylvania, on May 5, 1867; her father was a judge and one of the town's founders. She had received an excellent bookish education in her father's private library. For a while she also attended a boarding school in Indiana, but had to return home at the age of thirteen because she was considered to be too frail of health to be away from home. When her father died a few years later, leaving a heavily encumbered estate, she made her way to Pittsburgh where she quickly conceived the idea that she was going to become a newspaper writer. She read a piece in the Pittsburgh *Dispatch* entitled "What Are Girls Good For," and sent in a spirited response to it. The response was not published, but she was asked to write another piece on the same subject for the Sunday paper. In time this led to her being taken on the staff of the *Dispatch* at $5 a week.[8]

Originally Cochrane was supposed to write only on society, theater, and the arts—the usual pattern—but industrial Pittsburgh brought out her inquisitional faculties and she tramped through factories and workshops writing exposés of the abuses she found there. Since she developed an emotional style of high indignation it was only natural that her aspirations would eventually be directed to the New York *World*, where Joseph Pulitzer had made his paper famous for its crusades, exposés, and stunts. She wrote several letters to Pulitzer telling him about her experiences and offering to go up in a hot air balloon he was sponsoring in St. Louis. But she received no response. While in New York she lost her purse containing $100, nearly all the money she had in the world, and desperate, she pushed her way through the human guard dogs at 31 Park Row, and by some miracle that has never been explained, found herself standing before John Cockerill. She did not enter empty handed however. She had with her a list of "stunts" or investigations she felt that she was admirably fit to carry out. While Cochrane was no beauty, Cockerill obviously found something attractive and charismatic about her; he took her to see Pulitzer who was also impressed. In part Pulitzer may have been moved by her story of losing $100, for he gave her $25 to tide her over until it was decided what to do with her.

In a few days they decided to give Cochrane a chance. She was put on the payroll and allowed to follow up one of her own ideas. She wanted to check herself into the city's insane asylum on Blackwell's Island and see what she could find out about patient care there. The idea had strong appeal to Pulitzer since there had already been a lot of complaints about the place. To prepare herself Elizabeth read ghost stories, practiced making eerie laughs at her image in the mirror and read whatever she could about mad behavior. Donning old clothes she dropped by a woman's shelter and tried out her act, which caused her to be delivered to the lunatic wards on Blackwell's Island. Four physicians declared her to be insane. When she started acting normal the doctors were even more certain that she was a lunatic. After she got out she wrote a series of articles on her experiences, telling how patients were abused and beaten, describing the hospital as a "human rat trap, easy to get into, impossible to get out of."[9]

The exposé of Blackwell's Island caused a great stir in New York and brought about a grand jury investigation and even some rudimentary reforms. More importantly, the stunt convinced Pulitzer to offer Cochrane a full-time job and let her follow her own ideas for future stories. She was, without a doubt, a consummate actress, but, just as important for the *World*, she was a keen observer and a reporter with deadly accuracy and attention to detail. In the weeks and months that followed, Cochrane worked at a glove counter in a shop; visited the city dispensaries to see how illnesses of the poor were handled; and worked in a kitchen of an old ladies' home. She got herself arrested to see how women were treated in the city's jail—and the indignities she uncovered there had the effect of making the city employ matrons for the handling of women prisoners. She was probably the first woman journalist to uncover what today would probably be called sexual harassment. She got a job in a box factory which was said to have an overactive bunch of "mashers." She opened a campaign to run out of Central Park the many men who stalked young girls—villains with waxed whiskers who lured innocent maidens into their handsome carriages for destinations unknown.

So many and so newsworthy were these exploits that Elizabeth Cochrane became the best-known woman journalist in New York. For a while it was said that New Yorkers regularly scrutinized the face of every old woman or beggar or prostitute, thinking that it might be that "Bly" girl in one of her many disguises. But Joseph Pulitzer was delighted by it all and determined that this was the kind of success that could not be argued with.

Naturally none of these probes or stunts had the effect of making Nellie Bly a household name. The round-the-world trip in late 1889 and early 1890 was something altogether different. When it was over the name Nellie Bly would be known throughout the civilized world. The trip was begun as a typical stunt, with Pulitzer envisaging only a modest circulation gain from it. Working from a carefully prepared itinerary, Nellie Bly sailed from New York on the steamship *Augusta Victoria* on November 14, 1889, wearing a durable cloth suit and a Scotch check ulster and gillie cap. Pictures of this outfit eventually became famous throughout the world. (If Nellie had worn a dear stalker cap she would have been a perfect model for a female Sherlock Holmes.) She carried two satchels, containing, among other things, a tooth brush, a bank book, a pair of easy fitting shoes, and several changes of flannel underwear.

In spite of the need for speed, the trip as scheduled offered time for some short diversions. One was a visit to the author Jules Verne who wished the exuberant girl well but expressed his doubt that the trip could be made in less than eighty days. All along the route provisions were made for Nellie to send special dispatches to the *World* in New York. All were received and all were printed, giving rise to mounting tension. She lost five days in Colombo waiting for a ship to show up. She encountered a monsoon between Singapore and Hong Kong. By the time she reached Yokohama, Japan, her name was known to nearly everyone in the English-speaking world through the miracle of telegraphy. Japanese crowds gathered around this American youngster as if she were a creature from outer space.

Every dispatch, every cable, brought big headlines in New York: "Nellie Bly on the Fly," "Nellie Bly's Mad Rush," etc. The *World* offered a trip to Europe to the person who most closely estimated her arrival time in New York. Of course there was fast train service across the United States, which there had not been when Verne wrote his book in 1873, so Nellie Bly arrived in New York on January 29, 1890, having traveled 24,899 miles in 72 days, 6 hours, and 11 minutes. Cannons were shot off in the Battery and Brooklyn. Bands and crowds greeted the heroine as she stepped off the ferryboat from Jersey City. There were piles of telegrams from well wishers all around the world. Among the most pleasing, no doubt, was one from a gallant Jules Verne: "I never doubted the success of Nellie Bly. She has proved her intrepidity and courage."[10]

Stunts by their very nature do not linger long in the public memory, and Nellie Bly's trip around the world would hardly deserve more than a footnote in history today, except that from the female perspective this trip had a great deal to do with opening the doors to women in the journalistic professions. Not that women streamed into newspaper offices or that the old barriers to women immediately came down. Still, Nellie Bly's celebrated voyage brought the idea of the "girl reporter" to the surface of consciousness. Editors could still balk at the idea of hiring women for general duty assignments, but it was no longer possible to say that women could not be reporters. Clearly there *were* women reporters, and they were around to stay.

As for Elizabeth Cochrane herself, the later course of her career was about typical for her day and age. In 1895 she retired into matrimony, marrying a wealthy Brooklyn manufacturer more than twice her age. She moved into high society for a time, but after her husband's death she passed through some rough times. In 1920 Arthur Brisbane of the *Journal* got her to cover an execution at Sing Sing, and she wrote one of her best stories about this event. She died in 1922 at the age of fifty-five almost forgotten by the world, but by this time hordes of women were working on metropolitan papers. Some of these women recalled Nellie Bly when her obituaries were published. Most seemed to remember that she was an enormous woman, of heroic proportions, at least six feet tall, when in fact, she was only 5'3".

From a strictly feminist perspective, it might be possible to say that the stunts of Nellie Bly and a few others like her in the 1880s and 1890s did not advance the cause of women in journalism in any fruitful way. It is true that women became much more numerous in journalism and made their presence felt in every department of the newspaper business—except, it is said, in the area of political cartooning, where they never took hold at all. But their actual numbers continued to be small. Furthermore, even when women were welcomed in metropolitan city rooms, they often complained, and justifiably, that they were seldom assigned to front-page stories. The one exception to this, and perhaps it was an important exception, was the kind of story in which the female viewpoint could be used to sell papers through sensationalism.

It is not surprising that Nellie Bly worked for Pulitzer's *World*. And it is also not surprising that very early on William Randolph Hearst became a hearty believer in the usefulness of "girl reporters." Even before he moved to New York he had in his employ the tremendously talented and energetic Winifred Black who wrote under the name Annie Laurie—borrowed from yet another song title. A Wisconsin-born redhead, Black (her maiden name was Winifred Sweet) learned the art of emotive writing. What is perhaps more important is that she rapidly learned to write in clear, forceful English, abandoning all traces of Victorian propriety still found in newspaper writing in the 1890s. She developed her own brand of personal, vivid writing, short sentences and paragraphs with hard jolts. Her appeal was extravagantly emotional.

Annie Laurie's specialty was spreading the alarm about social ills, and she adopted some of the stunt techniques of Nellie Bly. She had herself admitted to the charity wards of the city hospital and exposed the scandalous treatment of women patients; she went to a leper colony; she interviewed the madam of a brothel; rendering all of these experiences in lurid and sentimental prose. However, Black was also an aggressive and resourceful reporter—probably the equal of any that Hearst had on the staff—so she was also assigned to big breaking news stories. If there was a spectacular murder, or a famous trial, or a major disaster, she was invariably one of the first reporters on the scene. She had a fearlessness and a skill in organization that allowed her to push her way in when women would ordinarily be banned. For example she was the only woman to reach the scene of the great Galveston tidal wave in 1900.

The most characteristic quality of Winifred Black was a refusal to give up on any story however difficult or forbidden. She was in Denver at the time of the famous San Francisco earthquake in 1904 and broke into tears because she would not be the first on the scene. When she stopped by the offices of the Denver *Post* there was a telegram waiting from Hearst. It contained but one word, "Go!"—She went.

Some years earlier, when President Benjamin Harrison visited California only one press representative was allowed to board his private train.
Black was not chosen. Nonetheless, she managed to secret herself aboard
the train and hide under a table in the dining car. She got her interview.[11]

Winifred Black was perhaps the first of the women reporters who came
to be called in newspaper lingo "sob sisters," this because of her emotion-
ally laced style. The pejorative was not entirely justified in the case of Black
since during her years as a newspaperwoman she served as drama critic, society editor, city editor, and managing editor as well as crusading reporter.
Nonetheless, beginning in the 1890s, there appeared a number of clones of
"Annie Laurie," who made names for themselves—usually in the "yellow
press"—as specialists in the heart-wrenching news story, which they rendered in shrieking abandon. One was Dorothy Dix who began her career on
the New Orleans *Picayune*; she later worked for Hearst's *Journal* in New
York. Another was Ada Patterson who got her first job because she had seen
a man hanged when the male reporter who was supposed to cover the story
got drunk. She wrote the story for the St. Louis *Republican*.

Newspaper editors and publishers had become aware that sensational trials needed the feminine touch; accordingly every gruesome murder trial or
legal ordeal of the rich and famous warranted coverage by the best "sob sisters" in the land. On the occasion of the murder trial of Harry K. Thaw in
1907, the nation's foremost sob sisters were all seated at tables in the center
of the room. Present were Winifred Black, Ada Patterson, Dorothy Dix, and
Nixola Greeley-Smith, a granddaughter of Horace Greeley—not precisely
a sob sister herself, but one of the best women journalists of the day. All
were there to give a sympathetic "feminine" account of the trial's alluring
young heroine, Evelyn Nesbit. One of the most striking adolescent femmes
fatales in the American record, Evelyn Nesbit had visited world-famous ar-
chitect Stanford White in his studio where she regularly comported herself
nude in a red velvet swing. She later married a mentally unstable millionaire
named Harry K. Thaw who shot White, her earlier lover, on the roof garden
of Madison Square Garden, probably in a fit of confused jealousy. No better
trial for female reporters could be imagined. They had before them one of
the great female protagonists in trial history.

But it must not be thought that sob sistering was the main use to which
women were put on metropolitan newspapers in those years. If so, the opportunities for women in newspaper work would have been very limited indeed. The truth is, beginning in the 1880s, the women who started drifting
into newspaper offices in fairly large numbers attended to chores that were
far more prosaic and habitual than those performed by the likes of Winifred

Black and Nixola Greeley-Smith. The rapid proliferation of evening papers and the expansion of Sunday papers brought about a perceived need for more "women's interest" material. Women readers were important newspaper subscribers, and new features of every kind had to be found for them. Newspapers were beginning to run material that they had never run previously—on society, child rearing, home decoration, and a wide variety of other "feminine" topics. These things became the instant preserve of women staff members, and, for the most part, have remained so to this day. Some male reporters and editorial writers may have considered such material trivial or second rate, but in no sense was it secondary in terms of readership and circulation. What was needed was not merely a female slant but female substance, and clearly female journalists could best supply it.

Even before newspapers began augmenting their feature sections in the 1880s and 1890s there was already a strong tradition of female journalism in the magazine field. There was a veritable explosion of new women's magazines at the end of the nineteenth century, and long before that there was one of the most profitable ventures in American publishing—*Godey's Lady's Book*—founded in 1830 by Louis A. Godey, and edited for forty years by the indomitable Sarah Josepha Hale. Hale, also the author of a number of books as well as the classic children's poem "Mary Had a Little Lamb," virtually invented the woman's magazine. *Godey's Lady's Book* published articles on art, flowers, gardening, homemaking, female education, and, of course, fashion. The magazine was so prosperous that as early as 1859 it was running colored plates in its fashion section. Its prosperity also allowed it to publish work by most of the major authors of the day. Emerson, Hawthorne, Longfellow, Harriet Beecher Stowe, Oliver Wendell Holmes, all wrote for *Godey's Lady's Book* at one time or another. The magazine was among the most successful publishing ventures in the nineteenth century—probably the best-known magazine in America before the Civil War. Louis Godey estimated the budget of his magazine at $100,000 by 1851. By 1860 the circulation was an unbelievable 150,000 and Godey himself was a millionaire.[12]

The sterling success of *Lady's Book* also gave rise to a large number of popular women writers in America, a good number of them encouraged directly by Sarah Hale and Louis Godey. These writers, "women scribblers" as Nathaniel Hawthorne ungallantly called them, wrote novels, poems, and books of every description. For example, Lydia H. Sigourney, who for a brief time was associate editor of the magazine, was probably the most prolific woman author in American history. She wrote over 2,000 poems and stories that were published in over 300 periodicals. She also published forty-six volumes of poetry, essays, travel, fiction, history, and the like. In her spare time she wrote cookbooks.

By the 1880s and 1890s when newspapers were just beginning to take the woman reader seriously, women journalists had already made a tremendous impact in the magazine field. Frequently they rose to positions at the top. There were numerous other editors beside Hale, such as Ann S. Stephens, editor of *Peterson's Magazine*. A few women even owned major magazines. Miriam Folline Leslie edited a magazine started by her husband Frank Leslie called *Frank Leslie's Lady's Journal*, an offshoot of his enormously popular *Frank Leslie's Illustrated Newspaper*. When her husband died in 1880 she had her own name legally changed to Frank Leslie (not Mrs. Frank Leslie), and published the magazines herself with great success.

Nearly all of the women's features that began appearing in newspapers in the 1880s and 1890s had been previously pioneered in women's magazines. But there was one feature—enormously popular—that was left for the newspaper to discover: the advice column. As might be expected, it was the commercially minded *Journal* of Hearst that took the first step in this direction. In 1898, Hearst's managing editor, Arthur Brisbane, called into his office two young ladies who had been assigned to the household page. He showed them a letter that he had just received from a reader saying that her husband was being subtly lured away by a woman he regularly met for lunch. Brisbane wondered if this and other letters like them might be put to some kind of use, even though they were not suitable for the "letters to the editor" section. One of the girls, Marie Manning, thought that a column of such letters might be a popular item. She agreed to undertake it. The only fear was that maybe not enough readers' letters would be received to fill up the column on a regular basis.

The column, known as "Advice to the Lovelorn," was begun on July 20, 1898. Marie Manning had no experience with this kind of material, but she had been in newspaper business since she was twenty—a space writer for Pulitzer's *World* and then for the *Journal*. She took the pen name Beatrice Fairfax, because she was reading Dante at the time and owned a place in Fairfax County, Virginia. For a few days—and only a few days—she had no questions to answer. For the first few columns she had to write her own questions and answer them herself. Shortly, however, the letters came pouring in, and Manning required an assistant and a secretary to handle the load. Within a few months, office boys had to go across Park Row to the post office to tote enormous sacks of mail for "Beatrice Fairfax"—sometimes 1,500 letters a day. The most oft-asked question was "What can I do to be popular?" Another very common question, characteristic perhaps of the last days of Queen Victoria, was "Is it ladylike to permit a man to hold and kiss my hand, when I'm engaged to someone else?" Beatrice Fairfax always said no.[13]

"Advice to the Lovelorn," ran for many years and was later taken over by other women using the Fairfax pen name. In time it was distributed to several hundred papers through Hearst's King Syndicate. Of course it was not possible to monopolize this gold mine, and within three years Hearst was running another, competing, and equally popular "lovelorn" column. The writer was Dorothy Dix, already a prominent sob sister in the Hearst organization. Dorothy Dix was the pen name of Elizabeth Meriweather Gilmer, a southern girl who had actually attempted something like a lovelorn column even before Marie Manning. She had, in fact, written advice to women on her first newspaper job at the New Orleans *Picayune*.

Elizabeth Gilmer was a sheltered southern girl, self-educated in her uncle's extensive library. She spent a few years in a finishing school and then went into newspaper work. When Gilmer began her column in New Orleans it was strictly an advice column, with no letters from readers, but later, in 1901, after she went to work for Hearst, her column, called "Dorothy Dix Talks," included letters three days a week and homilies or sermonettes the other days. Dorothy Dix became one of the great advice givers in American history. Her column (later anchored in the New York *Post*) provided brisk competition to "Advice to the Lovelorn." There were, accordingly, two competing columns of this type (just as there were later in the century with "Dear Abby" and "Ask Ann Landers"). Both columns were still being written in the 1930s. Gilmer continued to write her own material and also penned a number of books, including *How to Win and Hold a Husband*, published in 1939. She lived until 1951.

During the early years, both Fairfax's and Dix's columns concentrated their efforts on matters of the heart, and the readership was almost exclusively female. After World War I they sought to bring in wider issues of human relations and some 25 percent of query letters came from men.

In the view of some, advice to the lovelorn, or articles about children and cooking, had the effect of relegating ladies of the press to small arenas. Must women be nothing but sob sisters, advice givers, dispensers of household hints? Suffragettes would be quick to point out that if this was the extent of the female contribution, women would be consigned to the second rank of journalism for all time. (Of course it is hardly fair to say that women like Nellie Bly, Annie Laurie, Dorothy Dix, and others were trivial figures; they were exceptionally good reporters and top writers as well.) In any case, by the 1920s, the procrustean bed into which women had long been forced would be cast aside. There were by this time mainstream women reporters, columnists, editors, critics, who could not only hold their own with men, but often surpassed them. It is true that they were still often spared the most disagreeable police assignments, and many could justifiably complain that they did not get access to the front page, but few male reporters would try to argue that they could not handle the big story.

By the 1920s doors had flung open to women almost everywhere. The New York *Times* had long been resistent to women on its staff for obvious reasons. In the Ochs/Van Anda era stunts were an anathema, and there were no pages of household hints and lovelorn columns. So there was no easy way for women to maneuver their way in. There had been a few women in the society departments and holding secretarial positions, but none in hard news. Shortly before World War I, however, a girl fresh from Kansas, Jane Grant, showed up at the *Times* and was introduced to Carr Van Anda. All he could offer her was a job as a stenographer in the society department. Being both bright and aggressive she laid siege to Ralph Graves, the city editor, and convinced him to let her cover "hotel news." During World War I she took leave of her job and went to France with the YMCA and sang for the soldiers. When she came back she found herself getting better assignments. (Grant eventually married a GI she had met during the war—Harold Ross, an editor of *Stars and Stripes*. Later, in 1925, she helped Ross found the *New Yorker* magazine.)

There were a few other women on the *Times* even before the war. One was Mary Taft. After the war Rachel McDowell left the *Herald* (now a Munsey property) and began writing religious news for the *Times*. Nancy Hale, formerly of *Vanity Fair*, became a general duty reporter. Winifred Mallon joined the staff of the Washington bureau. The most celebrated woman writer of the *Times* in those years was the much-honored Anne O'Hare McCormick who joined the paper in 1921 and later became a major foreign correspondent. She won a Pulitzer Prize in 1937 and wrote for the *Times* until her death in 1954.[14]

If the *Times* was slow to open up to women, by the 1920s women were nonetheless a major force in newspaper reporting and no list of "star reporters" of the time could be composed without including a good number of women. If women were denied the very best assignments, they were no longer relegated to softer duties. Nellie Revell, who for thirty years was a writer on papers in Chicago, Denver, San Francisco, and New York, covered prizefights, murder trials, everything else that would come to a general duty reporter, and she was able to boast that she had never written a single line for a "woman's page" or a line of society news.

Equally sure that there was no such thing as "woman's viewpoint" was Genevieve Forbes Herrick of the Chicago *Tribune*, who, like a number of women, had to start out in sheltered jobs at the back of the city room, but then burst forth in full glory. She covered, among other things, the Loeb-Leopold case, Al Capone, and Queen Marie of Romania. Herrick was imbued with a robust sense of fun that she shared with earlier female reporters such as Elizabeth Cochrane and Winifred Black. She once returned from Europe disguised as an Irish hired girl so that she could be incarcerated on Ellis Island and report on conditions there.

By the 1920s New York especially was a veritable showcase for first-rate women reporters. Long on the *Tribune* (later the merged *Herald Tribune*) was Scottish-born Ishbel Ross who came to New York by way of the Toronto *Daily News*. The legendary Stanley Walker in his book *City Editor*, insisted that "there is general agreement among newspapermen who worked with her that she was the best newspaper woman who ever worked in New York."[15] She was not only an efficient, well-organized, disciplined, and highly resourceful reporter, but a first-rate writer as well. In the 1930s she gave up newspaper work for novel writing, and also wrote the first and still the most sprightly account of women in American journalism, *Ladies of the Press*.

By the 1920s and 1930s, the idea that women must write differently from men had been overcome. The old sob sister style had disappeared. It is true that the tabloids and other sensational papers still sent women to cover the great trials, but the women who did this now wrote stories that were no different in style from their male counterparts. Grace Robinson, who covered notable trials for the New York *Daily News*, was a reserved, dignified, diminutive person, often called "mouselike" by fellow reporters, but she was considered among the best in the business. What is more important, even though she wrote for a tabloid, her writing was completely lacking in the emotional hand-wringing of old—just good, crisp, lucid writing. Dorothy Kilgallen of the Hearst papers covered the nation's high-profile trials for the better part of four decades, but did so with cold, analytical detachment. One of her colleagues, Bob Considine, recalled that she was unexcelled in hard professionalism. "She'd always be the first to the phone, had the cleanest first sentence, hit the heart of a story with a few swift strokes."[16]

Looking back at American newspapers from early times it would be fair to say that the profession of journalism was among the first to attract women, to open its doors to them, and among the first to reap the benefits of their skills. Yes, there continued to be barriers to women in the field, but more often they were the barriers erected by society itself rather than the profession. For the most part newspapermen esteemed the talents of their female colleagues and liked them as people, whatever stereotyped ideas might have persisted in the recesses of their minds. Keeping women out had become nearly impossible, and the effort was ultimately perceived to be foolish. Quite plainly, the women were just too good.

14

The Newspaper Sage: From Our Town to Olympus

It must never be forgotten that the American newspaper in its age of greatness was never simply a source of daily information and fact. The newspaper had become a forceful and undeniable participant in the body politic. It was the newspaper, after all, that gave birth to reform in the cities. It was George Jones's clear-sighted but faltering New York *Times* that busted the Tweed ring at a time when no court, no state legislature had the will to do so. It was Pulitzer's *World* and not the ballot box that gave voice and power to the newly arriving multitudes from Europe. It was the muckraker and the editorial writer who gave birth to civic reform and the progressive era, not the politician or the government regulator. Exposure of the trusts and of railroad cartels came from the pages of the nation's newspapers at a time when judges, even United States senators, were known to be nothing but pawns of irresponsible robber barons.

It was little wonder, then, that during the golden age of the newspaper in America so many bright youngsters of the land were drawn to careers in journalism. The newspaper was the way that people encountered the world around them. It was also the only regular source of interpretation and analysis that could make sense of the cascade of events that constitute life in a democratic republic. The newspaper made public response possible. Accordingly, for the better part of a century the daily newspaper was looked to as the foundation stone of intelligent thought and informed opinion. People trusted the newspaper to make sense of the world for them, and, for the most part, newspapers were worthy of the trust. Because they performed that very important function, newspapers would attract to themselves some of the best minds at work in America.

Even before this time—as soon as newspapers cut loose from the vicious and contentious partisanship of the early republic—Americans looked to their newspaper editors as guides to the drift of public affairs. William Cullen Bryant, for half a century editor of the New York *Evening Post*, was long respected as the leading citizen—the most trustworthy citizen—of New York City, mostly on the basis of his grave, even-handed editorials. Before the Civil War, Horace Greeley, in spite of the vagaries and inconsistencies of his opinions, became our first public or national sage, honored for the vigorous advocacy of his widely distributed editorials in the weekly edition of the *Tribune*.

Over the years a bond of intimacy grew between the people and their newspapers; people came to trust newspapers not only to tell them what was happening, but to analyze the complex world that was rapidly unfolding. The writers of editorials, and later of opinion columns, became central figures in the life of the nation. These writers were uncommonly good, much better, some might say, than the people deserved. In our own time there has been considerable grumbling about manipulation of public opinion by the press. Editorial writers and columnists are often referred to as "pundits"—a word that frequently takes on a pejorative coloring, although it is derived from the Hindu word *pandit*, a learned man, or scholar. In some ways Americans are suspicious of all experts, whatever their field.

Nonetheless, for a long time, American newspapers enjoyed a great deal of trust, probably because those who owned them and those who edited them tended to be quirky individualists who were stridently independent and just as happy to be wrong as right. They were trusted because they were near at hand, intimate, familiar. They put out their papers mainly for their own city or town and made tireless efforts to make that community intelligible. It was probably part of the genius of E. W. Scripps that his papers had no boilerplate editorials, no "received opinion." The Scripps paper in Cleveland was written for Cleveland, and the Scripps paper in Cincinnati was written for Cincinnati. It took a long time for newspapers to get over the idea that their mission was to be anything other than free and independent spirits, rooted in their time and place. While they kept to this primeval notion, they largely retained the loyalty of their readers.

The most characteristic and beneficial trait of the American newspaper, then, during the last years of the nineteenth century and the early years of the twentieth, was a quality of intimacy, of personal bond between those who managed the news or wrote the editorials and the reading public. When that bond of intimacy was lost, as when Pulitzer's psychosomatic illnesses removed him from the day-to-day operation of the *World*, or when Whitelaw Reid's political aspirations left no imaginative force at the head of the *Tribune*, their papers grew stale or remote. (Both these papers were revived and returned to greatness in the passage of time with fresh infusions of editorial talent, especially in the 1920s.)

For this reason, the history of the American newspaper sparkles with the contributions of solitary editors and publishers who shaped public opinion in their own communities, usually without raising any fears that they were dictators of thought and fashion. People admitted that, right or wrong, these editors had the community's interests at heart, that above all else they wanted to cherish and understand this community they shared with their readers. Whatever the case, no country has been more blessed than the United States with publishers and editors of newspapers in cities outside the great metropolises, even some small towns, who have exercised powers far beyond their localities. This is because Americans—not only political orators—have faith in the "grass roots." Such a phenomenon would be inconceivable say, in France, where it would be unheard of for any newspaperman to mobilize public opinion except from the heart of Paris.

Probably no better or more characteristic example of this can be found than in the long career of William Allen White, who in 1895, at the age of twenty-seven, bought up the failing Emporia (Kansas) *Gazette*, and remained its publisher, editor, and principal oracle for nearly half a century. White had been born in Emporia and attended the University of Kansas, but he had no particular thought as a youth of settling down for a lifetime in his hometown. After working as an editorial writer for William Rockhill Nelson's Kansas City (Missouri) *Star*, White must have been bitten by more than the newspaper bug. He came to share Nelson's belief that the newspaper editor needed to be solidly rooted in his community. But that did not mean some jejune or sentimental attachment. If there was something wrong with the place it was the first job of the newspaper editor to fix it.

The Emporia *Gazette* bought by White was a worn-out populist party paper with a mere 600 subscribers. White believed that the populist demagoguery had done a great disservice to his native state, and during the election year of 1896 he printed an editorial "What's the Matter With Kansas?" in which he blamed the stale local populism and its "shabby, wildeyed, rattle-brained fanatics," as well as presidential candidate William Jennings Bryan, for the state's decline.[1] This editorial, reprinted around the country, made a national figure of this small-town newspaperman, a reputation that stayed with him until his death in 1944. It also made him a darling of the Republican party for a time, although he would never become a Republican of the old guard. He was, through and through, a Teddy Roosevelt–type progressive; he joined in the battle against the trusts, against child labor, advocated railroad rate control and workman's compensation and the conservation, of natural resources.

Although White's national reputation was well deserved—he was a graceful and charming writer—and partially rested on his books and on his articles in *McClure's*, *Judge*, and *American Magazine*, he always believed that his strength lay in his lifelong attachment to Emporia. The small town, he believed, was a vantage point, a place from which to view the world in both detachment and intense involvement. Yes, there is always that larger world out there—issues of the tariff or minimum wage—but one had no way of taking the measure of these things without first having a grip on the smaller, more fathomable world of one's immediate environment.

In 1916 White penned a brief tribute to America's rapidly disappearing country newspapers. The *Gazette*, of course, was not a country newspaper, but a daily with a circulation of 6,000. But White's reason for never leaving Emporia was his belief that the first function of the newspaper was to present "the sweet intimate story of life," and that if as a nation we do not start with that, we are moving into a shadowy realm of things unknown with no map to guide us. So, yes, understanding ourselves always means starting with the most basic and elemental verities of life.

When the girl at the glove-counter marries the boy in the wholesale house, the news of their wedding is good for a forty-line wedding notice, and the forty lines in the country paper gives them self-respect. When in due course we know that their baby is a twelve-pounder named Grover or Theodore or Woodrow, we have that neighborly feeling that breeds real democracy. . . . Therefore men and brethren, when you are riding through this vail of tears upon the California Limited, and by chance pick up the little country newspaper . . . don't throw down the contemptible little rag with the verdict that there is nothing in it. But know this, and know it well; if you could take the clay from your eyes and read the little paper as it is written, you would find all of God's beautiful, sorrowing, struggling, aspiring world in it, and what you saw would make you touch the little paper with reverent hands.[2]

The country newspaper did not, of course, drive the United States in 1916, and less would it do so in the years ahead. On the other hand, in White's day many newspaper reporters and editorialists believed that if you cannot understand and explain the world that is just before your eyes, the world of your own family, church, Grange, Rotary, or ladies' sewing circle, the bigger world of national or international politics would always be beyond you, outside your grasp.

It is for this reason that the years between the Civil War and World War I represent a kind of renaissance of regional journalism and grass-roots editorial opinion. With the time-honored pattern of personal ownership and intellectual control continuing, owner-editors were often recognized as persons of considerable national stature. The pattern was obvious in the South, with Henry W. Grady, striding like a colossus over Atlanta, his name and writings known throughout the land. In Louisville there was Henry "Marse" Watterson, the very picture of a Kentucky colonel, who ran the *Courier-Journal* for fifty years. Writer of many cogent editorials and known personally by all the presidents of his day, Watterson was perhaps one of the prime representatives of this shining era of "personal, one-man papers—blatant but independent."[3]

Regional editors of considerable stature could be found throughout the country. There was Harvey W. Scott, the best-known newspaperman in the Pacific Northwest and editor of the Portland *Oregonian* from 1865 to 1911. Another "small town" editor, a far more charming writer than Scott, was E. W. Howe of the Atchison (Kansas) *Globe*, who came to be known nationally as "the Sage of Potato Hill." Howe developed the art of the pithy editorial paragraph, and thousands of his highly polished ruminations were read throughout the land for decades.

To understand the contribution of nearly all of the indigenous newspaper thinkers of these years, it is necessary to keep in mind that they were never precisely philosophers or even thinkers in any specialized sense. They were hybrids of the practical and the theoretical mind; they were rooted always in the day's news and in the particularity of their time and place. James Thurber, the famous American humorist, was born in Columbus, Ohio, and worked for newspapers there after graduating from Ohio State University in 1919. Later in life he wrote a volume of Columbus sketches, *The Thurber Album*, which contains numerous portraits of eccentric but brilliant newspapermen he knew in his Ohio days. One of the Columbus editors he held in the highest esteem was Robert O. Ryder, editor of the *Ohio State Journal* from 1904 to 1929. A leisurely, pipe-smoking gentleman of scholarly mien, Bob Ryder was the son of a classics professor at Oberlin College, and he himself had been a Latin teacher for a while before getting into newspaper work. But he had early decided that the objects of his rapt attention would not be Latin elegies, instead the elegiac moods that could be gleaned from this "old Palladium of liberty of ours," that is, his native state of Ohio, its capital, and his own quiet tree-lined neighborhood on the east side of town which he called "Franklin Avenue, U.S.A."

Bob Ryder arrived at his office from Franklin Avenue every day in his electric runabout at precisely 5 P.M., having spent the earlier part of the day puffing on his Bull Durham pipe tobacco and contemplating the behavior of the neighbor ladies and the condition of the flower beds and trees. The offices of the *Ohio State Journal* looked out over the grounds of the state capitol, and after picking up his mail he sat in his modest private office at a table and wrote out by longhand his day's editorials (he had no typewriter) and sent them to the composing room through a pneumatic tube. He read newspapers from all parts of Ohio and there were always clippings from them on his table. They formed the basis for a very popular column of his called "Round About Ohio." Ryder concentrated all of his efforts on the editorial page and left the daily running of his paper to the city editor and managing editor. Nonetheless he read everything that went into the *Journal* and was adored by every man on his staff—certainly a superhuman achievement for a newspaper editor.

A mild, pleasant man of 6'2", Ryder was seldom inclined to be contentious; he was not what was usually called a reformer. Nonetheless, said Thurber, he slayed many a dragon in his day. When the Ku Klux Klan attempted to set up shop in Ohio he was the first to denounce it and did not desist until its disciples had folded their sheets and left town. Above all, however, Ryder was, like Ed Howe, our ultimate master of the newspaper paragraph—an art form now irretrievably lost. He must have written 50,000 of these during his career, spending the better part of the day at home polishing them to perfection. Newspaper "paragraphs" were miniature familiar essays. They dealt "with the appearance of flowers in January, snow in May, mysterious showers of rocks on farmhouses, strange animals 'lurking and prowling about and acting huge and feral,' and other peculiar happenings in 'this glorious old commonwealth of ours.' "[4]

Thurber believed that the art of the newspaper paragraph, consisting of "the daily grinding of gleams and sparkles of humor and satire from the grist of human nature and the news of the world, is a special and demanding comic art," was much in demand in the early years of the twentieth century. In fact, a good deal of Ryder's output was good enough that it was reprinted in the New York *Morning World* and the *Literary Digest*. When Harold Ross, a onetime wandering newspaperman, founded the *New Yorker* magazine in 1925, he sought out the talents of other newspapermen who had practiced the art of paragraphing and filled up the front sections of his magazine with some splendid specimens of the art—Thurber wrote many himself. The requisite qualities in the writer, of course, were a light touch and a direct confrontation with everyday realities. No abstract theorizers were wanted here. The most successful practitioners of the art put in regular hours like office workers, and were not able to "indulge in the relaxing frailties and postures of temperament. The best paragraphs, to be sure, come out of the quiet mind and the tranquil time, but the true paragrapher has had a tough training in reporting and editing, and he can write in any mood or weather."[5]

Probably, too, part of the greatness of the art of newspaper paragraphing was that it allowed the editorial page to keep its human scale and personal warmth. Today it often seems impossible for people to find a neighborly aspect on the editorial page of a great city paper, or even a small-town paper for that matter. Editorial writers today more often seem to belong to some elite cadre; they address us from some pulpit on high; they are hired thinkers, remote eminences, all crabbing for attention. The newspaper paragrapher or editorialist of yore was something altogether different. He sought the society of his neighbors and fellow citizens. He wanted to confront his readers directly, one-on-one so to speak, and the best of them succeeded marvelously.

None of this means to suggest that all of the wisdom of newspapers in these same years was to be found at the grass-roots level. Of course it was all too often true that the editorial page on many older papers, like those of the *Times* or the *Tribune* in New York, were stodgy and unexciting, or that those of the yellow press were inflammatory or simplistic. Arthur Brisbane, Hearst's chief editor in New York, insisted that his paper's editorials should be understandable to a child of ten, and he redesigned the editorial page with big bold type, cartoons, and a kind of popular opinionizing and pseudo-philosophy that came to be known as "Brisbanalities."

There were, of course, exceptions to these extremes. There were editorial writers like E. P. Mitchell of the *Sun*, who could engage serious issues with clarity and literary skill, but in the big cities of the 1890s the editorial writer groaning away in his stall at the Boston *Post* or the Philadelphia *Bulletin* or the Chicago *Daily News* was seldom more than a cultured hack grinding out safe and tepid generalities.

Still, first-rate newspaper editorializing had never died. It is easy to forget that even in the vortex of the age of yellow journalism the editorial function was taken seriously. Joseph Pulitzer, for example, always insisted on the highest intellectual standards for his editorial page on the New York *World*. His front page might well have been filled with scandal, with stunts, with sensation-mongering, but back inside, his editorial page was reflective, philosophical, idealistic, and always wide-ranging in its coverage. This was never more so than when Frank I. Cobb became chief of the editorial page in 1905.

The New York *Post*, always one of the most admired papers in American since the days of William Cullen Bryant, continued to demonstrate intellectual force and moral suasion, even though it never became a circulation leader. E. Lawrence Godkin became editor of the *Post* in 1883 and remained so until 1900. Even before taking over that paper, Godkin was an eminent national figure. English born, educated at Queens College, Belfast, Godkin emigrated to the United States in 1856, joined the bar, then moved into journalism. During the Civil War he served as a correspondent for the London *Daily News*. When the war came to a close Godkin had reached the conclusion that the United States needed, above all else, a serious intellectual weekly paper like the London *Spectator*—a paper that would engage the attentions of the nation's cultural and political leaders. The paper Godkin envisioned was the *Nation*, first published in July 1865. It was a sixteen-page quarto filled with extensive commentary on American life, political analysis, and literary criticism.

The *Nation* was an almost instant success as an organ of opinion, and in its early years it had no real competitors. It was never, however, much of a money maker, and in 1881 Godkin sold the magazine to the wealthy German-born financier, Henry Villard, who by this time had already bought the New York *Post*. Villard, who was to make millions in the railroads of the Northwest, was decidedly liberal in attitude and had, in fact, married the only daughter of the crusading William Lloyd Garrison. Villard brought Godkin into the *Post*, first as associate editor and then as editor. More importantly, he brought the *Nation* in as a weekly supplement of the *Post*: it remained such for thirty-three years. Villard offered his editor a free hand, although that presented few hazards since there was a strong bond of sympathy between the two. Villard, a strong partisan of all the strains of German liberalism, which he shared with Carl Schurz (who had been his first editor on the *Post*), made a good match with Godkin's classical English Whig attitudes gleaned from Bentham and Mill. All believed in laissez-faire policies of free trade, reconciliation with the South (including the removal of the carpetbaggers), public education (including the establishment of the land grant system of universities), and women's suffrage. They strongly condemned the speculative intrigues of the 1870s, corrupt municipal politicians, schemes to bring about inflation such as the coinage of silver, and all expansionist policies on the part of the U.S. government. In the last years of his life, the Spanish-American War left Godkin with the bitter feeling that the United States was going down the same road as the Europeans toward war and the struggle for dominance.

E. L. Godkin was a kind of patrician liberal who believed that everything would turn out well if the nation's men of affairs, people of privilege and intelligence, acted responsibly in the nation's best interest. His readership, on both the *Post* and the *Nation* was, he said, the world of "gentlemen and scholars." The capitalist world that was erupting around him, with its fierce competition, greed, the growth of trusts and cartels, the suborning of judges and legislatures, was beyond his comprehension; the remedy he offered was that those with money or power should take full responsibility for the destiny of the nation.

Unfortunately Godkin did not have the power or the influence to change the course of American history in the last decades of the nineteenth century and to deflect the cruelties and self-serving energies of the capitalist era. He was, nonetheless, a voice that was heard; he had an influence on several generations of American intellectuals, social reformers, and idealistically minded citizens. He was a clear, ironic, penetrating, far-seeing writer with the ability to peel the layers off the most complex social and economic issues. William James, perhaps the best-known American philosopher of his day, believed that Godkin was the strongest intellectual force at work in American life in the dreary years of voracious capitalism and yellow journalism. He wrote:

To my generation his was certainly the towering influence in all thought concerning public affairs, and indirectly his influence has assuredly been more persuasive than any other writer of the generation, for he influenced other writers who never quoted him, and determined the whole current of discussion.[6]

Godkin, in short, was read where it counted: in the studies of professors, ministers, social thinkers, and the thousands of young reformers about to become the next generation of newspaper writers and politicians. Godkin, and a handful of others like him around the country, was living proof, if often rather threadbare proof, that the older traditions of liberty, decency, and public reflection were not dead and would survive to a new time, and he always offered some small hope that the next generation would be better.

And the next generation *was* better. The early decades of the twentieth century generally witnessed vast improvements in the editorial columns of daily papers, with a number of young writers and intellectuals coming on the scene. The best of these writers were individuals who would play a significant role on the national stage. A number wrote books that allowed them to be independent men of letters, although they were usually quite satisfied to be considered—first and foremost—newspapermen. This was because they did not regard the newspaper as a place to be escaped from as soon as their reputations were secure. They believed that being rooted in newspaper work was what gave them their inspiration and their authority.

It would be hard to think of two more able individuals who devoted themselves to the American scene in the first half of the twentieth century than Henry L. Mencken of Baltimore, and Walter Lippmann of New York. Both were born in the 1880s (Mencken in 1880 and Lippmann in 1889), and both were active until after World War II—Lippmann continued writing political commentary for newspapers and magazines until shortly before his death in 1974. Their equals cannot be found in print journalism in our own time. They wrote during the high tide of the newspaper in America, and they made the most of golden opportunities. On the face of it two more unlike individuals would be hard to find. Lippmann was a serious social philosopher with a gift for style and the desire to find a delicate balance, an equilibrium. Mencken a Swiftian satirist of brilliant and malignant wit wanted nothing more than to raise storms and bloody noses. This was the only way, he believed, to get the attention of the placid, cud-chewing American people. Lippmann was probably the most determined and coherent political thinker ever to devote himself to newspaper work in America. Mencken was probably the most brilliant and eruptive stylist to stir the waters of American journalism. Robert Frost called Mencken America's greatest essayist, and although some may argue with that judgment, it is certainly not far-fetched.

Lippmann and Mencken, both the products of prosperous commercial families in the East, developed very early in their lives a metropolitan or cosmopolitan point of view. They would not quite have agreed with the likes of William Allen White or Bob Ryder that an understanding of America could come from lying in the soft bosom of the old genteel America of small towns and good neighborliness. They did not precisely reject the visions of loveliness or security that might be found in Emporia, or the small colleges or county seats of Ohio "that old Palladium of Liberty"; nor did they reject the notion that newspapers must form an intimate bond with the environment around them. It is just that these were two individuals who had to face all of the traumas and anxieties of national life, the brutal consequences of industrialization, of an irresponsible and venial patrician class, of shabby machine politics, of a poorly educated electorate that would take no responsibility for government, of stereotyped manners and morals, of low culture and gaudy amusement. It was not that the generous optimism of people like White and Ryder was without foundation, it is just that the application of it had lost its power. Mencken and Lippmann felt that they had to deal, head on, with a far more complex, stubborn and painful world, and their conclusions about this world were not wholly optimistic.

Of the two Mencken arrived on the scene first. Son of a well-off cigar manufacturer in Baltimore, he joined the Baltimore *Herald* in 1899 right out of high school. He had no desire to go to college and all his life he believed that college professors were mostly pedants, creatures of low imagination and clotted vision. Since he was an individual of boundless energy and talent, Mencken rose quickly in the hierarchy. By 1903 he was city editor of his paper, and in 1905 he was briefly managing editor. The following year, however, he joined the city's leading paper, the *Sun*, referred to locally as the *Sunpaper*, and remained with that organization in various capacities for over forty years.

Mencken was not mainly interested in management, however; even editorial writing in the traditional sense did not suit his fancy. He much preferred writing on his own, and by the time he joined the *Sun* he had written numerous magazine articles and was at work on several books. An omnivorous reader, Mencken was widely acquainted with modern European literature. But his greatest preoccupation was with the welter of American life; accordingly he never allowed himself to be parted from regular reporting. Until 1948 he covered most major presidential conventions, believing these gaudy circuses offered a clue to the nature of American life and the essential frailty of the democratic process.

By 1910 Mencken had begun his association with the magazine the *Smart Set* of which he would shortly become editor. But he never left his home base in Baltimore for New York even as he became a well-known writer; indeed, he continued to live nearly all his life in Baltimore in a row house at 1524 Hollins Street. In 1910, a new opportunity opened up for Mencken at the *Sun*. The staid old paper, owned since the 1830s by the Abell family, was sold to a new publisher, Charles H. Grasty, a lively crusader type who had come up under Nelson at the Kansas City *Star*. Grasty shook up the *Sun*, put in an afternoon edition (people now spoke of the *Sunpapers*), and brought both editions into the twentieth century. Under Grasty Mencken was assigned to write editorials, and beginning on April 18, 1910, he began a regular column on the editorial page, signed only by his initials, H.L.M.

The following year the column was given a title, "The Free Lance," by which name it remains one of the great classics of American journalism. "The Free Lance" was rambunctious, irreverent, iconoclastic, funny, impertinent, youthful, and wide-ranging. Mencken's assignment was to tilt his lance at anything he wished, and he went after everything in sight, whether sacred or profane. Whatever good, solid, banal, and callow people were for, Mencken was invariably against. His aim was "to combat, chiefly by ridicule, American piety, stupidity, tin-pot morality, cheap chauvinism in all their forms." His most important bolts of lightning were reserved for the Baltimore scene, its prominent citizens, its crooked reformers, "its honorary pallbearers," as he called them. He also attacked bureaucracy, Christian Science, chiropractic science, blue laws, the Anti-Saloon League, and the Rotary. The "good" people were against prostitution, so he was for it; they were against woman's suffrage, so he was for it, although invariably his arguments in support of these things were ironical and deceptive: quixotic ideas that were disarming to the reader accustomed only to safe platitudes and stereotyped ideas.

"The Free Lance" quickly became one of the best-known and talked-about institutions of Baltimore. It is said that many citizens of the town ripped open the paper as soon as they got it—even before they looked at the headlines—to see what mischief Mencken was up to. He seldom disappointed them; the man was incapable of writing a line without sparkle, wit, and intellectual force. He came to be called the "Sage of Baltimore." His talents were soon recognized by newspaper editors and writers around the country. Henry Watterson of the Louisville *Courier-Journal* was rapturous in his praise: "Think of it. The staid old Baltimore *Sun* has got itself a Whangdoodle. Nor is it one of the bogus Whangdoodles which we sometimes encounter in the sideshow business—merely a double-cross betwixt a Gin Rickey and a Gyascutis—but genuine, guaranteed, imported from the mountains of Hepsidam."[7]

Mencken was, in fact, such a good writer that it was a foregone conclusion that he would shortly be a figure on the national stage. Over the next two decades he would be the editor (and major contributor) to two national magazines, *The Smart Set* and *The American Mercury*. The latter magazine, launched in 1924, became the leading "literary magazine" of the 1920s. It has been widely remarked that along every college walk in the land the green covers of the *Mercury* could be seen flashing among the students' texts, making Mencken, if only for a few years, the idol of America's youth.

But Mencken continued to think of himself as primarily a working newspaperman. He believed that in a country like the United States one's inspiration should come from the rough passage of daily events. He did not like to think of himself as precisely an editorial writer but as an essayist in general practice. ("The Free Lance" as a regular feature in the *Sunpapers* lasted until 1915; thereafter Mencken took to the editorial page only when it suited him, but, with his literary reputation riding high, most of his better things found a national outlet.) If there were any fat cats around, any frauds, any illusionists, any political mountebanks, any self-satisfied movie directors, any pompous business leaders, Mencken could always be counted on to skin them alive. On a daily basis he was ready to take on any delusions of the popular culture, any misplaced faith that our style of politics was anything other than childish and stupid. He might often be wrong, and he could be mean, but his words always had a powerful impact and sawed through to the bone.

A few sample Menckenisms will suffice. Here is a comment on President Calvin Coolidge in 1924:

In his whole life he has probably never thought an original thought, but he has at least shown a talent for dramatizing the thoughts of others. In the present campaign he has very neatly seized the leadership of the Babbitts. Every idea that is honorable and of good report in Pullman smoke-rooms, on the verandas of golf clubs, among university presidents, at luncheons of the Kiwanis Club and where sweaterers and usurers meet—all this rubbish he has wielded into a system of politics, nay, of statecraft, of jurisprudence, of epistemology, almost of theology, and made himself the prophet of it.[8]

On the oratorical style of President Warren G. Harding:

I rise to pay my small tribute to Dr. Harding. Setting aside a college professor or two and half a dozen dipsomaniacal newspaper reporters, he takes the first place in my Valhalla of literati. That is to say, he writes the worst English that I have ever encountered. It reminds me of a string of wet sponges, it reminds me of tattered washing on the line; it reminds me of stale bean soup, of college yells, of dogs barking idiotically through endless nights. It is so bad that a kind of grandeur creeps into it. It drags itself out of the dark abysm (I was about to write abscess) of pish, and crawls insanely up the topmost pinnacle of posh. It is rumble and bumble. It is balder and dash.[9]

On the misery of school days:

School days, I believe, are the unhappiest in the whole span of human existence. They are full of dull, unintelligible tasks, new and unpleasant ordinances, brutal violations of common sense and common decency. It doesn't take a reasonably bright boy long to discover that most of what is rammed into him is nonsense, and nobody really cares very much whether he learns it or not. . . . His actual companions, forced upon him by the inexorable decrees of a soulless and irrational state, are school-ma'ams, male and female, which is to say persons of trivial and unromantic achievement, and no more capable of inspiring emulation in a healthy boy than so many midwives or dog-catchers.[10]

Mencken was perpetually angry that a great material society like the United States had been unable to establish a fully adult civilization. He hated our childish forms of entertainment—baseball, the movies, astrology—our mindless system of schooling and churchgoing, our Puritanism (which is to say our suspicion of the manners and morals of our neighbors), and above all our lunatic belief that freedom to choose at the ballot box will result in the selection of "good men," which is to say, of politicians of honor, dignity, and intelligence.

Walter Lippmann, another American journalist whose star was in the ascendancy during the 1920s proclaimed that Mencken was "the most powerful personal influence on this whole generation of educated people." He attributed this tremendous influence to Mencken's tenacity in digging for everything found in the American soil whether it be putrid or not, his refusal to be deflected by abstract ideas or by any of the luxuries provided to those who enjoy the shelter of the ivory tower.

Most educated men are so preoccupied with what they conceive to be the best thought in the field of their interest, that they ignore the follies of uneducated men. A Jacques Loeb would spend very little of his time on biology as taught in an Oklahoma high school. Even William James, who was more interested in the common man than any great philosopher of our time, was looking always for grains of wisdom in the heaps of folly. But Mr. Mencken is overwhelmingly preoccupied with popular culture. He collects examples of it. He goes into a rage about it. He cares so much about it that he cannot detach himself from it.[11]

Perhaps only another individual steeped in the world of daily journalism could grasp the potential richness of this field of the popular or general culture. But Walter Lippmann, perhaps the greatest political philosopher ever to devote himself to the editorial pages of the American newspaper, had a genuine appreciation for the genius of Mencken, although he was himself a man of considerably different temperament. He did not share Mencken's volcanic force. For years he sought, day in and day out, to pour oil on troubled waters, to put together the pieces resulting from every political explosion. Quite curiously, in the end, like Mencken, he drew rather darksome conclusions about the character of American civilization.

Born in New York City of a wealthy German-Jewish family, Lippmann was accorded all of the luxuries of an upper-class education including extensive European travel in his adolescent years. He graduated from Harvard University in 1910 with a degree in philosophy. Even as an undergraduate, Lippmann's intellectual powers must have been evident: George Santayana, who mostly remained aloof from his American colleagues, was obviously impressed and made this brilliant youngster his teaching assistant. Clearly Lippmann could have gone on to an illustrious academic career, but during his college years he had also been bitten by the newspaper bug. He had worked as a reporter for the Boston *Common*, which undoubtedly steered him away from the academic path. With the full idealism of youth he went to work for Lincoln Steffens, preparing articles on municipal and corporate corruption that appeared in *Everyman's Magazine*. As a forward-looking member of the progressive movement he became associated with Herbert Croly and his recently launched magazine the *New Republic*. During World War I he took a post in the Wilson administration, an experience that left him troubled and skeptical. By this time Lippmann had already written his first book, *A Preface to Politics*, which would earn him a solid reputation before he was thirty. With the war over, and with a growing skepticism about the institutions of democratic society, Lippmann began thinking once more of the possibilities inherent in daily journalism. He discovered that he shared the faith of Milton and John Stuart Mill that the press was, or ought to be, "the bible of democracy, the book out of which a people determines its conduct."[12] Accordingly, in 1922, Lippmann accepted an offer to manage the editorial page of the New York *World*.

The *World* had been considerably improved since Pulitzer's death under the editorship of Frank I. Cobb, and Lippmann was now precisely where he wanted to be: writing editorials on a daily basis. With the *World*'s editorial page as his forum page he rapidly became one of the most influential figures in American life; his opinions were widely quoted, most especially where it was important: in intellectual circles and the seats of power. His influence would continue to grow, especially in the 1930s when he began writing a daily column called "Today and Tomorrow" for the New York *Herald Tribune*. He would conduct this column until 1966, and it would be one of the monuments of that form—perhaps the best newspaper column in the history of American journalism.

Undoubtedly one of the reasons for Lippmann's influence was that he was a serious political philosopher who also had the ability to write powerfully and simply. Too, he had garnered a reputation as a public intellectual by writing a series of books in which he pondered not so much the specific political issues of the day, but the wider questions of democracy: of law, of government, of public opinion, of the role of the press, and so on. Even as he was waiting to go on the job at the *World* in 1922 he was writing probably his best-known book, *Public Opinion*. It is a work that has had a tremendous influence on American political thought in the years since its publication; its principal ideas have become part of our national vocabulary.

Basically, *Public Opinion* was highly skeptical of the mechanics of democracy. Democracy is a form of government that replaces the sovereignty of the king (or of cabinet and legislature) with sovereignty of the people. But such a form of sovereignty can only work if the people are well-informed on the major issues of the day, and in a modern industrial society, and in an evolving international community, such issues become complex and overly demanding. Are the people up to the task of guiding the government? Lippmann feared that they are not. They may well exercise their right to vote at the ballot box, they may shout for what they want, but whether they understand the issues that confront the nation is an altogether different matter. Lippmann believed that the vast majority of citizens were too busy managing their own lives and making a living to master the issues of statecraft. Furthermore, he was equally skeptical of the means by which the average citizen gets information about the questions of the day. Lippmann's knowledge of the American newspapers told him that there was not enough information and analysis in them to enlighten any large number of individuals. Too, in a popular democracy, government itself has quite enough reasons to keep the citizenry in the dark about the major issues. Politicians want to get reelected so they are highly motivated to reduce all ideas to cerebral rubber stamps, simplistic phrases, popular uproars—"sound bites" as they say in our day. Lippmann's World War I service in Washington led him to see how government itself uses propaganda and other forms of managed news to keep public opinion fragmented and weak.

Some of these same ideas were amplified and developed in later books of Lippmann's—*The Phantom Public* (1925); *A Preface to Morals* (1929); *The Good Society* (1937); and *The Public Philosophy* (1954)—all of them best-sellers when they came out, and tremendously influential among the nation's intelligentsia. Some people who had known Lippmann in his youth were troubled by his deep skepticism about the political transaction in America. Some professed to believe that Lippmann had abandoned the liberalism and progressivism of his youth for some kind of reactionary conservatism. Actually this would be to completely misunderstand Lippmann's work. For Lippmann, words like liberalism and conservatism were simply other simplistic concepts in which politicians kept the public in thrall. Such terms were merely mental crutches to lean on and fend off the obligation to think. Of course the simplistic concepts and confections that kept Henry Mencken laughing were a daily burden to Lippmann who wrestled with them seriously throughout his life. In every day's news he struggled, sometimes vainly, but often successfully, with the profound issues that confronted the American public. He never gave up trying to figure out how best to get democracy to work, and his herculean efforts in that regard had no equal in his time.

As to the American press, as to newspapers he worked for during his lifetime, Lippmann was not only skeptical but often pessimistic. Were the editorial pages of the typical daily paper nothing but superficial excursions into the simple-minded shibboleths that demagogues wanted to keep heated up so as to control the electorate? Was the American newspaper condemned to weak coverage, flights into yellow journalism, to sentiment and sensationalism? Had newspapers given up trying to think, to be the bible of democratic man? One might well say so. On the other hand, with figures like Walter Lippmann in the field, there always remained more than just a glimmer of hope that the press could perform its vital task. As long as there were people like Lippmann upon the stage there seemed to be a calming reassurance that American journalism, and maybe even American democracy, was very good indeed.

15

The Foreign Language Press

The foreign language newspaper can hardly be ignored in the history of American journalism because of the vast number of these papers that existed over the years and because of the considerable impact they had on society until fairly recent times. These papers maintained a vital link to the old world from which millions of immigrants came to the American shore, but they also helped to ease the transition to an often bewildering new society into which these newcomers were unceremoniously thrust. It is not really surprising that by 1917, the year the United States entered World War I, there were 1,323 foreign language newspapers being published in the United States (and this excludes papers written for American Indians). This was the high tide of foreign newspaper circulation in America.[1]

A person stopping by a newsstand on the streets of New York in 1910 or 1915 would certainly have been bewildered by the array of foreign language newspapers on display, some printed in a familiar Roman typeface, others in the cyrillic alphabet or German script or Chinese characters. There would have been papers readily available for immigrants and first-generation Americans written in German, Italian, Yiddish, Hungarian, Serbian, Russian, Greek, Slovakian, Chinese, Japanese, Spanish, even Rumanian and Latvian, as well as others.

There would, of course, be a big difference between the appearance and quality of these papers. Some would have been scraggly folded sheets of four pages. A few would differ barely at all in heft and bulk from the nearby New York *World* or New York *Times*. To all appearances the leading foreign language papers were simply variants of the large metropolitan dailies. But many papers were the products of weak enterprise, probably turned out on small hand presses by a staff of one or two. Such ephemeral products might disappear tomorrow to be replaced by others hoping for better luck. But some of the major foreign language papers were giants in the newspaper field, with circulations over 100,000. The *New Yorker Staats-Zeitung*, dating from 1845, had a circulation of 250,000 at one time. It was probably the most influential foreign language daily in America and had its own building on "German newspaper row." Like its English competitors it had a large staff of reporters and editors, a full complement of printers, pressmen, deliverymen, and advertising salesmen. It was printed on the Hoe rotary press, just like the *Tribune* and the *World*, and hurried down chutes for fast delivery to all areas of New York City. The paper had sections for women, business news, features, book reviews, music and drama criticism—everything one might expect in a daily paper. Even a superficial inspection of the contents would suggest that here was a typical American paper that just happened to be written in a foreign language.[2]

A large foreign language press seems not at all unusual when one considers that America had been and remains a land of immigrant peoples. Naturally the pattern of foreign language newspapers changed with the passage of time. In recent years the United States has received large numbers of people from Korea, the Philippines, Vietnam, and Cuba. Newspapers for these groups would not have been needed in the nineteenth century, but sizable communities now demand this cultural benefit. Perhaps in time these newspapers will disappear or find their functions nearly obliterated, as did those of earlier groups that surrendered to assimilation, such as the Dutch, Finnish, Norwegian, Swedish, Greek, Slovene, Rumanian, and so on.

The foreign language press in America began in colonial times. The vast majority of people coming to the British colonies of North America before the Revolution were of three stocks: English or Welsh, Scotch-Irish, or German. There were a number of other settlements too, such as the Dutch enclave in New York and New Jersey, and a short-lived Swedish settlement along the Delaware River in New Jersey, but none of these gave rise to newspapers, nor did any of the small number of French- or Spanish-speaking people living here and there. The Dutch failure is most surprising since the New Amsterdam colony was an extensive one that lasted from 1624 and 1664. It may be explained by the fact that the commercially minded Dutch regarded their territory here as only a business venture. This nearsightedness and the failure to colonize aggressively probably account for the eventual loss of their territory.

The most important foreign language group in colonial times was, of course, the Germans, and they were the first to provide newspapers for their settlers. Over the course of American history there were more papers in the German language than any other. Until well after the Civil War German newspapers constituted half of the national total of foreign language papers. When dailies arrived on the scene, German newspapers were invariably in the lead. As late as 1914, one-third of all foreign language dailies were German.[3]

The first of these papers, as one might expect, appeared in the German settlements of Pennsylvania. None of the many little states that constituted eighteenth-century Germany had sought colonies in North America, but thousands of Germans, fleeing poverty, tyranny, or religious persecution accepted the liberality of William Penn and settled in eastern Pennsylvania. So great became this influx of German immigrants that by the Revolution Benjamin Franklin estimated that one-third of the population of Pennsylvania was German.[4] Large numbers of Lutherans, Moravians, Mennonites, and United Brethren settled in the colony, especially near Germantown, and it was here that the first foreign language newspaper appeared.

Actually, Benjamin Franklin, observing the growing number of Germans in the area—most of them literate—was the first to get in the act, putting out the *Philadelphische Zeitung* in 1732. But lacking German type, familiarity with the language, and having no standing in the community, Franklin gave up after two issues. In a few years, however, a successful paper was begun by Christopher Saur.[5] This paper was called the *Hoch Deutsche Pennsylvanische Bericht* ("High German Pennsylvania Report"), and it first appeared on August 20, 1739. Saur was a typical immigrant of the time. He had arrived from the Palatinate in 1724 at the age of thirty. He took up several trades: he made optical instruments, dealt in medicinal herbs, made button molds, repaired clocks, sold Franklin's stove, worked as a carpenter and tailor, and finally began printing books in German. It was the printing business that eventually led to his newspaper.

Saur was a Dunkard. Dunkards were opposed to the Lutherans and other reform sects, so that his paper occasionally stirred up religious controversy even though it did not run editorials as such. The popularity of the paper, however, was due to the fact that it contained news of the German community, which was now extensive in size and consisted of a large number of literate individuals.

The Saur paper became a family enterprise that was later taken over by his son. Its name was changed to the simpler *Germantauner Zeitung* ("Germantown News") and it continued to publish through the Revolution. It was issued twice a month, later weekly. The paper contained commercial adver-tisements, news of ship arrivals, church news, and occasionally brief reports from the old country. It advertised lotteries to raise funds for schools and churches or to fund public improvements, but never referred to taverns or worldly forms of entertainment.[6]

Saur did not have a monopoly for long, however. After 1762 he had com-petition from John Heinrich Miller who began a rival paper, the *Wochentli-che Philadelphische Staatsbote* ("Weekly Philadelphia Public Messenger"). The two papers shared the vicissitudes of most English lan-guage papers in the period before the Revolution. Miller's paper forged ahead for a while because he strongly supported the revolutionary move-ment, while Saur remained a loyalist. On the other hand, when the British occupied Philadelphia Miller was forced to flee, and Saur had the field to himself. Unfortunately another reversal of fortune occurred at the end of the Revolution when Miller returned. Saur and his son, both once very prosper-ous men, retreated to Nova Scotia on the tail of the British Army.

With the war over, however, there was a burst of activity in the German newspaper field. Thirty-eight German papers were started in Pennsylvania between the Revolution and 1800, some of them, like the *Adler* ("Eagle") of Reading, were long-lived institutions.[7] The *Adler* lasted until 1913. During the Revolution German immigration had dried up, and it remained a mere trickle until about 1830 when it again had a dramatic spurt. Still, Germans from the older immigration began to migrate in sizeable numbers to Dela-ware, Maryland, Virginia, and western Pennsylvania, so there were German language papers established in those places also. A few were started before 1800; as early as 1789 there appeared a *Virginische Zeitung*, and in 1793 *Der General Staatsbote* in Frederick, Maryland. One of the sons of Christo-pher Saur returned to establish a German weekly in Baltimore in 1796. It was *Der Neue Unpartheyische Baltimore Bote und Marylander Staats Reg-ister*, the first of many German-language papers in that city with a rapidly growing German population.

A second wave of German immigration began about 1830, and although it was not a great wave like that following the failure of the 1848 Revolution, it sent large numbers of Germans trekking westward, into the western part of Virginia, Ohio, and beyond. Eventually there would be large concentra-tions of Germans in midwestern cities including Cincinnati, St. Louis, Cleveland, and Milwaukee, giving rise to prosperous German newspapers in those cities. Most of the German immigrants had little contact with the Pennsylvania Germans (sometimes incorrectly called Pennsylvania

Dutch), who by this time had evolved a strange form of fractured German that adopted some anglicized words and an English word order.

It was the large number of Germans pouring into Cincinnati that brought into existence the first German language daily. This was the *Cincinnati Volksblatt*, established in 1836 and stepped up to daily status in 1843. As a matter of strict fact this was not the first foreign language daily to be published in the United States. The first apparently was the French *Courrier Français*, which had a brief life between 1794 and 1798.[8] (Interestingly enough, French papers never became an important force in American journalism either at this time or later.) The *Cincinnati Volksblatt* became a major American paper of many years' duration. It was published continuously until World War I.

Wherever Germans settled in large numbers, newspapers would follow, and in the major cities the dailies would become affluent, powerful, and influential. In Philadelphia the *Alte und Neue Welt* became the leading German paper, and served, like the New York *Staats-Zeitung*, as a model for other such papers around the country. (It was written in standard German, not the Pennsylvania-German argot which had largely been confined to the north and west of Philadelphia.) St. Louis, an extremely important German community, had two major papers, the *Anzeiger des Westens*, and the *Westliche Post*, and numerous lesser ones. Cleveland had *Germania*, Chicago the *Illinois Staats-Zeitung* and Pittsburgh the *Freiheitsfreund*.

German newspapers openly involved themselves in American political issues. Most of them also followed political developments in Germany, especially in times of crisis. During the Revolution of 1848, few German papers remained silent about what was going on. They ignored American issues for the moment. When they did deal with the American political scene most of the German papers followed the Democrat line. A few subsidized Whig, and later Republican papers flared up during presidential campaigns, but most of the new German immigrants were workingmen and artisans and tended to become Democrat voters. Things changed briefly as the Civil War neared. For example, George Schneider, one of the "forty-eighters," and, after 1851, publisher of the *Illinois Staats-Zeitung*, led the revolt of Chicago's Germans against Stephen A. Douglass's Democratic organization at the time of the Kansas-Nebraska Act.[9] Schneider was even one of the organizers of the Illinois Republican party. But most German metropolitan papers returned to the Democratic fold after the Civil War and remained there until they had to deal with the issue of Woodrow Wilson's feigned "neutrality" in World War I.

According to the census of 1870 there were 1,690,533 persons born in Germany living in the United States, and probably about five or six million German-speaking people in the country. The vast majority were literate. Eighty percent of the foreign language papers at this time were German papers.[10] Over the next two decades the total number of German language papers would double, but by 1890 the percentage of these in the foreign language press would fall considerably because of the enormous number of immigrants now arriving from southern and eastern Europe. But the German newspapers continued to provide the moral and intellectual leadership as well as expertise in advertising and business practices.

The *New Yorker Staats-Zeitung* was probably the leading foreign language newspaper throughout the nineteenth century. It was founded in 1834 as a Democratic campaign organ but was later taken over by Jacob Uhl who made it a mainstream paper. It became a daily in 1849. Oswald Ottendorfer, one of the 1848 refugees, joined the paper in 1850. When Uhl died Ottendorfer helped his widow, Anna, run the paper and later married her. He continued as publisher until 1890, and apparently was exceptional both as editor and far-seeing business manager. By 1872 the paper had a rotary press capable of printing 12,000 sheets an hour. The following year the *Staats-Zeitung* moved into its own building on Printing House Square and acquired all of the latest facilities. It had a circulation of about 50,000 at this time.

In 1870 the *Staats-Zeitung* was an eight-page paper. The first page was usually devoted to telegraphic news and reports from European correspondents. Pages two and three contained advertising, page four had the lead article, often written by Ottendorfer himself. Pages six contained a literary item, a German classic perhaps, or serial novel. Pages seven and eight were usually devoted to local news. As time went on more of the paper consisted of things American, although it never failed to deal with major developments in Germany—the Franco-Prussian War, for example.

As a publisher, Ottendorfer tended to be conservative. He adopted all of the latest business techniques for promoting his paper. He used layouts and design features much like those of the other New York dailies. Carl Wittke, an historian of the German press in America, attributed the success of the *Staats-Zeitung* to its finding a full complement of local advertising and to various devices for building circulation. The paper was run to make a profit, not as a propaganda sheet.[11]

By the time Oswald Ottendorfer retired in 1890, his paper had increased to twelve pages and also had an afternoon and Sunday edition. Its circulation had risen to 90,000, which made it the largest-circulation German newspaper in the world. Management eventually passed to Herman Ridder, previously the publisher of a German Catholic paper, who later went on to an illustrious career in the newspaper industry. He was one of the founders of the Associated Press and president of the American Newspaper Publishers Association. His sons took over the management of the business in the twentieth century at a time when the German language papers were beginning their decline.

The German language press was kept prosperous for many years not only by a large readership but by successful promotions and rich sources of advertising revenues. The metropolitan dailies, whether in New York, Chicago, St. Louis, or Cincinnati, were filled with paid announcements for sale of real and personal property. They contained announcements of businesses for sale, of German bankers and brokerage houses, of land agents, and currency exchanges. Railroad and steamship companies advertised their rates. The papers were filled with local advertisements for saloons and beer gardens, hotels, any watering spots that might have some nostalgic reference to scenes and places in the fatherland. Liquor advertisements could be found in profusion. So, too, were the notices of German book dealers and publishers offering German classics as well as the works of German-American writers. Not a few English-speaking businesses also sought to reach this large minority audience.

By the 1880s, of course, with new waves of immigration coming from around the globe—from eastern and southern Europe, from the Orient—it was no longer possible to think of the foreign language press as being predominately German. There would shortly be major daily papers published in Italian, Polish, Yiddish, Spanish, Bohemian, Japanese, and Chinese, most of these appearing in major cities where large immigrant populations existed. It is also not possible to ignore the large number of immigrants arriving from countries like Norway and Sweden in these same years, and these groups created a need for newspapers as well, although their geographical distribution, which was largely in the upper Midwest, ordained a different kind of newspaper content and distribution.

Immigration from the Scandinavian countries began fairly early—the 1840s saw the first waves—and rose to a torrent in the 1880s. A great deal of the immigration was brought about by aggressive promotions by western railroads which sent agents abroad offering cheap land and inexpensive rail fares from the East Coast to the upper Mississippi valley. Most Scandinavians were not political refugees, they migrated for economic reasons. Forced to live on rocky or mountainous soil, many Swedes and Norwegians lived on the margin of subsistence. Too, the rule of primogeniture, which ordained that the first son got everything and the others nothing, created obvious hardships. Some Scandinavians were desirous of escaping the confinements of the cold, pietistic, and inflexible dogmas of Lutheranism. They brought their religion with them, but it was slowly softened under the more forgiving American skies.

Although both Norwegians and Swedes wanted to preserve much of their home culture, they were also addicted to the American educational system and rapidly became English-speaking. Nonetheless, there were a great many solidly Norwegian and Swedish communities that demanded their own organizations, lodges, singing societies—and newspapers. The number of Norwegian- and Swedish-language newspapers (there were later a very small number of Danish papers as well) was not inconsiderable. Nearly all were monthlies or weeklies. Well over a million Swedes migrated to the United States, most of them settling first in Illinois, later, beginning in the 1880s, in Minnesota, which quickly came to be called the "Swedish state." Many other American cities had a fair number of Swedes also, and newspapers arose there in substantial numbers. In addition to the large number of Swedish papers in and around Minneapolis, there were important papers in Chicago and New York. Certainly New York has never been thought of as a center of Swedish immigration, but a great number of Swedes were employed for building the Brooklyn Bridge in the 1880s, and there were thus extensive settlements in Brooklyn.

Norwegian immigration was considerable. Between 1826 and 1915 emigration from Norway to the United States was over three-quarters of a million. Norway lost a larger percentage of its population to American emigration than any European country except Ireland.[12] Accordingly there were a considerable number of Norwegian language newspapers. The first was the *Nordlyset* ("Northern Light"), founded in Norway, Wisconsin, in 1847. Over the next century some 500 Norwegian newspapers and other periodicals would appear, their distribution giving some idea of the profile of the population: 216 of these were in Minnesota; 85 in Illinois; 82 in Wisconsin; 62 in North Dakota; 57 in Iowa; 42 in Washington (State); and 30 in New York (State). Of cities, Minneapolis had the largest number with 113.[13]

Most people today who conjure up a vision of the immigrant Norwegian think immediately of the thrifty, stoical, hard-working farmers of the upper Midwest, many of whom started out living in sod huts and endured conditions that could be harsher than those of the old country. This brings to mind the cruel, implacable scenes so well portrayed in the novels of Ole Rolvaag such as *Giants in the Earth*. In the beginning few Norwegians were reached by newspapers; later they may have received a Norwegian paper by post from Minneapolis or Fargo along with the Sears-Roebuck catalog. The city newsstand was not the usual venue for Norwegian papers, but they could be found on display in urban neighborhoods with large Norwegian populations. Not all Norwegian immigrants followed the farming vocation. New York City had more than a sprinkling of Norwegian sailors, carpenters, joiners, and others who followed the maritime industry. There were 6,000 Norwegians living in Brooklyn in 1869. A long-lived paper, the *Nordisk Tidende* ("Norway Times") started in 1891, and as late as 1940 still reached 55,000 first- and second-generation Norwegians, most of them living in the Bay Ridge section of Brooklyn.[14]

Norwegian newspapers naturally interested themselves in American political issues. Most of them in the Midwest tended to be Republican, although by the beginning of the twentieth century there were the expected socialist publications in the big cities. Moral–political issues were hotly debated. There were a number of temperance papers directed toward Norwegians. A prominent one was *Reform*, which had its birth in Eau Claire, Wisconsin, in 1889. By and large, though, most Norwegian papers attempted to deal with issues of general concern to the immediate community and to the particularities of Norwegian-American life.

Probably the most influential of Norwegian newspapers for many years was the Chicago-based *Skandinaven* started in 1866 by John Anderson with the help of Victor F. Lawson (originally Lassen), who went on to fame as publisher of the Chicago *Daily News*. Anderson, an indefatigable promoter, saw to it that every immigrant train arriving in Chicago was met and that free copies of his paper were given to any Norwegian who could not afford to buy it. The *Skandinavan* thus went out onto the vast prairies with a blessing on its head.

Another reason for the success of the *Skandinavan* was that it was an integral part of a larger publishing enterprise—something not at all unusual with the foreign language press. The paper had a *Boghandel* ("book trade") which was very productive and published some 500 titles until to 1941.[15] These included novels, works dealing with Norwegian history, and many other topics. In addition to its books, *Skandinavan* offered a "Husbibliothek" ("Home Library"), a monthly publication for women readers. Edited by Ingeborg Rasmussen, a member of the newspaper's editorial staff for many years, the target audience was naturally the Norwegian housewife. But Rasmussen, like many of her female contemporaries on staff for foreign language papers, was interested in wider social issues, particularly women's suffrage and the opportunities for women outside the home.

It is nearly impossible to make any generalizations about the content and function of the foreign language papers in America during their great years between 1880 and 1930. Most of them made an effort to bridge the gap between the new world and the old. Some immigrants were rapidly assimilated into American society and rapidly accepted English as their principal language. Some, often the "old folk," preferred the home language and newspapers printed in it. For the vast majority, foreign language papers were a supplement to the easily available English papers, which invariably carried a great deal more news. Second-generation citizens most commonly used their foreign language papers to sustain a bond to the culture of their homeland, a bond that became more tenuous or purely nostalgic with the passage of time.

Whatever the case, foreign language papers ran the gamut from the few city dailies like the *Staats-Zeitung* which were nothing but variants of the English dailies, to small-sheet monthlies that could do little more than serve up news of some immediate community or comforting messages from back home. The former was the most characteristic pattern. It certainly was the norm for most Norwegian papers as well as for Chinese and Japanese papers and many others. On the other hand, some small foreign language papers principally served as a pipeline back to the old world. Such was the case with the few newspapers appealing to immigrants from Switzerland. The Swiss immigration was small, most of it concentrated in the Midwest, most of it German-language. (A few Italian Swiss settled in California.) A Swiss paper was established in Cincinnati, but later moved to Tell City, Indiana, the center of Swiss immigration in that state. This was a German-language paper called the *Volksblatt*, which consisted almost exclusively of news items from Switzerland and a small literary section.[16]

To give some idea of the difficulty of finding categories to describe the function of the foreign language press in America, one could hardly do better than to mention the large number and the cultural significance of Yiddish newspapers in the United States. There were an enormous number of these papers between 1880 and World War II—most being in New York, of course—but what was most remarkable, at the height of their prosperity, they outstripped even the German papers in circulation, if never affluence. What makes the story of these papers especially fascinating is that they form a chapter in a larger picture of Jewish immigration to America that went back to colonial times. Curiously, they reversed the usual pattern in which foreign language papers gave way to English papers. The first Jewish papers in America were written in English. German and Yiddish papers came only later.

The reason for this is not hard to find. Before the middle of the nineteenth century the number of Jews in the United States was exceedingly small. The first group of Jews to land on American soil were twenty-three Sephardic Jews who settled in New Amsterdam in 1654. This immigration was opposed by the irascible governor Peter Stuyvesant, but forced on him by the Dutch West India Company which had established the colony. These first Jewish immigrants had no synagogue, but had a burial ground near present-day Chatham Square in New York City. Their numbers did not substantially increase by further immigration. By the end of the American Revolution there were apparently only two to three thousand Jews in the United States, most of them also Sephardic Jews from Spain or Portugal.

Eventually there would be two sizable waves of Jewish immigration to the United States—the first between 1850 and 1880 consisting of Jews from Germany and Austria-Hungary, most of them German-speaking; the second between 1880 and World War I from eastern Europe, most of these Yiddish-speaking. This last group was a tidal wave that eventually inundated all of the previous Jewish immigrant groups. Before these two waves, the Jews were so few in number that they had little choice but to be assimilated linguistically. The 50,000 Jews in the United States in 1850 (one-third of them in New York), were English-speaking.

For this reason the first Jewish publication in America was an English language monthly, *The Jew*, founded in 1823 by Solomon Henry Jackson, the city's first Jewish printer.[17] After this a few English language papers, journals, and magazines were established for the Jewish community. The situation changed considerably with the influx of German-speaking Jews. This was a diverse group—many arrived with the "forty-eighters," these mostly educated; a few were wealthy men who merged into high finance or established successful businesses. Some, however, were poor and became peddlers, ragpickers, or junk dealers. Few had any experience with farming so they had to stick to the cities where the road upward was hard. Still, by dint of hard enterprise and strong support from their families, many climbed the American success ladder in a generation or two. Most of the German Jews quickly learned English, and when they did read about their own community it was in English-language publications, but some in the big cities read German dailies.

The next wave of Jewish immigration—that of the mostly Yiddish-speaking Jews from eastern Europe—was not so easily assimilated. The first problem was with the magnitude of the influx, which began slowly enough in the 1880s but became a torrent in the early years of the twentieth century. In the 1880s some 200,000 eastern European Jews came to the

United States; in the 1890s some 500,000; in the period between 1900 and 1914, about 1.5 million. Some of these had skills that could not easily be transferred to the new world; others had lived in small agricultural communities and floundered helplessly in the large American cities in which most of them settled. The majority came to cities like New York, Philadelphia, and Baltimore where their presence could hardly be overlooked. By 1910, nearly one-fourth of the population of New York City consisted of these newcomers, most of them crowded into tenements on the lower east side, with others pushing into equally squalid conditions in the Williamsburg and Brownsville sections of Brooklyn or central Harlem. The world of these immigrants and the frequently wretched circumstances of their lives was well described in Jacob Riis's *How the Other Half Lives* (1890) and many subsequent works.

Yiddish is a Germanic language with Slavic and Hebrew elements. Most of the immigrants speaking it arrived from the "Pale of Settlement"—Poland, Ukraine, Lithuania. Most were literate but not highly educated, so transition to American life was difficult. In New York many went into the needle trades or worked in cigar factories or other small "sweatshops." Some were street peddlers, but most were desirous of improving their lot, and there was a narrow stratum of an intellectual elite ready to help them out.

Yiddish newspapers appeared fairly early. The first was the *Yidische Tseitung* ("Yiddish Journal"), published in New York in 1870. It did not enjoy a long life, dying seven years later. But its subtitle gives some idea of the aspirations that would always characterize the Yiddish press. It was called "A Weekly Paper of Politics, Religion, History, Science and Art." The first daily was the *Post*, which appeared in 1871, but this, too, was short-lived. It was not until 1897 that the most famous and long-lasting of the Yiddish papers made its debut. This was the *Forverts*, variously the "Jewish Daily Forward," or *Forward*. The paper's great success can be attributed to its determined effort to address the needs of the millions of newer immigrants, few of them intellectuals, as they grappled with the working conditions of the sweatshops and the living conditions of the tenements. At the same time the paper also attempted to forge some kind of cultural unity in the Jewish community. The thrust of the *Forward* was a socialistic philosophy. It was devoted to the reform and trade union movements, and thus did a remarkable job of addressing the actual concerns of the multitude.

The *Forward* took as its editor in 1901 one of the legendary figures of American journalism, Abraham Cahan. He remained the guiding light of the paper until his death a half-century later. Cahan was born in Lithuania in

1860 and was educated at the Teachers College in Vilnius. He arrived in New York in 1882, before the large waves of immigration from his homeland began. A revolutionary in his own country, he quickly allied himself with the socialist movement in the United States and started a socialist paper within a few years. At the same time, he rapidly learned the English language and spent some of his early years teaching it to newcomers. When the large waves of immigrants began arriving he agonized over the questions of how they should be reached, whether they should be Americanized, and how their native culture should be preserved. As late as the 1890s the newcomers were faced with having to read Yiddish papers that were written in a kind of stilted cultural Yiddish. It was either that or the German papers, or papers in Hebrew, which were then few in number and most of them ephemeral.

When Cahan launched his early socialist paper *Di Neie Tzeit* ("The New Era") in 1886 he began using the simplest form of Yiddish, avoided the pretentious-sounding "Deitschmerisch" used by his educated contemporaries and heard on the Jewish stage.[18] He wanted to reach the multitude with the language they had learned at the family hearth. When he became editor of the *Forverts* he followed the same approach. His aim was to reach the masses, much as Pulitzer and Hearst were doing for English readers, although perhaps for somewhat more soulful reasons. Cahan had the double objective of making the new world intelligible while retaining cultural and spiritual traits of the Pale of Settlement. He regarded socialism as the ideal that would make the new world understandable and tolerable—indeed he thought it to be the secularized form of Judaism.

As to preserving tradition and the home culture, the *Forward* devoted much of its space to presenting the best work of Yiddish writers then available—poets, dramatists, novelists. Among the writers who contributed to the *Forward* over the years were Sholem Asch, Abraham Reisin, Sholem Aleichem, and Isaac Bashevis Singer. Equally important were Cahan's efforts to form a close bond with his readers. One of his major contributions to this end was a column called "Bintl Brief" ("Bundle of Letters") in which readers wrote to the editor with the problems they encountered in everyday life. Cahan and his associates responded with warmth, intelligence, and sympathy. The "Bintl Brief" was one of the superb achievements of American journalism, and in many ways it was characteristically American.

The *Jewish Daily Forward* became a surprising financial success. After the waves of immigration from eastern Europe beginning in 1903 its circulation soared. The Forward Association built a ten-story building at 173–175 East Broadway in New York. (It is now an historical landmark, although the paper moved uptown in the 1970s.) In 1923 the *Forward* had the largest circulation of any foreign language newspaper in the United States—153,639.[19] Abraham Cahan was now among the most illustrious Jewish figures in the United States, and not only among Jews. He wrote a great deal in English for other papers such as the New York *World* and the *Evening Post*. His work also appeared in the *Atlantic Monthly*. For four years he collaborated with Lincoln Steffens on the *Commercial Advertiser*. He wrote several novels in English, the most famous of which is probably *The Rise of David Levinsky* (1917). Henry Mencken praised this work fulsomely in *The Smart Set* and formed a lifelong friendship with the *Forward* editor. Although the *enfant terrible* of Baltimore could hardly have been taken by Cahan's socialism, he remembered the man himself with high respect. He described Cahan in 1918, then fifty-eight years old, as "a notably handsome man with an erect bearing," a man with "a mop of wavy hair that gave him, somehow, a dignified appearance."[20]

Although the *Forward* became the shining star in the firmament of the Yiddish press, it was hardly the only Yiddish-paper of importance. There were, over time, twenty-seven Yiddish-language dailies in New York,[21] and some of them competed vigorously with the *Forward*. There was the *Yiddishes Tageblatt* ("Jewish Daily News") that went back to 1885. It contained an English page and was mostly for the orthodox. Also successful for many years was the *Morgen Zhurnal* ("The Morning Journal"), established in 1901, which was conservative and Republican in politics. It had a circulation of 111,000 by 1916. There was the *Tog*, established in 1914, as a liberal pro-Zionist paper. Later there were far left leaning papers like *Morgen Freiheit* (1922), and of course there were always religious papers. Besides New York there were Jewish dailies in Cleveland and Philadelphia. Chicago had the first Yiddish daily outside of New York, the *Yiddisher Kurier*, founded in the 1890s; it was followed by a number of others.[22]

The history of the foreign language press in America has always been one of ebb and flow. Old, solid papers die and others replace them. Members of ethnic groups are assimilated and no longer desire to read the language of their parents or grandparents. The Yiddish press is as good an example of this as any. Having reached a pinnacle in circulation in about 1923–24, the dailies began to disappear one by one as Yiddish speakers were assimilated and not refreshed by new immigration. After the Nazi genocide it was clear that there was no longer a stock of Yiddish-speaking natives, and that this charming and eccentric language that has added so much to American English (having given us words like bagel, chutzpah, kibitzer, kosher, schlemiel, or the "Yinglish" beatnik, and many other locutions and catch phrases) is a dying language that cannot be resuscitated. There are no longer any Yiddish dailies in North America. The *Forward* was the last to give up, going to weekly publication in 1983. It became an English-language paper—and a lively one—in 1990.

The fate of the German-language press was still more dramatic. At one time constituting as much as one-third of the foreign papers printed in America, the German papers were dealt a cruel blow by World War I. Before America entered the war most of them sided with Germany against Britain, so they were forced to do a torturesome about-face in 1917. Most of them came around to support the American cause and the war effort, although a few were closed by restrictive and, some would say, undemocratic legislation during the war years. Too, most of these papers staggered under the force of anti-German hysteria that was rife at that time. German language instruction was discontinued in many high schools. German names and words were banished: sauerkraut became "liberty cabbage" for a while, and hamburger became Salisbury steak. "Schmierkase" became cottage cheese—and never changed back. (These frenzied corrections were by no means restricted to the United States. The British royal family changed its name from Saxe-Coburg and Gotha to Windsor in 1917.)

The German press picked up slightly in the 1920s, but then began a slow decline. The famous *New Yorker Staats-Zeitung* merged with one of its major rivals, the *Herold* in 1934, and continued as a daily until 1975, although clearly this and other surviving German papers were not read by people who *needed* them, but only by the few who wanted some nostalgic link to the heritage of the past.

A similar fate met the presses of a number of other foreign language groups that were once gigantic, the Italian papers being a good example. There were many Italian dailies in cities with big Italian populations, and these papers enjoyed a brisk circulation, especially in neighborhoods that were well defined. The leading Italian paper in the United States for over a century was *Progresso*, founded in 1880. In New York's "Little Italy" this paper enjoyed an enormous circulation in the 1930s and began a slow decline only after World War II. It struggled along gamely until 1988, however, and then gave up.

The gap was immediately filled by *America Oggi* ("America Today"), which began the same year, but conditions of reaching the target audience had completely changed. Nominally, *America Oggi* is a New York paper, but its offices are located in Westwood, New Jersey. It has a circulation of about 30,000. Its editor, Andrea Mantineo, reported to the New York *Times* that "our readers have moved and spread out, and that makes it difficult for us to track them down."[23] Newsstand sales of such papers are now of minor significance. Most of them go out in the mail.

Editors of some of the older papers use all the modern techniques for reaching new readers or members of the younger generation. Some use games, contests, or giveaways. Others have solved their circulation problems by going bilingual or running a few pages in English. However, if there is any doubt about the resiliency of the foreign language press in America, one can always point to the crop of newcomers that have miraculously appeared as if from thin air. The last decades of the twentieth century have seen the appearance of many new papers in Latino, Chinese, and Russian. There are now sixty Vietnamese newspapers in the United States, most of them on the West Coast. They enjoy considerable success. The advertising revenues are good.

America, it has long been said, is a melting pot. People give up their old ways, their home language, and become Americans. Perhaps. But the process of melting never seems to end, and as long as it goes on, foreign language newspapers will probably continue to be an important presence, a much valued ingredient, in our national life.

16

Tabloids

In the first two decades of the twentieth century many hoped that yellow journalism would become a mere footnote in history—a disagreeable reminder of the shameful events leading up to the Spanish-American War. On the other hand, the forces of sensationalism had never been completely stifled. William Randolph Hearst was still on the scene, and with his political ambitions dampened, he began in earnest his quest to buy up newspapers around the country, most of them filled up with his own trashy boilerplate, and appealing, as usual, to the lowest common denominator. If there had been any hope that yellow journalism would completely burn itself out, Hearst's vigorous acquisitions in those years provided baleful evidence to the contrary.

An even more obvious sign that yellow journalism was still alive in the 1920s was the appearance of a new kind of newspaper: the tabloid. The tabloid was a small-format newspaper, about half the size of the typical daily paper, and thus easy to tuck under the arm and open up on the subway or streetcar. The format itself was not invented in the 1920s. Most newspapers of the early republic were of tabloid size. The "bedsheet papers" that had become almost universal by 1920 were products of the nineteenth century. What characterized the new tabloids was a renewed dedication to sensationalism and a strong dependence on illustration, especially photographs. In this second incarnation tabloids were to have a great impact on American journalism. Of course sensationalism had been used with success since the first appearance of the penny papers in the 1830s. Illustrated papers had also been tried before. So none of the ingredients of the 1020s-style tabloid newspaper were completely novel. Still, the total package had quite an impact.

The tabloid daily that Americans came to know in the 1920s was an English invention. Its inventor was a young man of "humble middle-class origins" named Alfred Harmsworth, one of the most successful newspaper publishers of all time. Harmsworth (who later became a baronet—Lord Northcliffe) got into the newspaper business in the 1880s with a human-interest weekly called *Answers*; it was intended for working-class readers who were marginally literate, but scantily educated. In 1894 Harmsworth got into big-time journalism by establishing a paper called the *London Evening News*; two years later he founded another paper called the *London Daily Mail*, cheerfully billed as "the busy man's newspaper." It was clear that Harmsworth had been carefully following the innovations of Pulitzer and Hearst in the United States, for his new papers brushed aside the long, tiresome columns of type that characterized traditional English newspapers and replaced them with big headlines, racy stories, features, contests, and other simple confections.

So successful were these efforts that in 1905 Harmsworth looked around for new fields to conquer. He established a paper called the *Daily Mirror*, which was to be "written *by* women *for* women." This was not a success. Looking for a way out Harmsworth reduced the price of the paper and shrank the size. The *Daily Mirror* was transformed into what was called a "half-penny illustrated"—the English name for tabloid. This revised version of the *Mirror* was simplistic, sensational, brisk, amusing, and full of pictures. Circulation skyrocketed: by 1909 the paper was selling 1,000,000 copies a day, the largest circulation of any newspaper in the world at the time.[1]

In spite of Harmsworth's success in this area, no American publisher seemed willing to adopt the idea. Even before he made a tabloid of his *Mirror* Harmsworth paid a visit to Joseph Pulitzer in New York, and as a courtesy was allowed to produce, for a single day, what he thought the "newspaper of the twentieth century" would be. On January 1, 1901, the *World* was printed in a tabloid format and it sold an extra 100,000 copies. Pulitzer, however, thought that this rise in circulation was only due to people's curiosity, so no attempt was made to follow up. Nearly two decades would pass before the idea came to fruition in America.

Harmsworth was right that the United States was ripe for this experiment, although there were ample reasons for skepticism. New York had already had a tabloid-format illustrated paper in the 1870s, the *Daily*

Graphic. The paper was filled with line drawings (photography was not yet available for newspaper printing) and tended toward the sensationalistic. The venture was not a great success, however, so the concept seemed an ill omen. A few other similar experiments were made but they were not long-lasting either. One tabloid that did have an enormous success was the weekly *Police Gazette*, and it wallowed freely in all of the tawdriness and titillation of the day—grisly train wrecks, rapes, murders, child abductions, pugilistic contests, police raids on "disorderly houses," and every pecca-dillo then considered an affront to prim Victorian society. Although it was a smashing success, few newspaper publishers thought of it as a newspaper even though it was printed on newspaper stock. Always on the edge of por-nography, it was mainly read by lusty male enthusiasts at barber shops, race tracks, or stables.

It was only after World War I that the daily tabloid newspaper in the mod-ern sense made its appearance in the United States. Two young men from Chicago were willing to give it a try. They were the grandsons of Joseph Medill, and, since 1914, publishers of the Chicago *Tribune*: Joseph Medill Patterson and Robert R. McCormick. The two cousins had served in the army during the war and on numerous occasions in France had discussed the possibility of starting a Harmsworth-style tabloid in the United States, probably in New York. (Competition for their own paper in Chicago would have been an unwelcome idea.) The cousins had discussed the idea with Harmsworth who not only gave them encouragement, but threatened that if they did not come out with a New York tabloid he would do it himself.

Immediately at war's end plans were laid for what would become the New York *Daily News*. In Chicago, the *Tribune* had been rolling in money during the war, so there were few doubts about financing. Nor were there doubts about which of the two men would run the New York paper. Joseph Medill Patterson, moved by sympathies for the masses and possessed of so-cialistic leanings (or perhaps only pretensions), was the ideal candidate. His ostentatiously patrician cousin, McCormick, who never had any desire to do anything but run a true-blue Republican paper, was glad to stay in Chi-cago and publish "The World's Greatest Newspaper." The split worked out perfectly for both men.

The New York tabloid had its birth on June 26, 1919, and was printed on rented presses of the *Evening Mail* in City Hall Place. Originally called the *Illustrated Daily News*, the title would be shortened before the year was over to the *Daily News*. The paper attempted to follow the formula of Harmsworth's *Daily Mirror* as closely as possible, although in the begin-ning most of the features and photographs were coming in from the Chicago

Tribune. The first edition of the paper, very cheaply printed, had a huge picture on page one of the Prince of Wales, due to visit the United States later in the summer and already a heartthrob of American women. There were abbreviated news stories throughout, all playing up some human-interest angle. On the back page there were pictures of some lovelies who had entered a beauty contest the paper had run as a promotional device.

While using all of the enticements and techniques that had been successful in London, the first edition of the paper was not very impressive to New York's newspaper observers. The New York *Sun* made fun of this pint-sized street urchin, and most editors in the city were certain that they had little to fear from this cheap-looking newcomer. William Randolph Hearst, whose papers had the most to fear, had equipped a tabloid plant at 55 Frankfort Street in case the *Daily News* should be a success, but the initial public response was unenthusiastic so he gave up the idea of entering the market. Throughout the summer of 1919 the interlopers from Chicago were not having much success; circulation slumped, and most people in the know predicted an early death for the paper. There was one local sage who thought otherwise. Carr V. Van Anda, editor of the New York *Times*, felt certain that the paper would make the grade. "This paper," he said, "should reach a circulation of 2,000,000."[2]

By midsummer of 1919 the paper's circulation dipped to 26,000 and two of its four reporters were fired. It looked for a while as if all of the excess profits from the *Tribune* were going down the drain. Within a year, however, the paper began to take hold among New York's multitudes. Even on newsstands that stocked only foreign language papers the *News* sold well because of its front-page pictures. (The usual practice at that time was to have one glaring headline and from one to four photographs, sometimes with extensive captions.) Inside, the paper featured short, snappy news stories, with major public issues given highly abbreviated treatment. Many items that would appear in the *Times* were given no treatment at all. The paper was strong on puzzles, contests, comics, and, after the first year, sin and sex. It was easy for intellectuals and cultural critics to assume that the paper was read only by subliterates or morons, but the writing was good, and would get better, and the mix of materials was very well crafted to meet a perceived public demand.

Within a year of its birth, the *Daily News* was doing splendidly. Two editions, each of twenty pages, were being printed, with a circulation of 150,000. By 1922 the circulation reached 400,000, and by 1924, 750,000. It was the largest selling daily newspaper in the country by the time it was five years old. The magical figure of 2,000,000, predicted by Carr Van Anda, was actually reached—in 1940![3]

Needless to say, the meteoric rise of the *News* gave great discomfiture to William Randolph Hearst who had earlier scoffed at the tabloid idea but now found the circulation of his morning *American* so threatened that he had no choice but to enter the field. In numerous public utterances he remained contemptuous of the tabloid idea, but he eventually reached the point where he had to react if he was to continue to compete at the low end of the newspaper spectrum. To test the waters he changed his Boston paper, the *Advertiser*, to a tabloid. But Boston, always called a "poor farm" by newspaper publishers, proved to be the wrong place for experimentation, as Frank Munsey had found out earlier. Accordingly, Hearst laid plans to confront the *Daily News* directly on its own turf. For a short while he tried a tabloid "supplement" to the *American*, and, when this did not work, he gave birth to his own daily tabloid in New York. It was called the *Daily Mirror*, and it appeared on the street on June 24, 1924.[4]

This new entry into the tabloid market resembled nothing but a carbon copy of the *Daily News*, and if anyone wondered what the *Mirror* mirrored, the answer would have been: the *Daily News*. The typography and general appearance of the two papers were almost identical. Hearst directed his editors to follow slavishly everything the *News* did. The *News* ran a "Tongue Teaser" contest, so the *Mirror* had a column of "Tongue Twisters." Hearst made no effort to deny that his paper was a copycat version, a flagrant imitation, of the *News*. The front page of the *Mirror* closely resembled the front page of the *News*. The Hearst people hoped that a lot of people would buy the paper under the impression that they were getting the *News*.

The main difference between the two papers was that the *Mirror* was an even more skimpy, low-flying paper than its role model; it carried far less serious news and wallowed far more unabashedly in the troughs of gossip, sin, and scandal. Hearst's formula for the paper was that it be "90 percent entertainment, 10 percent information." And the formula apparently worked; after only two years the *Mirror* had a circulation of 370,000. Since another new tabloid, Bernarr Macfadden's *Daily Graphic* was finding at least 200,000 readers, and since none of the city's principal papers seemed to be affected by this tabloid glut, one can only conclude that the tabloids had tapped into a group of citizens who simply had not bought newspapers before.

By 1926 the tabloid mania was at full tilt, and the tabs in New York went at each other with hammer and tong. The latest entry in the field, the *Daily Graphic*, was probably the most shamefully libidinous of the three papers.

Founded by health and physical culture faddist Bernarr Macfadden, who had made a fortune on two magazines, *Physical Culture* and *True Story*, the *Graphic* earned its notoriety by an effusive use of photography, even fake photography when necessary. Using a technique called "composography," by which photographs could be torn apart and merged with file photographs that might be posed for expressly by models, the *Graphic* was able to produce pictures illustrating news scenes not otherwise obtainable. For example, all of the tabloids carefully followed the marriage of an elderly and wealthy real estate magnate Edward Browning to a fifteen-year-old shopgirl, Frances Heenan. Browning became known to all the tabloids as "Daddy Browning"; his youthful inamorata was called "Peaches." Their marital bumps and pratfalls were fully covered by the *News* and the *Mirror*, but only the *Graphic* could render the intimacies of their honeymoon. It showed "Peaches" in her negligee, clutching a teddy bear, or the bridal couple having a pillow fight. The *Graphic* "got" these pictures by hiring models to pose for the desired scenes and then removing the heads and putting file photos of "Peaches" and "Daddy" in their place. Of course the *Graphic* clearly marked these as "Composite Photographs," thus avoiding the inevitable lawsuits. Adding this shameless twist to the trend toward lurid photojournalism only amplified the cries against tabloid journalism—"gutter journalism" it came to be called, or "sewer journalism."

Bernarr Macfadden, the old beet-juice drinker and muscle flexer, had no trouble justifying nudity in his paper on the grounds that it was "healthy." (He later went on to publish nudist magazines.) He justified running a "composite" photograph of King George and Queen Mary of England taking a bath together in a large marble tub, as a "healthful" influence on society. Whether titillating or merely grotesque, journalistic liberties of this kind could only give a bad name to the profession.

The *News* and the *Mirror* never stooped to these levels, but by the mid-1920s they were in fierce competition with each other to cover the most sensational and lurid happenings of the day. If there was some nasty society divorce, some gruesome murder or high-profile criminal trial (and the 1920s seem to have been richly endowed with these), the tabloids devoted pages upon pages to them. The celebrated Hall-Mills murder case in New Jersey became the special preserve of the *Mirror*, which took literally thousands of photographs during the trial and ran many of them on a daily basis.

In the spring of 1927 all of the tabloids were busy covering the trial of corset salesman Judd Gray, who helped murder the husband of his sweetheart, Mrs. Ruth Snyder. The *Daily News* got the best on this one. When it came time for the guilty lovers to die in the electric chair, *News* photographer Tom Howard, against prison rules, strapped a tiny camera to his ankle and got a picture of Mrs. Snyder straining in the chair just after the juice had been turned on. This shot filled the whole of the first page in the next morning's paper. It sold 250,000 extra copies. Large public demand brought forth another 750,000 copies of the front page later on.[5] While this was hardly Pulitzer Prize photojournalism, the picture remains one of the most famous news photos of all time.

Sensationalistic tabloid journalism reached its apogee in the mid-1920s. The Depression brought a check on the public's appetite for scandal, even if it never completely eradicated it. The *Graphic*, hardly a real newspaper in any case, went into bankruptcy in 1932. Hearst's *Mirror* continued to lag behind the *Daily News* but struggled on until 1963. Hearst sold the paper during the Depression but then bought it back. It is said that the *Mirror* was kept afloat by the daily column of Broadway roustabout Walter Winchell and a few good sports writers. The *News* is no longer the circulation leader of the nation at the end of the twentieth century, but it continues as the subway rider's favorite tabloid. Its circulation is now below a million.[6]

Of course the sensational tabloid spread far and wide in the 1920s; New York was not its only home. Following pretty much in the pattern of the *Daily News* were the Boston *Daily Record*, the Philadelphia *News*, the New Orleans *Tribune*, and several others. None survived to a happy maturity. It might be fair to say that some of the appeal of the 1920s-style tabloid survives in the so-called supermarket tabloids of the late twentieth century. The writing in these papers (magazines we should probably call them) is much more banal and insipid than the daily tabs of old; the photography far less clever and imaginative.

With the dramatic success of the tabloid trend, it is not surprising that there would be an effort to experiment with nonsensational or "clean" tabloids. Among those willing to try this route was Cornelius Vanderbilt Jr., an heir to the Vanderbilt fortune, who established the Los Angeles *Illustrated News* as well as similar tabloids in San Francisco and Miami. These papers built up sizable circulations, but never garnered the support of advertisers. They eventually withered. The Washington *News* and the Philadelphia *Sun* were also of this type but did not enjoy long and prosperous lives. There were a few success stories: the Chicago *Times* was established in 1929 and attempted to be a tersely written mainstream paper in tabloid format. When Marshall Field III combined this paper with his Chicago *Sun* in 1947, he retained the tabloid format. The Chicago *Sun-Times* has been and continues to be a leading paper, written and edited on a high level. In New York, the Long

Island *Newsday*, founded in 1940, became a highly successful and even respected paper in the New York City area.[7]

It might be possible to lament the rise of the salacious tabloid in the 1920s and applaud its retreat from daily journalism in the years since. On the other hand the tabloid was not an altogether deleterious influence on American journalism. It was, at the very least, a dash of pepper or smelling salts. It got many a mainstream publisher jumping to his feet looking for ways to infuse new vitality into papers that had become sleepy or moribund. The presence of photography could no longer be denied, and the newly found art of photojournalism did much to breathe fresh air into the lives of hidebound publishers. The New York *Times*, for example, needed such a transfusion in the 1920s. When the decade began, it was a rare day when the *Times* would have even a single picture on page one—just the inevitable ribbons of type. Within a few years pictures began to appear, and today, no issue of the New York *Times* can be found without all kinds of photographs, maps, and other illustrations. The slimmed-down national edition of November 8, 1996, for example, displayed two large photographs and a map on page one. Altogether there were on that day forty-six photographs and nineteen charts, graphs, maps, and other visuals (exclusive of advertising illustrations).

The photography revolution, spawned in large part by the appearance of the tabloids in the 1920s, did not destroy "print" journalism as some feared at the time; instead it provided a boost—a zest and vitality—that was very much needed in the face of brisk competition from radio and news magazines. Forever after, "print" in the newspaper business would have to mean more than "type" on paper.

17

A Bright and Shining Moment

In the 1920s the American newspaper reached the pinnacle of its glory—and influence. It would shortly be challenged by radio, that new "electric" medium of mass communication, although throughout the 1920s radio would be a weak force as a conveyor of news. Nightly "newscasting" did not begin until the late 1920s, at which time the networks hired former newspapermen like H. V. Kaltenborn, Floyd Gibbons, and Lowell Thomas to read news over the air, most of it coming from major newspapers or press services. It was not until the Munich crisis of 1938 that the major radio networks began to assemble their own large news-gathering staffs.[1]

It was a great time for the press; the better newspapers sparkled now as they had never sparkled before. News-gathering and professional standards for reporters, editorial writers, and columnists were at their zenith. Public trust in newspapers would probably never again be as high as it was at that time. The papers' owners were delighted as circulation and advertising revenues soared. In 1926 *Editor and Publisher* declared that "this was the greatest era in newspaper history. . . . Newspapers have never before been so large in volume, complete in contents, and lavish in service." By the mid-1920s, *Editorand Publisher* reported aggregate daily circulation reached a record high of 36,000,000; advertising revenues reached $775,000,000.[2]

It was, of course, a time of general prosperity, and a great many up-to-date papers, metropolitan dailies, built new office buildings, some of them luxurious—a far cry from the tatterdemalion, down-at-heel quarters that traditionally housed newspaper offices and plants. At the very beginning of the decade, for example, the Chicago *Tribune* built an office skyscraper appropriately called the "Tribune Tower," which replaced a 1902 building that was still called the "new" Tribune Building. The grandiose Tribune Tower, doubtless far more elegant than Pulitzer's "Dome" of the 1880s, was excoriated by modern architects for its gothic battlements and conceits, but it seemed appropriate for an aggressive booster paper that unashamedly called itself "The World's Greatest Newspaper." The *Daily News* in Chicago also built an elegant new skyscraper. So, too, did the *Public Ledger* in Philadelphia, and later the tabloid upstart *Daily News* in New York.

During the 1920s newspapers experienced a prosperity and a popularity they would never again attain. Home delivery brought one, or even several, newspapers into the homes of most Americans on a daily basis. City street corners were invariably dotted with newsstands where bellicose urchins in checkered caps hawked the latest edition straight off the press with cries of "EXTRA! EXTRA!" Most metropolitan papers, morning and evening, seemed to have editions around the clock, using every possible pretext for extra editions—the landing of Lindbergh in Paris, the result of some famous criminal trial, the results of a knockdown in a prizefight or the score of a World Series game. People rushed to the street to get the latest news, "hot off the press."

During these years the newspaper as a cultural icon was always at the forefront of the American consciousness. Newspaper people played a pivotal role in popular culture—in the funny papers, in pulp fiction, in the movies. The newspaper reporter had become a popular folk hero by the 1920s, displacing other popular heroes of an earlier generation: the frontiersman, the whaler, the cowboy, the river pilot, and the railroad engineer. Ben Hecht and Charles McArthur, both with newspaper experience, wrote a popular Broadway comedy, *Front Page*, which also made a spectacular hit as a movie. By the late 1920s and early 1930s stories about working newspapermen became a magnet to moviegoers, and even the biggest starts, like Clark Gable and Frederic March, did not hesitate to accept roles as hard-boiled city reporters. (Gable in fact was in a number of such movies.) These roustabouts in $10 pants often wound up with an heiress at the end, usually believed to be a well-deserved fate by a public that was mesmerized by reporters and the workings of a metropolitan newspaper. Nor were the women left out—the movies and the funny papers had their girl "star reporters" as well. And the movie parts went to leading actresses like Glenda Farrell and Bette Davis.

There was something both luminescent and endearing about the newspaper scene in these last years before the dark clouds of the Depression closed in. Whatever excesses may have been characteristic of the age, and yes, this was the jazz age, the age of the flivver and the flapper, of Jersey Lightning and bathtub gin, of raccoon coats and college pranks, of flagpole sitting, the Ku Klux Klan and mah-jongg; it was an age of danger too, although people found that out only later. Above all it was an age of frenzied excitement and unbridled optimism. Newspapers had learned how to reflect all these things. At no other time in American history had so many people itched to get their hands on a daily newspaper. The newsboy's call of "Extra, Extra, Read All About It" was something of an aphrodisiac, a magnet, a Lorelei.

Newspapers, certainly the leading papers, seemed to have that ineffable quality we call personality, or spirit. Today workers in the mass media—newspapers or television—constantly lament that people do not trust them. The journalist or television investigative reporter seems to be linked with politicians and lawyers as objects of suspicion and distrust. The media megaliths they work for often have no personality at all. How different things were in the 1920s, when one had one's favorite newspaper with its quirky columnists and star reporters. They may well have had their illicit passions, but these could all be encompassed by human understanding. Thus, we took delight in reporters who snagged an heiress (even if it was only in the movies), or who took off to write the great American novel, or who ended up in an attic with cheap hooch behind the radiator. At least they had charm and it was the kind of charm ordinary people could understand. The pawns and pralines of today's newspapers and television networks seem as remote from us as a congressional caucus, as cold and self-serving as a lawyer's plea bargain.

In the 1920s the newspaper made one last stab at being an intimate part of our culture, of enjoying life with the general public, sharing fun with us. Newspapers for one last time aspired to be *our* newspapers, and they did it, for the most part, in a gay, uproarious, and lighthearted manner.

Sorrowfully, there were several notable papers that began a slide to oblivion in the 1920s. The venerable New York *Post*, one of the great American papers throughout the nineteenth century, was in serious trouble during these years and began a decline into mediocrity. (The onetime paper of Hamilton, Bryant, and Godkin eventually became a lurid Rupert Murdoch tabloid!) The *Sun* continued to be a highly respected home-delivery paper, maybe the best evening paper in New York, but, truthfully, it had not survived the machinations of Munsey and its days were also numbered.

From the perspective of leadership, it is necessary to point out that a great many publishers who dominated the newspaper field for several generations were passing from the scene in the 1920s. Victor F. Lawson of the Chicago *Daily News* died in 1924. Henry Watterson had given up the editorship of the Louisville *Courier-Journal* in 1919 and died two years later. William Rockhill Nelson had died back in 1915 and his paper went through some troubled years before regaining its full stature. Edwin A. Grozier, who had made a clear-cut success of the Boston *Post*, died in 1924. E. W. Scripps, his chain now in the firm grip of Roy W. Howard, died the same year. Frank Munsey died, unmourned, in 1926.

With some of the illustrious old warhorses passing from the scene, it might seem easy to conclude that the one-man domination of newspapers was weakening. But such was far from the case. Roy W. Howard was every bit the equal of Scripps in management. And if the colorful Nelson was no longer alive, the Midwest had his worthy successor in Gardner Cowles who became a similar press lord in Des Moines, Iowa, as owner of the *Register and Leader*. His family later became a big player in Minneapolis as well, buying up the *Star* and *Tribune* among other papers. And no more fanciful press lord can be imagined than Col. Robert R. McCormick of the Chicago *Tribune*. Sitting in regal splendor among the battlements of the Tribune Tower, McCormick ran a paper often described as pugnacious, bigoted, even rabid. (In a fury at the State of Rhode Island, Colonel McCormick once had the Rhode Island star gouged out of the flag prominently displayed on the front page of his paper.) But it was a paper that nobody could be indifferent to, and for a number of decades during the colonel's lifetime, the *Tribune* was the circulation leader among all non-tabloid newspapers in America.

Many major cities remained poorly served by newspapers during the prosperous 1920s. Washington D.C. had scarcely a paper worthy of a nation's capital. The *Post*, so famous today, was then an undistinguished Republican paper owned by playboy Edward B. "Ned" McLean, a onetime crony of President Harding. In Philadelphia, newspaper magnate Cyrus H. K. Curtis, publisher of the *Saturday Evening Post* and the *Ladies' Home Journal*, tried to be the Frank Munsey of Philadelphia, buying up the *Public Ledger*, the *Evening Telegraph*, the *Press*, and the *North American*. But Curtis was never as successful in creating top newspapers as he was in creating successful magazines. In his time, the Curtis papers were nearly all bested by the conservative-leaning *Evening Bulletin*.

In Baltimore the newspaper competition had been heavy, but spirited: both Hearst and Munsey owned papers there. The *Sun*, going back to the 1830s, was always the leading paper, and after 1920, with the Abell family out of the picture, and with Paul Patterson as president of the Sun Company and H. L. Mencken as perpetual gadfly, the *Sun* moved forward as a newspaper of the top rank.

Once again, however, New York proved in these years to be indisputably the newspaper capital of America. And if the tabloids seemed to demonstrate that New Yorkers had an unquenchable thirst for the low and tawdry, there was also plenty of evidence to prove that the city that had nurtured Greeley and Bennett, Bryant and Godkin, Dana and Pulitzer still had the guts to produce great newspapers.

There is ample evidence that this last decade before the Depression gave us something of a renaissance of newspapers. If proof be needed it can be found in the achievements of two newspapers of star quality in the 1920s, newspapers that would unfortunately not survive the twentieth century, but which would glisten brightly in the firmament for a time. The first was Joseph Pulitzer's *World*, reborn after the maestro's death and given a few more great years in the early 1920s before it went sadly to its grave. The other was the newly formed New York *Herald Tribune*, an amalgamation of the papers of Bennett and Greeley which, by common consent, had worn themselves out before the 1920s. In its revitalized form this newcomer showed a gargantuan talent for newspapering. The effulgence of the *World* and the *Herald Tribune*, even if short lived, even if puzzling in the course of human events, gives some idea of the force that American newspapers once exhibited, for here were two of the best newspapers ever published.

Looking back, the brief renaissance and then agonizing death of the *World* may be hard to understand by the vast majority of those living today—people born after 1931. But it cannot be forgotten that during the lifetime of Pulitzer, and even in its last years, the *World* was somehow *the* New Yorker's paper, and the newspaperman's paper as well. The *World* was the paper that a beginning reporter from Dubuque or Tucumcari wanted to work on. It was the paper of papers in the minds of journalists. And to its readers the *World*, for all its faults, was an institution that one could understand on a personal level. Probably no newspaper in American history had a stronger bond with its readers. It had dabbled in unseemly yellow journalism, had grown weak for a time, had grown thin and emaciated, but great masses of New Yorkers felt strong emotional ties to this, *their* paper; its eventual passing was like the passing of one's father or grandfather. When the *World* was about to go out of existence in 1931 a woman from Queens wrote in—and her letter was typical of thousands of others—pleading that the paper not be allowed to die: "As a grammar school girl I used to consume my breakfast with the *World* propped up against my sugar bowl. . . . If there is any way out of it don't give up the *World!* Save it for us."[3]

The *World* was a member of one's family; somehow it could always be trusted. By the early 1920s it hardly had the best news-gathering organization in the city—those laurels belonged to the *Times*—but the *World* was like one's best friend—not just a lofty institution. The *Times* had substance and authority; the *World* had something infinitely more agreeable to many people, it had personality. The same thing could be stated from the perspective of working newspapermen, reporters, and editors: the *World* always had high dramatic impact and sharp focus. More important, to the average New Yorker, it was universally believed it to be incorruptible.

When Joseph Pulitzer died in 1911 the *World* had already recovered from its "yellow phase" and was on the road to recovery. There were problems, serious in nature, that would hobble the paper toward the end. One was the legacy of Pulitzer himself. He was his paper's own wicked fairy godfather, laying a curse on his journalistic offspring even before his death, writing an inscrutable and poorly thought-out will. The two Pulitzer papers, the *World* and the St. Louis *Post-Dispatch*, were left to Pulitzer's three sons: Ralph, Joseph Jr., and Herbert. Ralph the eldest was expected to lead, but Herbert, only a boy when his father died, received six-tenths of the stock.[4] While Herbert emerged as little more than a playboy, Joseph Jr., in whom his father had no confidence, took over the *Post-Dispatch* and turned out to be the most skillful newspaperman of the lot—he went on to guide the St. Louis paper into its greatest era. Ralph surely possessed the knowledge and ability to run the *World* and did in fact do so until the late 1920s and with some success. But he was forever crimped and paralyzed by his father's lack of confidence, which may have accounted for some of the problems that plagued the paper at the end.

Still, Ralph, running the *World* after 1911, managed to preside over a remarkable transformation of the paper. He was, from the beginning, exceedingly lucky in having with him the greatest editorial page editor of his day, Frank I. Cobb, who was the moving spirit of the paper from 1905 until his death in 1923. Although the *World* did not neglect its traditional crusades, promotions, and sensational exploits, it turned away from the dregs of yellow journalism and back to the immense source of strength that the paper had in the 1880s.

Unfortunately Cobb died in 1923, surely a major blow to the *World*. Nonetheless, with the addition of men like Walter Lippmann and Arthur Krock there was little diminution in the quality of the editorial page. They were assisted as editorial writers by Maxwell Anderson and Laurence Stallings, later famous for their play *What Price Glory?,* by Charles Merz, who would subsequently become editor of the New York *Times*, and by Allan

Nevins, soon to be recognized as one of the great American historians. The *World* persisted in having the problem that it had even in Pulitzer's best days, a sharp contrast between lightweight news coverage and hard-edged and highly intellectual editorial commentary.

But in the early 1920s, even before Cobb's death, the news pages of the *World* also showed a decided improvement. Much of this was due to the powerful impact of a new managing editor, Herbert Bayard Swope, who took the reins in 1921. Swope had come up the ranks at the *World* and had been the paper's star reporter, a man of tremendous vigor and enterprise, a man of relentless memory, a man who seemed to be pals with everybody from the president to the corner shoeshine boy. One of his recent biographers referred to Swope as "the most charming extrovert in the Western world."[5] Swope had not reached his position at the top of the *World* through charm alone. He had been a great reporter in his day, perhaps the best in New York. He had won the first Pulitzer Prize for reporting in 1917. He had an encyclopedic memory for facts and could seldom be bested in quiz games by anyone on his staff. He seemed to know everything in the *World Almanac*, the *World*'s own prize reference source. Some people thought he knew everything else as well.

Immediately on taking over the editorship of the *World* Swope began to show his stuff. The writing on the news pages became tighter, lighter, more dramatic. Swope did not have as many news pages at his disposal as the *Times* or the *Tribune*, but Swope believed that he could wrap up the news with much more flair. But this did not lead to superficiality. Following the old fighting tradition of Pulitzer, it was decided to take some story, some issue, and go into it in real depth, arouse people's interest in a big way. Swope explained his philosophy of news handling in simple terms: "I take one story each day and bang the hell out of it."[6] The issues chosen were not sordid tales or tabloid confections; they invariably involved some major local or public policy issue.

Swope's greatest contribution to American newspaper history was his invention of what came to be called the "op-ed" page. Unable to take control of the editorial page itself, still in the able hands of Frank Cobb, Swope added a new page to his paper opposite the editorial page—thus its name, "op-ed"—and filled it with bright columnists, often contributions from writers outside the paper. In New York he had plenty of talent to choose from. Almost immediately Swope had two experienced journalists who wrote regular columns, Heywood Broun, with "It Seems to Me," and Franklin P. Adams ("F.P.A.") with his "Conning Tower." Both of these individuals were full-fledged members of the famous Algonquin Round Table, and through their efforts Swope was able to reach out to a great number of other New York artists, poets, and intellectuals as well as a wide variety of others who could pump gaiety and excitement into the paper. Through the doors of the Tower at 63 Park Row swung some of the most lively contributors in journalism. If they did not come in on their own, Swope, and people like Adams and Broun, who were among the most skilled logrollers of all time, would bring them in. Gathered under the gilded dome in the mid-1920s was probably the most gifted and exciting assemblage of writers ever found in one place on the planet.

Among those who wrote for the *World* during the Swope era were such luminaries as Alexander Woollcott, Dorothy Parker, George S. Kaufman, E. B. White, Ring Lardner, Marc Connelly, Edna Ferber, Russel Crouse, Samuel Hoffenstein, John O'Hara, Elinor Wylie, Albert Payson Terhune, Howard Dietz (who signed himself as "Freckles"), Irvin S. Cobb, H. L. Mencken, Will Rogers, H. G. Wells, and many others.

Even without these charming irregulars the *World* was well loaded with talent on its own staff. The paper had probably the best-known cartoonist in New York at the time, Rollin Kirby (winner of the first Pulitzer Prize for cartooning). Also on the staff of cartoonists were Bud Fisher and the inimitable H. T. Webster. The fourteenth and fifteenth floors of the "Golden Dome" housed the brain trust, with such heavyweights as Walter Lippmann, Arthur Krock, Allan Nevins, Charles Merz, Maxwell Anderson, and Laurence Stallings. There were also John L. Heaton and E. R. Paulin. There was James M. Cain, recently arrived from the Baltimore *Sun*, later the author of *The Postman Always Rings Twice*.

The *World* had peerless talent in other areas. For a long time they had the best music critic ever to write for an American newspaper, James Gibbon Huneker, who was followed by the gifted composer Deems Taylor. Harry Hansen ran the books page and was one of the most highly respected book reviewers in the nation. Robert Benchley also reviewed books for a while, and Quinn Martin was a pioneering film reviewer. The paper had some of the best foreign correspondents active in the 1920s: William Bolitho, John Balderston, and Samuel Spewack. During the years of high tide the paper also had some of the best star reporters in the field, among them Dudley Nichols, Oliver H. P. Garrett, Norman Krasna, Morris Markey, St. Clair Mc Kelway (the latter two would become staff writers for the *New Yorker* magazine), Martin Green, Donald Henderson Clarke, Joseph van Raalte, and C. S. Weinschenck.

Arthur Krock, who later moved on to an illustrious career at the *Times,* probably gave a perfect summary of the eminence of the *World* in the 1920s when he remarked that at no newspaper in the world was the atmosphere charged with more electricity and youthful energy. At no place else was the conversation so good (even though the food in the Dome's cafeteria was awful). To no working newspapermen were the words, "I'm from the *World*," filled with more portent and more pure joy. The paper itself was produced with aggressive independence, ingenuity, and color. "The *World* was a great newspaper; a compassionate and constructive force in the public interest; a lethal enemy of official sham and officially inspired misinformation, a literary product of the first rank in the essential categories of journalism on its highest level."[7]

Unfortunately the blaze of glory that showed from the great dome on Park Row would not be of long duration. This newspaper, which newspaper publishers and working newsmen around the country believed to be the standard newspaper of the world, the paper by which others would be judged, had its Achilles' heel, which brought it to the ground as the 1920s came to an end. The Achilles' heel was Joseph Pulitzer's poorly thought-out will and indecisiveness on the part of the family owners at the top.[8] A big mistake was made in 1925 when the price was raised from two to three cents. No other New York papers followed and the *World*'s circulation plummeted. Too, the morning edition was being strongly muscled-out by the new tabloids. Furthermore there had been numerous longstanding weaknesses in the business department. In 1928 Swope quit as editor and it seemed to be all downhill from there. With the Pulitzer sons indecisive the paper was sold in 1931 to Roy W. Howard, who killed the morning *World* and merged the afternoon paper with his own afternoon *Telegram*. In this form the name *World*, but not the old essence, continued for another thirty-five years. Alas, the name *World* can no longer be found on New York newsstands, and the once famous *World* dome at 63 Park Row was razed in 1954. Americans of the present day have little knowledge of what was, at one time, one of our leading cultural institutions.

One of the reasons for the decline of the *World* after 1925 was the appearance on the New York newspaper scene of a sprightly morning newcomer—the New York *Herald Tribune*. In a sense the newcomer was not new at all. It was a combination of two famous old papers, James Gordon Bennett's *Herald* and Horace Greeley's *Tribune*. The circumstances of the merger were curious and provide much more than a footnote in journalistic history. James Gordon Bennett Jr., the aging playboy and wine bibber, had died in Paris in 1918, and his paper, although still keeping a loyal following, had gotten into financial problems toward the end of his life. In 1920 the remains were sold to Frank Munsey, that shameless newspaper poacher whom Bennett often referred to scornfully as "that grocer." The deal with Munsey also included the legendary English-language Paris *Herald*.

Whitelaw Reid, the editor and publisher of the New York *Tribune* died in 1912, leaving his paper, with a circulation of only about 50,000, to his wealthy wife Elisabeth Mills Reid. Due to Whitelaw Reid's political aspirations and sorry neglect, the paper became moribund by 1912. Certainly it looked like the dullest paper in New York. Mrs. Reid was determined that her son, Ogden Mills Reid, should become the editor of the paper, and she was willing to pour any amount of money from her vast fortune into getting the paper back on track. Between 1912 and 1920 the stodgy *Tribune* was reinvigorated, "desolemnized" by Ogden Reid and some youthful colleagues. It was completely redesigned; pictures, maps, line drawings began to appear; headlines became larger; there was a graceful Sunday rotogravure section; expanded features; bylines were introduced, which gave way to livelier writers—and copy. A zesty youthful crowd came onto the paper. It is interesting to note that the columns of both Heywood Broun and Franklin P. Adams were started at the *Tribune*. Only later were these valuable features lured away by Swope at the *World*.

There continued to be a problem for both the *Herald* and the *Tribune*, however. There were too many morning newspapers in New York—seventeen English-language dailies in the city in 1923, a situation regularly complained about by Frank Munsey. On this point Munsey was right. The *Herald* and the *Tribune* were basically Republican papers chasing the same readership. Munsey was sure that the two papers would prosper if merged. Accordingly he approached Mrs. Reid and offered to buy the *Tribune*. The patrician Mrs. Reid, no more impressed by this bloodless newspaper grabber than anyone else in the journalistic community, refused to sell. Munsey pressed the issue a number of times, but Mrs. Reid and her son would not budge. Doubtless, however, they perceived the validity of Munsey's arguments. The two papers overlapped. After several months of sparring, Munsey took the opposite tack and offered to sell the *Herald* to the Reids, a somewhat bitter pill for him to swallow since the *Herald* was the paper of which he was the most proud. The Reids took over the *Herald* on March 17, 1924. Included in the $5 million price was the Paris edition of the paper, which would henceforth be known as the Paris *Herald Tribune*—to this day the most important American paper published in Europe.

At the time the *Herald* and the *Tribune* were combined into the New York *Herald Tribune*, the reputations of the two papers had been reversed; the *Herald*, long one of the most sparkling papers in the nation, had become dreary under the tutelage of Munsey; the *Tribune* had begun to shine. It was already coming to be known as the "writer's paper" in New York, attracting the most seasoned hands from the New York newspaper field. After the merger, and especially after 1925 when the *World* began its slide, the best and brightest wanted to work on the *Herald Tribune*.

The new paper was ready to take on New York. Already it had abandoned the aging Tribune Tower at 154 Nassau Street, and, moving with the tide, built a completely modern building on West 40th Street in New York, only a few blocks from the *Times*. This new building, which opened in 1923, had been carefully designed for modern newspaper production and was probably the best newspaper office in the country at the time. In a seven-story structure, devoted exclusively to the *Tribune*, the layout provided for the smooth flow of news from the editorial offices above to the composing, printing, and distributing functions on the lower floors—this in contrast to so many older newspaper offices, where layout was governed by outmoded nineteenth-century hierarchical functions.

Whenever the word layout is mentioned in connection with newspapers, the *Herald Tribune* still comes to the mind of professionals. There has probably been no newspaper in American history that better combined beauty of typography and layout with dignified presentation and news handling. The 1920s may have been a decade of gaudy exuberance, with the tabloids embodying the most garish taste of the era; the *Herald Tribune*, on the other hand, managed to capture the euphoria and youthful zest of the age without sacrificing dignity and high professional competence. Within a few years it would be hard to deny that the *Herald Tribune* was the most beautiful-looking newspaper in America.

Actually much of this typographical excellence came about several years before the merger. In 1916 the Reids hired away from the New York *Times* a brilliant editor named Garet Garrett. An old-fashioned up-the-ladder newspaperman, Garrett had started out in Chicago as a printer's apprentice, then worked himself up to the top at the *Times*. He was actually hired to revamp the financial news at the *Tribune*, but within a year he had been made managing editor. In this role he brought about many innovations, but perhaps the most important was to the typography and layout of the paper. In 1917 most American papers still ran monotonous columns of type and used a confusing jumble of different heads. The major headings were invariably all capital letters of different sizes and these muddied up the effect of the story below. Garrett selected a single typeface for the paper, one designed in the late eighteenth century by Giambattista Bodoni. It had both a classical beauty and high readability. Capital and lower-case letters were used in headings, along with a beautiful italic of the Bodoni family. Since the reading typeface had long descenders, there was more white space between the lines, so the text had a clean, spread-out, and elegant look.[9]

By the time the *Herald* and the *Tribune* merged, the *Tribune* was already an exceedingly handsome paper. The *Tribune*'s typography was naturally selected for the new paper, and page one was crowned by a striking logotype that featured, in addition to the paper's name, an allegorical dingbat that had been introduced back in 1866 to celebrate the twenty-fifth anniversary of the *Tribune*. Of course this was a splendid refinement, but it would have been of small consequence had the paper not followed suit with extreme attention to all aesthetic detail. However, more than typography was involved. There was always a strong effort to make some kind of harmony between the news mix and the appearance of a page. During the 1930s and 1940s the *Herald Tribune* had on its staff an eccentric and unheralded individual named Everett Kallgren, officially the night editor and known to the staff as "the Count." A man with only one eye—but that eye keener than the two of most men—the Count had the job of making up the pages, cutting things to fit, changing the headlines, creating in that day's paper a mosaic that would combine sensitivity to the news requirements with a keen sense of harmony and aesthetic balance. Never had a paper looked so airy and substantial at the same time. Little wonder that during Kallgren's tenure on the paper, the Ayer Cup for typographic excellence was awarded eight times to the *Herald Tribune*; the paper also received honorable mention twelve other times during this period—a record unmatched by any other paper.[10]

Ogden Reid and his wife, Helen Rogers Reid, ran the paper although it continued to be owned by Elizabeth Mills Reid until her death in 1931. Ogden Reid, who had been editor of the *Tribune* since his father's death, was a genial, mild-mannered Yale graduate who drifted into alcoholism in the 1930s and 1940s but who nonetheless loved the paper and was not without executive talent. Always standing behind him, some would say in front of him, was his tenacious wife, Helen, a Wisconsin girl who had once been Elizabeth Reid's secretary and later married the son of the family. A diminutive woman, barely five feet in height, she was an unstoppable dynamo. Nominally heading the advertising department, which she completely reinvigorated, she was always a force on the editorial floors as well. Often called "Queen Helen," sometimes affectionately, sometimes not, Helen Reid was the very picture of the newspaper matriarch so often portrayed in modern television drama. After her husband's death in 1947 she went on to be the publisher of the paper, acknowledged then for what she had long been, a major force in American journalism.

Because of Ogden Reid's somewhat loose and benign control, the day-to-day management of the *Herald Tribune* drifted largely into the hands of the senior editors and these, as luck would have it, were top rate. By the late 1920s the *Herald Tribune*, with the help of carefully chosen editors, was run meticulously like the most expensive Swiss watch. Dedication to high professionalism and craftsmanship filtered down to the rank and file.

One of the key figures on the *Herald Tribune* was a slight but dapper Texan named Stanley Walker, who became perhaps the most legendary city editor in American newspaper history. Author of a classic book on journalism entitled, appropriately, *City Editor,* Walker personally defied all of the stereotypes of the position. A man who seldom shouted or pounded his desk, he got his results by promoting the idea that city reporting was an important and dignified business. Reporters were called Mister. There was no screaming around the room, no mood of chaos or disorganized euphoria. Probably Walker's greatest ability was to pace himself, to keep everything on an even keel even when some maddening story was breaking. He probably gave as many orders to his minions as any city editor and talked on the phone as incessantly as any—to city councilmen, showmen, labor leaders, archbishops, visiting heads of government, aviators, taxi drivers—but always without seeming to become flustered. He had all the nervous energy of the fabled city editor, but delivered it with smooth torque. Within months of coming on the job he turned the city room of the *Herald Tribune* from the proverbial anarchistic rumpus room to a smooth high-toned operation.[11]

A great deal of Walker's success was due to the fact that he cared mightily about newspaper style. He knew well that he did not have the ability to compete with the *Times* in manpower and depth of coverage, but he could insist that what went into the paper be better written, more crisp, more colorful. He paid very close attention to style, he complimented reporters who turned in good copy, excoriated those drawn to pomposities or what he called "Taj Mahals of flubdub." His idea was always to instill pride in the men under him; instill the belief that they could turn out the best-written paper in New York, and for the most part they did. Although the Reids and the paper's business managers always saw themselves in competition with the *Times,* the reporters never saw it that way. The *Herald Tribune* was the real article; the *Times* was just another dull paper in their minds. By the mid-1930s, *Time* magazine had proclaimed that the *Herald Tribune* had the best city staff of any newspaper in the country.[12] And there developed a widely held belief that the *Herald Tribune* was the best written American paper as well.

Stanley Walker became city editor of the *Herald Tribune* in 1927 when he was thirty years of age. At this time, and during the next few years, as the

World lay dying, the paper became the kind of magnet for talent that the *World* had been in the early days of Swope. Among those on whose talents Walker could draw (although they were not all assigned to the city staff) were St. Clair McKelway, Alva Johnson, Beverly Smith, James T. Flexner (a Harvard Ph.D. who just dropped in without any journalistic experience, but went on to write a Pulitzer-winning biography of George Washington), Herbert Asbury, John O'Reilly, Edward Dean Sullivan, Dennis Tylden Lynch, Joseph Alsop, and Lucius Beebe. Beebe was a blue-ribbon eccentric and son of a wealthy Boston banker, who arrived wearing formal dress and top hat. He had to be told, "For God's sake Lucius, go home and get dressed." Beebe went on to write some thirty books on subjects as diverse as railroads, high society, night clubs, Boston brahmins, gastronomy, and men's fashion.

It was perhaps in its key functionaries that the *Herald Tribune* was most amply blessed. The paper had the best rewrite man in the business—probably the best rewrite man of all time, in Robert B. Peck. Writing a syndicated column was Mark Sullivan, who went on to produce a monumental six-volume history of the United States in the first quarter of the twentieth century, *Our Times*. The sports department had one of the country's best sports writers in William O. McGeehan, a survivor from the old *Herald*. (Later on the pride of the paper's sports pages would be Red Smith, often called the most literate sports writer of all time.) The paper had the strongest drama critic of the day in Percy Hammond, who once humorously defined his art as "the venom of contented rattlesnakes."[13] The paper had one of the most imaginative political cartoonists of the day, Jay Norwood ("Ding") Darling, winner of two Pulitzer Prizes.

The *Herald Tribune* was especially well endowed with women writers and editors. The paper had on its staff the Scottish-born Ishbel Ross, frequently said to have been the best female general-duty reporter to work in New York. Also, for many years, beginning in 1924, Irita Van Doren was editor of the paper's Sunday Book Review supplement, highly esteemed in New York literary circles. The Sunday magazine was edited by Marie (Missy) Mattingly. In the 1930s the paper added to its firmament Dorothy Thompson, a well-seasoned foreign correspondent, then the wife of novelist Sinclair Lewis.

Probably the most glittering jewel in the crown of the *Herald Tribune*—and irrefutable evidence of the paper's catholicity of taste—came with the addition of Walter Lippmann's column "Today and Tomorrow," probably the best serious newspaper column ever to appear in an American paper. When the *World* died everybody, it seemed, wanted Lippmann. Roy

Howard would have been delighted to put him in charge of the editorial page of the *World Telegram*. He was also offered a professorship at Harvard and the presidency of the University of North Carolina. Most tempting, perhaps, Adolph Ochs offered to make him head of the *Times'* Washington bureau.[14] But promised a completely free hand by the Reids to write whatever he liked, Lippmann took up the *Herald Tribune*'s offer. Many found it incredulous that this onetime socialist and progressive philosopher could make an alliance with a traditionally "conservative" paper. But "Today and Tomorrow" made its debut on September 8, 1931, and ran for over thirty years. Lippmann always enjoyed all the freedom he could have wished for.

The quality of American newspapers did not markedly deteriorate during the dark days of the Great Depression, and the equally dark days of World War II that followed. But some of the youthful spirit went out of newspapers during these years. Maybe this was because much of the gusto and *joie de vivre* went out of American life. Gone with the stock market crash of 1929 was the belief in the invincibility of the American way of life. Gone too were short skirts, bathtub gin, all-night parties, girls dancing on table tops, genuine heroes like Lindbergh and Perry and Babe Ruth. No more Ziegfield. No more vaudeville. Everything seemed to droop, like women's hemlines.

To be sure, great newspapers continued to shine after 1929. Papers like the New York *Times* and the *Herald Tribune* lost none of their luster. On the other hand, the tabloids that people once thought of as "colorful" now seemed somehow drab, limp in the arms of the subway straphanger. In the frightening year of 1933 the Newspaper Guild was founded with the goal of "organizing" the low-paid newspaper reporter. Maybe this was a needed development; on the other hand, nothing was more cheerfully less bureaucratic, less organized, than the art of reporting had once been. Soon the Japanese would be in Manchuria. Soon there would be columns of storm troopers marching in Vienna and Prague. People would be getting their international news by radio from the sepulchral voices of Edward R. Murrow and William L. Shirer. Everything about the news would now seem far away.

By this time the simple pleasures had gone out of the art of newspapering. Herbert Bayard Swope when he was on the New York *World* remarked that "journalism was life reflected in ink." A great newspaper is never, he wrote, "just a specific product, but an atmosphere."[15] Above all, what the newspaper had once provided was a personal atmosphere, a kind of close-knit bond with its community. There was not just one kind of bond, but for a long time what people demanded was that it be intimate, modest, and understandable to plain folk. Even the woolly headed philosophizing of Horace Greeley could be forgiven because people understood that "old Horace" was merely trying to do what everyone else was trying to do—understand the kaleidoscopic world we live in.

The idea that a newspaper was both a specific product and an atmosphere took root in America as it did nowhere else. Naturally our papers differed markedly in quality and personality, but all of them struggled to be, in Lincoln's phrase, "of the people, by the people, and for the people." There were the small country weeklies with what William Allen White called "the sweet intimate story of life," there were the antic paragraphers and "colymnists" of the hinterland. There was Dana's old four-page New York *Sun*, every line of it lovingly and imaginatively written. There was Pulitzer's *World* in the 1880s reaching out to the masses of newcomers stepping on shore at Castle Garden and Ellis Island, needing someone to look out for them and speak for them. Even William Cullen Bryant and E. L. Godkin, who addressed their New York *Post* to "ladies and gentlemen," were really trying to speak for everybody and to everybody. In those days the American newspaper was all that one could reasonably expect it to be: spectator, educator, entertainer, guardian of a great trust, and faithful friend.

Notes

CHAPTER 1

1. The *Transcript* was not the first daily paper to sell for $4 a year. Lynde had apparently gotten this idea from Seba Smith who the year before had issued a much smaller $4 paper in Portland, Maine.

2. Frank Luther Mott, *American Journalism: A History, 1690–1960*, New York, 1969, pp. 218–220.

3. Robert W. Jones, *Journalism in the United States*, New York, 1947, p. 228.

4. Mott, p. 322–323.

CHAPTER 2

1. These circulation figures from the 1830s are in Alfred McClurg Lee, *The Daily Newspapers in America*, New York, 1937.

2. John T. Cunningham, *Made in New Jersey: The Industrial Story of a State*, New Brunswick, NJ: Rutgers University Press, 1954, p. 49.

3. Lyman Horace Weeks, *A History of Paper Manufacturing in the United States, 1690–1916*, New York, 1916, pp. 212–213.

4. For a more extensive account of the introduction of woodpulp into paper manufacture, see Weeks, pp. 234–238.

5. Frank Luther Mott, *American Journalism*, New York, 1969, p. 204.

6. For a description of the Hoe "lightning press," see George A. Isaacs, *The Story of the Newspaper Printing Press*, London, 1931. See also Frank E. Comparato, *Chronicles of Genius and Folly*, Culver City, CA, 1979; also cf. Mott, pp. 314–316.

7. Douglas C. McMurtrie, *The Westward Migration of the Printing Press in the United States*, Mayence: *Gutenburg Jahrbuch*, 1930.

8. Arthur M. Schlesinger, Jr., *The Age of Jackson*, Boston, 1995, p. 73.

9. Mott, p. 265.

10. There is an excellent history of the *Evening Post* up to 1920: Allan Nevins, *The Evening Post: A Century of Journalism*, New York, 1922.

CHAPTER 3

1. Quoted in Glynden G. Van Deusen, *Horace Greeley: Nineteenth Century Crusader*, Philadelphia, 1953, p. 56.

2. Oliver Carlson, *The Man Who Made News: James Gordon Bennett*, New York, 1942, p. 109.

3. From the New York *Herald*, quoted in Willard G. Bleyer, *Main Currents in the History of American Journalism*, Boston, 1927, p. 187.

4. This announcement appeared daily in the New York *Herald*, from February 28 to March 12, 1838.

5. *Herald*, February 28, 1837.

6. Carlson, p. 142.

7. *Herald*, September 6, 1836.

8. Quoted in Carlson, p. 170.

9. Springfield *Republican*, June 7, 1872, quoted in Michael Schudson, *Discovering the News*, New York, 1978, p. 51.

10. Carlson, p. 395.

11. Van Deusen, p. 21.

12. Ibid., p. 35.

13. Greeley Papers (New York Public Library), June 11, 1838.

14. New York *Tribune*, December 3, 1845, quoted in Van Deusen, p. 51.

15. Mott, p. 268.

16. Stephen Bates, *If No News Send Rumors: Anecdotes of American Journalism*, New York, 1989, p. 71.

17. Vernon Louis Parrington, *Main Currents in American Thought*, Vol. II, "Horace Greeley: Yankee Radical," 1958, p. 247.

18. For further information about the relationship between Fuller and Greeley, see L. V. Reavas, *A Representative Life of Horace Greeley*, New York, 1872, pp. 529–537. See also Greeley's own *Recollections of a Busy Life*, New York, 1868.

CHAPTER 4

1. Quoted in Daniel J. Boorstin, *The Americans: The National Experience*, New York, 1965, p. 125.

2. Douglas C. McMurtrie, *The Western Migration of the Printing Press*, Mayence, *Gutenburg Jahrbuch*, 1930, p. 20.

3. Ibid.

4. Michael Emeryand Edwin Emery, *The Press and America*, Englewood Cliffs, N J: Prentice-Hall, 1992, p. 116.

5. Frank Luther Mott, *American Journalism*, New York, 1969, p. 283.

6. Bessie Louise Pierce, *A History of Chicago*, Vol. I, New York, 1937, p. 44.

7. Mott, p. 287. For more information about Twain's newspaper career, see Chapter 11 of this book.

8. The Overland Stage from St. Louis was not established until 1858—but even this journey took three weeks, about as long as sailing around the Horn.

9. For a fuller account of the ideas of Frederick A. Douglass, see Waldo E. Martin, *The Mind of Frederick Douglass*, University of North Carolina Press, 1984. See also Benjamin Quarles, *Frederick Douglass*, Washington, 1969.

10. For a good compact summary of these developments, see Emery and Emery, pp. 123–127. For further information, see Carter E. Bryan, "Negro Journalism in America Before Emancipation," *Journalism Monographs*, No. 12 (September 1969).

CHAPTER 5

1. Oliver Carlson, *The Man Who Made News: James Gordon Bennett*, New York, 1942, p. 346.

2. Allan Nevins, *The New York Post: A Century of Journalism*, New York, 1922, pp. 267–268.

3. Michael Schudson, *Discovering the News*, New York, 1967, p. 65.

4. Quoted in Richard Kluger, *The Paper: The Life and Death of the New York Herald Tribune*, New York: Knopf, 1986, p. 80.

5. Carlson, pp. 342–343, 346.

6. Ibid., p. 344.

7. Michael Emery and Edwin Emery, *The Press in America*, New York, 1982, p. 182.

8. Bruce Catton, *Pictorial History of the Civil War*, New York, 1960, p. 497.

9. Emery and Emery, p. 134.

10. Quoted in Mott's *American Journalism*, from F. L. Bullard, *Famous War Correspondents*. For Coffin's own account of his Civil War experiences, see his *Four Years of Fighting*, Boston, 1886. There is an extensive account of war reporting in J. J. Mathews, *Reporting the Wars*, Minneapolis, 1957. A good many of the correspondents wrote autobiographies or memoirs; see Mott, p. 407 for a bibliography.

11. Schudson, p. 67.

12. Edmund Wilson, *Patriotic Gore: Studies in the Literature of the Civil War*, New York: Oxford University Press, 1962, p. 635ff.

CHAPTER 6

1. Frank M. O'Brien, *The Story of the Sun*, New York, 1928, p. 79.

2. James Harrison Wilson, *The Life of Charles A. Dana*, New York, 1907, p. 61. This was the standard biography of Dana, but his newspaper career is best covered in the various books about the *Sun*. See for example, O'Brien (above) and Candace Stone, *Dana and the Sun*, New York, 1938.

3. Oliver Carlson, *The Man Who Made News: James Gordon Bennett*, New York, 1942, p. 394.

4. O'Brien, pp. 159–160.

5. Ibid., p. 156.

6. Ibid., p. 263.

7. Ibid., p. 270.

8. Allan Nevins, *The Evening Post: A Century of Journalism*, New York, 1922, p. 546.

9. Stanley Walker, *City Editor*, New York, 1934, p. 292.

10. Edward P. Mitchell, *Memoirs of an Editor*, New York, 1924, p. 112. This book gives a good account of Dana as an editor and of the *Sun's* golden years.

11. Quoted in Mott, p. 378.

CHAPTER 7

1. *Sixth Census of the United States* (1840); *Eighth Census of the United States* (1860).

2. *Twelfth Census of the United States* (1900); see also Arthur M. Schlesinger, *The Rise of the City, 1878–1898*, New York, 1932.

3. Robert W. Jones, *Journalism in the United States*, New York, 1947, p. 258.

4. Frank Luther Mott, *American Journalism*, New York, 1969, p. 504.

5. George P. Rowell, *Centennial Exhibition of Newspapers*, Philadelphia, 1876, p. 184.

6. Mott, p. 507.

7. Some large presses in the post–Civil War period were manufactured by the Bullock Company of Philadelphia, and a few Walter presses were imported from England.

8. George A. Isaacs, *The Story of the Newspaper Printing Press*, London, 1931, p. 69.

9. Richard Kluger, *The Paper: The Life and Death of the New York Herald Tribune*, New York: Knopf, 1986, p. 152.

10. Mott, p. 490.

11. For a biography of Reid, see Royal Cortissoz's two-volume *The Life of Whitelaw Reid*, New York, 1921, a flattering family-sponsored work. More objective but less detailed is Bingham Davis, *Whitelaw Reid: Journalist, Politician,*

Diplomat, University of Georgia Press, 1975. Also lively accounts in Kluger, pp. 140ff.

12. For an account of Bennett's more outlandish escapades, see Richard O'Connor, *Scandalous Mr. Bennett*, Garden City, NY, 1962.

13. See George H. Douglas, *Rail City: Chicago U.S.A.*, San Diego, 1981, pp. 77–79.

14. For an account of this aspect of Grady's career, see Raymond B. Nixon, *Henry W. Grady: Spokesman for the New South*, New York, 1943.

CHAPTER 8

1. Michael Emery and Edwin Emery, *The Press and America*, Englewood Cliffs, NJ: Prentice-Hall, 1992, pp. 172–174.

2. W. A. Swanberg, *Pulitzer*, New York, 1967, pp. 104–107; 120–121. See also Marvin Trachtenberg, *The Statue of Liberty*, New York, 1977, pp. 183–184.

3. Don C. Seitz, *Joseph Pulitzer: His Life and Letters*, New York, 1924, p. 52.

4. Frank Luther Mott, *American Journalism*, New York, 1969, p. 370.

5. Seitz, pp. 107–108.

6. Quoted in *The Story of the St. Louis Post-Dispatch*, St. Louis, 1949, p. 3.

7. Mott, p. 434.

8. Burton J. Hendrick, *The Training of an American*, Boston, 1928, p. 158.

9. Quoted in Swanberg's *Pulitzer*, p. 70.

10. Ibid., p. 154.

11. Ibid., p. 168.

12. Mc Lean had bought the *Morning Journal* from Albert Pulitzer in 1894, paying $1 million for it. Admitting defeat, he sold it one year later to Hearst for only $180,000.

13. W.A. Swanberg, *Citizen Hearst*, New York, 1961, pp. 25–26.

14. *American Magazine* (November, 1906).

15. Emery, p. 194.

16. *Citizen Hearst*, p. 59.

17. Emery, p. 196.

18. *Citizen Hearst*, pp. 107–108.

19. Samuel Eliot Morrison, *Oxford History of the American People*, New York, 1965, p. 801.

20. New York *Evening Post*, February 19, 1898.

21. For a fuller treatment of Hearst's quasi-military exploits in the Spanish-American War, see "Hearst at the Front," in *Citizen Hearst*, pp. 150–169.

22. Swanberg, *Pulitzer*, pp. 253, 255.

23. For a complete list of Hearst's newspaper and magazine holdings at this time, see *Editor & Publisher*, March 6, 1937, p. 1.

CHAPTER 9

1. Meyer Berger, *The Story of the New York Times*, New York, 1951, p. 99.

2. Quoted in Harrison E. Salisbury, *Without Fear or Favor*, New York, 1980, p. 66.

3. Michael Emery and Edwin Emery, *The Press in America*, Englewood Cliffs, NJ: Prentice-Hall, 1992, p. 234.

4. Berger, p. 117.

5. Ibid., p. 127. In a table on pages 569–570, Berger offers complete circulation figures for the *Times*, weekdays and Sunday, from 1896 to 1950.

6. For a description of this neighborhood that became Times Square, see Gerald R. Wolfe, *New York: A Guide to the Metropolis*, New York, 1975, pp. 235–240.

7. For a more detailed account, see Berger, pp. 162–165.

8. The entire front page of the *Sun* on this date, including the inaccurate headline, is pictured in Walter Lord, *A Night to Remember*, New York, 1978, p. 179.

9. Berger, p. 160.

10. Ibid., p. 253.

11. Emery, p. 238.

12. Berger, pp. 153–154.

CHAPTER 10

1. Meyer Berger, *The Story of the New York Times*, New York, 1951, p. 560.

2. Frank Luther Mott, *American Journalism*, New York, 1969, p. 447.

3. The poem appeared in the *Evening Post*, on April 20, 1865.

4. As originally published, this sketch was called "Jim Smiley and His Jumping Frog."

5. Among the books of Petroleum Nasby were *The Nasby Papers* (1864), and *Swingin' Round the Cirkle* (1867). Cyril Clemons wrote a book about the humorist, *Petroleum V. Nasby*, in 1936.

6. W. A. Swanberg, *Pulitzer*, New York, 1967, p. 206.

7. Robert W. Jones, *Journalism in the United States*, New York, 1947, p. 413.

8. Charles Press, *The Political Cartoon*, Rutherford, NJ, 1981, p. 115.

9. Ibid., pp. 263–264. This contains a humorous account of the birth of the daily political cartoon. See also Walt McDougall, *This is the Life!* New York, 1926, which has a fuller version of the story.

10. Pierre Couperie, et al., *A History of the Comic Strip*, New York, 1968, p. 29.

11. Ibid., p. 23.

12. For a convenient account of syndication and ready-print practices, see Jones, pp. 352–363.

13. George Perkins, et al. (ed.) *Reader's Encyclopedia of American Literature*, New York, 1991, p. 318.

14. An informal memoir of Howard R. Garis and the "Bedtime Stories" can be found in Roger Garis, *My Father Was Uncle Wiggily*, New York, 1968.

15. From *Universal Review*, September 1890, quoted in Mott.

CHAPTER 11

1. Frank Luther Mott, *American Journalism*, New York, 1969, p. 648. These statistics refer only to English-language dailies of general circulation.

2. Quoted in Oliver H. Knight (ed.) *I Protest: The Selected Disquisitions of E.W. Scripps*, Madison, WI, 1966, p. 270.

3. Negley D. Cochrane, *E. W. Scripps*, New York, 1933, p. 59.

4. Ibid., p. 106.

5. Mott, p. 553.

6. Robert W. Jones, *Journalism in the United States*, New York, 1947, p. 397.

7. Victor Rosewater, *History of Cooperative Newsgathering in the United States*, New York, 1930.

8. Jones, p. 403.

9. For Scripps's own reasons for founding the United Press, see Cochrane, pp. 82–103.

10. Quoted in Charles R. McCabe (ed.), *Damned Old Crank*, New York, 1951, p. 219. More on the discovery and rise of Roy Howard will be found in Cochrane, pp. 222–230.

11. Mott, p. 592.

12. Theodore Peterson, *Magazines in the Twentieth Century*, Urbana, IL: University of Illinois Press, 1964, p. 10.

13. George Britt, *Forty Years—Forty Millions: The Career of Frank A. Munsey*, New York, 1935, p. 115.

14. Quoted in Emery, p. 291.

CHAPTER 12

1. *Journalist*, February 1890.

2. Stanley Walker, *City Editor*, New York, 1934, p. 37.

3. H. L. Mencken, *Happy Days*, New York, 1940, p. 203.

4. H. L. Mencken, *Newspaper Days*, New York, 1941, p. 7.

5. Ibid., p. 8.

6. Frank Luther Mott, *American Journalism*, New York, 1969, p. 489.

7. Walker, p. 43.

8. For the text of Lee's letter making this proposal, see Robert W. Jones, *Journalism in the United States*, New York, 1947, pp. 503–504.

9. Ibid., p. 505.

10. Mott, p. 489.

11. See Albert A. Sutton, *Education for Journalism in the United States*, Northwestern University Press, 1945.

12. W. A. Swanberg, *Pulitzer*, New York, 1967, p. 304.

13. The details of the development of contract agreements can be found in the *Guild Reporter* and *Editor & Publisher* for these years.

14. See Richard Lingemann, *Theodore Dreiser: At the Gates of the City, 1871–1901*, New York, 1986, also Dreiser's own account of his newspaper career, *Newspaper Days*, New York, 1922.

CHAPTER 13

1. For a fuller version of the careers of these women, see Marion Marzolf, *Up From the Footnote: A History of Women Journalists*, New York, 1977.

2. Alexis de Tocqueville, *Democracy in America*, Vol. II, Phillips Bradley (ed.), New York: Knopf, 1945, p. 198.

3. An amusing account of the career of Anne Royall can be found in Ishbell Ross, *Ladies of the Press*, New York, 1936, pp. 27–30.

4. Ross, p. 32.

5. For a fuller account of the life of Victoria Woodhull, see Joanna Johnson, *Mrs. Satan: The Incredible Saga of Victoria C. Woodhull*, New York, 1967.

6. Marzolf, p. 20.

7. Robert W. Jones, *Journalism in the United States*, New York, 1947, p. 532.

8. See Mignon Rittenhouse, *The Amazing Nellie Bly*, New York, 1956; a lively short account can be found in Ross, pp. 48–59.

9. Ross, p. 51.

10. Ibid., p. 56.

11. Ibid., pp. 63, 64.

12. Jones, pp. 297–301.

13. Ross, pp. 80–81.

14. Marzolf, pp. 56–57.

15. Stanley Walker, *City Editor*, New York, 1934, p. 288.

16. Quoted in Marzolf, p. 59.

CHAPTER 14

1. This editorial, originally published on August 15, 1896, was reprinted in White's *Autobiography*, New York, 1946, pp. 523–527.

2. Quoted in Daniel J. Boorstin, *The Americans: The Democratic Experience*, New York, 1973, p. 136.

3. Tom Wallace, "There Were Giants in Those Days," *Saturday Evening Post*, August 6, 1938, p. 12.

4. James Thurber, *The Thurber Album*, New York, 1952, pp. 265–266.

5. Ibid., p. 276.

6. Quoted in Allan Nevins, *American Press Opinion*, New York, 1928, p. 299.

7. Quoted in Carl Bode, *Mencken*, Carbondale, IL, 1969, p. 41.

8. Baltimore *Evening Sun*, August 25, 1924.

9. Baltimore *Evening Sun*, March 7, 1921.

10. Baltimore *Evening Sun*, October 8, 1928.

11. Walter Lippmann, "H. L. Mencken," in *Men of Destiny*, Seattle, 1969, pp. 64–65.

12. Quoted in Ronald Steele, *Walter Lippmann and the American Century*, Boston, 1980, p. 172.

CHAPTER 15

1. Sally M. Miller, *The Ethnic Press in the United States*, New York, 1987, p. xiii.

2. This view was expressed by Carl Wittke in his excellent study of the German press, *The German Language Press in America*, New York, 1973, p. 6.

3. Michael Emery and Edwin Emery, *The Press and America*, Englewood Cliffs, NJ: Prentice-Hall, 1992, p. 227.

4. Allan Nevins and Henry Steele Commager, *A Short History of the United States*, New York, 1942, p. 30.

5. Variously spelled Sauer, Sower, and Sowr.

6. Wittke, p. 18.

7. Miller, p. 133.

8. Frank Luther Mott, *American Journalism*, New York, 1969, p. 121.

9. Miller, p. 137. See also Alfred E. Zuker, *The Forty-Eighters: Political Refugees of the German Revolution of 1848*, New York, 1950.

10. Wittke, p. 201.

11. Ibid., p. 83.

12. Carl Wittke, *The Saga of the Immigrant*, Cleveland, 1967, pp. 279–280.

13. Miller, p. 262.

14. Kenneth T. Jackson (ed.), *Encyclopedia of New York City*, New Haven, CT: Yale University Press, 1995, p. 814.

15. Miller, p. 266.

16. For an account of the Swiss immigration, see Wittke, *We Who Built America*, Cleveland: Western Reserve University Press, pp. 297–301; for more on the Swiss newspapers, see his *The German Language Press in America*, p. 196.

17. Emery, p. 227.

18. Cahan wrote a five-volume autobiography, *Blater Für Mein Leben*, of which only one volume has been translated into English. As *The Education of Abraham Cahan*, Philadelphia, 1969, this first volume gives an account of Cahan's early newspaper efforts. Cf. pp. 307ff.

19. Mordecai Soltes, *The Yiddish Press: An Americanizing Agency*, New York, 1950, p. 184.

20. H. L. Mencken, *My Life as Author and Editor*, New York, 1993, p. 247.

21. Jackson, p. 820.

22. Miller, pp. 215, 217.

23. New York *Times*, July 22, 1996, p. C7.

CHAPTER 16

1. Simon Michael Bessie, *Jazz Journalism*, New York, 1938, p. 75.

2. Ibid., p. 82. This book gives a pungent account of the tabloid era of the 1920s. Also, see John Dhapman, *Tell It to Sweeney: The Informal History of the New York Daily News*, New York, 1961, an account written in the breezy "news" style.

3. This was the highest circulation of any American newspaper at that time. The *Daily News* was outsold, however, by the *London Daily Express*, with 2,665,000.

4. For a more detailed discussion of Hearst's moves into the tabloid field, see W. A. Swanberg, *Citizen Hearst*, New York, 1961; a brief summary will be found in Bessie, pp. 134–156.

5. A reproduction of this front page of the *Daily News* can be found in Emery and Emery, *The Press in America*, Englewood Cliffs, NJ: Prentice-Hall, p. 284.

6. The 1996 edition of *Editor and Publisher International Yearbook* listed the current circulation of the *Daily News* as 738,091.

7. For an account of some of these efforts, see Bessie, pp. 162–183; also Emery, p. 286.

CHAPTER 17

1. For a brief history of the rise of radio news, see George H. Douglas, *The Early Days of Radio Broadcasting*, Jefferson, NC, 1987, pp. 98–126.

2. *Editor and Publisher, International Yearbook*, 1927, p. 19.

3. James W. Barrett. *The World, The Flesh and Messrs. Pulitzer*, New York, 1931, p. 23.

4. On Pulitzer's will, see W. A. Swanberg, *Pulitzer*, New York, 1967, p. 414. For a fuller and more emotional version, see Barrett, pp. 37–57.

5. Alfred Allan Lewis, *Man of the World*, New York, 1978, p. ix.

6. Ibid., p. 82.

7. Arthur Krock, *Memoirs: Sixty Years on the Firing Line*, New York, 1968, pp. 72–73.

8. A good general account can be found in Barrett. Certainly as the last city editor of the paper, Barrett was close to the events as they unfolded.

9. For a more detailed discussion of this revolution in typography, see Richard Kluger, *The Paper: The Life and Death of the New York Herald Tribune*, New York: Knopf 1986, pp. 199–200. For more information on Garrett, see George Ryant's 1968 doctoral thesis at the University of Wisconsin, "Garet Garrett's America."

10. Kluger, p. 316.

11. For a fuller discussion of Walker's technique of city editing, see "The Sawed Off Texan and Other High Spirits," in Kluger, pp. 239–268. See also Walker's own book, *City Editor*, New York, 1934.

12. Kluger, p. 254.

13. Peter Hay (ed.) *Broadway Anecdotes*, New York, 1989, p. 177.

14. Lippmann's move from the *World* to the *Herald Tribune* is chronicled in Ronald Steele, *Walter Lippmann and the American Century*, New York, 1980, pp. 273–282.

15. John K. Hutchins and George Oppenheimer (eds.), *The Best in the World*, New York, 1973, pp. xx–xxi.

Bibliographic Essay

The literature treating American journalism is vast, and the bibliography below makes no claim to being comprehensive. For the most part, bibliographies for the individual chapters will try to annotate briefly the works used in the preparation of this book and other items closely related to the principal matters under discussion. A reasonable attempt will be made to acquaint the reader with the most important source materials in the history of the American newspaper, although it has to be kept in mind that there is a much larger body of literature dealing with all the media of communication—magazines, radio and television, advertising, public relations, etc. There are also a great many interpretative works, most of them academic in nature, which attempt to place the media in a specific intellectual context. The sections below on General Histories and Bibliographies will give the casual reader direction in finding some of these works.

GENERAL HISTORIES OF JOURNALISM

One of the most thorough and readable histories of journalism presently available is Michael Emery and Edwin Emery, *The Press and America: An Interpretative History of the Mass Media*, 7th ed., Englewood Cliffs, NJ, a solid and well-written reference work, admirable as a textbook. It offers a treatment of all the media, but its coverage of newspapers is especially strong, and has excellent and up-to-date bibliographies. For many years the classic work in the field was Frank Luther Mott's *American Journalism: A History: 1690–1969*, New York, 1969, 3rd ed. While there is some treatment of magazines here, this is basically a newspaper history, especially strong on individual papers, their character, changes of management, names of editors and publishers, and developments in mechanical and business fields.

Any serious student of American newspapers would do well to look at some of the earlier classics in the field. George H. Payne, *History of Journalism in the United States*, New York, 1920, is especially good on the period before 1800. Some of the efforts from the nineteenth century can be very rewarding, e.g., Frederic Hudson, *Journalism in the United States from 1690 to 1872*, New York, 1873. It is thorough for its time but not a modern historiography. Other well-known and standard works are: James Melvin Lee, *History of American Journalism*, Boston, 1923, rev. ed.; William Grovesnor Bleyer, *Main Currents in the History of American Journalism*, Boston, 1927; Alfred McClurg Lee, *The Daily Newspaper in America*, New York, 1937, especially strong on social and economic issues; W. A. Dill, *Growth of Newspapers in the United States 1724-1925*, Lawrence, KS, 1925; Robert W. Jones, *Journalism in the United States*, New York, 1927, a rather anecdotal work, very informative in some areas, weak in others.

Other more recent works of considerable interest are: Edith M. Bartow, *News in These United States*, New York, 1952; John W. Tebbel, *The Media in America*, New York, 1974, a brief survey account; also an earlier work of the same author, with Kenneth Stewart, *Makers of Modern Journalism*, told mostly in biographical terms. There is Michael Schudson, *Discovering the News*, New York, 1978, which purports to be "A Social History of American Newspapers," but seems rather to provide a framework for newspapers within the history of ideas. A somewhat slender volume it nonetheless has valuable bibliographic notations. Robert A. Rutland's, *The Newsmongers*, New York, 1973, is a rather breezy popular treatment; Sidney Kobre, *Development of American Journalism*, Dubuque, IA, 1969, a sociological analysis that is particularly strong on regional papers.

Some of the best treatments of the newspaper in American life can be found in works of general history and intellectual history. Especially to be recommended are Daniel Boorstin, *The Americans*, New York, 1958, especially Vol. I, "The Colonial Experience," and Vol. 2, "The National Experience." Also very helpful are: Vernon L. Parrington, *Main Currents in American Thought*, New York, 1927 (available as three volumes bound as one) with good studies of some major newspaper figures. Although not highly specific to newspapers there is much of interest in classic works of American history such as James McGregor Burns, *The American Experience*, New York, 1981–1989, 3 vols.; Samuel Eliot Morrison and Henry Steele Commager, *The Growth of the American Republic*, New York, 1969. Richard Hofstadter, William Miller, and Daniel Aaron, *The United States: The History of a Republic*, Englewood Cliffs, NJ, 1972. Merle Curti's *The Growth of American Thought* is an excellent work in intellectual history.

Naturally many books devoted to "media history" contain information on newspapers. Some of these are written in a dreary academic style but can be useful because of their comprehensive nature. An evaluation of some of these can be found in the bibliographies of Emery and Emery, *The Press and America*, p. 633. Others will be identified in the bibliographical entries below.

BIBLIOGRAPHIES, INDEXES, ENCYCLOPEDIAS

There is a wealth of bibliographical material available, some specific to newspapers, most extending to the broader area of all media of communication. A very helpful recent work is William David Sloan, *American Journalism History: An Annotated Bibliography*, New York, 1989. Very useful to the working journalist would be Roland E. Wolseley and Isabel Wolseley, *The Journalist's Bookshelf*, Indianapolis, 1986. This work is conveniently broken down into categories such as "Biography," "Ethics," "Editing," "Religious Journalism," and so on. Another recent bibliography with a specific focus is Richard A. Schwartzlose, *Newspapers: A Reference Guide*, Westport, CT, 1987. Having a somewhat broader coverage of all media is Eleanor Blum and Frances Wilhoit, *Mass Media Bibliography: Reference, Research and Reading*, Urbana, IL, 1990. See also, Lucy Shelton Caswell (ed.), *Guide to Sources in American Journalistic History*, Westport, CT, 1989.

The good standard histories of journalism invariably have solid bibliographies that will probably be useful to the general reader. Mott's *American Journalism* has good annotated bibliographies but is now out of date. The bibliographies in *The Press and America* by Emery and Emery, still in print, are accessible, well selected, and easy to use.

As to indexes of newspaper collections, the most useful index is *Newspapers on Microfilm*, of the Library of Congress. Since the Library of Congress has the most complete collection of American newspapers, this is probably the most comprehensive index to extant papers. There is still considerable value in Clarence S. Bingham's *History and Bibliography of American Newspapers, 1690–1820*, Worcester, MA, 1937, not only because of the complete listing of these early papers but because of considerable information about their ownership, development, and general history. A standard index for many years was Winifred Gregory's *American Newspapers, 1821–1936*, New York, 1936, although since many newspaper archives have put their old papers on microfilm, this can no longer be taken as a guide to newspapers available in their original form.

Over the years there have been a number of directories of the newspaper industry, most of them annuals. The first of these was *George P. Rowell & Co. Newspaper Directory* (1869). This was followed by *N.W. Ayer & Sons American Newspaper Annual*, which eventually became the *Directory of Newspapers and Periodicals*. A standard and important reference source is *Editor & Publisher International Yearbook*, a series that started in 1921.

A number of newspapers have produced indexes of their own contents over the years. By far the best known today is the *New York Times Index*, published continuously since 1913. In recent years the *Times* has rounded out this unique reference work by indexing papers going back to its inaugural issue in 1851. The only other American newspaper currently indexing itself is the *Wall Street Journal*.

There are a number of encyclopedias that cover media, newspapers, journalists, and the like. Of special interest is Donald Paneth (ed.) *The Encyclopedia of American Journalism*, New York, 1983, which has over 1,000 entries and good bibliographies. Particularly relevant to the lives of major journalists is Joseph P. McKerns, *The Biographical Dictionary of American Journalism*, Westport, CT, 1989, with accounts of five hundred people in various phases of newspaper work. A lavish, illustrated account of the lives of newspaper men and women will be found in several volumes of the *Dictionary of Literary Biography*, edited by Perry J. Ashley, Chicago, 1983–. Of special interest to our subject is Vol. 23, covering 1873–1900, and Vol. 25, covering 1900–1925. There are some 750 biographical entries in William H. Taft's *Encyclopedia of Twentieth Century Journalists*, New York, 1987. For coverage of the mass media, see Robert V. Hudson, *Mass Media*, New York, 1971.

ARCHIVES, COLLECTIONS, AND EXHIBITS

It hardly needs to be said that the best way to become acquainted with American newspapers is to look at the originals. In recent years more and more newspaper archives have put their old papers on microfilm, which is not entirely satisfactory since an element of verisimilitude is lost. Of course libraries, even large and well-healed research libraries, are obliged to go this route for lack of space. Even more important, most papers since 1870 are on high-sulphur paper stock, which has consigned them to oblivion. Many would have been turned to dust without microfilming. On the other hand, the rag paper stock from colonial times has often passed the test of time, with the originals remaining in good condition. But not many libraries have copies, and those that do are reluctant to give them into the hands of casual users.

There is an excellent recent compilation of newspaper archives with a detailed description of what is found in them. The book is *Untapped Sources: American Newspaper Archives and Histories*, by Jon Vanden Heuvel, published in New York (1991) by the American Society of Newspaper Editors. It contains references to collections of army newspapers, ethnic papers, religious papers, and many others.

The largest single archive of American newspapers is found in the Library of Congress. The best collection of colonial newspapers is at the American Antiquarian Society. Major historical societies have important newspaper collections. Among these are the New York Historical Society, the Chicago Historical Society, the Wisconsin State Historical Society, the Pennsylvania Historical Society, the Western Reserve Historical Society, and the New Jersey Historical Society. Large research universities also house large newspaper collections. Among the most important are: Harvard University, the Bancroft Library of the University of

California, University of Chicago, Yale University, University of Missouri, the University of Illinois, the University of Texas, and Duke University.

Permanent exhibits of American newspapers have been few in number. A major new museum devoted to newspapers opened in 1997 in Arlington, Virginia, just across the Potomac River from Washington, D.C. In a 72,000-square-foot building called Newseum there is a major news history gallery with exhibits covering newspapers, magazines, award winning photojournalism, and cartoons. The permanent exhibit also covers radio and television broadcast news. Newseum has a satellite gallery in New York at 580 Madison Avenue.

Another important exhibit is "Newspapers in America," at the Museum of Science and Industry in Chicago. Newspapers are included in a major exhibit at the Smithsonian Institution in Washington entitled "Information Age: People, Information and Technology." Many public libraries have newspaper exhibits from time to time. It is perhaps not at all surprising that museums abound that devote themselves to film, radio, television, photography, advertising, and so on. Relevant to our subject matter, there are cartoon exhibits in Boca Raton and Orlando, Florida, and San Francisco.

CHAPTER 1: PENNY PAPERS: THE PRINTED WORD FOR DEMOCRATIC MAN

There is no book that deals with the penny paper phenomenon as such. "The New York Penny Press and the American Romantic Movement," a 1984 dissertation by Gary L. Whitby at the University of Iowa gives a more complete picture of the developments of the 1830s than most of the general histories. One may also want to look at Donald Lewis Shaw and John W. Slater, "Sensationalism in American Press News: 1820–1860," *Journalism History*, 12 (Autumn-Winter), 1985. There is a fair amount of information in the standard history of the New York *Sun*, Frank M. O'Brien, *The Story of the Sun*, New York, 1918. On the *Sun*'s great "moon hoax" one may wish to look at Fred Fedler, *Media Hoaxes*, Ames, IA, Iowa State University Press, 1989.

The whole field of the popular press in these years is detailed in a scholarly manner in James L. Crouthamel, *Bennett's New York Herald and the Rise of the Popular Press*, Syracuse University Press, 1989. (See further references to James Gordon Bennett in the entry for Chapter 4 below.) For a broader treatment of this area, see Richard A. Schwarzlose, *The Nation's Newsbrokers*, Vol. I, *The Formative Years, from Pretelegraph to 1865,* Evanston, IL: Northwestern University Press, 1989.

To get an idea of the other trends that were developing at this time, it is probably a good idea to look at works dealing with some of the major newspapers and editors of the day. There is a good history of the Boston *Transcript*, Joseph E. Chamberlin, *The Boston Transcript: A History of Its First Hundred Years*, Boston, 1930. Gamaliel Bradford's "Samuel Bowles," *Atlantic Monthly*, 116 (October 1915) contains a good brief account of the famous editor of the Springfield *Republican*. An excellent history of the New York *Post* and its longtime editor William Cullen Bryant can be found in Allan Nevins, *The Evening Post: A Century of Journalism*, New York, 1922. There is an interesting life of the energetic and hot-tempered James Watson Webb of the New York *Courier and Enquirer*: James L. Crouthamel, *James Watson Webb: A Biography*, Middletown, CT: Wesleyan University Press, 1969. Some information about one of the early successful penny papers outside New York will be found in Gerald W. Johnson, et al., *The Sunpapers of Baltimore*, New York, 1937.

Much useful information is to be had in biographies of some of the leading editors of the federalist era. For example, there is John W. Osborne, *William Cobbett: His Thought and His Times*, Rutgers University Press, 1956. There is James Tugg, *Benjamin Franklin Bache and the Philadelphia Aurora*, University of Pennsylvania Press, 1991. Also, Jacob Axelrad, *Philip Freneau: Champion of Democracy*, University of Texas Press, 1967. The earlier standard life of the great antifederalist editor is Lewis Leary, *That Rascal Freneau*, Rutgers University Press, 1941.

Some idea of the "commercial" uses of the press in these years can be found in David P. Forsyth, *The Business Press in America, 1750–1865*, New York, 1964.

CHAPTER 2: THE QUEST FOR A REAL NEWSPAPER

There is a considerable literature on the technological developments needed to produce newspapers, magazines, and other publications of mass circulation. A good deal of material is available about printing in colonial times. Lawrence C. Wroth's *The Colonial Printer*, Portland, ME, 1938 is a comprehensive work. There are also a number of works dealing with printing in individual colonies, including another work of Lawrence Wroth's, *A History of Printing in Colonial Maryland, 1686–1786*, Baltimore, 1922. Also, C. R. Hildeburn, *Sketches of Printers and Printing in Colonial New York*, New York, 1895; and Milton W. Hamilton, *The Country Printer: New York State: 1735–1830*, Port Washington, NY, 1964.

Many readers will probably be interested in more general histories of printing that cover early times to the present. Included in this category is Colin Clair, *A Chronology of Printing*, New York, 1969; Douglas C. McMurtrie, *The Book: The Story of Printing and Bookmaking*, New York, 1943; R. A. Peddie, *Printing: A Short History of the Art*, New York, 1927. Siegfried Steinberg, *Five Hundred Years of Printing*, Baltimore, 1961. Also, W. Turner Berry and E. Edmund Poole, *Annals of Printing: A Chronological Encyclopedia From the Earliest Times to 1950*, London, 1966. James Moran, *Printing Presses from the Fifteenth Century to Modern Times*, University of California Press, 1973. S. H. Steinberg, *Five Hundred Years of Printing*, Hammondsworth, 1955.

With specific reference to printing in America, see John Clyde Oswald, *Printing in the Americas*, New York, 1937, which contains many facsimile pages from newspapers. Also Douglas C. McMurtrie, *A History of Printing in the United*

States, in several regional volumes, New York, 1936. An earlier source that is very useful is J. Luther Ringwalt (ed.) *American Encyclopedia of Printing*, Philadelphia, 1871.

As to the development of the newspaper presses, especially in the nineteenth century, with the coming of rotary and "lightning" presses, see George A. Isaacs, *The Story of the Newspaper Printing Press*, London, 1931; James Grant, *The Newspaper Press: Its Origin, Progress, and Present Position*, London, 1871. Of individual achievements, see, Jacob Kainen, *George Clymer and the Columbian Press*, San Francisco: San Francisco Book Club of California, 1950. Also, Rollo G. Silver, "Efficiency Improved: The Genesis of the Web Press in America," American Antiquarian Society, 1970, *Proceedings*, 1970, pp. 325–350. There is a detailed history of the Hoe Company, a family dynasty and leader in the field of rotary press manufacture in the United States for over a century and a half: Frank E. Comparato, *Chronicles of Genius and Folly: R. Hoe & Company and the Printing Press as a Service to Democracy*, Culver City, CA, 1979. This work is massive and fully detailed and might be overwhelming to the ordinary reader not interested in printing. A good earlier source on the subject is Henry L. Bullen, "Richard Marsh Hoe and the Evolution of Fast Printing Presses," in *Inland Printer* (September 1922); another good short survey can be found in Calder M. Pickett, "Technology and the New York Press in the Nineteenth Century," *Journalism Quarterly* (Summer 1960), pp. 398–407.

As to other print technologies there are a number of works available. There is Thomas Mackeller, *The American Printer: A Manual of Typography*, Philadelphia, 1886; George A. Kubler, *A Short History of Stereotyping*, New York, 1927. A good history of paper and paper manufacturing is Lyman Horace Weeks, *A History of Paper Manufacturing in the United States, 1690–1916*, New York, 1916.

CHAPTER 3: GIANTS OF A NEW AGE: JAMES GORDON BENNETT AND HORACE GREELEY

There are vast sources of information about both James Gordon Bennett and Horace Greeley. The reader cannot only refer to the many specialized works, but to the histories of American journalism treating this time period. Quite naturally, many general works in American history have references to these two major figures, perhaps more to Greeley because of his role as a politician and political thinker.

Undoubtedly the best work on Bennett is the biography, Oliver Carlson, *The Man Who Made News*, New York, 1942. Not only is this a solid treatment of Bennett's life, it is built around the reasonable premise that in building up the *Herald* Bennett had discovered or invented what we today call news, moving away from the old indiscriminate heaping of facts or journal keeping. Another work, equally important, which lays out the journalistic implications in full detail, is James L.

Crouthamel, *Bennett's New York Herald and the Rise of the Popular Press*, Syracuse University Press, 1989. Another biography of Bennett also covers the career of James Gordon Bennett, Jr. This is Don C. Seitz, *The James Gordon Bennetts*, Indianapolis, 1938, a lively anecdotal account.

The *Herald* was much maligned during Bennett's lifetime. But there were some favorable contemporary accounts. Appreciative of Bennett's contribution in the early days was "The Herald—Onward," *Democratic Review*, November 1852. Insightful as to Bennett's career as an editor is "James Gordon Bennett's Scintillations," *Galaxy* (August 1872). There was an early biographical treatment of Bennett, now, unfortunately, rather inaccessible: [Isaac C. Pray], *Memoirs of James Gordon Bennett and His Times*, New York, 1855. Scholarly publications have picked up on Bennett's contributions in individual areas. Unfortunately there is no good study of Bennett's contribution to the development of business news. But there is Judith M. Buddenbaum, "The Religious Journalism of James Gordon Bennett," *Journalism History* (Summer/Autumn 1987). Some ideas of Bennett's approach to reporting can be found in Wallace B. Eberhard, "Mr. Bennett Covers a Murder Trial," *Journalism Quarterly* (Autumn 1970).

A really comprehensive and analytical life of Horace Greeley is long overdue. The standard life of Greeley, and it is certainly a detailed treatment, is Glynden G. Van Deusen, *Horace Greeley: Nineteenth Century Crusader*, Philadelphia: University of Pennsylvania Press, 1953. Also available and of course interesting is Greeley's own *Recollections of a Busy Life*, New York, 1868. Dealing specifically with the *Tribune* and with Greeley's political life is Jeter Allen Isley, *Horace Greeley and the Republican Party, 1853–1861: A Study of the New York Tribune*, Princeton, NJ: Princeton University Press, 1947. Although it deals mainly with the twentieth-century *Herald Tribune*, which brought together Bennett's and Greeley's papers in a remarkable synthesis, Richard Kluger's *The Paper: The Life and Death of the New York Herald Tribune*, New York: Alfred A. Knopf, 1986, has a considerable amount of information about the early days of both papers. It is a well-written, lively and thoughtful history.

An excellent contemporary source on Greeley is James Parton's *Life of Horace Greeley*, New York, 1855. Another work from the nineteenth century that is useful is Francis Nicoll Zabriski, *Horace Greeley the Editor*, New York, 1890. Also, L. V. Reavas, *A Representative Life of Horace Greeley*, New York, 1872, which has good information about the relationship between Horace Greeley and Margaret Fuller.

There have been many recent studies of Greeley, some of the most important listed in the Emery and Emery bibliography. A classic analysis of Greeley's influence is John R. Common, "Horace Greeley and the Working Class Origins of the Republican Party," *Political Science Quarterly* (September 1909). An excellent study of Greeley's seemingly contradictory ideas and a fair-minded resolution of them is found in Vernon L. Parrington, "Horace Greeley: Yankee Radical," *Main Currents in American Thought*, Vol. II, Boston, 1927.

CHAPTER 4: NEWSPAPERS MOVE WEST—FERMENT IN THE SOUTH

Many general histories of the westward movement have considerable information about the development of newspapers in the western territories and states. An excellent description of the dynamics of western journalism, especially the "booster press" can be found in Daniel Boorstin, *The Americans: The National Experience*, New York: Random House, 1965. An account of the spread of printing presses in the West can be found in Douglas C. McMurtrie, *The Western Migration of the Printing Press, Gutenburg Jahrbuch*: Mayence, 1930, p. 20. McMurtrie is the undisputed authority on the western press in the nineteenth century and is the author of a number of monographs in this area. He was the editor of *A History of California Newspapers from the Sacramento Daily Union of December, 25, 1858*, New York, 1927. Some of his other works are *Early Printing in Wisconsin*, Seattle, 1931, and *Early Printing in Colorado*, Denver, 1935.

Other notable histories of the western press are George S. Turnbull, *History of Oregon Newspapers*, Portland, 1939; Sam Acheson, *35,000 Days in Texas: A History of the Dallas News and Its Forbears*, New York, 1938; George S. Hage, *Newspapers on the Minnesota Frontier, 1849–1860*, Minnesota Historical Society, 1967. There is an interesting dissertation about the early press in the Washington territory: Barbara L. Cloud, "Start the Presses: The Birth of Journalism in the Washington Territory," University of Washington, 1979. Colorful histories serving up the ambiance of western journalism are Robert P. Karolevitz, *Newspapering in the Old West*, Seattle, 1965, a pictorial history; also, John Myers, *Print in a Wild Land*, Garden City, NY, 1967.

There is a considerable literature about the newspaper uses of the newly developed telegraph and other speed techniques coming into use before the Civil War. Victor Rosewater, *History of Cooperative News-Gathering in the United States*, New York, 1930, has much on telegraphy, also information about the formation of the New York Associated Press. Alvin F. Harlow, *Old Wires and New Waves*, New York, 1936, is a classic in its field; it treats not only the development of telegraphy but its use by newspapers. Also see Richard A. Schwartzlose, *The Nation's Newsbrokers*, Vol. I: *The Formative Years: From Pretelegraph to 1865*, Evanston: Northwestern University Press, 1989; and Robert Luther Thompson, *Wiring a Continent: The History of the Telegraph Industry in the United States, 1832–1866*, Princeton, NJ: Princeton University Press, 1947.

On the topic of the ferment before the Civil War, once again, there is considerable treatment of the role of newspapers in general histories. It is important to remember that the few decades before the Civil War produced newspaper editors who occupied themselves almost exclusively with the issue of abolition. Accordingly, histories of the abolition movement will contain a great deal of information about newspapers. Among the biographies of editors of antislavery papers are Wendell P. Garrison and Francis J. Garrison, *William Lloyd Garrison*, 4 vols., New York, 1885–94, containing a full history of the *Liberator*. A recent biography of Garrison is John L. Thomas, *The Liberator: William Lloyd Garrison*, Boston, 1963. Also, Joseph C. Lovejoy and Owen Lovejoy, *Memoir of the Rev. Elijah P. Lovejoy*, New York, 1838, dealing with the seed years of the movement; William Birney, *James C. Birney and His Times*, New York, 1910.

On the life and career of Frederick Douglass, one should probably begin with Douglass's own chronicle of his career as an abolitionist editor, *My Bondage and My Freedom*, New York, 1855, of which there are numerous recent reprints. There is a good recent biography of Douglass, William S. McFeely, *Frederick Douglass*, New York: Norton, 1991. The earlier standard biography was Philip S. Foner, *Frederick Douglass*, New York, 1963. A considerable literature dealing with the history of black journalism has appeared, much of it especially strong on this period. See especially Martin E. Dann, *The Black Press, 1827–1890*, New York, 1971; Roland E. Wolseley, *The Black Press USA*, Ames, IA: Iowa State University Press, 1990. (Only the early chapters deal with this period.) I. Garland Penn's *The Afro-American Press and Its Editors*, Springfield, MA, 1891, gives much source material for the abolitionist period and after. For more bibliographical information on black journalists, see the notes for Chapter 17 below.

Concerning the stance of the southern press in these years, see Donald E. Reynolds, *Editors Make War: Southern Newspapers in the Secession Crisis*, Nashville: Vanderbilt University Press, 1970. For a good description of the leading southern secessionist editor, see Laura A. White, *Robert Barnwell Rhett*, New York, 1931.

CHAPTER 5: THE CIVIL WAR—THE INDISPENSABILITY OF NEWS

The best way to get an idea of how American newspapers covered the Civil War is to resort to the old files and newspapers themselves. Most of the major papers of the country were covering all news in much greater depth than they were only a decade before. Clearly Bennett's *Herald* had the best coverage of the war, although Raymond's *Times* and Greeley's *Tribune* gave Bennett brisk competition.

There is a considerable literature dealing with the journalism of the Civil War. Most of it falls into two categories: general works dealing with coverage of the war and the relationship of the newspaper to the war, and individual accounts by war correspondents, or "specials" as they were then called. A good overview of wartime journalism is Joseph J. Mathews, *Reporting the Wars*, Minneapolis, MN: University of Minnesota Press, 1957, which covers wars of American involvement since the mid-eighteenth century. On Civil War reporting there are two classic works by J. Cutler Andrews, *The North Reports the Civil War*, Pittsburgh: University of Pittsburgh Press, 1955, and *The South Reports the Civil War*, Princeton, NJ: Princeton University Press, 1970.

Other useful works that deal with particular problems or sectional interests are Robert S. Harper, *Lincoln and the Press*, New York, 1951; Donald R. Reynolds, *Editors Make War: Southern Newspapers in the Secession Crisis*, Nashville: Vanderbilt University Press, 1970; Ralph Ray Fahrney, *Horace Greeley and the Tribune in the Civil War*, Chicago: University of Chicago Press, 1929; William L. Klement, *The Copperheads in the Middle West*, Chicago: University of Chicago Press, 1960.

As to war reporting, one can look at surveys such as Emmett Crozier, *Yankee Reporters: 1861–1865*, New York, 1956. F. L. Bullard's *Famous War Correspondents*, Boston, 1914, contains short biographies of war correspondents of both the North and South. There are numerous accounts built around individual correspondents, either autobiographical or biographical. Among the most interesting are W. E. Griffis, *Charles Carleton Coffin*, Boston, 1898. Coffin's own account is available in his *Four Years of Fighting*, Boston, 1866. Also, Royal Cortissoz, *The Life of Whitelaw Reid*, New York, 1921; *Memoirs of Henry Villard*, 2 vols., Boston, 1904; Thomas W. Knox, *Camp-Fire and Cotton-Field*, New York, 1865; G. A. Townsend, *Campaigns of a Non-Combatant*, New York, 1866; and A. B. Paine (ed.), *A Sailor of Fortune: Personal Memoirs of Capt. B. S. Osbon*, New York, 1906.

CHAPTER 6: DANA AND THE NEW YORK *SUN*: THE NEWS STORY AS ART

There is certainly room now for a fresh treatment of the life and work of Charles A. Dana and the contributions of the *Sun* to modern journalism. On the other hand, the traditional works are sentimental but useful. The authorized life of Dana is James Harrison Wilson, *Charles A. Dana*, New York, 1907. A somewhat more lively biography was Charles J. Rosebault, *When Dana Was the Sun*, New York, 1931. The most important study of Dana's contributions as an editor is Candace Stone, *Dana and the Sun*, New York, 1938. On the *Sun* specifically, see Frank M. O'Brien, *The Story of the Sun*, New York, 1918. A good deal of other information about the *Sun* in Dana's time and after can be found in the memoirs of his longtime colleague and successor as editor E. P. Mitchell, *Memoirs of an Editor*, New York, 1924.

A moralistic approach to the *Sun* style of journalism and a rueful lament for the loss of Dana's Brook Farm idealism can be found in Vernon Parrington's *Main Currents in American Thought*, Vol. II, Boston, 1927. Parrington is willing to admit that Dana was a "folk hero," but seems unable to appreciate his contributions to journalism.

A good collection of *Sun* writing in the 1870s and 1880s is very much lacking, but there is a collection of editorials from the period, *Casual Essays of the Sun*, New York, 1905. It does include "Yes Virigina, There Is a Santa Claus."

For an idea of the newspaper landscape in those years when the *Sun* was shining brightly, one can refer to some of the journalistic autobiographies of the time. There is, for example, John W. Forney, *Forty Years of American Journalism*, Philadelphia, 1887; Alexander K. McClure, *Reflections of a Half Century*, Salem, MA, 1902; and Franc B. Wilkie, *Personal Reminiscences of Thirty-Five Years of Journalism*, Chicago, 1891. One may also look at other contemporary works, such as Simeon North, *History and Present Condition of the Newspaper and Periodical Press of the United States*, Washington D.C.: U.S. Printing Office, 1884, a work published as part of the 1880 census.

CHAPTER 7: NEWSPAPERS IN THE GILDED AGE

To understand the vagaries and inconsistencies of newspaper development in the Gilded Age it is probably best to begin with general historical works that make detailed intellectual analyses of the time. One classic historical work is Charles A. Beard and Mary R. Beard, *The Rise of American Civilization*, Vol. II; *The Second American Revolution*, New York, 1930, which follows the rise of the age of capitalism and industry in America. Or, Allan Nevins, *The Emergence of Modern America, 1865–1878*, New York, 1927. One can also look at Richard Hofstadter, *The Age of Reform*, New York, 1955; Henry Steele Commager, *The American Mind*, New Haven, CT: Yale University Press, 1950; Howard Mumford Jones, *The Age of Energy*, New York, 1970; Blake McKelvey, *The Urbanization of America, 1860–1915*; Matthew Josephson, *The Robber Barons*, New York, 1934; Arthur M. Schlesinger, *The Rise of the City, 1878–1898*, New York, 1932; Norman J. Ware, *The Labor Movement in the United States 1860–1895*, New York, 1929.

Of specific relevance to the history of newspapers during the last quarter of the nineteenth century is the development of advertising. It is not possible to give a detailed account of the literature here, but especially good for our purposes are; Daniel Pope, *The Making of Modern Advertising*, New York, 1983; and James Wood, *The Story of Advertising*, New York, 1958. Neil Borden's *The Economic Effects of Advertising*, Chicago, 1942, traces the relationship between national manufacturing and the advertising business. Especially good on the development of department store advertisement in the 1880s is George Juergens, *Joseph Pulitzer and the New York World*, Princeton, NJ: Princeton University Press, 1966.

There has been a considerable amount written about the leading editors and publishers of this period. For a good account of the lives and careers of both Whitelaw Reid and James Gordon Bennett, Jr., see Richard Kluger, *The Paper: The Life and Death of the New York Herald Tribune*, New York: Alfred A. Knopf, 1986. The old standard biography of Whitelaw Reid is Royal Cortissoz's *The Life of Whitelaw Reid*, 2 vols., New York, 1921, an overly glowing family-sponsored account. A shorter and more objective recent biography is Bingham Duncan, *Whitelaw Reid: Journalist, Politician, Diplomat*, University of Georgia Press,

1975. For a history of the *Tribune* under Reid's rule, see Harry W. Baehr, Jr., *The New York Tribune Since the Civil War*, New York, 1936. Vivid, and more penetrating than his biography of Reid, is Royal Cortissoz's *The New York Tribune: Incidents and Personalities in Its History*, New York, 1923.

It is not fitting to leave the history of the *Tribune* without some mention of the development of the linotype, Reid's "rattle box." The story of Ottmar Mergenthaler and his invention is best told in Thomas Dreier's *The Power of Print—and Men*, published in 1936 by the Mergenthaler Company, New York. This work celebrated the semicentennial of the invention. A similar celebration of the typewriter is *The Story of the Typewriter, 1873–1973*, published by the Herkimer (NY) Historical Society, 1923. Pertinent to the labor problems that arose during this time of technological transition is a privately printed pamphlet celebrating the *Tribune*'s centennial, Henry McIlvaine Parsons, *A History of 100 Years of Unions at the New York Tribune*, New York, 1941.

As to James Gordon Bennett, Jr., perhaps the best available work is Don C. Seitz, *The James Gordon Bennetts*, Indianapolis, 1928. Over half of this book is devoted to Bennett the younger. It is a more or less sympathetic rendering. More recent is Richard O'Connor, *Scandalous Mr. Bennett*, New York, 1962. An amusing and well-written account of Bennett Jr., as the "Magnifico of Maxim's" can be found in Lucius Beebe's *The Big Spenders*, Garden City, NY, 1966.

There are numerous works on the regional editors and publishers who were prominent during the last quarter of the nineteenth century. On William Rockhill Nelson of the Kansas City *Star*, see Icie F. Johnson, *William Rockhill Nelson and the Kansas City Star*, Kansas City, 1935; also a recent fresh perspective, William L. McCorkle, "Nelson's *Star* and Kansas City, 1880–1898," Ph.D. thesis, University of Texas, 1968. An earlier appreciation of Nelson by his well-known Kansas neighbor William Allen White is "The Man Who Made the Star," *Colliers* (June 26, 1915), 12ff.

On other Midwestern figures of importance, see Charles G. Clayton, *Joseph B. McCullagh of the St. Louis Globe-Democrat*, Carbondale, IL: Southern Illinois University Press, 1969. More specific to the *Globe-Democrat*, but built around McCullagh, is Jim Hart, *A History of the St. Louis Globe-Democrat*, Columbia, MO: University of Missouri Press, 1961. Looking at the Chicago scene there is Melville E. Stone, *Fifty Years a Journalist*, Garden City, NY, 1921. The early part of this book deals with Stone's Chicago career, the latter part with the building of the Associated Press. Charles H. Dennis's *Victor Lawson: His Time and His Work*, Chicago, 1935, is a good source on the Chicago *Daily News*.

Of well-known Southern editors Henry Grady is the subject of an excellent biography: Raymond B. Nixon, *Henry W. Grady: Spokesman for the New South*, New York, 1943. On Henry "Marse" Watterson, see Joseph L. Wall, *Henry Watterson: Reconstructed Rebel*, New York: Oxford University Press, 1956. Watterson's own readable and mellow autobiography, *"Marse Henry," An Autobiography*, New York, 1919 is a charming read. Some idea of Watterson's editorial skills can be gleaned from Arthur Krock's collection, *The Editorials of Henry Watterson*, New York, 1923.

Of course the most influential editors in the country continued to be in New York during the Gilded Age, many of them struggling heroically to comprehend this new and frenetic capitalist order. The highly esteemed editor of the New York *Post* during these years was E. L. Godkin, and he was the subject of a biography by his successor as editor Rollo Ogden: *Life and Letters of Edwin Lawrence Godkin*, New York, 1907. There is a good biography of Charles R. Miller of the *Times*: F. F. Bond, *Mr. Miller of the Times*, New York, 1931.

CHAPTER 8: DANGEROUS CROSSROADS: PULITZER AND HEARST

The journalism of the 1880s and 1890s has been treated under a number of different labels. Sometimes it is more generously spoken of as "the new journalism," or "people's journalism"; at other times, especially when referring to the unbridled competition during the Spanish-American War, it is referred to as "yellow journalism." Whatever the terms used, nearly all of the standard histories of American newspapers have detailed coverage of this time period, and one may refer to some of those sources.

The "new journalism" is almost universally said to begin with Pulitzer, and, in fairness to this the most spectacular and imaginative giant of his age, one can separate out his great achievements at the *World* before the yellow phase. His best biographers have all attempted to do this. The first important biography of Pulitzer was written by Pulitzer's longtime business manager, Don C. Seitz: *Joseph Pulitzer: His Life and Letters*, New York, 1924. James W. Barrett, one of Pulitzer's editors who stayed with the *World* until the end, wrote *Joseph Pulitzer and His World*, New York, 1941. The best and most exhaustive account of Pulitzer's life and career is W. A. Swanberg, *Pulitzer*, New York, 1967. A good analysis of Pulitzer and the *World* is to be found in George Jeurgens, *Joseph Pulitzer and the New York World*, Princeton, NJ: Princeton University Press, 1966. A study of Pulitzer's development and early career in St. Louis is Julian S. Rammelkamp, *Pulitzer's Post-Dispatch, 1878–1883*, Princeton, NJ: Princeton University Press, 1966. Also very useful is Homer W. King's *Pulitzer's Prize Editor: John A. Cockerill*, Durham, NC: Duke University Press, 1965.

William Randolph Hearst has quite naturally been the subject of numerous biographies, some of them vitriolic. Most of the early works seem to get lost in the contradictory qualities of the man. Such is the case with John K. Winkler, *Hearst: An American Phenomenon*, New York, 1928. By the 1930s it was easy to put Hearst, with his vast empire and prodigal spending, into the villain category. This was done up thoroughly by Ferdinand Lundberg in *Imperial Hearst: A Social Biography*, New York, 1936, a work that goes along with other works of that age such as Matthew Josephson's *The Robber Barons*, in mounting an angry attack on

America's plutocrats. In somewhat the same vein, but more balanced, was Oliver Carlson and E. S. Bates, *Hearst: Lord of San Simeon*, New York, 1936. Better and fuller biographies of Hearst came after World War II. From the standpoint of Hearst's newspaper career the best biography is probably John Tebbel, *The Life and Good Times of William Randolph Hearst*. More accessible to the general public, and certainly avoiding atrabilious editorializing is W. A. Swanberg, *Citizen Hearst*, New York, 1961. Anyone interested in Hearst's newspaper career will also find of some interest Oliver Carlson's *Brisbane: A Candid Biography*, New York, 1937, a study of Hearst's longtime top lieutenant.

Interestingly there is no full-scale study of the phenomenon of "yellow journalism," although nearly all of the standard histories of American journalism have detailed treatment of the yellow age. Willard G. Bleyer's *Main Currents in the History of American Journalism*, Boston, 1927, does a good job of documenting Hearst's manipulating of the news through sensationalism. A view of the ways that yellow journalism led to the jingoisms of the 1890s and eventually to the Spanish-American War can be found in Joyce Milton, *The Yellow Kids: Foreign Correspondents in the Heyday of American Journalism*, New York, 1989. Also, numerous general histories of the war give ample coverage to the journalistic dimension. See, for example, Walter Millis, *The Martial Spirit: A Study of Our War With Spain*, Boston, 1931.

CHAPTER 9: THE RISE OF THE NEW YORK *TIMES*

There is no comprehensive critical history of the New York *Times*. In the last few decades a number of books about the *Times* have appeared, most of them dealing with office intrigues, struggle for dynastic supremacy, etc. One has to go back a long way for a good general history. The first real history of the paper was *History of the New York Times 1851–1921*, New York, 1921, by Elmer Davis, a book published by the *Times* itself. Then there was a centennial history, *The Story of the New York Times 1851–1951*, by Meyer Berger, New York, 1951. Berger, a longtime *Times* writer, grew up on the lower east side of New York and was famous for pieces about New York City that were written with color and charm. His book is enjoyable, anecdotal, reliable, but it too was essentially a *Times* inside product, so the keen edge of the historian is lacking. (Sadly the book contains not a single footnote, citation, or reference of any kind.) At the time of the centennial the *Times* also published a work to go along with the Berger history: *One Hundred Famous Pages from the New York Times*.

Unfortunately there is no really good critical biography of Adolph Ochs, a serious gap in the annals of journalistic history. One may, however, look at Gerald W. Johnson's amiable account of the life of Ochs, *The Honorable Titan*, New York, 1946. There is a brief biography of Carr V. Van Anda by Barnett Fine, *A Giant of the Press*, New York, 1933.

Even though the *Times* had not grown to its full estate in the nineteenth century, there is a fairly extensive literature about Henry Raymond and the early New York *Times*. There is a good biography of Raymond by Francis Brown, *Raymond of the Times*, New York, 1951. There is also an earlier source that contains a good deal of solid information about the *Times* in the nineteenth century: Augustus Maverick, *Henry J. Raymond and the New York Press*. Not a great deal has been written about the George Jones era at the *Times*, although this was a significant period for the *Times* historically. A good deal can be found in the standard histories that cover the Tweed Ring, New York politics, and Tammany Hall. One can look, for example, at Seymour J. Mandelbaum's *Boss Tweed's New York*, on the *Times*'s successful effort to dislodge this arch scoundrel from New York politics.

For those interested in the pre-Ochs New York *Times*, there is a biography of the paper's editor in the 1880s and 1890s, Charles R. Miller. It is F. F. Bond's *Mr. Miller of the Times: The Story of an Editor*, New York, 1931. Since Miller continued with the *Times* and ran the editorial page in the Ochs era, this book is somewhat informative about the *Times* up until the 1920s.

CHAPTER 10: OF EVENINGS, AND SUNDAYS, AND FUNNIES, AND SUCH

There is no book that devotes itself to the "evening paper" trend of the 1880s and after, nor of the Sunday paper explosion of the 1890s. The best general account of the development of the urban evening papers is in Frank Luther Mott's *American Journalism*, especially Chapter 27 (pp. 446ff), which gives some idea of the reason for the trend and offers a discussion of the principal papers that started up in this period or made a conversion. Mott also has a thorough treatment of the expanding Sunday paper after 1870 (pp. 480–482; and of the Sunday paper wars of the 1890s (pp. 524–527). The biographies of Pulitzer and Hearst mentioned in the bibliography for Chapter 9 naturally take up this subject. Available on the Sunday paper is a thorough doctoral dissertation, "The Metropolitan Sunday Newspaper in the United States: A Study of Trends in Content and Practices," by William A. Hachten, Minneapolis, MN: University of Minnesota, 1960.

On the literary men, occasional columnists and familiar essayists who were once such an important part of the American newspaper, there are a number of works that cover prominent individual figures. There are two good works on Eugene Field of the Chicago *Daily News*: Slason Thompson, *Eugene Field*, New York, 1901, and Charles H. Dennis, *Eugene Field's Creative Years*, Garden City, NY, 1924. There is Elmer Ellis, *Mr. Dooley's America*, New York, 1941; Ellis also edited *Mr. Dooley at His Best*, New York, 1938. There is Frank Wilson Nye, *Bill Nye: His Own Life Story*, New York, 1926; also Opie Read *I Remember*, New York, 1930. On the famous paragrapher and "Sage of Potato Hill," see E. W. Howe, *Plain People*, New York, 1929. See also Calder M. Pickett, *Ed Howe: Country Town Philosopher*, Lawrence, KS: University Press of Kansas, 1969.

The famous nineteenth-century newspaper humorists like Petroleum Nasby and Artemus Ward are invariably anthologized in collections of American humor. One of the best of the recent ones is Russell Baker, *Russell Baker's Book of American Humor*, New York: Norton, 1993. The literature treating of Mark Twain is too great to be dealt with here, but easily accessible.

There is a considerable literature dealing with both political cartoons and "the comics." The casual reader might do well to begin with a rather general work in the area such as William Murrell, *A History of American Graphic Humor*, New York, 1938. With specific reference to political cartoons, see Stephen Hess and Milton Kaplan, *The Ungentlemanly Art: A History of American Political Cartoons*, New York, 1968; also Charles Press, *The Political Cartoon*, Associated University Presses, 1981. There are a number of collections of editorial cartoons; in a definite historical context is Allan Nevins and George Weitenkampf, *A Century of Political Cartoons*, New York, 1944.

As to the history of the "comics" or "funny pages," see Pierre Couperie and Maurice C. Horn, *A History of the Comic Strip*, New York, 1968. Jerry Robinson, *The Comics: An Illustrated History of Comic Strip Art*, New York, 1974. Also, Coulton Waugh, *The Comics*, New York, 1947, an encyclopedic work; and Richard Marschall, *America's Great Comic Strip Artists*, New York, 1989.

CHAPTER 11: NEWSPAPER CHAINS AND PRESS ASSOCIATIONS

E. W. Scripps was the subject of much discussion in the years following his death; much less so recently, even though interest in Hearst remains high. There are several biographies of Scripps available. Negley D. Cochran's *E. W. Scripps*, New York, 1933, is a good first-hand account by one of Scripps's editors. Colorful but less informative is Gilson Gardner's *Lusty Scripps*, New York, 1932. See also, Charles R. McCabe (ed.) *Damned Old Crank*, New York, 1951. A good deal about the early Scripps can be found in the autobiography of his first partner, Milton McRae, *Forty Years in Newspaperdom*, New York, 1924. Albert Britt's *Ellen Browning Scripps*, Oxford University Press, 1961, not only sheds light on Scripps himself but on this remarkable woman journalist whose influence on her brother can hardly be overestimated.

The best approach to the life of Frank Munsey is through the general histories of journalism and the many works on newspapers written in the wake of Munsey's career as an amalgamator and assassin of newspapers. There is a biography, hardly sympathetic but well enough detailed: George Britt, *Forty Years—Forty Millions: The Career of Frank A. Munsey*, New York, 1935.

The history of the various press associations and news-gathering organizations has been fairly well documented. On the rise of such associations see Richard A. Schwartzlose, *The Nation's Newsbrokers*, Vol. I, *The Formative Years to 1865*, Evanston, IL: Northwestern University Press, 1989, probably the definitive study of this period. There is an earlier and shorter work that is quite adequate, Victor Rosewater, *History of Cooperative Newsgathering in the United States*, New York, 1930. Several articles by Richard Schwartzlose document the incubator period of news associations. See his "Harbor News Association: Formal Origin of the AP," *Journalism Quarterly* 45, Summer, 1968, pp. 253ff, and "Early Telegraphic News Dispatches: Forerunner of the AP," *Journalism Quarterly* 51, Winter, 1974, pp. 595ff. Good background material on the rise of telegraphy in communication can be found in Alvin F. Harlow, *Old Wires and New Waves: The History of the Telegraph, Telephone and Wireless*, New York, 1936.

For the history of the later press associations, the second volume of Schwartzlose's excellent history, *The Nation's Newsbrokers: The Rush to Institution, From 1865 to 1920*, Evanston, IL: Northwestern University Press, 1990, will probably be the best guide. See also Robert W. Desmond, *The Information Process: World News Reporting 1900–1920*, Ames: University of Iowa Press, 1980. This book covers the activities of the AP, the UP, and INS. Elmo Scott Watson, *A History of Newspaper Syndicates in the United States, 1865–1935*, Chicago, 1936.

There is a history of the Associated Press, Oliver Grambling, *AP: The Story of News*, New York, 1940, highly anecdotal and now out of date. A good deal of information about the Associated Press at the end of the nineteenth century will be found in Melville E. Stone, *"M.E.S." His Book*, New York, 1918. The last half of Stone's autobiography also deals with the AP. It is *Fifty Years a Journalist*, Garden City, NY, 1921. There is a lively history of the United Press: Joe Alex Morris, *Deadline Every Minute: The Story of the United Press*, New York, 1957

CHAPTER 12: FANTASY AND REALITY: THE NEWSPAPER REPORTER

There is no comprehensive history of newspaper reporting, although the standard histories of journalism give a fairly clear idea of the development of the profession. There are some memoirs of reporters (see below), which may provide the most intimate and reliable picture of the reporting life.

Naturally there are books that deal with reporting in specific time periods. Especially well represented are the major wars, which have given rise to histories of war coverage and "war correspondents." Outside of wartime there have been treatments of "foreign correspondents," nearly all suggesting that the lives of such individuals are far more eventful and exciting than the lives of police reporters or society reporters at home.

Certainly war reporting is a very inviting topic. There is an excellent doctoral dissertation on reporting the Mexican War. It is Thomas W. Reilly, "American Reporters and the Mexican War, 1846–1848," Ph.D. thesis, University of Minnesota, 1975. Civil War reporting has been a subject of enduring interest. See, for example, Emmet Crozier, *Yankee Reporters, 1861–1865*, New York: Oxford

University Press, 1956; also Joseph J. Mathews, *Reporting the Wars*, Minneapolis: University of Minnesota Press, 1957. This book deals with "coverage" even of wars in the eighteenth century, even though the word "reporter" was not in use at that time. (A number of memoirs or lives of major correspondents—Whitelaw Reid, for example—are available; some make for very good reading.) Most of the books dealing with the reporting of the Spanish-American War focus on the excesses of yellow journalism, although one can look at works by and about some of the participants such as Frederic Remington and Richard Harding Davis. See also, Joyce Milton: *The Yellow Kids: Foreign Correspondents in the Heyday of American Journalism*, New York, 1989. A good account of reporting during World War I can be found in Emmet Crozier, *American Reporters on the Western Front, 1914–1918*, New York: Oxford University Press, 1959.

There are some comprehensive accounts, such as Mathews's mentioned above, and profiles of famous war correspondents such as F. L. Bullard, *Famous War Correspondents*, Boston, 1914. Also on the lives and doings of "foreign correspondents," see John Hohenberg, *Foreign Correspondence: The Great Reporters and Their Times*, New York: Columbia University Press, 1964.

The late nineteenth and early twentieth centuries gave rise to a great many memoirs of working newspapermen that evoke the flavor of the profession during those times. See, for example, Will Irwin, *The Making of a Reporter*, New York, 1942. (A scholarly study of Irwin's career as a reporter is Robert V. Hudson, "Journeyman Journalist, An Analytical Biography of Will Irwin," Ph.D. thesis, University of Minnesota, 1970.) There is Julian Ralph, *The Making of a Journalist*, New York, 1903. The autobiography of Irwin S. Cobb, *Exit Laughing*, Indianapolis, 1941, is an amusing book that also offers an interesting analysis of newspaper history. Cobb discusses several "ages": "The Time of the Editor," "The Time of the Reporter," etc.

There are a considerable number of books dealing with the lives and careers of the muckrakers at the turn of the century. The bibliography in Emery and Emery gives a good sampling of these. There is, for example, *The Autobiography of Lincoln Steffens*, New York, 1931; also, *An American Chronicle*, New York, 1945, which is the autobiography of Ray Stannard Baker, and many others. There is a copious literature, growing much larger in latter decades, dealing with the subject of women reporters, their trials and tribulations—see the entries for Chapter 13.

Two splendid works by major literary figures who came up through the reporting ranks are Theodore Dreiser, *A Book About Myself: Newspaper Days*, New York, 1922, which gives an excellent account of the joys and hardships of the wandering newspaperman in the 1880s and 1890s. The University of Pennsylvania Press put out a fuller edition of this work in the 1980s, with naughty bits that were once expurgated now restored. But it is available only in a high-priced format. H. L. Mencken's *Newspaper Days*, New York, 1941, is not precisely an autobiography, but a series of vignettes dealing with Mencken's early newspaper career written with wit and sparkle, and offering lots of insights into the reporter's craft and daily life.

A good short portrait of the reporting life as lived in the golden years from 1900 to 1930 can be found in "Notes on a Noble Calling," in Stanley Walker's *City Editor*, New York, 1934.

CHAPTER 13: WHEN THE WOMEN MARCHED IN

There are a number of good histories of women in American journalism and there has been a considerable amount written about particular figures such as Nellie Bly, Victoria Woodhull, and Margaret Fuller, including full-length biographies.

Probably the classic work among the general histories remains Ishbel Ross's *Ladies of the Press*, New York, 1936. It is written by one of the great women reporters and covers the field up to the 1930s with swift wit and intelligence. On Ross herself, incidentally, there is an interesting dissertation, Beverly Merrick, "Ishbel Ross: On Assignment With History: The Formative Years, 1895–1923," Ohio University, 1989.

Of recent surveys, perhaps the best is Marion Marzolf, *Up From the Footnote: A History of Women Journalists*, New York, 1977. It is a more structured work than that of Ross and contains very useful bibliographies. Of other recent works see Marion Golden Schlipp and Sharon M. Murphy, *Great Women of the Press*, Carbondale, IL: Southern Illinois University Press, 1983; also Julia Edwards, *Women of the World: The Great Foreign Correspondents*, Boston, 1988, which covers a period of 140 years. Lively accounts of women reporters will be found in John Jakes, *Great Women Reporters*, New York, 1969. A good short account of the early women journalists is Susan E. Dickinson, "Women in Journalism," in *Women's Work in America*, ed. Annie Meyer, New York, 1891. A lively editor's account of women reporters is Stanley Walker's "A Gallery of Angels," in his *City Editor*, New York, 1934.

There is a growing interest in the contributions of women printers and journalists in colonial times. Detailed information may be found in Elisabeth Dexter, *Colonial Women of Affairs*, New York, 1924. There have been not a few articles on women in colonial and revolutionary times, e.g., Leonard J. Hooper, "Women Printers in Colonial Times," *Journalism Educator*, April 1974; Susan Henry, "Margaret Draper: Colonial Printer Who Challenged the Patriots," in *Journalism History*, Winter 1974. Also Nancy Fisher Chudacoff, "Women in the News 1762–1770," *Rhode Island History*, Fall 1973.

On the period of the first half of the twentieth century, when women were making inroads as editors and correspondents, see Maurine Beasley, *The First Women Washington Correspondents*, Washington D.C., 1976. Also by Beasley is "The Curious Case of Anne Royall," *Journalism History* Winter, 1976. See also, Kathleen Endres, "Jane Grey Swisshelm, 19th Century Journalist and Feminist,"

Journalism History Winter, 1975. Naturally Margaret Fuller has been accorded book-length treatment a number of times. Two recent works with a strong feminist slant are: Bell Gale Chevigny, *The Woman and the Myth, Margaret Fuller's Life and Writings*, Old Westbury, NY, 1976, and Paula Blanchard, *Margaret Fuller: From Transcendentalism to Revolution*, New York, 1978. Of older treatments of Fuller, see Mason Wade, *Margaret Fuller: Whetstone of Genius*, New York, 1940; also Arthur W. Brown, *Margaret Fuller*, New York, 1964.

Of the gusty era of the late nineteenth century when women journalists were knocking over the barricades, of special importance is Mignon Rittenhouse, *The Amazing Nellie Bly*, New York, 1956. A more recent work on Nellie Bly is Brooke Kroeger's *Nellie Bly: Daredevil, Reporter, Feminist*, New York: Times Books, 1994. See also *Mrs. Satan: The Incredible Saga of Victoria V. Woodhull*, New York, 1967. The best-known of the woman muckrakers was surely Ida Tarbell, and one can look to her own *All in a Day's Work*, New York, 1939.

Well-known women journalists of the twentieth century have been subjects of a number of good books. See, for example, Marion Sheehan, *The World at Home: Selections From the Writing of Anne O'Hare McCormick*, New York, 1956. Mary Margaret McBride wrote an interesting autobiography, *A Long Way From Missouri*, New York, 1959. There is a very substantial biography of Dorothy Thompson: Marion K. Sanders, *Dorothy Thompson: A Legend in Her Time*, Boston, 1973. A bibliography on more recent women in journalism, including television reporters and anchors can be found in Emery and Emery, p. 685.

CHAPTER 14: THE NEWSPAPER SAGE: FROM OUR TOWN TO OLYMPUS

This chapter celebrates some of the most respected figures in American journalism, strong leaders of public opinion, sages admired in their own time and place, and, in a few cases, throughout the nation. Earlier sections of this bibliography have dealt with the literature treating some of them: William Cullen Bryant, Horace Greeley, William Allan White, Henry Watterson, and numerous others. Some of the figures discussed here—giants of the late nineteenth century or early twentieth century—have given rise to a good deal of commentary.

Surely E. L. Godkin, longtime editor of the New York *Post* was one of the most trusted and admired figures of the late nineteenth century. Although his paper was not one of the circulation leaders of the nation he was always a figure of tremendous influence. There is an excellent but now dated biography of Godkin, Rollo Ogden, *Life and Letters of Edwin Lawrence Godkin*, New York, 1907. Naturally, too, Allan Nevins's famous history of the *Post* is an excellent source of material about the great liberal editor: *The Evening Post: A Century of Journalism*, New York, 1922. A somewhat wider context for Godkin can be found in John G. Sproat, *"The Best Men": Liberal Reformers in the Gilded Age*, Oxford University Press, 1968. Godkin has been of continuing interest to journalistic historians. See Henry F. Pringle, "Godkin of the *Post*," *Scribner's*, December 1934; Allan Nevins, "E. L. Godkin: Victorian Liberal," *Nation*, July 22, 1950; Randall L. Murray, "Edwin Lawrence Godkin: Unbending Editor in Times of Change," *Journalism History*, Autumn 1974.

Anyone interested in Godkin and his times could hardly do better than look at some of the collections of his own writings, many of which, naturally, appeared in the *Post*. See for example his *Reflections and Comments* (1895), *Problems of Democracy* (1896), and *Unforseen Tendencies of Democracy* (1898).

It hardly needs to be said that a vast literature has built up around H. L. Mencken. One should go first to the numerous collections of his own writings, such as the Six Series of *Prejudices*, New York, 1919–1927. Excellent selections from these have been made by James T. Farrell and Alistair Cooke. Mencken's own selection of his work is *The Mencken Chrestomathy*, New York, 1949. Of special value to those interested in Mencken's newspaper career is his own *Newspaper Days*, New York, 1941. A posthumously published memoir is Mencken's *Thirty-Five Years of Newspaper Work*, ed. by Fred Hobson, et al., Baltimore: Johns Hopkins University Press, 1994. There is a first-rate recent collection specific to Mencken's newspaper writing: Marion Elizabeth Rodgers, *The Impossible H. L. Mencken*, New York: Doubleday, 1991.

There are several good biographies of Mencken. Carl Bode, *Mencken*, Carbondale: Southern Illinois University Press, 1969; also, and written by a working newsman, William Manchester, *Disturber of the Peace: The Life of H. L. Mencken*, Amherst: University of Massachusetts Press, 1986. There have been several books dealing with Mencken's ideas. See George H. Douglas, *H. L. Mencken: Critic of American Life*, Hamden, CT, 1978; also Charles A. Fecher, *Mencken: A Study of His Thought*, New York, 1978. Naturally there are many books dealing with Mencken as a literary critic, magazine editor, and cultural gadfly. See Betty Adler, *H.L.M., The Mencken Bibliography*, Baltimore: Johns Hopkins University Press, 1961, and continuing issues of *Menckeniana*, published by the Enoch Pratt Public Library of Baltimore.

Undoubtedly the best work on Walter Lippmann is Ronald Steele, *Walter Lippmann and the American Century*, Boston, 1980, which serves as both a biography and a guide to the man's thought. But there have been other scholarly books on Lippmann: John Luskin, *Lippmann, Liberty and the Press*, Tuscaloosa: University of Alabama Press, 1972; and Hari N. Dam, *The Intellectual Odyssey of Walter Lippmann*, New York, 1973. Marquis Childs and James Reston's *Walter Lippmann and His Times*, New York, 1959 is a collection of essays. Other works relevant to Lippmann as a journalist are, David Elliott Weingast, *Walter Lippmann: A Study in Personal Journalism*, New Brunswick, NJ: Rutgers University Press, 1949, and Frederick H. Schapsmeier, *Walter Lippmann: Philosopher-Journalist*, Washington DC, 1969. There are books and many articles dealing with Lippmann's "public philosophy," and the bibliography in Steele's biography is a fine guide to these.

Very much needed is a good collection of the whole range of Lippmann's "Today and Tomorrow" columns and other journalistic pieces; on the other hand, there are compilations from various time periods. For example, *Interpretations, 1931–1932*, New York, 1933, covers the early depression years. *The New Imperative*, New York, 1935, covers the New Deal era. *The Cold War*, Boston, 1947, covers the post-war age, and there are numerous others. Clinton Rossiter and James Lare attempted a thematic presentation of Lippmann's work in *The Essential Lippmann*, New York, 1963.

Today Lippmann is doubtless more often read in his full-length works of political philosophy such as *A Preface to Politics*, *Public Opinion*, *The Phantom Public*, *Essays in the Public Philosophy*, all masterpieces of their kind. A full list is found in Steele p. 633.

CHAPTER 15: THE FOREIGN LANGUAGE PRESS

The foreign language press in America was several centuries old when it first began to receive extensive scholarly attention. But the best works on the subject have appeared only in the last several decades when many once-prominent language groups have given up on newspapers, certainly daily newspapers.

The first important work about the foreign language press was the work of a sociologist, Robert E. Park, whose detailed scholarly study *The Immigrant Press and Its Control* was published in 1922. On the other hand, a great deal of information about the foreign language press can also be found in general histories of various immigrant groups—the German, the Irish, the Swedish, the Russian, and so on.

A good recent compilation of the scholarship in this area is Sally M. Miller, *The Ethnic Press in the United States*, Westport, CT, 1987. This work is broken down into twenty-seven linguistic groups, each treated by an authority on the subject. There was an earlier and much less exhaustive work, Edward Hunter, *In Many Voices: Our Fabulous Foreign-Language Press*, North Park, GA, n.d. For research purposes one has access to Lubomyr R. and Anna T. Wynar, *Encyclopedic Directory of Ethnic Newspapers and Periodicals and Newspapers in the United States*, Littleton, CO, 1976. Naturally anyone seriously interested in the topic has recourse to the archives and collections where these newspapers are available on microfilm.

There are a number of books and a great many articles dealing with specific linguistic groups. The German language press has been especially well treated as might be expected. The best work in the field is surely Carl Wittke's *The German Language Press in America*, Lexington, KY: University Press of Kentucky, 1957. (A distinguished historian of the immigrant experience, Wittke is also the author of *The Saga of the Immigrant*, Cleveland: Western Reserve University Press, 1967, which has a great deal in it about newspapers.)

Other serious works dealing with single linguistic groups are: Jonas A. Backlund, *A Century of Swedish-American Press*, Chicago, 1952; limited in time-span but otherwise very good is Arlow W. Andersen, *The Immigrant Takes His Stand: The Norwegian-American Press and Public Affairs, 1847–1872*, Northfield, MN, 1953. See also, Marion T. Marzolf, *The Danish Language Press in America*, New York, 1979.

There is a sizable literature dealing with Yiddish newspapers in America; alas, some of the best of it is written in Yiddish. There are not many full-length books in English, but see Mordecai Soltes, *The Yiddish Press*, New York, 1925. A good deal has been written about Abraham Cahan and the *Jewish Daily Forward*. Unfortunately only one volume of Cahan's autobiography has been translated, *The Education of Abraham Cahan*, New York, 1969, and this does not deal with the great days of the *Forward*. But rewarding on Cahan and the work he did on the *Forward* is Moses Rischen (ed.), *Grandma Never Lived in America: The New Journalism of Abraham Cahan*, Bloomington, IN: Indiana University Press, 1986.

There is a recent thorough history of the Italian-American press: Pietro Russo, *Italian American Periodical Press, 1836–1980*, Staten Island: Center for Migration Studies, 1983.

Fuller bibliographies listing many articles on the periodical press in foreign languages may be found in Miller's *The Ethnic Press in the United States*.

CHAPTER 16: TABLOIDS

Naturally a great deal has been written in general histories of journalism about the rise of the tabloids. Much other information may be found in books dealing with the decade of the 1920s (see Chapter 17). There are a number of accounts devoted to the tabloids themselves. Probably the best survey of the beginnings of the tabloid age is Simon M. Bessie, *Jazz Journalism*, New York, 1938. There is a lively history of the New York *Daily News*: John Chapman, *Tell It to Sweeney: The Informal History of the New York Daily News*, New York, 1961. More general works covering photo and feature journalism are: *Hello Sweetheart: Get Me Rewrite*, Chicago, 1988 (this was originally published as *Behind the Front Page*); also, Helen M. Hughes, *News and the Human Interest Story*, Chicago: University of Chicago Press, 1940. Covering a broader time frame but limited to New York is John D. Stevens, *Sensationalism and the New York Press*, 1991, New York: Columbia University Press, 1991. Bernarr McFadden is treated in *Jazz Journalism*, already mentioned, but see also William H. Taft, "Bernarr McFadden: One of a Kind," *Journalism Quarterly*, Winter 1968, pp. 627ff.

There are a number of books dealing with knockabout journalism in other parts of the country. A great deal has been written about the flamboyant Bonfils and Tammen of the Denver *Post*. See, for example Gene Fowler's *Timber Line*, New York, 1933, a sparkling account of the Denver *Post*'s most gaudy days; also Bill Hosokawa, *Thunder in the Rockies: The Incredible Denver Post*, New York, 1976. The various books on Hearst (see Chapter 8) give an account of the master's efforts to reinvigorate yellow journalism in the 1920s and his excursions into the tabloid field.

CHAPTER 17: A BRIGHT AND SHINING MOMENT

To get the pulse of the 1920s it is undoubtedly important to consult some of the many general works that treat the age. Among those that are especially helpful are: Frederick Lewis Allen, *The Big Change*, New York, 1952, and Allen's *Only Yesterday: An Informal History of the 1920s*, New York, 1959; Geoffrey Perrett, *America in the Twenties: A History*, New York, 1982; Charles A. Beard and Mary R. Beard, *America in Mid Passage*, New York, 1939 (a part of the Beards' multivolume history of American civilization). The early years of the twentieth century, including this period, are covered in massive detail by the six volumes of Mark Sullivan's *Our Times*, New York, 1926–1928. Sullivan was a newspaperman by vocation, and a longtime editorial writer for the New York *Herald Tribune*.

On the rise of radio as competition for print journalism, see Erik Barnouw, *A History of Broadcasting in the United States*: Vol. I, *A Tower in Babel*, New York: Oxford University Press, 1966; also George H. Douglas, *The Early Days of Radio Broadcasting*, Jefferson, NC: McFarland, 1987.

There are a number of books that deal with the shifting newspaper scene of the 1920s. One of the best is Oswald Garrison Villard's *Some Newspapers and Newspaper-Men*, New York, 1923. It has evaluations of figures like Frank Munsey, Col. Robert R. McCormick, essays on leading papers like the New York *World*, the Baltimore *Sun*, and numerous others, all from a high-minded progressive stance, but always judicious in that handling. Some standard papers of repute also have individual histories that are particularly relevant to this time frame. See, for example, Gerald W. Johnson, Frank R. Kent, H. L. Mencken, and Hamilton Owens, *The Sunpapers of Baltimore*, New York, 1937.

As to the renaissance and then rapid decline of the New York *World*, see James Boylan (ed.), *The World and the Twenties: The Golden Age of New York's Legendary Newspaper*, New York, 1973. Probably the most intimate account of the *World* and its decline is to be found in a small book by the paper's last city editor, James W. Barrett, *The World, The Flesh and Messers Pulitzer*, New York, 1931. Some idea of the style and the reportage of the *World* can be found in John K. Hutchens and George Oppenheimer (eds.), *The Best in the World*, New York, 1973. Much information about the *World* can also be found in two solid biographies of Herbert Bayard Swope, Alfred Allan Lewis, *Man of the World*, New York, 1978, and E. J. Kahn, *The World of Swope*, New York, 1965.

The New York *Herald Tribune* is fortunate enough to have one of the best histories ever written of a single newspaper, Richard Kluger's *The Paper: The Life and Death of the New York Herald Tribune*, New York: Knopf, 1986. While the book is perhaps not the best source for the early days on the original *Herald* under

Bennett and the *Tribune* under Greeley, it serves that period adequately. It is splendid in its coverage of the merged paper after 1924, especially strong on the era of Ogden Reid and Helen Rogers Reid, and the final years of the paper in the 1950s and 1960s. Anyone interested in more detail on the years before the 1930s would also do well to look at an earlier history, Harry W. Baehr's *The New York Tribune Since the Civil War*, New York, 1936. Also of some interest is Royal Cortissoz's *New York Tribune: Incidents and Personalities in Its History*, New York, 1923. A recent biography of Whitelaw Reid also provides good background: Bingham Duncan, *Whitelaw Reid: Journalist, Politician, Diplomat*, Atlanta: University of Georgia Press, 1975. (See the bibliography for Chapter 8 on Whitelaw Reid.)

Of the years leading up to the merger at the *Herald* one may look at the various works on James Gordon Bennett Jr. already mentioned. On the famous European edition of the paper, begun as the Paris *Herald*, see Al Laney, *Paris Herald: The Incredible Newspaper*, New York, 1946, and Charles L. Robertson, *The International Herald Tribune*, New York: Columbia University Press, 1987. For a more personal account see Erik Hawkins, *Hawkins of the Paris Herald*, New York, 1963.

To get the spirit and the tempo of the New York *Herald Tribune* in the 1920s and 1930s one can hardly do better than consult Stanley Walker's *City Editor*, New York, 1934. By no means is it a history of the Tribune; rather it is a compendium of newspaper practices and culture of the golden age and a splendid guide to the city rooms of New York. Also very interesting is a work by a successor to Walker as the paper's city editor: Joseph G. Herzberg, *Late City Edition*, which contains essays by various members of the *Herald Tribune* staff explaining a number of newspaper functions: the morgue, the copydesk, and so on. Among other things the book has a piece by the great rewrite man Robert B. Peck.

The bibliographical notes in Kluger offer much more detail and many more sources of information about this splendid American newspaper.

Index

About the Author

GEORGE H. DOUGLAS is Professor of English at the University of Illinois. A New Jersey native, his father was a long-time writer and editor at the *Newark Evening News*. As a boy Douglas was an inveterate visitor to the paper's city room and was awed by the roar of the rotary presses. He is the author of eleven books and many dozens of articles dealing mostly with American literature and social history. Among his books are *The Early Days of Radio Broadcasting*, *H. L. Mencken: Critic of American Life*, *All Aboard: The Railroad in American Life*, *Skyscraper Odyssey*, and *The Smart Magazines*.